The Twelve Stars of Our Republic
by Edwin Williams

Address:
HardPress
8345 NW 66TH ST #2561
MIAMI FL 33166-2626
USA
Email: info@hardpress.net

THE

TWELVE STARS

OF OUR

REPUBLIC:

OUR

NATION'S GIFT-BOOK TO HER YOUNG CITIZENS.

ELEGANTLY ILLUSTRATED.

NEW YORK:

EDWARD WALKER, 114 FULTON STREET.

1850.

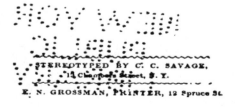

STEREOTYPED BY C. C. SAVAGE,
13 Chambers Street, N. Y.

E. N. GROSSMAN, PRINTER, 13 Spruce St.

ADVERTISEMENT.

To MY YOUNG COUNTRYMEN —

    Permit me with fraternal earnestness and regard, to direct your attention to this constellation of brilliant names in the broad firmament of our Republic. With all the skill that mind and art can command, I have caused this volume to be prepared for your instruction and delight. The memoirs were written by that eminent statician, EDWIN WILLIAMS; and the introduction was penned by my much esteemed friend, B. J. LOSSING, the author of my book entitled, Seventeen Hundred and Seventy-Six, and editor of my Young People's Mirror. These names will insure your confidence and esteem. Intrinsic value marks every line; and from this mine of instruction you may draw up an abundance of the pure gold of practical knowledge, concerning the progress of our government, so essential in fitting you for the responsibilities and honor of a good American citizen and wise legislator. Contemplate these twelve bright stars with an earnest desire to be worthy of their companionship; for with such aspirations, if you do not become one of the brilliant cluster, you will shine brighter in an humbler sphere, and shed a degree of lustre upon yourselves and your country. That you may thus profit by exertions in your behalf, is the sincere wish of   Your friend,

THE PUBLISHER.

CONTENTS.

DESCRIPTION OF THE EMBELLISHMENTS.

INDEPENDENCE HALL.—This venerable and venerated edifice, wherein the great act that proclaimed freedom to America was performed, is on Chestnut street, between Fifth and Sixth streets, Philadelphia. It was originally built by the legislature of Pennsylvania, for a statehouse. It was begun in 1729, and finished in 1734, at a cost of $280,000. The two wings were erected in 1739-'40. The architectural design of the house and steeple was furnished by Dr. John Kearsley. The old bell that rang merrily on the adoption of the Declaration of Independence, was imported from England in 1752, but being cracked at the trial-ringing, it was recast by Isaac Norris, of Philadelphia, and upon it was placed the inscription, "Proclaim liberty to the land, and to the inhabitants thereof." That office it performed twenty years afterward. The old bell still hangs in the steeple, but hopelessly cracked. The hall where the Declaration was signed is, in appearance, the same as in the Revolution, and is situated upon the street floor, on the left of the principal entrance. The Declaration of Independence was written by Thomas Jefferson, at his private lodgings, in the house of a Mr. Graaf, on the southwest corner of Market and Seventh streets, Philadelphia.

It is related, that, on the morning of the day when the Declaration was adopted, the venerable bellman ascended the steeple, and a little boy was placed at the door of the hall to give him notice when the vote should be concluded. The old man waited long at his post, saying, "They will never do it; they will never do it." Suddenly a loud shout came up from below, and there stood the boy, clapping his hands and shouting, "Ring! Ring!" Grasping the iron tongue of the bell, backward and forward he hurled it a hundred times, proclaiming "liberty to the land, and to the inhabitants thereof."

BUNKER HILL MONUMENT.—This noble monumental structure marks the spot where the first regular battle of the Revolution took place. It is upon an eminence in Charlestown, near Boston, and is composed of granite from the neighboring hills. The corner-stone was laid on the anniversary of the battle, the 17th of June, 1825, by the venerable Lafayette, then the nation's guest, and it was dedicated by an eloquent oration from the lips of Daniel Webster. The monument is a hollow obelisk, 221 feet high, and 30 feet square at the base, and is ascended by an interior spiral flight of stairs of 295 steps. For a long time, want of funds caused the progress of its erection to cease, but in September, 1840, the ladies of Boston, assisted by contributions from all parts of the Union, held a fair, from which they realized about $40,000. The work was immediately recommenced, and the monument was finished in 1842. On the 17th of June, 1843, a celebration was had in honor of its completion, and again Daniel Webster was the orator. A large number of soldiers of the Revolution, some of whom were in the battle 68 years before, were present, together with the president of the United States (John Tyler) and all his cabinet. The whole weight of the monument is estimated at 7,000 tons, and so well and firmly is the foundation laid, that it will stand for ages, a noble memento of the first battle of our WAR FOR INDEPENDENCE.

THE CAPITOL OF THE UNITED STATES, in the city of Washington, is considered one of the finest statehouses in the world. It is beautifully located upon an eminence 73 feet above the Potomac river, and from its dome is a noble view of the whole metropolis, and of the surrounding country. The building is constructed of white freestone, and covers an area of more than an acre and a half. The length of the front is 352 feet, including the wings; the depth of the wings is 121 feet. A lofty dome, which covers a magnificent rotunda within, rises from the centre building. Two lesser domes rise from the wings. Along the eastern front is a projection 65 feet wide, with a noble portico of 22 lofty Corinthian columns. On the western front is a projection of 83 feet, including the steps, and a portico of 10 columns. By the side of the steps on the eastern front is a beautiful marble group by Persico, representing Columbus and an Indian girl, and in niches in the walls under the portico, are fine marble allegorical statues. The height of the building to the top of the dome, is 120 feet. The rotunda is 95 feet in diameter, adorned near the dome with basso-relievos representing scenes in American history. Its walls are decorated with fine historical paintings, for which Congress appropriated $10,000 each. The library room of Congress is 92 by 34 feet in size, and 36 feet in height, and contains 25,000 volumes in arched alcoves. In the second story of the south wing is the hall of representatives, of a semi-circular form, 96 feet long and 60 feet high, with a dome supported by 24 columns of variegated marble, with Italian marble capitals of the Corinthian order. The senate-chamber occupies a similar position in the north wing. It is also semi-circular, 75 feet long and 45 feet high. Below the senate-chamber is the room of the supreme court of the United States. The building contains 70 rooms for the accommodation of committees and officers of Congress. The grounds around the Capitol include 22 acres, and are highly ornamented with shrubbery and gravel-walks, the whole enclosed by an iron railing. The building cost $2,160,000.

THE PRESIDENT'S HOUSE is a mile northwest of the Capitol, upon a gentle eminence, 44 feet above the river, toward Georgetown. It is an elegant edifice of white freestone, two stories high, with a lofty basement. It is 170 feet long and 86 wide. The north front is ornamented with a fine portico of 4 lofty Ionic columns, projecting with three columns. The outer intercolumniation is for carriages to drive under to shelter company when alighting. The building stands in the centre of 20 acres of ground, beautifully laid out in gravelled walks, and ornamented with flowers and shrubbery. The apartments within are admirably adapted for the uses they are designed for, and are elegantly furnished.

INTRODUCTION.

"WE hold these truths to be self-evident—that all men are created equal; that they are endowed by their Creator with certain unalienable rights; that among these are life, liberty, and the pursuit of happiness. That to secure these rights, governments are instituted among men, deriving their just powers from the consent of the governed; that whenever any form of government becomes destructive of these ends, it is the right of the people to alter or abolish it, and to institute a new government, laying its foundation on such principles, and organizing its powers in such form, as to them shall seem most likely to effect their safety and happiness."

Such were the lucid apprehensions of the true character and mission of government which were entertained by the founders of our republic, and expressed by them in their solemn declaration of the political independence of the Anglo-American colonies. From the moment when the English felled the first tree at Jamestown, or the Pilgrims cleft the snow on Plymouth beach, loyalty had been the co-worker with religion in planting English institutions in wilderness America, and in strengthening, by population and the industrial arts, the puissance of the British realm. Magna Charta was the political bible on whose teachings and guaranties the English colonies rested all their hopes of civil and religious freedom; and the spirit of the British constitution was never lost sight of in their social arrangements and legislative enactments, even when oppression had aroused the lion of rebellion and the blow was struck which dismembered the empire. That act, itself, was a vindication of the dearest rights of a British subject which the constitution recognized, and professed to defend.

When the "Seven Years' War" ended in 1763, at a cost to Great Britain of five hundred and sixty millions of dollars, and a thriftless ministry otherwise exhausted the treasury, it became necessary to devise some means to replenish the public coffer to save the government from a ruinous fiscal embarrassment. The wealth and prosperity of the American colonies had long been a theme for gratulation in Old England; and the cheerfulness with which men and money had been raised for the public service through the late war, was an assurance that further drafts upon their generosity would not be dishonored. Such drafts were made, but in the wrong way. Money was *demanded*, not *asked* for, and taxation was imposed without the consent of those upon whom the burden was laid. The burden, it is true, was not grievous in itself, but the political principle involved was one which lay at the foundation of civil freedom ; and if the assumed rights and powers of the parliament of Great Britain were to be tacitly assented to, abuse after abuse of privileges might enter so wide a door, until the liberty guarantied by the British constitution would be destroyed, and the colonists would be reduced to the vassalage of serfdom.

These evils far-seeing statesmen of America clearly perceived, and warned the people to awake to the same perceptions. The warning was heeded. They winced under the lash of commercial restrictions, and they rebelled, as far as loyalty to their sovereign would permit, when the stamp-act cast off the disguise of ministers and revealed the despotism that stood ready with its fetters to bind the free Britons of America. Henceforward contentions arose. The British parliament assumed the right to tax the colonies of Great Britain, without their consent. The colonies raised the standard inscribed, " TAXATION AND REPRESENTA- TION *one and inseparable.*" Ten long years they humbly petitioned and remonstrated. They loved the parent-country, revered her institutions and laws, and were proud of their connexion with such an empire. But their loyal prayers were answered by other and greater oppressions. Insults succeeded oppressions, threats succeeded insults, and armies came hither to execute those threats. The colonies confederated, and by representatives, consulted and acted for the general good. They still clung to the hope of reconciliation ; but at length that radiant star waned in the firmament, clouds gathered in the political heavens, and the alternative was presented of resistance and freedom, or submission and slavery. The choice was soon made, and the weapons were speedily prepared to sever the last tie that bound America to Britain— the ligament of *political union.*

In June, 1776, Richard Henry Lee, of Virginia, one of the master-spirits of the revolution, stood up boldly in the continental Congress, and, denouncing the British government as an instrument of oppression most foul, and the king as a tyrant whose behests freemen were not bound to heed, sent a small slip of paper to the desk of Charles Thomson, the secretary of Congress. He rose with solemn countenance, but clear, firm voice, and read as follows : " *Resolved,* That the United Colonies are, and of right ought to be, free and independent states ; that they are absolved from all allegiance to the British crown ; and that all political connexion between them and the state of Great Britain is, and ought to be, totally dissolved." These words were few, but pregnant with great consequences. They formed the dedicatory oration at the planting of the tree of liberty—they were the first notes of that full diapason of harmonious defiance which arose loud and clear, from every hill and valley of our beautiful land, and awoke responsive echoes among the hopeful in the old world.

Royalty, relying upon justice and a lingering hope of reconciliation, yet lingered in the continental Congress, and some shrunk back from the fearful responsibilities assumed by that resolution. But Lee, the Adams's, Jefferson, Witherspoon, Franklin, and others less conspicuous as speakers, were bold and firm in its support, and their strength seemed to increase in proportion to the growing timidity of a few. "I should advise," said Samuel Adams, "persisting in our struggle for liberty, though it were revealed from heaven that nine hundred and ninety-nine were to perish and only one of a thousand were to survive and retain his liberty! One such freeman must possess more virtue, and enjoy more happiness, than a thousand slaves; and let him propagate his like, and transmit to them what he hath so nobly preserved." Such sentiments like electricity, pervaded the whole solemn council, confirmed the wavering, and strengthened the already resolute. A declaration, in conformity with the resolution, setting forth the causes which impelled the colonies to a separation from the parent-state, was prepared, and on the fourth of July votes from all the colonies were obtained in favor of the resolution and the adoption of the declaration. On that day the decree went forth affirming that the "United Colonies are, and of right ought to be free and independent states; that they are absolved from all allegiance to the British crown, and that all political connexion between them and the state of Great Britain is, and ought to be, totally dissolved; and that, as free and independent states, they have full power to levy war, conclude peace, contract alliances, establish commerce, and to do all other acts and things which independent states may of right do." This declaration was signed on that day only by John Hancock, the president of Congress, and thus sent forth to the colonial assemblies and to the army. The great body of the delegates signed it on the second of August following.

The adoption and signing of the declaration of independence, was but the initial act in the founding of our republic. It was an easy matter to *declare* the states free, but all men saw the vastness of the the labor that must be performed, and the privation and sorrow that must be endured in *supporting* that declaration. Already the great energies of the British government were concentrating in efforts to crush the now formidable rebellion here. Armies were already in our midst —fleets were hovering upon our coasts—German hirelings were filling transports to come hither to plunder and destroy; and in every neighborhood, aye, in almost every household, more dreaded secret enemies who, through principle or interest, adhered to the crown, weakened the patriot cause and strengthened the oppressor's arm.

In all the colonies the royal governments were overturned, and constitutions were adopted by the people represented in council, consonant with the spirit of the declaration of independence, and conformable to the political wants of each state. So extended was the geographical area, and so dissimilar were the social habits and industrial pursuits of the thirteen insurged states, that there could be said to exist scarcely a semblance of political union, except in the federal Congress and the federal army, and these depended for existence and vitality upon the presence of a common danger and a desire for the promotion of the common welfare. Confusion was everywhere visible, and nothing but a stronger confederation, bound by a covenant of political union, promised to hold the colonies long together. This was at length effected; and on the fifteenth of November, 1777, ARTICLES OF CONFEDERATION were adopted, and became the organic law of the land.

This step toward a permanent federal government was good as far as it went; but it was soon perceived that the reserved sovereignty of the individual states, and the jealousies that naturally arose out of sectional relations, rendered the general Congress weaker than before, and quite inadequate, in power, to carry on the complicated operations of government with efficiency. But the strife of war and the contention of parties within, occupied too much of the mind and energies of the people to allow of further legislation upon that subject, and it was left for the establishment of peace to devise a better government. This was finally done; and in September, 1787, the present CONSTITUTION OF THE UNITED STATES was adopted by the convention appointed to "revise the articles of confederation." It was ratified by the several states, after long and vigorous debate, and on the 30th of April, 1789, GEORGE WASHINGTON was elected the first president of the United States, in conformity to the provisions of the federal constitution. This was really the crowning act of the Revolution—this was the birth-day proper of our happy republic, for all that preceded it were but the labor-throes of progress in bringing forth this comely child, the pride and glory of the earth.

Although Washington was the first president of the republic under the federal constitution, yet he was not the first president, in fact, of the United States. The presidents of Congress during the first insurgent period, and afterward under the articles of confederation, held the same political relation to the people (though with much less power) as the president now does. They were each, in turn, the chief magistrate of the nation, and as such it is proper to associate them, by brief mention, with the twelve whose biographies compose this volume. There were fourteen of them during a period of fourteen years and eight months, or from September, 1774, to May, 1789. They were elected to serve only for a session of the body that raised them to the dignity—were merely chairmen of that body—and yet their office was the highest in the gift of the people. We will notice them in the order of their election and service.

PEYTON RANDOLPH.—The first continental Congress met in Carpenter's hall, Philadelphia, on the 5th of September, 1774. There were fifty-five delegates elected, representing twelve of the thirteen colonies, and all were present but those of North Carolina, who did not arrive until the 14th. Georgia was not represented. Peyton Randolph was appointed president, and Charles Thomson secretary. Mr. Randolph was a native of Virginia, and descended from one of its oldest and most respected families. Like other young men of the aristocracy, he was educated in England. He chose the profession of the law, and such were his talents that he was appointed attorney-general of the province as early as 1756. In that year he engaged with one hundred gentlemen to band as volunteers and march against the Indians on their western frontier. He was for some years a member of the house of burgesses of Virginia, and at one time its speaker. He was one of the delegates from Virginia to the first continental Congress, was chosen the chairman, or president, of that body, and was also chosen president of the second Congress, that met in Philadelphia on the 10th of May, 1775. On account of sickness he was obliged to resign his station on the 24th of that month and return to Virginia. He afterward resumed his seat as a delegate in Congress, and died at Philadelphia, of apoplexy, on the 22d of October, 1775, aged 52 years. Toward the close of the session of 1774, he was obliged to be absent, and his place was filled, the remainder of the term, by

HENRY MIDDLETON, a delegate from South Carolina. His term of office was but of a few days' continuance, for the session terminated on the 26th of October. Mr. Middleton was very little known in public life. He was the son of Arthur Middleton, the first royal governor of South Carolina, and, with his more distinguished son Arthur (one of the signers of the declaration of independence), early espoused the patriot cause. He was a man of great wealth, and therefore his stake was greater in the issue. Both himself and son suffered severely in estate during the conflict. He remained a member of Congress until 1776, when he retired from public life. Of the time of his death we have no record at hand.

JOHN HANCOCK.—When Peyton Randolph left the presidential chair on the 24th of May, 1775, John Hancock, a delegate from Massachusetts, was elected to fill the vacancy. Mr. Hancock was the son of John Hancock, a pious minister of Braintree, in Massachusetts, and was born in 1737. He graduated at Harvard college, in 1754. On the death of his uncle, Thomas Hancock, a benefactor of the college, he received a large fortune, entered into commercial business, and soon became one of the leading merchants of Boston. He was chosen a member of the Massachusetts assembly, for Boston, in 1766, with James Otis, Thomas Cushing, and Samuel Adams. One of his vessels, named Liberty, was seized on coming into Boston, in 1768, charged with evading the revenue laws. Already the public mind was greatly agitated by the Stamp Act and other measures of parliament, and Mr. Hancock was one of the leaders of the opposition in the assembly. The seizure of his vessel caused a serious riot, and from that time he was marked as an agitator, by the royal government. In all the phases of political events from that period until the breaking out of the revolution, he was a firm adherent to the patriot cause. He was a delegate for Massachusetts in the first continental Congress, and so decidedly rebellious did his course appear, that General Gage, in issuing a proclamation of "pardon to all rebels," excluded John Hancock and Samuel Adams, whose offenses, it was declared, were " of too flagitious a nature to admit of any other consideration than that of condign punishment." He remained a member of Congress until the 1st of November, 1777, and was president of that body from May 24th, 1775, until he vacated his seat as delegate. Ill health was the cause of his withdrawal, for a time, from public business. He was chosen the first governor of Massachusetts under its new constitution, in 1780, and was annually elected to that office for five years, when he resigned. He was again elected governor in 1787, and remained in office until his death on the the 8th of October, 1793, aged 56 years.

HENRY LAURENS.—Mr. Laurens, a delegate from South Carolina, succeeded John Hancock on the 1st of November, 1777. He took an active part in the politics of his native state, and early espoused the republican cause. He was president of the provincial Congress of South Carolina, in 1775, and while acting in that capacity he drew up a form of association, in a decided tone, to be signed by all the friends of liberty. A temporary constitution was adopted for his state in 1776, and under it he was elected vice-president. The next year he was elected a delegate to the general Congress, and was its president until December, 1778. He was deputed by Congress, in 1780, to solicit a loan from Holland, and to negotiate a treaty with the United Netherlands. The vessel in which he sailed was captured on the banks of Newfoundland. He was sent to England and committed to the Tower, on a charge of high treason, where he was confined more than a year, and was treated with great severity. His papers discovered matters which led to a war between England and Holland. He was released at the close of the year 1781. He went to Paris, and there, with Franklin and Adams, signed the preliminaries of peace, in November,

1782, having been appointed by Congress one of the commissioners. He returned to America in 1783, and died at Charleston, South Carolina, on the 8th of December, 1793, aged 69 years. His son, Henry L., inherited from him an estate worth about three hundred thousand dollars, on condition that he should burn his body on the third day after his death. His daughter married Dr. Ramsay, one of the earliest historians of the revolution.

JOHN JAY succeeded Mr. Laurens in the presidential chair, on the 10th of December, 1778. He was the son of Peter Jay, a descendant of a French Huguenot who emigrated from Rochelle, France, to New York, about 1696. He was born December 12, 1745, and was educated at King's (now Columbia) college. He married the daughter of William Livingston, governor of New Jersey, and early espoused the republican cause. Although very young, he was a distinguished lawyer when appointed a delegate from New York to the Congress of 1774. He was the writer of the eloquent address to the people of Great Britain, adopted at that session, and penned many of the finest productions of the succeeding Congresses. He was in New York, assisting in forming the constitution and government of that province, in 1776, and, consequently, his name was not attached to the declaration of independence. He presented a draught of the constitution of the state of New York, in March, 1777, which was adopted. From the May following until August, 1779, he was chief justice of his state ; but his duties as president of Congress obliged him to resign that post. In September, 1779, he was appointed minister plenipotentiary to the court of Spain. There he remained until 1782, but was unsuccessful in his principal negotiations, on account of reputed bad faith on the part of France. He was appointed a commissioner to negotiate a peace with Great Britain, in 1782, and he signed the definitive treaty, September 3, 1783. He returned to America in 1784, having been appointed by Congress secretary of state for foreign affairs. This was a very important station, and therein his services were exceedingly valuable. He was not a member of the convention that framed the federal constitution, but assisted it by suggestions and advice, and aided Hamilton and Madison in writing the Federalist. Washington appointed him chief justice of the United States, in 1789, and in 1794 he was appointed minister plenipotentiary to the court of St. James, where he effected the treaty that bears his name. He was elected governor of New York, in 1795, and re-elected in 1798. He withdrew from public life in 1801, and for nearly thirty years lived in pleasant retirement upon his estate at Bedford, Westchester county, New York, where he died May 17, 1829, aged 84 years.

SAMUEL HUNTINGTON was born in Windham, Connecticut, in 1732. He had a strong and active mind, but it had not the advantages of a collegiate education. He studied law, and commenced the practice of his profession in Norwich, in 1760. He was a representative in the general assembly in 1764, and the following year he was appointed king's attorney for the province. In 1774, he was made assistant judge of the superior court, and in 1775 was elected to a seat in the council. The same year he was elected a delegate to the general Congress, of which body he was a member until 1781, and was one of the signers of the declaration of independence. He succeeded Mr. Jay in the presidency, September 28, 1779. On retiring from Congress, he again took his seat upon the bench and in the council of his state. He was again in Congress in 1783, and the next year was appointed chief justice of Connecticut. He was elected governor of his state in 1786, and held the office until his death, which occurred at Norwich, on the 5th of January, 1796, at the age of 63 years.

THOMAS M'KEAN, of Delaware, succeeded Mr. Huntington as president of Congress, on the 10th of July, 1781. He was the son of William M'Kean, an Irishman, and was born March 19, 1734. He studied law in New Castle, and settled in that county, of which he was a representative in the legislature, in 1762. He was a member of the colonial, or Stamp Act Congress, in 1765, and having, from that time, warmly espoused the cause of the colonists against Great Britain, he was elected a delegate to the first general Congress, in 1774. At that period he was a resident of Philadelphia. He remained a delegate in Congress from Delaware until 1783, and at the same time he was chief justice of Pennsylvania. He voted for and signed the declaration of independence. He was a warm friend of the federal constitution, and in the Pennsylvania convention he urged its adoption. In 1799, he was elected governor of Pennsylvania, in which office he remained until 1808. From that period, he enjoyed the retirement of private life until his death, which occurred on the 24th of June, 1817, in his 83d year.

JOHN HANSON.— We have been unable to collect any details of the life of Mr. Hanson. He was elected a delegate to Congress from Maryland, in the summer of 1781, and remained in that body until the establishment of peace, in 1783. He was elected by his colleagues president of Congress, on the 5th of November, 1781, and held the office just one year. He died in Prince George's county, Maryland, November 13, 1783.

ELIAS BOUDINOT.— This distinguished patriot was of Huguenot extraction. He was a native of New Jersey, and studied law under Richard Stockton, one of the delegates in Congress from that state who signed the declaration of independence. He became a distinguished lawyer, was an active patriot, and in 1777 Congress appointed him commissary-general of prisoners. The same year he was elected a delegate to Congress, where he remained until 1783. He succeeded John Hanson as president of that body, on the 4th of November, 1782, and in that capacity he signed the definitive treaty of peace. After the war, he resumed the profession of the law, but was again called to serve in Congress, under the new constitution, in 1789, where he represented his state for six years. Washington appointed him director of the mint of the United States, in 1796, where he continued until 1805, when he left the cares of public life, and retired to Burlington, New Jersey. He was then a trustee of Princeton college, and that year established its cabinet of natural history, at a cost of $3,000. He assisted in the formation of the American Bible Society, in 1816, and was elected its first president. He made a donation to it of ten thousand dollars, and afterward contributed liberally toward the erection of its depository. He was active and liberal in many benevolent operations, and on the 24th of October, 1821, at the age of 81, he went to receive his reward.

THOMAS MIFFLIN.— General Mifflin was the first of the military profession called to preside over Congress. He succeeded Dr. Boudinot on the 3d of November, 1783. He was a native of Pennsylvania, and was born of Quaker parents, in 1744. He was of an active and zealous temperament, and at a very early period of the controversy, took sides with the republicans. He was a member of the first Congress, in 1774, and when it adjourned, he took up arms. He was appointed quartermaster-general, on the organization of the continental army, in 1775. For this offence he was disowned by the society of friends. In 1777, he became associated with Gates and others, in endeavors to take from Washington the chief command, and for this act his reputation was injured. He was re-elected to Congress in 1783, and was president when, at its session at Annapolis, that year, Washington resigned his commission, and the definitive treaty of peace was ratified. In 1787, he was a member of the convention that framed the federal constitution, and in 1788 he succeeded Franklin as president of the supreme executive council of Pennsylvania. He was chosen governor of the state in 1790, and by his eloquence, more than his official power, he gathered the militia and controlled the elements of disorder that appeared in the " Whiskey Insurrection" in Pennsylvania, in 1794. He was governor until 1799, and died January 20, 1800, aged 56 years.

RICHARD HENRY LEE, one of the earliest and most active friends of the cause of freedom, was a native of Virginia. He was born at Stratford, Westmoreland county, January 20, 1732. He was educated in England, and, as early as 1755, he was a member of the house of burgesses. He was then very diffident, and it was many years before he could so far overcome the weakness as to attempt to make a speech. He originated the first open resistance to British tyranny in

2

the time of the Stamp Act, in 1765, and then his eloquence began to beam forth.   He also, in connexion with Dabney Carr, proposed the organization of committees of correspondence, in 1773. He was a member of the first Congress, in 1774; and in 1776 he submitted to that body the resolution which declared the United Colonies free and independent states.   Some of the most powerful documents drawn up by committees, were from his pen. He withdrew from Congress in 1778, but was re-elected in 1784, and on the 30th of November of that year he succeeded General Mifflin in the presidential chair.   He was chosen one of the first senators from Virginia, after the adoption of the federal constitution.   He resigned the office in 1792, and died at his seat in Westmoreland county, Virginia, June 19, 1794, aged 62 years.

NATHANIEL GORHAM was born in Charlestown, Massachusetts, in 1738.   He was often a member of the Massachusetts legislature, where his sound common sense, rather than brilliancy of talents, made him influential.   He was an active but not very prominent patriot during the trying scenes of the Revolution.   In 1784, he was elected a delegate to Congress, and was chosen president of that body on the 6th of June, 1786.   He was a judge of the court of common pleas for his district, for several years, and a member of the convention that formed the federal constitution.   He died June 11, 1796, aged 58 years.

ARTHUR ST. CLAIR was a native of Edinburgh, Scotland.   He was born in 1734, and came to America with Admiral Boscawen, in 1755. He served in Canada, under Wolfe, and after the peace of 1763, he was appointed to the command of Fort Ligonier, in Pennsylvania. In 1776, he was appointed a colonel in the continental army, and raised a regiment destined for service in Canada.   In August, of that year, he was appointed a brigadier, and was in the battles of Trenton and Princeton.   In February, 1777, he was made a major-general, and on the 5th of June was ordered by General Schuyler to the command of the garrison at Ticonderoga.   Owing to a lack of troops, provisions, and ammunition, sufficient to well man the works, he was obliged to evacuate that post, on the approach of Burgoyne, on the night of the 5th of July.   He was at Yorktown when Cornwallis surrendered, and from there he went south to reinforce General Greene in Georgia. After the war, he resided in Pennsylvania, was elected to Congress in 1786, and was made president of the same on the 2d of February, 1787. The Northwestern territory was organized in 1788, and he was appointed its governor, which station he held until 1802, when Ohio was admitted into the Union as an independent state.   He declined being a candidate for governor.   During his administration there was much trouble with the Indian tribes, and his military operations against them were disastrous.   He left his office almost ruined in fortune.   He made claims against Congress for services and disbursements, which were disallowed, and he died almost penniless, at Laurel Hill, near Philadelphia, August 31, 1818, aged 84 years.

CYRUS GRIFFIN was a native of England, but for several years previous to the Revolution he was a resident of Virginia, and member of the house of burgesses. He sided with the republicans against the government of his fatherland, and throughout the war adhered consistently and firmly to the patriot cause. He was elected a delegate to the general Congress, in 1778, and again served his adopted state in that capacity in 1787. He was elected president of that body on the 22d of January, 1788. After the adoption of the federal constitution, and the reorganization of the judiciary, he was appointed a judge of the district court of Virginia. At his first court, held at Richmond, John Marshall, afterward chief justice of the United States, was admitted as counsel. He died at Yorktown, Virginia, on the 10th of December, 1810, aged 62 years.

CHARLES THOMSON, who was chosen secretary of the first continental Congress, in 1774, and who for fifteen consecutive years performed the arduous and important duties of that station, may very properly be noticed among these brief memoirs, for his services, in fact, were more really valuable — he was more truly the presiding officer in those assemblies — than the president. Perfectly familiar with every political movement at home and abroad, which related to his country, and in constant correspondence, both secret and open, with the leading men of the day, he was consulted on all occasions, and his opinions had weighty influence. Mr. Thomson was born in Ireland, and came to this country with his three elder brothers, in 1741. He landed at New Castle; his industry was all that he could depend upon for support. He was educated by Dr. Allison, the tutor of several of the signers of the declaration of independence, and afterward he was the teacher at the Friend's academy, at New Castle. He went to Philadelphia, and was fortunate enough to obtain the friendship and advice of Dr. Franklin, who was his firm friend through life. When the first Congress met, in 1774, he was called upon to keep minutes of their proceedings, and from that time until he resigned his office, in July, 1789, he was the sole secretary. His mind was always strongly imbued with religious principles, his morals were strictly pure, and so upright was he in all his ways, that the Indians gave him a name which signified "the man of truth." He married Hannah Harrison, the aunt of the late president of the United States. After the Revolution, he devoted much time to the study of the Bible; and he translated the Septuagint, from the original Greek, which was published in four volumes in 1808. He died at Lower Merion, Montgomery county, Pennsylvania, August 16, 1824, aged 94 years.

Judge Griffin was the last of the presidents under the old confederation, and was succeeded by Washington, on the 30th of April, 1789, when the new system of government, under the federal constitution, commenced its prosperous career. The history of that career from the period when the population of the states did not exceed four millions, until the present, when twenty millions are reckoned, is well developed in the memoirs which compose this volume, and requires no notice at our hands. The picture is one of great beauty and magnificence; and if the old Roman had cause to boast of his citizenship, surely an American, with all the glory and beneficence of free institutions around him, has cause to be proud of his citizenship, and to be grateful to his Creator for giving him such a goodly heritage.

No department of literature, in a moral point of view, is more pleasing, instructive, and useful, than biography; for while it portrays the history of the times of the subject, if he be an active man in public life, it develops the secret springs of history, which the study of individual acts can alone reveal. Nowhere, in the whole range of this department, can a more interesting and instructive series of biographies be found, than is presented in those of the presidents of the United States, exhibiting as they do the planting, the incipient germination and the wide-spread fruition of a great republic, based upon the broadest foundations of a peaceful policy, and secured by the overshadowing influence of universal intelligence among the people. It is a wonderful history; and the life of each president is a brilliant commentary upon the influence of early moral culture in laying the basis of character to secure future greatness; and the *equality* which opens the door to the attainment of the highest honors, to every citizen.

In former times, when the people chose their rulers, a successful warrior generally received their suffrages; and it too often happened that he used his skill and popularity in establishing for himself a despotic throne upon the wreck of the very instrument that raised him to power—the free exercise of the will of the people. Happily for us, the glitter of military glory has not often blinded us, and only three of our twelve presidents have been soldiers by profession and from choice. Washington, our first and well-beloved, was a soldier only when common danger threatened the land, and freedom called for aid in the unequal struggle. When that danger was passed he delivered his commission to the power that gave it, and laid aside his sword to hold the implement of more beneficent subjugation — the plough. And the glory which each military president derives from his success in battle, is like the ephemeral brilliancy of the dewdrop that fades in an hour, compared to that more enduring brightness which his position as the head of a great republic causes him to receive from the confidence of a free people, and to reflect upon the pages of the history of his race. And yet, estimating right by the standard of equitable human policy, and endowing government, by imputation, with sentiments of self-love and self-preservation, they never drew their blades in a wrong cause, nor sullied the fair fame of themselves or their country by their unrighteous use. They were never lifted in support of despotism or oppression, or cruelly stained with the blood of the friends of freedom. It is also a pleasant reflection, that a combination of legislative talent and rare personal virtues in each, chiefly aided him in attaining the lofty position of the presidential chair, for without these, his military deeds, however brilliant, might have challenged the admiration of his countrymen, but could never have secured their consent to intrust him with the guidance of the helm of state. A bad man can never fill the seat of Washington while virtue and intelligence remain with the people.

Although our political system, like every other production of human wisdom, is, in a measure, defective, yet in its practical operation in attaining the great object for which governments are instituted — the happiness and prosperity of the people — it is 'eminently good. So radical was the change wrought by the Revolution, that many of the leading men of that period were distrustful of the capacities of the people for self-government, without some powerful check in the hands of ministers by which the freedom of will and action might be controlled. This distrust, and a jealous regard for state-rights, caused opposition to the federal constitution, and it was two years and a half from the adoption of that instrument before every state had ratified it. The political postulate of Paine, that "the best system of jurisprudence is a strong people and a weak government," was considered dangerous in practice, and perilous, if adopted, to the very existence of the new republic. On the other hand, men of equal sagacity, who had labored with the others, shoulder to shoulder, during the Revolution, were disposed to give the people the "largest liberty." Political parties, distinguished as Federalists and Republicans, were thus formed at the starting point of our permanent national career, and for twenty years each labored hard to convince the world that the other would assuredly pull down the pillars of the state, and crush the hopes of freedom beneath them. But the republic stood firm. Population increased. New industrial resources, whence public wealth and private happiness were drawn, were hourly developing. The waves of population, of commerce, and of agriculture, beat against the Alleganies, rose above them, and finally poured their flood into the great valleys of the Ohio and Mississippi. The "wilderness blossomed as the rose." New states were added to the original thirteen; and thirty years' experience taught cautious doubters that the people were fully capable of self-government. Increasing prosperity at home, and respect abroad, have since marked our progress; and now our inhabited territories extend from ocean to ocean; our thirteen states have grown to thirty; our four millions of people have increased to twenty millions; our sails of commerce are upon every sea; and our political doctrines, enforced only by happy illustrations in our own history, are at this moment revolutionizing the hoary political systems of the old world. Our declaration that "all men are born free and equal," repudiated the "divine right of kings," the immunities of aristocracies, and the privileges of castes. These three classes of burdens weigh heavily upon social advancement, and obstruct the upward progress of nations. We cast them off, and outstripped Europe in the race for eminence. Her people are now struggling with mighty energy to shake off these incubi; and as every effort casts up to the light of righteous scrutiny the foul practices and intentions of despotism, the beauty of our own system becomes more apparent by contrast, and our duty to be grateful appears a glorious privilege.

The spectacle which is quadrennially presented here of a change of rulers, both in the method and in the practical result, is a notable exhibition of the capacity of our people for self-government, and their undoubting reliance upon the strength and justice of our political system. Party spirit, which, when controlled by intelligence, prudence, and judgment, is a powerful element of purity in a free state, pervades our whole people when a new election for chief magistrate approaches. Two eminent men of the nation are selected as candidates for the office. The character of each, public and private, is immediately placed beneath the scrutiny of the microscope of party zeal, and his faults and virtues, his weakness and his strength, are measured by an exalted standard, and published to the world. A foreigner, uninstructed in our ways, landing in our midst at the time of our election canvass, would believe that the elements of destruction were rife; that our government was on the verge of dissolution; and that Anarchy was about to snatch the sceptre from Order and Justice. The day of choice passes by; the great voice of the nation has spoken; the tumult of party warfare ceases; the placards of praise and censure of candidates disappear; the threatening aspect of party spirit is changed to serenity; and a cheerful acquiescence of the minority in the expressed will of the majority silences every murmur of complaint. Partisans, bitter and uncompromising in the contest, meet upon the common ground of friendly intercourse, and walk arm in arm as happy brothers amid the profuse blessings of free institutions. Faith, strong and abiding, in the promises of the constitution, and the virtue and intelligence of the people, assure all that he who is elevated to the post of honor, governed by the wise checks and balances of organic law, and a desire to appear worthy to fill the seat of the wise and good who have ruled before him, will employ every power he possesses in efforts to sustain the true glory of the republic. That faith has never yet been betrayed.

The nine presidents who sleep in the grave have an enduring monument in the love and esteem of the whole nation, and those who remain with us are honored and beloved.

The economy of our government, the light burdens which are imposed upon the people for its support, and the general freedom of labor, are important features in our system, and present a strong contrast to the expensive operations of royalty and the cruel exactions of aristocracy. Here, the emoluments of office are small, and unrighteous sinecures are unknown. No national church establishment, with its host of non-producers, exacts tithes; no ponderous standing army, with its legions of drones, draws the life-blood from the veins of industry; nor does the pomp, and pageantry, and costly trappings of royalty, and the erection, decoration, and support of gorgeous palaces, deprive enterprise and labor of their just reward. The toiler is fairly paid for the sweat of his brow; and no man, unless it be the black bond-slave, is so much the servant of another that his manhood is obliterated and he is made to feel like a dependent serf of the soil, compelled to utter in secret, if he dare utter it at all, the complaining question of the old man upon the banks of Ayr:—

> "If I'm yon haughty lordling's slave,
>   By Nature's law designed,
> Why was an independent wish
>   E'er planted in my mind?
> If not, why am I subject to
>   His cruelty and scorn?
> Or why has man the will and power
>   To make his fellow mourn?"

Here, the road to honor, wealth, and distinction, is free and unobstructed, and every youth of our republic may have the opportunity to travel that highway and win them. The spirit of our institutions is utterly unmindful of the assumptions of caste, whether based upon ancestry or wealth; and the poorest young man in our land has an equal right to the enjoyment of the highest distinctions, with the proudest child of rank and riches. Indeed, the history of our republic abounds with striking examples of exaltation to honor of men who began their career in the humblest walks of life; and some of the wisest living statesmen whose minds control public opinion, shape the course of party tactics, and direct the grave affairs of the nation, were children of poverty and obscurity. These various considerations combined — the noble character of our past rulers — the wisdom and beneficence of our political system — the just confidence of the people in the practical wisdom of our organic laws — the fair rewards of labor — the light burdens imposed for the support of government — and the equality which opens wide the pathway of honor to each — should form an irresistible inducement for every youth to aspire to the exalted station of a *good citizen*, and a cause for emotions of profound gratitude to the great Disposer of events for a birthright so valuable.

Young men, read these memoirs attentively, and ponder seriously upon the exhibition of human character and national greatness which they develop. Reflect upon your exalted position as a component of the sovereignty of a great republic, and the responsibilities which consequently rest upon you. As your fathers pass away, you must step in and fill their places. Learn to perform their duties well; and learn, too, to feel that the exercise of their duties is an exalted privilege, for while it ministers to your personal gratification it gives you a powerful influence over the destinies of our race. The people of the old world, for the present moment shrouded in gloom and bound in fetters, are lifting up their eyes to you for light and freedom. With you is intrusted the vestal fire of liberty. Let it never grow dim in your keeping, but feed its living flame with generous self-sacrifices, that the struggling nations may never be without a sure beacon to guide them in their pathway of blood to the temple of emancipation. Young men, a glorious field of usefulness is before you. A white harvest calls for zealous reapers. Human progress, with all its varied labors and felicities, beckons you on. Be not unfaithful—be not idle—but work, work, work.

> "Young men of every creed! up and be doing now;
> The time is come to "run and read," with thoughtful eye and brow.
> Extend your grasp to catch things unattained before;
> Touch the quick springs of Reason's latch, and enter at her door.
> The seeds of mind are sown in every human breast;
> But dormant lie, unless we own the spirit's high behest
> Look outwardly, and *learn*; look inwardly and *think*;
> And Truth and Love shall brighter burn o'er Error's wasting brink.
> Give energy to thought, by musing as ye move;
> Nor dream unworthy aught, or trifling for your love.
> Plunge in the crowded mart, there read the thoughts of men;
> And Human Nature's wondrous chart shall open to your ken!
> Shun drunkenness—'tis sin! the deadliest fatal ban
> Which ever veiled the light within, and palled the soul of man!
> In freedom walk sublime, as God designed ye should;
> Pillared props of growing time, supporting solid good.
> Tread the far forest; climb the sloping hill way-side,
> And feel your spirits ring their chime of gladness far and wide.
> Where'er your footsteps tend, where'er your feelings flow,
> Be man and brother to the end—compassionate the low!
> Curb Anger, Pride, and Hate; Let Love the watchword be;
> Then will your hearts be truly great, God-purified, and free!"

BIOGRAPHICAL SKETCH

OF

GEORGE WASHINGTON.

THE family of Washington, in Virginia, is descended from English ancestors, who were anciently established at Turtfield and Warton, in Lancashire, from a branch of whom came Sir William Washington, of Leicestershire, eldest son and heir of Lawrence Washington, Esq., of Sulgrave in Northamptonshire. Sir William had, besides other younger brothers, two, named John and Lawrence, who emigrated to Virginia in 1657, and settled at Bridge's creek, on the Potomac river, in the county of Westmoreland. John, the father of Lawrence Washington, died in 1697, leaving two sons, John and Augustine. Augustine died in 1743, at the age of forty-nine, leaving several sons by his two marriages. George, the president, was the eldest by his second wife, Mary Ball, and was born at Bridge's creek, on the 22d (or 11th, old style) of February, 1732.

Each of the sons of Augustine Washington inherited from him a separate plantation. To the eldest, Lawrence, he bequeathed the estate on the Potomac river, afterward called Mount Vernon, which then consisted of twenty-five hundred acres, and also other lands and property. The second son, Augustine, received an estate in Westmoreland. To George were left the lands and mansion where his father lived at the time of his disease, situated in Stafford county, on the east side of the Rappahannock river, opposite Fredericksburg ; and to each of the other four sons an estate of six or seven hundred acres. The youngest daughter died in infancy, and for the only remaining one a suitable provision was made in the will. Thus, it will be seen, that Augustine Washington left all his children in a state of comparative independence. His occupation had been that of a planter, and the large estates he was enabled to leave his family had been acquired chiefly by his own industry and enterprise.

Left a widow, with the charge of five young children, the eldest of whom was eleven years of age, Mrs. Washington, the mother of George, exhibited her resources of mind in the superintendence of their education and the management of the complicated affairs of her deceased husband, who by his will had directed that the proceeds of all the property of her children should be at her disposal until they should respectively come of age. This excellent woman had the happiness to see all her children come forward with a fair promise into life, filling the sphere allotted to them with equal honor to themselves and to the parent who had been the only guide of their principles, conduct, and habits. She lived to witness the noble career of her eldest son, till he was raised to the head of a nation, and applauded and revered by the world. Her death took place at the age of eighty-two, at her residence in Fredericsburg, Virginia, August 25, 1789.

Under the colonial governments, particularly in those of the south, the means of education were limited. Those young men who were destined for the learned professions were occasionally sent to England, when their parents were sufficiently wealthy to bear the expenses ; while the planters generally were satisfied with such a home education for their sons as would fit them for the duties of practical life, by means of a private tutor, or a teacher of the common schools then in existence. The simplest elements of knowledge only, such as reading, writing, arithmetic, and keeping accounts, were taught at schools of this description, to one of which George Washington was sent, and to such slender advantages was he indebted for all the aids his mind received in his juvenile years.

While at school he was noted for an inquisitive, docile, and diligent disposition, but displaying military propensities and passion for active sports. He formed his playmates into companies, who paraded, marched, and fought mimic battles, in which he was always the commander of one of the parties. He had also a fondness for running, jumping, wrestling, and other active sports and feats of agility.

His early proficiency in some branches of study is shown by his manuscript schoolbooks, which, from the time he was thirteen years old, have been preserved. These books begin with geometry, and he had already become familiar with arithmetic in the most difficult parts. Many pages of the manuscript in question are filled with what he calls *Forms of writing*, such as notes of hand, bills of exchange, bonds, land-warrants, leases, deeds, and wills, written out with care, and in a clerk's hand. Then follow selections in poetry of a moral and religious cast, and *Rules of Behavior in Company and Conversation*, which code of rules it is believed had an influence upon his whole life. Of an ardent temperament and strong passions, it was his constant effort and ultimate triumph, through the varied scenes of his eventful life, to check the one and subdue the other. His intercourse with men, private and public, in every walk and station, was marked with a consistency, a fitness to occasions, a dignity, decorum, condescension, and mildness, which were at once the dictates of his own good sense and judgment, and the fruits of unwearied discipline.

The last two years which he passed at school were devoted to the study of geometry, trigonometry, and surveying, for which he had a decided partiality. He thus qualified himself for his subsequent profession as a surveyor, in the practice of which he had an opportunity of acquiring information respecting vacant lands, and of forming those opinions concerning their future value which afterward greatly contributed to increase his private fortune. Except the above branches of the mathematics, his acquirements did not extend beyond the subjects usually taught to boys of his age at the common schools. It is even doubtful whether he received any instructions in the principles of language. By practice, reading, and study in after-life, he gradually overcame his early defects in composition till at length he wrote with accuracy, purity of idiom, and a striking appropriateness of phraseology and clearness of style. No aid was derived from any other than his native tongue. He never even commenced the study of the ancient classics. While in the army, after the French officers had joined the Americans, he bestowed some attention on the French language, but at no time could he write or converse in it, or indeed translate any paper.*

In the year 1746, while he was yet at school, a midshipman's warrant was obtained for him in the British army, by his eldest brother, Lawrence, who had been an officer in the British service, and served at the siege of Carthagena and in the West Indies. George, who was then fourteen years of age, was desirous thus early of embracing the opportunity presented for a naval life, but the interference of an affectionate mother deferred the commencement and changed the course of his military career.

Soon after leaving school, in his sixteenth year, he went to reside with his brother Lawrence, at his seat on the Potomac river, which had been called Mount Vernon, in compliment to the admiral of that name. The winter passed in the study of mathematics and in the exercise of practical surveying. At this time he was introduced to Lord Fairfax, and other members of the Fairfax family, established in that part of Virginia. With this family, his brother Lawrence was connected by marriage, and to his intimate acquaintance with them was George Washington mainly indebted for the opportunities of performing those acts which laid the foundation of his subsequent successes and advancement.

Lord Fairfax was possessed of large tracts of wild lands in the valleys of the Allegany mountains, which had not been surveyed; and so favorable an opinion had he formed of the abilities and attainments of young Washington, that he intrusted to him the responsible service of surveying and laying out the lands in question. He set off on this surveying expedition soon after he had attained his sixteenth year, accompanied by George Fairfax, a young man who was a relative of Lord Fairfax. The enterprise was arduous, and attended with privations and fatigues, but the

* Sparks's Life of Washington.

task was executed in such a manner as to give satisfaction to his employer, and establish his reputation as a surveyor.   Having received a commission or appointment as a public surveyor, he devoted three years to this pursuit, which at that time was lucrative and important.

At the age of nineteen he was appointed one of the adjutant-generals of Virginia, with the rank of major.   His military propensities had increased with his years, and he prepared himself by the study of books on the military art and by the manual exercise for the life of a soldier. But he had scarcely engaged in this service, when he was called upon to accompany his brother Lawrence on a voyage to the West Indies for his health.   They sailed for Barbadoes in September, 1751, and soon after landing on that island, George was seized with the smallpox.   The disease was severe, but with good medical attendance he was able to go abroad in three weeks.   Leaving his brother Lawrence to embark for Bermuda, he returned to Virginia in February, having been absent over four months.   His brother soon followed him, without recovering his health, and died the following summer.   Large estates were left by the deceased brother to the care and management of George, who was appointed one of the executors, with a contingent interest in the estate of Mount Vernon and other lands.   But his private employments did not prevent his attention to his public duties as adjutant-general, the sphere of which office was enlarged by new arrangements.

The plan formed by France for connecting her extensive dominions in America, by uniting Canada with Louisiana, now began to develop itself. Possession was taken by the French of a tract of country then deemed to be within the province of Virginia, and a line of posts was commenced from Canada to the Ohio river.   The attention of Lieutenant-Governor Dinwiddie, of Virginia, was attracted by these movements, and he deemed it his duty to send a messenger to the French officers and demand, in the name of the king of Great Britain, that they should desist from the prosecution of designs which violated, as he thought, the treaties between the two crowns.   Washington, at his own desire, was selected for this hazardous enterprise, and he engaged in it with alacrity, commencing his journey the day on which he was commissioned, in October, 1753.   His course was through a dreary wilderness, inhabited for the most part only by Indians, many of whom were hostile to the English.   Conducted by guides over the Allegany mountains, he suffered many hardships, and experienced many narrow escapes, but succeeded in reaching the French forts on the Allegany branches of the Ohio.   After delivering the lieutenant-governor's letter to St. Pierre, the French commanding officer, and receiving an answer, he returned, with infinite fatigue and much danger, from the hostile Indians, to Williamsburg.   The manner in which he performed his duty on this occasion raised him much in public opinion, as well as in that of the lieutenant-governor.   His journal, which extended to sixty days, was published by authority, and laid the foundation of Washington's fame, as it gave strong evidence of his sagacity, fortitude, and sound judgment.

As the French commandant on the Ohio showed no disposition, in his answer sent by Washington, to withdraw his forces from that country, the assembly of Virginia determined to authorize the governor and council to raise a regiment of three hundred men, to be sent to the frontier, for the purpose of maintaining the rights of Great Britain to the territory invaded by the French. The command of this regiment was given to Colonel Fry. Major Washington was appointed lieutenant-colonel, and obtained permission to march with two companies in advance of the other troops to the Great Meadows. In a dark rainy night, May 28, 1754, Colonel Washington surrounded and surprised a detachment of the French troops, a few miles west of the Great Meadows. The Americans fired about daybreak upon the French, who immediately surrendered. One man only escaped, and the commanding officer of the party, M. de Jumonville, and ten of his men were killed. Being soon after joined by the residue of the regiment, also by two companies of regulars, and Colonel Fry having died, the command devolved on Colonel Washington. This body of men, numbering less than four hundred, were, in the following month of July, attacked by about fifteen hundred French and Indians, at Fort Necessity, situated at the Great Meadows, and after a contest which lasted a whole day, the French offered terms of capitulation, and articles were signed, by which the fort was surrendered, and the garrison allowed the honors of war, and permitted to return unmolested into the inhabited parts of Virginia. Great credit was given to Colonel Washington by his countrymen, for the courage displayed on this occasion, and the legislature were so satisfied with the conduct of the party as to vote their thanks to him and the officers under his command. They also ordered three hundred pistoles to be distributed among the soldiers, as a reward for their bravery.

Soon after this campaign, Washington retired from the militia service, in consequence of an order from the war department in England, which put those of the same military rank in the royal army over the heads of those in the provincial forces. This order created great dissatisfaction in the colonies, and Washington, while refusing to submit to the degradation required, declared that he would serve with pleasure when he should be enabled to do so without dishonor.

The unfortunate expedition of General Braddock followed in 1755. The general, being informed of the merit of Washington, invited him to enter into his family as a volunteer and aid-de-camp. This invitation Colonel Washington accepted, as he was desirous to make one campaign under an officer supposed to possess some knowledge in the art of war. The disastrous result of Braddock's expedition is well known. In the battle of the Monongahela, in which General Braddock was killed, Washington had two horses shot under him, and four balls passed through his coat, as his duty and situation exposed him to every danger. Such was the general confidence in his talents, that he may be said to have conducted the retreat.

Soon after his return to his home at Mount Vernon, Colonel Washington was appointed by the legislature of the colony, commander-in-chief of all the forces raised and to be raised in Virginia, which appointment he accepted, and for about three years devoted his time to recruiting and organizing troops for the defence of the colony. In the course of his duties in this service, he had occasion to visit Boston on business with General Shirley, who was then the British commander-in-chief in America. This journey of five hundred miles, Washington, accompanied by his aid and another officer, performed on horseback in the winter of 1756. He stopped several days in the principal cities on the route, where his military character and services in the late campaign procured for him much notice.

While in New York he was entertained at the house of Mr. Beverly Robinson, between whom and himself an intimacy subsisted till it was broken off by their opposite fortune twenty years afterward in the revolution. The sister of Mrs. Robinson, Miss Mary Phillips, was an inmate of the family, and being a young lady of rare accomplishments, her charms made a deep impression upon the heart of the Virginia colonel. He imparted his secret to a confidential friend whose letters kept him informed of every important event. He soon learned that a rival was in the field, and was advised to renew his visits ; but he never saw the lady again, till she was married to that same rival, Captain Morris, his former associate in arms, and one of Braddock's aids-de-camp.*

In 1758, Colonel Washington commanded an expedition to Fort Du Quesne, which terminated successfully, and the French retired from the western frontier. By gaining possession of the Ohio the great object of the war in the middle colonies was accomplished, and having abandoned the idea he had entertained of making an attempt to be united to the British establishment, he resigned his commission in the colonial service, in December, 1758, after having been actively engaged in the service of his country more than five years.

Having paid his addresses successfully the preceding year to Mrs. Martha Custis, Colonel Washington was married to that lady on the sixth of January, 1759. She was three months younger than himself, and was the widow of John Parke Custis, and daughter of John Dandridge. Distinguished alike for her beauty, accomplishments, and wealth, she was possessed also of those qualities which adorn the female character, and contribute to render domestic life attractive and happy. Mr. Custis, her first husband, had left large landed estates, and forty-five thousand pounds

* Sparks's Life of Washington.

sterling in money. One third of this property his widow held in her own right, the other two thirds being equally divided between her, a son, and daughter, the former six years old, the latter four, at the time of her second marriage.

An accession of more than one hundred thousand dollars was made to Colonel Washington's fortune by his marriage, in addition to what he already possessed in the estate of Mount Vernon, and other lands which he had selected during his surveying expeditions, and obtained at different times. His extensive private affairs now required his constant attention. He was also guardian to the two children of Mrs. Washington, and this trust he discharged with all the care of a father, till the son became of age, and the daughter died in her nineteenth year. This union was in every respect felicitious, and continued forty years ; the lady surviving her distinguished husband, only about eighteen months. To her intimate acquaintances, and to the nation, the character of Mrs. Washington was ever a theme of praise. Affable, courteous, and charitable, exemplary in her deportment ; unostentatious and without vanity, she was much esteemed in private life, and filled with dignity every station in which she was placed.*

To the delightful retreat of Mount Vernon, the late commander of the Virginia forces, released from the cares of a military life, and in possession of everything that could make life agreeable, withdrew, three months after his marriage and gave himself up to domestic pursuits. These were conducted with so much judgment, steadiness, and industry, as greatly to enlarge and improve his estate. He had a great fondness for agricultural pursuits, and in all the scenes of his public career, there was no subject upon which his mind dwelt with so lively an interest as on that of agriculture. The staple product of Virginia, particularly in the lower counties, was tobacco, to the culture of which Washington chiefly directed his care. This he exported to England for a market, importing thence, as was then the practice of the Virginia planters, implements of agriculture, wearing apparel, and most other articles of common family use. For the study of English literature he had a decided taste, and his name is frequently to be found as subscriber to such works as were published in the colonies.

The enjoyments of private life at Mount Vernon, and the exercise of a generous hospitality at that mansion, continued uninterrupted for a period of about fifteen years ; with the exception of his absence from home during the session of the Virginia legislature, to the house of burgesses of which colony Washington was first elected a representative from the county of Frederic, during his last military campaign, without his personal solicitation or influence. He took his seat in that body at Williamsburg in 1759, and from that time till the beginning of the revolution, a period of fifteen years, he was constantly a member of the house of burgesses,

* Sparks.

being returned by a majority of votes at every election.   For seven years he represented jointly with another delegate the county of Frederic, and afterward the county of Fairfax, in which he resided.   There were commonly two sessions in a year, and sometimes three.   He gave his attendance punctually and from the beginning to the end of almost every session.

His influence in public bodies was produced more by the soundness of his judgment, his quick perceptions, and his directness and sincerity, than by eloquence or art.   He seldom spoke, never harangued, and it is not known that he ever made a set speech, or entered into a stormy debate. But his attention was at all times awake, and he was ever ready to act with decision and firmness.   His practice may be inferred by the following counsel.   In a letter to a nephew, who had been chosen and taken his seat as a member of the assembly, he says : " The only advice I will offer, if you have a mind to command the attention of the house, is to speak seldom, but on important subjects, except such as properly relate to your constituents, and in the former case make yourself perfectly master of the subject.   Never exceed a decent warmth, and submit your sentiments with diffidence.   A dictatorial style, though it may carry conviction, is always accompanied with disgust."

In the Virginia legislature, Washington acquitted himself with reputation, and gained no inconsiderable knowledge of the science of civil government.   During this period the clashing claims of Great Britain and her colonies were frequently brought before the colonial assembly.   In every instance he took a decided part in the opposition made to the principle of taxation claimed by the mother-country, and went heart and hand with Henry, Randolph, Lee, Wythe, and the other prominent leaders of the time.   His disapprobation of the stamp-act was expressed in unqualified terms.   He spoke of it in a letter written at the time, as an " unconstitutional method of taxation," and " a direful attack on the liberties of the colonists."   And subsequently he said : " The repeal of the stamp-act, to whatever cause owing, ought much to be rejoiced at.   All, therefore, who were instrumental in procuring the repeal, are entitled to the thanks of every British subject, and have mine cordially."   He was present in the Virginia legislature, when Patrick Henry offered his celebrated resolutions on this subject, and from his well-known sentiments expressed on other occasions, it is presumed that Washington concurred with the patriotic party which supported these early movements in favor of colonial rights and liberties.

In the subsequent acts of the people of the colonies in resisting the claims and aggressions of the British government, Washington cordially sympathized, and approved of the most decisive measures proposed in opposition, particularly of the agreements not to import goods from Great Britain.   " The northern colonies," he remarks in a letter to George Mason, " it appears, are endeavoring to adopt this scheme.   In my opinion, it is a good one, and must be attended with salutary effects, provided it can be carried pretty generally into execution." In these sentiments Mr. Mason concurred, and with a view to bring about a concert of action between Virginia and the northern colonies, he drew up a series of articles in the form of an association. The house of burgesses met in May, 1769, and as Mr. Mason was not a member, Washington took charge of the non-importation agreement paper, which, on being presented by him, after the dissolution of the assembly, was unanimously adopted by the members who assembled in a body at a private house. Every member subscribed his name to it, and it was then printed and distributed in the country for the signatures of the people. Washington was scrupulous in observing this agreement, enjoining his correspondents in London to send him none of the articles enumerated in the agreement of association, unless the offensive acts of parliament should be repealed.

In the autumn of 1770, Washington, accompanied by a friend, visited the western lands of Virginia on the Ohio river, for the purpose of selecting tracts awarded to the officers and soldiers for their services in the French war. Proceeding to Pittsburg on horseback, he there embarked in a canoe, and descended the Ohio river to the Great Kenhawa, a distance of 265 miles. After examining the lands on the latter river and making selections, he returned up the Ohio, and thence to Mount Vernon.

The Virginia assembly, which had been prorogued by the governor, Lord Dunmore, from time to time, until March, 1773, is distinguished as having brought forward the resolves instituting a committee of correspondence, and recommending the same to the legislatures of the other colonies; Washington was present and gave his support to those resolves. At the next session, which took place in May, 1774, the assembly adopted still more decisive measures. The news having reached Williamsburg at the commencement of the session, of the passage of the act of the British parliament for shutting up the port of Boston, the sympathy and patriotic feelings of the burgesses were strongly excited, and they forthwith passed an order deprecating this procedure, and setting apart the first of June to be observed as a day of fasting and prayer to implore the Divine interposition in behalf of the colonies. The governor thereupon dissolved the house the next morning.

The delegates, eighty-nine in number, immediately repaired to the Raleigh tavern, organized themselves into a committee, and drew up and signed an association, among other matters, advising the committee of correspondence to communicate with the committees of the other colonies, on the expediency of appointing deputies to meet in a general correspondence. Although the idea of a congress had been suggested by Doctor Franklin the year before, and proposed by town meetings at Providence (Rhode Island), Boston, and New York, yet this was the first public assembly by which it was formally recommended.

3

Twenty-five of the Virginia delegates, who had remained in Williamsburg, among whom was Washington, met on the twenty-ninth of May, and issued a circular letter to the people of Virginia, recommending a meeting of deputies from the several counties at Williamsburg, on the first of August, for the purpose of a more full and deliberate discussion. Meetings were accordingly held in the several counties, resolutions were adopted, and delegates appointed to the proposed convention. In Fairfax county, Washington presided as chairman, and was one of a committee to prepare a series of resolves, expressive of the sense of the people. These resolves are twenty-four in number, and were drawn by George Mason ; they constitute an able and luminous exposition of the points at issue between Great Britain and the colonies. They are of special interest as containing the opinions of Washington at a critical time, when he was soon to be raised by his countrymen to a station of the highest trust and responsibility.*

In a letter to his friend Bryan Fairfax, dated July 20, 1774, Washington writes as follows :—

" Satisfied, then, that the acts of the British parliament are no longer governed by the principles of justice, that they are trampling upon the valuable rights of Americans, confirmed to them by charter and by the constitution they themselves boast of, and convinced beyond the smallest doubt, that these measures are the result of deliberation, and attempted to be carried into execution by the hand of power, is it a time to trifle, or risk our cause upon petitions, which with difficulty obtain access, and afterward are thrown by with the utmost contempt ? Or should we, because heretofore unsuspicious of design, and then unwilling to enter into disputes with the mother-country, go on to bear more, and forbear to enumerate our just causes of complaint ? For my own part, I shall not undertake to say where the line between Great Britain and the colonies should be drawn ; but I am clearly of opinion that one ought to be drawn, and our rights clearly ascertained. I could wish, I own, that the dispute had been left to posterity to determine, but the crisis is arrived when we must assert our rights, or submit to every imposition that can be heaped upon us, till custom and use shall make us tame and abject slaves."

One of the principal acts of the Virginia convention, which met at Williamsburg on the first of August, 1774, of which body Washington was a member, was to adopt a new association, whose objects were resistance to parliamentary aggressions, by non-intercourse with Great Britain. The convention appointed Peyton Randolph, Richard Henry Lee, George Washington, Patrick Henry, Richard Bland, and Edmund Pendleton, delegates to the first continental Congress, which met at Philadelphia, on the fifth of September. Two of Washington's associates, Mr. Henry and Mr. Pendleton stopped on their way at Mount Vernon,

* These resolves are in Washington's writings, vol. ii., appendix, page 488.

whence they all pursued their journey together and were present at the opening of the Congress. As the debates of that distinguished assembly were never made public, the part performed by each individual can not now be known. In its transactions, however, Washington took an active part, and Mr. Wirt in his life of Patrick Henry relates an anecdote which shows in what estimation he was held by his associate members of Congress. Soon after Patrick Henry returned home, being asked whom he thought the greatest man in Congress, he replied : " If you speak of eloquence, Mr. Rutledge of South Carolina is by far the greatest orator ; but if you speak of solid information and sound judgment, Colonel Washington is unquestionably the greatest man on that floor."

Replying to a letter from his friend Captain Mackenzie of the British army, then stationed at Boston, in which that officer spoke of the rebellious conduct of the Bostonians, their military preparations, and their secret aim at independence, Washington wrote, while attending the Congress, giving his sentiments and views on the state of public affairs. The following are extracts :—

" Although you are taught to believe that the people of Massachusetts are rebellious, setting up for independence, and what not ; give me leave, my good friend, to tell you that you are abused, grossly abused. Give me leave to add, and I think I can announce it as a fact, that it is not the wish or interest of that government, or any other upon this continent, separately or collectively, to set up for independence ; but this you may at the same time rely on, that none of them will ever submit to the loss of those valuable rights and privileges which are essential to the happiness of every free state, and without which, life, liberty, and property, are rendered totally insecure.

" Again, give me leave to add, as my opinion, that more blood will be spilled on this occasion, if the ministry are determined to push matters to extremity, than history has ever yet furnished instances of in the annals of North America, and such a vital wound will be given to the peace of this great country, as time itself can not cure, or eradicate the remembrance of."

What is here said of independence is confirmed by the address of the first Congress to the people of Great Britain. " You have been told that we are seditious, impatient of government, and desirous of independency. Be assured that these are not facts, but calumnies." That such were at this time the sentiments of the leaders in America, there can be no reasonable doubt ; being accordant with all their public acts and private declarations.

It is not easy to determine at what precise date the idea of independence was first entertained by the principal persons in America. The spirit and form of their institutions led the colonists frequently to act as an independent people, and to set up high claims in regard to their rights and privileges ; but there is no sufficient evidence to prove, that any province, or any number of prominent individuals, entertained serious thoughts of separating entirely from the mother-country, till very near the actual commencement of the war of the revolution.*

While Washington and his principal coadjutors had no confidence in the success of petitions to the king and parliament, and looked forward to the probable appeal to arms, they were still without any other anticipations than by a resolute vindication of their rights to effect a change in the conduct and policy of the British government, and restore the colonies to their former condition.

On returning from Congress to his farm, Colonel Washington was soon interrupted in his private occupations by the calls of his fellow-citizens of Virginia, to assist in organizing military companies for the defence of the colony, and to prepare for the approaching contest with Great Britain. He was consulted as the first military character in Virginia, and it seemed to be the expectation of the people that in the event of a war he would be placed in command of the Virginia forces. Being solicited to act as field-officer in an independent company, he wrote to his brother as follows : " I shall very cheerfully accept the honor of commanding it, if occasion require it to be drawn out, as it is my full intention to devote my life and fortune in the cause we are engaged in, if needful."

Washington was a delegate to the second Virginia convention, which met at Richmond on the 20th of March, 1775, and approved of the proceedings of the continental Congress of 1774. A committee, of which Washington was a member, was appointed, on motion of Patrick Henry, and reported a plan of defence, by embodying, arming, and disciplining the militia. He was also on a committee to devise a plan for the encouragement of domestic arts and manufactures. The people were advised to form societies for that purpose, and the members of the convention agreed that they would use home manufactures in preference to any others,

---

* Among those who from the first seemed, to have a presentiment that reconciliation with Great Britain was out of the question was Patrick Henry. As early as 1773, according to Mr. Wirt, he alluded to the probability of a Declaration of Independence, and predicted that after being assisted by France, Spain, and Holland, " our independence would be established and we should take our stand among the nations of the earth !" Down to the year 1775, however the idea of independence was not generally prevalent or popular among the great mass of the American people. Doctor Timothy Dwight of New Haven, Connecticut, for many years president of Yale college, and for a time a chaplain in the revolutionary army, confirms this statement in his writings. " In the month of July, 1775," he says, " I urged in conversation with several gentlemen of great respectability, firm whigs, and my intimate friends, the importance, and even the necessity, of a declaration of independence on the part of the colonies, and alleged for this measure the very same arguments which afterward were generally considered as decisive ; but found them disposed to give me and my arguments, a hostile and contemptuous, instead of a cordial reception. These gentlemen may be considered as representatives of the great body of the thinking men in this country. A few may perhaps be excepted, but none of these durst at that time openly declare their opinions to the public."
Dwight's Travels, vol. i., page 159.

themselves. The former delegates were again chosen by the convention to represent Virginia in the next continental Congress, and Washington with his colleagues repaired to Philadelphia, where that body assembled on the 10th of May, 1775.

Hostilities having commenced between Great Britain and the colonies, Congress first proceeded to consider the state of the country and to provide for defence. The military fame and reputation of Washington were universally acknowledged by his countrymen and duly appreciated by his associates in the national councils. He was appointed chairman of the various committees charged with the duty of making arrangements for defence ; including the devising of ways and means, making estimates, and preparing rules and regulations for the government of the army. The forces under the direction of Congress were, on motion of John Adams, called " the continental army."

The selection of a commander-in-chief of the American armies, was a task of great delicacy and difficulty. There were several older officers than Colonel Washington, of experience and reputation, who had claims for the appointment, but it·was considered good policy to make the selection from Virginia, and all acknowledged the military accomplishments and other superior qualifications of Washington. The New England delegates were among the foremost to propose and the most zealous to promote the appointment of Colonel Washington. John Adams, one of the Massachusetts delegates, on moving that the army then besieging the British troops in Boston should be adopted by Congress as a continental army, said it was his intention to propose for the office of commander-in-chief, a gentleman from Virginia who was at that time a member of their own body. When the day for the appointment arrived (the fifteenth of June, 1775), the nomination was made by Mr. Thomas Johnson of Maryland. The choice was by ballot, and Colonel Washington was unanimously elected. As soon as the result was ascertained, the house adjourned. On the convening of Congress the next morning, the president communicated to him officially the notice of his appointment, and he rose in his place, and signified his acceptance in the following brief and appropriate reply :—*

" MR. PRESIDENT : Though I am truly sensible of the high honor done me in this appointment, yet I feel great distress from a consciousness that my abilities and military experience may not be equal to the extensive and important trust. However, as the Congress desire it, I will enter upon the momentous duty, and exert every power I possess in their service, and for support of the glorious cause. I beg they will accept my most cordial thanks, for this distinguished testimony of their approbation.

" But lest some unlucky event should happen unfavorable to my reputation, I beg it may be remembered by every gentleman in the room, that

* Sparks.

I this day declare, with the utmost sincerity, I do not think myself equal to the command I am honored with.

" As to pay, sir, I beg leave to assure the Congress, that, as no pecuniary consideration could have tempted me to accept this arduous employment, at the expense of my domestic ease and happiness, I do not wish to make any profit from it. I will keep an exact account of my expenses ; those I doubt not they will discharge, and that is all I desire."

In a letter to his wife, announcing his appointment, dated Philadelphia, June 18, 1775, Washington expressed similar sentiments to the foregoing, as follows :—

" My Dearest : I am now set down to write to you on a subject which fills me with inexpressible concern, and this concern is greatly aggravated and increased, when I reflect upon the uneasiness I know it will give you. It has been determined in Congress, that the whole army raised for the defence of the American cause shall be put under my care, and that it is necessary for me to proceed immediately to Boston to take upon me the command of it.

" You may believe me, when I assure you in the most solemn manner, that, so far from seeking this appointment, I have used every endeavor in my power to avoid it, not only from my unwillingness to part with you and the family, but from a consciousness of its being a trust too great for my capacity, and that I should enjoy more real happiness in one month with you at home, than I have the most distant prospect of finding abroad, if my stay were to be seven times seven years. But as it has been a kind of destiny that has thrown me upon this service, I shall hope that my undertaking it is designed to answer some good purpose. You might and I suppose did perceive, from the tenor of my letters, that I was apprehensive I could not avoid this appointment, without exposing my character to such censures, as would have reflected dishonor upon myself, and given pain to my friends. This, I am sure, could not, and ought not, to be pleasing to you, and must have lessened me considerably in my own esteem. I shall rely, therefore, confidently on that Providence which has heretofore preserved and been bountiful to me."

The appointment was made on the 15th of June, four days after which he received his commission from the president of Congress, declaring him commander-in-chief of all the forces then raised, or that should be raised, in the united colonies, or that should voluntarily offer their services for the defence of American liberty. The members of Congress by resolution, unanimously pledged themselves to maintain, assist, and adhere to him with their lives and fortunes, in the same cause. Four major-generals, eight brigadier-generals, and an adjutant-general, were likewise appointed by Congress for the continental army.

On the 21st of June. Gen. Washington hastened from Philadelphia to join the continental army at Cambridge near Boston. He was accompanied by Generals Lee and Schuyler, and escorted by a volunteer troop of light horse which continued with him to New York. On his way he was everywhere received by the people with enthusiasm, and the respect to which his new rank entitled him. The particulars of the battle of Bunker's hill reached him at New York, and increased his anxiety to hasten forward to the army. Leaving Gen. Schuyler in command at New York, Washington again pursued his journey, escorted by volunteer military companies, to Springfield, Massachusetts, where he was met by a committee of the provincial Congress of that colony, which attended him to Cambridge. He arrived at the latter place on the second of July, and took the command of the army the next day.

At this time Gen. Washington found the British intrenched on Bunker's hill, having also three floating batteries in Mystic river, and a twenty-gun ship below the ferry between Boston and Charlestown. They had also a battery on Copp's hill, and were strongly fortified on Boston Neck. The Americans were intrenched at various points so as to form a line of siege around Boston and Charlestown.

The effective force of the American army placed under the command of Washington, amounted to fourteen thousand, five hundred men, raised in the New England colonies.* Several circumstances concurred to render this force very inadequate to active operations. Military stores were deficient in camp, and the whole amount in the country was inconsiderable. Under all these embarrassments, the general observed, that "he had the materials of a good army; that the men were able-bodied, active, zealous in the cause, and of unquestionable courage." He immediately instituted such arrangements as were calculated to increase their capacity for service. The army was distributed into brigades and divisions, and on his recommendation, general staff-officers were appointed. Economy, union, and system, were introduced into every department. As the troops came into service under the authority of distinct colonial governments, no uniformity existed among the regiments. In Massachusetts, the men had chosen their officers, and (rank excepted) were in other respects, frequently their equals. To form one uniform mass of these discordant materials, and to subject freemen, animated with the spirit of liberty, and collected for its defence, to the control of military discipline, required patience, forbearance, and a spirit of accommodation. This delicate and arduous duty was undertaken by General Washington, and discharged with great address. When he had made considerable progress in disciplining his army, the term for which enlistments had taken place was on the point of expiring. The commander-in-chief made early and forcible representations to Congress on this subject, and urged them to adopt efficient measures for the formation of a new army. They deputed three of their mem-

* Several companies of riflemen from Virginia, Pennsylvania, and Maryland, joined the army at Cambridge in September, having marched from four to seven hundred miles.

bers, Mr. Lynch, Dr. Franklin, and Mr. Harrison, to repair to camp, and in conjunction with him and the chief magistrates of the New England colonies, to confer on the most effectual mode of continuing, supporting, and regulating, a continental army. By them it was resolved to enlist 23,722 men, as far as practicable, from the troops before Boston, to serve till the last day of December, 1776, unless sooner discharged by Congress.

In the execution of this resolve, Washington called upon all officers and soldiers to make their election for retiring or continuing. Several of the inferior officers retired. Many of the men would not continue on any terms. Several refused, unless they were indulged with furloughs; others unless they were allowed to choose their officers. So many impediments obstructed the recruiting service, that it required great address to obviate them. Washington made forcible appeals, in general orders, to the pride and patriotism of both officers and men. He promised every indulgence compatible with safety, and every comfort that the state of the country authorized. In general orders of the 20th of October, he observed :—

"The times, and the importance of the great cause we are engaged in, allow no room for hesitation and delay. When life, liberty, and property, are at stake ; when our country is in danger of being a melancholy scene of bloodshed and desolation ; when our towns are laid in ashes, innocent women and children driven from their peaceful habitations, exposed to the rigors of an inclement season, to depend perhaps on the hand of charity for support ; when calamities like these are staring us in the face, and a brutal savage enemy threatens us and everything we hold dear, with destruction from foreign troops ; it little becomes the character of a soldier to shrink from danger, and condition for new terms. It is the general's intention to indulge both officers and soldiers who compose the new army with furloughs for a reasonable time ; but this must be done in such a manner as not to injure the service, or weaken the army too much at once."

In the instructions given to the recruiting officers, the general enjoined upon them, "not to enlist any person suspected of being unfriendly to the liberties of America, or any abandoned vagabond, to whom all causes and countries are equal and alike indifferent."*

Though great exertions had been made to procure recruits, yet the regiments were not filled. Several causes operated in producing this disinclination to the service. The sufferings of the army had been great; fuel, clothes, and even provisions, had not been furnished them in sufficient quantities ; the small-pox deterred many from entering ; but the principal reason was a dislike to a military life. Much also of that enthusiasm which brought numbers to the field, on the commencement of hostilities had abated. The army of 1775 was wasting away by the expiration of the terms of service, and recruits for the new, entered slowly.*

Unfortunately, an essential error had been committed in constituting the

* Ramsay.

first military establishment of the Union, the consequences of which ceased only with the war. The soldiers were enlisted for the term of one year, if not sooner discharged by Congress. This fatal error brought the American cause more than once into real hazard.

General Washington had earnestly urged Congress to offer a bounty; but this expedient was not adopted till late in January; and on the last day of December, 1775, when the old army was disbanded, only nine thousand six hundred and fifty men had been enlisted for the army of 1776.

The general viewed with deep mortification the inactivity to which he was compelled to submit. His real difficulties were not generally known; his numbers were exaggerated; his means of acting on the offensive were magnified; the expulsion of the British army from Boston had been long since anticipated by many; and those were not wanting who insinuated that the commander-in-chief was desirous of prolonging the war, in order to continue his own importance.

Congress having manifested dispositions favorable to an attack on Boston, General Washington continued to direct his utmost efforts to that object. In January, 1776, a council of war resolved, " that a vigorous attempt ought to be made on the ministerial troops in Boston, before they can be reinforced in the spring, if the means can be provided, and a favorable opportunity should offer ;" and for this purpose that thirteen regiments of militia should be required from Massachusetts and the neighboring colonies. The colonies complied with this requisition ; but such was the mildness of the early part of the winter, that the waters continued open, and of course impassable.

Late in February, appearances among the British troops indicated an intention to evacuate Boston. But as these appearances might be deceptive, General Washington determined to prosecute a plan which must force General Howe either to come to an action or abandon the town.

Since the allowance of a bounty, recruiting had been more successful, and the regular force had been augmented to fourteen thousand men. The commander-in-chief had also called to his aid six thousand militia. Thus reinforced, he determined to take possession of the heights of Dorchester and fortify them. As the possession of this post would enable him to annoy the ships in the harbor, and the soldiers in the town of Boston, he was persuaded that a general action would ensue. Should this hope be disappointed, his purpose was to make the works on the heights of Dorchester preparatory to seizing and fortifying other points which commanded the harbor, a great part of the town, and the beach from which an embarkation must take place in the event of a retreat.

To facilitate the execution of this plan, a heavy bombardment and cannonade were commenced on the British lines on the second of March, which were repeated on the succeeding nights. On the east of them a strong detachment, under the command of General Thomas, took possession of the heights, and labored with such persevering activity through the night, that the works were sufficiently advanced by the morning nearly to cover them.

It was necessary to dislodge the Americans or to evacuate the town, and General Howe determined to embrace the former part of the alternative. Three thousand chosen men commanded by Lord Percy embarked, and fell down to the castle, in order to proceed up the river to the intended scene of action, but were scattered by a furious storm. Before they could be again in readiness for the attack, the works were made so strong that the attempt to storm them was thought unadvisable, and the evacuation of the town became inevitable.

This determination was soon known to the Americans. A paper signed by some of the selectmen, and brought out by a flag, communicated the fact. This paper was accompanied by propositions said to be made by General Howe, relative to the security of the town and the peaceable embarkation of his army. The advances of the American troops were discontinued, and considerable detachments were moved toward New York before the actual evacuation of Boston. That event took place on the seventeenth of March, 1776 ; and in a few days the whole fleet sailed out of Nantasket road, directing its course eastward ; immediately after which the American army proceeded by divisions to New York, where it arrived on the fourteenth of April.*

Washington and the continental army were received with enthusiasm by the inhabitants of Boston. The legislature of Massachusetts presented the commander-in-chief with an address, congratulating him on the successful result of the siege of Boston, and expressing their obligations for the great services he had rendered to his country. The continental Congress also passed a unanimous vote of thanks to him, and a gold medal was ordered to be struck commemorative of the evacuation of Boston, and as an honorable token of the public approbation of his conduct.

General Howe, with the British army of about ten thousand men, and one thousand refugees or tories, sailed for Halifax in seventy-eight ships and transports ; but anxious for the safety of New York, and apprehensive that the British commander might have concealed his real designs and directed his course to that important point, the American commander-in-chief had directed the march of his army to New York, as already stated. They went by land to Norwich, Connecticut, and thence by water through Long Island sound. When it was ascertained that the British fleet had put to sea, ten days after the evacuation of Boston, Washington set off for New York, passing through Providence, Norwich, and New London. At Norwich he had an interview with Governor Trumbull who came there to meet him. On the thirteenth of April he arrived in New York.†

General Washington found it impracticable, or inconsistent with his du-

* Marshall.   † Sparks.

ties to carry out his original design of visiting his family at Mount Vernon in the winter, and attending for a short space to his private affairs. Mrs. Washington therefore joined him at headquarters at Cambridge, in December, 1775, where she remained till the next spring. This was her practice during the war. She passed the winters with her husband in camp, and returned at the opening of the campaigns to Mount Vernon.

His large estates were consigned to the care of a superintendent, Mr. Lund Washington, who executed the trust with diligence and fidelity. Notwithstanding the multitude of public concerns, which at all times pressed heavily, and which he never neglected, the thoughts of General Washington constantly reverted to his farms. In the midst of the most stirring events of the war, he kept up an unremitted correspondence with his manager, in which he entered into details, gave minute instructions, and exacting reports, relating to the culture of his lands, and every transaction of business. From the beginning to the end of the revolution, Lund Washington wrote to the general, as often at least as two or three times a month, and commonly every week, detailing minutely all the events that occurred on the plantation. These letters were regularly answered by the general, even when the weight and embarrassment of public duties pressed heavily upon him.

An extract from one of his letters to Lund Washington on these topics, dated December, 1775, will show a trait of character, and the footing on which he left his household at Mount Vernon.

" Let the hospitalities of the house, with respect to the poor, be kept up. Let no one go hungry away. If any of this kind of people should be in want of corn, supply their necessities, provided it does not encourage them in idleness ; and I have no objection to your giving my money in charity, to the amount of forty or fifty pounds a year, when you think it well bestowed. What I mean by having no objection is, that is my desire that it should be done. You are to consider, that neither myself nor wife is now in the way to do these good offices. In all other respects, I recommend it to you, and have no doubt of your observing the greatest economy and frugality ; as I suppose you know, that I do not get a farthing for my services here, more than my expenses. It becomes necessary, therefore, for me to be saving at home."[*]

To detail all the operations of Washington in public affairs in the years which followed would be to repeat the history of the war of the American revolution, and, of course, greatly exceed the limits of the part of this work allotted to a memoir of his life. We can therefore only allude to the prominent events with which his personal history was connected during that eventful period, following him rapidly in his movements, until peace and the acknowledgment of American independence by Great Britain crowned his efforts in the cause of his country.

[*] Sparks.

The evacuation of Boston varied the scene, but did not lessen the labors of Washington. Henceforward, he had a much more formidable enemy to contend with. The royal army in Boston was, on a small scale, calculated to awe the inhabitants of Massachusetts into obedience, but the campaign of 1776 was opened in New York with a force far exceeding anything hitherto seen in America. Including the navy, as well as the army, it amounted to fifty-five thousand men, and was calculated on the idea of reducing the whole united colonies. The operations contemplated could be best carried on from the central province of New York, and the army could be supplied with provisions from the adjacent islands, and easily defended by the British navy. For these reasons, the evacuation of Boston, and the concentration of the royal forces at New York, had been for some time resolved upon in England.

The reasons that had induced the British to gain possession of New York, weighed with Washington to prevent or delay it. He had therefore, as already stated, detached largely from his army before Boston, and sent General Lee to take the command, following the main army himself immediately after the evacuation, and departure of the British army from Boston ; and he now made every preparation in his power for the defence of New York. Considerable time was allowed for this purpose, in consequence of the delay of General Howe at Halifax, where that officer waited for promised reinforcements from England.*

Besides the preparations for defence against the British army, Washington had to guard against the numerous disaffected persons and tories, or American loyalists on Long island, Staten island, and in the city of New York. By the persevering representations of Washington, Congress adopted measures for the apprehension of this class of enemies to the American cause. Many tories were apprehended in New York and on Long island ; some were imprisoned, others disarmed. A deep plot originating with the British governor Tryon, who continued on board a vessel at the Hook, was defeated by a timely and fortunate discovery. His agents were found enlisting men in the American camp, and enticing them with rewards. The infection spread to a considerable extent, and even reached the general's guard, some of whom enlisted. A soldier of the guard was found guilty by a court-martial and executed. It was a part of the plot to seize General Washington and convey him to the enemy.†

General Howe, with a part of the British fleet and army arrived at the hook from Halifax, in the latter part of June, and took possession of Staten island. The general then awaited the arrival of his brother Lord Howe, who was on his way from England with another fleet, and proposals from the British ministry for an accommodation to be offered to the Americans, before hostilities should be renewed.

* Ramsay.   † Sparks. *

General Washington had visited Philadelphia in the month of May, for the purpose of advising with Congress on the state of affairs and concerting arrangements for the campaign. He was absent fifteen days, examining on his way, Staten island and the Jersey shore, with the view of determining the proper places for works of defence. He seems to have been disappointed and concerned at dissensions in Congress which portended no good to the common cause. It was known, from late proceedings in parliament, that commissioners were coming out from England with proposals of accommodation. In a letter to his brother, dated at Philadelphia, May 31, 1776. Washington expresses his gratification that the Virginia convention had passed a vote with great unanimity, recommending to Congress to declare the united colonies free and independent states. "Things have come to such a pass now," he writes, "as to convince us, that we have nothing more to expect from the justice of Great Britain; also that she is capable of the most delusive arts; for I am satisfied that no commissioners were ever designed, except Hessians and other foreigners; and that the idea was only to deceive and throw us off our guard. The first has been too effectually accomplished; as many members of Congress, in short, the representation of whole provinces, are still feeding themselves upon the dainty food of reconciliation; and though they will not allow that the expectation of it has any influence upon their judgment with respect to their preparations for defence, it is but too obvious that it has an operation upon every part of their conduct, and is a clog to their proceedings. It is not in the nature of things to be otherwise; for no man that entertains a hope of seeing this dispute speedily and equitably adjusted by commissioners, will go to the same expense and run the same hazards to prepare for the worst event, as he who believes that he must conquer, or submit to unconditional terms, and the concomitants, such as confiscation, hanging, and the like."

Notwithstanding the hesitancy of some of the members of Congress, there was still a large majority for vigorous action; and while he was there, they resolved to reinforce the army at New York, with thirteen thousand eight hundred militia, drawn from Massachusetts, Connecticut, New York, and New Jersey; and a flying camp of ten thousand more, from Pennsylvania, Maryland, and Delaware.*

The Declaration of Independence by Congress, on the fourth of July, 1776, was received by General Washington, and read to the troops under his command on the ninth, at six o'clock in the evening; the regiments being paraded for the purpose. The document was read in the hearing of all, and received with the most hearty demonstrations of joy and satisfaction. In the orders of the day it was said, "The general hopes that this important event will serve as a fresh incentive to every officer and soldier to act with fidelity and courage, as knowing, that now the peace and

* Sparks.

safety of his country depend, under God, solely on the success of our arms, and that he is now in the service of a state possessed of sufficient power to reward his merit, and advance him to the highest honors of a free country."

Lord Howe arrived at Staten island on the twelfth of July, joining his brother, the general, with the expected additional forces from England. The command of the fleet had been conferred upon the former, and both the brothers were commissioners for restoring peace to the colonies. Lord Howe was not deterred by the declaration of independence from trying the influence of his powers for pacification, although he regarded the declaration as a circumstance unfavorable to the success of his mission. He sent on shore a circular letter, dated off the coast of Massachusetts addressed severally to the late governors under the crown (whom he supposed to be still in power), enclosing a declaration which he requested them to make public. It announced his authority to grant pardons, and to declare any colony or place under the protection of the king. Assurances were also given that the meritorious services of all persons who would aid in restoring tranquillity in the colonies would be duly considered.

These papers were transmitted by the commander-in-chief to Congress who directed their publication, that the people "might be informed of what nature were the commissioners, and what the terms with the expectation of which the insidious court of Britain had sought to amuse and disarm them."

About the same time Lord Howe despatched a letter to General Washington by a flag, which the general refused to receive, as it did not acknowledge the public character with which he was invested, being directed " To George Washington, Esq." The course pursued was approved by Congress, and a resolve was passed, that in future no letters should be received from the enemy, by commanders in the American army which should not be directed to them in the characters they sustained. A few days afterward General Howe wrote to Washington, repeating the same superscription as had been used by his brother. This letter was likewise refused, but an explanation took place through an interview between Colonel Patterson, adjutant-general of the British army and General Washington. General Howe was induced to change his superscription, and from that time all letters addressed by the British commanders to General Washington bore his proper titles.

In the conference between Washington and Colonel Patterson, the adjutant-general observed that " the commissioners were armed with great powers, and would be very happy in effecting an accommodation." General Washington replied " that from what appeared, these powers were only to grant pardons ; that they who had committed no fault wanted no pardon."

General Howe, perceiving that all attempts at conciliation were hopeless, prepared for the operations of the campaign. He however, delayed for some time active measures, as he was still waiting for further reinforcements. This period was employed by Washington in strengthening his works on New York island. Fort Washington, on an eminence in the north part of the island, on the east bank of the Hudson, and Fort Lee, on the opposite shore in New Jersey, were commenced, and between these forts the channel of the river was obstructed by hulks of vessels and chevaux-de-frise. Batteries were erected on the margins of the North and East rivers — redoubts were thrown up at different places, and the island generally placed in a state of defence

The British reinforcements had all arrived by the middle of August, and the aggregate of their army was estimated at over twenty-four thousand men. To this army, aided in its operations by a numerous fleet, was opposed the American army, a force unstable in its nature, incapable from its structure of receiving discipline, and inferior to the enemy in numbers, in army, and in every military equipment. In a letter dated the 8th of August, General Washington stated his army consisted of only seventeen thousand, two hundred and twenty-five men, of whom three thousand, six hundred and sixty-eight were sick. This force was rendered the more inadequate to its objects by being necessarily divided for the defence of posts, some of which were fifteen miles distant from others, with navigable waters between them. The army was soon afterward reinforced by regulars and militia, which augmented it to twenty-seven thousand men, of whom one fourth were sick. The diseases incident to new troops prevailed extensively, and were aggravated by a deficiency of tents.

The American troops were so judiciously distributed on York island, Long island, Governor's island, Paulus Hook, and on the sound toward New Rochelle, East and West Chester, that the enemy were very cautious in determining when or where to commence offensive operations. Every probable point of embarkation was watched, and guarded with a force sufficient to embarrass, though very insufficient to prevent a landing. From the arrival of the British army at Staten island, the Americans were in daily expectation of being attacked. General Washington was therefore strenuous in preparing his troops for action. He tried every expedient to kindle in their breasts the love of their country, and a high tone of indignation against its invaders. Thus did he, by infusing into every bosom those sentiments which would stimulate to the greatest individual exertion, endeavor to compensate for the want of arms, of discipline, and of numbers.

Early in the morning of the twenty-second of August, the principal part of the British army landed on Long island, under cover of the guns of the fleet; and extended their line from the Narrows, through Utrecht and Gravesend, to the village of Flatbush. On the twenty-seventh, the fifth day after landing, a general action took place between the two armies; the

Americans on Long island, then commanded by General Putnam, being attacked by the British army, under General Clinton. The variety of ground, and the different parties employed in different places, both in the attack and defence, occasioned a succession of small engagements, pursuits, and slaughter, which lasted for many hours.

The Americans were defeated in all directions. The circumstances which eminently contributed to this, were the superior discipline of the assailants, and the want of early intelligence of their movements. There was not a single corps of cavalry in the American army. The transmission of intelligence was of course always slow, and often impracticable. From the want of it, some of their detachments, while retreating before one portion of the enemy, were advancing toward another, of whose movements they were ignorant.

In the height of the engagement Washington passed over to Long island, and with infinite regret saw the slaughter of his best troops, but had not the power to prevent it ; for had he drawn his whole force to their support he must have risked everything on a single engagement. He adopted the wiser plan of evacuating the island, with all the forces he could bring off. In superintending this necessary, but difficult and dangerous movement, and the events of the preceding day, Washington was indefatigable. For forty-eight hours he never closed his eyes, and was almost constantly on horseback. In less than thirteen hours the field artillery, tents, baggage, and about nine thousand men, were conveyed from Long island to the city of New York, over the East river, and without the knowledge of the British, though not six hundred yards distant. The darkness of the night and a heavy fog in the morning, together with a fair wind after midnight, favored this retreat. It was completed without interruption some time after the dawning of the day.*

The loss of the Americans at the battle of Long island, was twelve hundred men, about a thousand of whom were captured. The loss of the British was less than four hundred.

Immediately after the success of the British arms on Long island, Admiral Lord Howe, as one of the king's pacificators, made another attempt at negotiation. He admitted General Sullivan, who had been taken prisoner, to his parole, and sent him to Philadelphia with a verbal message to Congress, the purport of which was, that although not authorized to treat with Congress as such, it being an illegal assembly, yet he was desirous of conferring with some of its members as private gentlemen only, whom he would meet at any place they might appoint. To this Congress sent a reply by General Sullivan, refusing to authorize any of their body to confer with his lordship in their private capacity ; but saying that they would send a committee to inquire into his authority to treat with persons authorized by Congress, and to hear his propositions for peace. Instructions

---

* Ramsay.

were at the same time sent to General Washington by Congress, that no propositions for peace ought to be received, unless directed in writing to the representatives of the United States ; and to inform those who might make application for a treaty, that Congress would cheerfully conclude a treaty of peace whenever such should be proposed to them as representatives of an independent people.

Doctor Franklin, John Adams, and Edward Rutledge, were appointed by Congress to confer with Lord Howe, whom they met for that purpose on Staten island. As Lord Howe declined conferring with the committee except as private gentlemen, he being unauthorized to recognise Congress as a legal body, the conference terminated without effecting anything. The commissioners absolutely refused to entertain any propositions except they were made to them as the representatives of a free and independent people. The interview was therefore closed, with the understanding, that war or absolute independence were the only alternatives the Americans chose to recognise.

General Howe now took measures to drive the Americans out of the city of New York. He made preparations to have troops landed from the ships on opposite sides of the upper part of the island, while the main body of the fleet entered the harbor, and took a position nearly within cannon-shot of the city. By this arrangement the Americans would be hemmed in, and be compelled to evacuate the city, or suffer the privations and dangers of a siege.

Viewing these preparations of the British commander with alarm, Washington called a council of war, on the twelfth of September, sixteen days after the battle of Long island, and recommended an immediate withdrawal of the troops. This measure was finally determined upon, and with great activity the Americans commenced removing the artillery and stores far above the city, to Dobb's ferry on the western shore of the Hudson. The commander-in-chief retired to the heights of Harlem, and a force of nine thousand men was stationed at Mount Washington, King's bridge, and other posts in the vicinity, while about five thousand remained near the city. The residue were placed between these extreme points, to act at either place as occasion might require.

On the fifteenth, a division of the British army, landed at Kipp's bay on the East river, three miles above the city, and attacked the American batteries erected there. The troops stationed at this place fled with precipitation, without waiting for the approach of the enemy. Two brigades were put in motion to support them. General Washington rode to the scene of action, and to his great mortification met the whole party retreating. While he was exerting himself to rally them, on the appearance of a small corps of the enemy, they again broke and ran off in disorder. Such dastardly conduct raised a tempest in the usually tranquil mind of Washington. He viewed with infinite concern this behavior of his troops, as threatening

4

ruin to his country.   His soul was harrowed up with apprehensions that his country would be conquered, her army disgraced, and her liberties destroyed, while the unsuccessful issue of the present struggle would, for ages to come, deter posterity from the bold design of asserting their rights.   Impressed with these ideas, he hazarded his person for some considerable time in the rear of his own men, and in front of the enemy, with his horse's head toward the latter, as if in expectation that, by an honorable death, he might escape the infamy he dreaded from the dastardly conduct of troops in whom he could place no dependence.   His aids, and the confidential friends around his person, by indirect violence, compelled him to retire.   In consequence of their address and importunity, a life was saved for public service, which otherwise, from a sense of honor and a gust of passion, seemed to be devoted to almost certain destruction.*

The troops referred to continued their retreat, until they reached the main body of the army at Harlem heights.   The division in or near the city, under the command of General Putnam, retreated with great difficulty, leaving behind them their heavy artillery, and a large portion of the baggage, provisions, and military stores, including the tents, which had not been removed.   The loss of the tents was severely felt by the army, at the approach of winter.   Fifteen of the Americans were killed, and three hundred taken prisoners.   The British army entered the city without much loss and took formal possession of it, to the great joy of the tories ; but they had hardly become quiet before a fire broke out, which raged until it had destroyed about a third of the city.

General Howe having organized a temporary government, and left some troops in the city, marched with the main body of his army up York island and encamped near the American lines in front of Harlem heights.   The British lines extended across the island, while their shipping defended their flanks.   Washington had made his strongest post at King's bridge, as that preserved his communication with the country.   On the day after the retreat from New York, a skirmish took place between advanced parties of both armies, in which the Americans gained a decided advantage, though with the loss of two gallant officers, Colonel Knowlton of Connecticut, and Major Leitch of Virginia.   This was the first advantage the army under the command of Washington, had gained in the campaign.   Its influence on the army was great, and the general gave public thanks to the troops engaged therein.

On the twenty-second of October, Washington fell back to White Plains in Westchester county, and on the twenty-eighth, a partial action was fought there, which resulted in the repulse of the Americans, with some loss.   Washington retired to Northcastle, five miles farther north, and Howe discontinued further pursuit, directing his attention to the American posts on the Hudson river.   Forts Washington and Lee, were taken by

* Ramsay.

the British army in November, the garrison in the former, consisting of nearly three thousand men, surrendering as prisoners-of-war, and the British losing about a thousand men in the assault. The garrison in Fort Lee made a hasty retreat and joined the main army, leaving behind them their cannon, tents, and stores, which fell into the hands of the victors.

It having become evident to General Washington, that General Howe had changed his plan of operations, and designed an invasion of New Jersey, he crossed the North river with the American army, and, retreating before Lord Cornwallis, who had entered New Jersey with six thousand men, he took post along the Hackensack river. His situation there was nearly similar to that which he had abandoned; for he was liable to be enclosed between the Hackensack and Passaic rivers. He therefore, on the approach of the enemy, passed over to Newark, on the west side of the latter river, where he stood his ground some days; but being incapable of any effectual opposition, he retreated to New Brunswick, on the day Lord Cornwallis entered Newark. At New Brunswick, Washington kept his troops in motion, and even advanced a detachment, as if intending to engage the enemy. Nor did he quit this position till their advanced guards were in sight. He then retreated toward Trenton, pursuing a route near the Raritan river, that he might be in the way to prevent General Howe from throwing in a strong detachment between him and Philadelphia. Although this retreat was effected without loss from the enemy, the small force which began it was daily lessening, by the expiration of the term of service for which they were engaged. This terminated in November with many, and in December, with nearly two thirds of the residue. No persuasions were availing to induce their continuance. They abandoned their general, when the advancing enemy was nearly in sight. General Lee who commanded the eastern troops at White Plains, was ordered by Washington to cross the North river, and join the retreating army in New Jersey. Lee was so tardy in obeying the order, that he was three weeks reaching Morristown. While on his march he lodged one night at a house about three miles from camp, where he was taken prisoner by a company of British light-horse. The command of his division devolved on General Sullivan, who marched it to the main army. Four regiments under General Gates, soon after arrived from Ticonderoga. These forces with others, joined Washington, after he had crossed the Delaware with his army of about three thousand men, which he accomplished on the seventh of December. The enemy did not attempt to cross the river, General Howe contenting himself with having overrun New Jersey. It was however expected, that, as soon as the ice should become sufficiently strong, the enemy would cross the Delaware, and bring all their force to bear upon Philadelphia. Anticipating this event, Congress adjourned to Baltimore; and General Putnam who took the command of the militia in Philadelphia, was instructed to prepare for an obstinate defence of that city.

In this very dangerous crisis, and which may be considered the most gloomy period of the war, Washington made every exertion to procure reinforcements. These exertions were in a great measure unavailing, except in and near Philadelphia. Fifteen hundred of the citizens of that metropolis marched to the aid of Washington. The American army now amounted to about seven thousand men, after the arrival of the forces under Sullivan and Gates. The two armies were separated from each other by the river Delaware. The British in the security of conquest, cantoned their troops in Burlington, Bordentown, Trenton, and other towns of New Jersey. On receiving information of their numbers and different cantonments, Washington observed —"Now is the time to clip their wings, when they are so spread." Yielding to his native spirit of enterprise, which had hitherto been repressed, he formed the bold design of recrossing the Delaware, and attacking the British posts on its eastern banks.*

In a letter to Joseph Reed, dated Bristol, Pennsylvania, December 23, 1776, Washington thus discloses his designs :—

" Christmas-day, at night, one hour before day, is the time fixed upon for our attempt on Trenton ; our numbers, sorry am I to say, being less than I had any conception of, but necessity, dire necessity, will, nay must, justify an attack."

The desperate situation of the American cause at this time is thus alluded to by him, in a letter to his brother, John Augustine Washington, dated, December 18, 1776 :—

" We were obliged to cross the Delaware with less than three thousand men fit for duty ; the enemy's numbers, from the best accounts, exceeding ten or twelve thousand men.

" Since I came on this side, I have been joined by about two thousand of the city militia, and I understand that some of the country militia are' on their way ; but we are in a very disaffected part of the province, and, between you and me, I think our affairs are in a very bad condition.

" You can form no idea of the perplexity of my situation. No man, I believe, ever had a greater choice of difficulties, and less means to extricate himself from them. However, under a full conviction of the justice of our cause, I can not entertain an idea that it will finally sink, though it may remain for a time under a cloud."

In the evening of Christmas-day, General Washington made arrangements for passing over the Delaware, in three divisions. At Trenton were three regiments of Hessians, amounting to about fifteen hundred men, and a troop of British light-horse. Small detachments of the British army were stationed at Bordentown, Burlington, Black Horse, and Mount Holly. General Cadwallader was to cross at Bristol, and attack the latter

* Ramsay.

posts ; General Ewing was to cross a little below Trenton, to intercept the retreat of the enemy in that direction, while the commander-in-chief, with twenty-four hundred continental troops, should cross nine miles above Trenton, to make the principal attack. But Generals Cadwallader and Ewing were unable to pass, from the quantity of floating ice which obstructed the boats. The division commanded by Washington, accompanied by Generals Greene, Sullivan, Stirling, Mercer, and St. Clair, alone succeeded. These troops began to cross early in the evening, but were so retarded by ice, that it was nearly four o'clock in the morning of the twenty-sixth, before the whole body with the artillery, was landed on the New Jersey bank of the river. They were formed in two divisions, and marched by different roads to Trenton, where they arrived within three minutes of each other, about eight o'clock in the morning. They met with but slight opposition, except from two or three pieces of artillery which were soon taken. The surprised Hessians attempted a retreat to Princeton, but were intercepted, and, finding themselves surrounded, soon laid down their arms and surrendered as prisoners-of-war. Between thirty and forty Hessians, among whom was Colonel Rahl, their commander, were killed. The American loss was two privates killed, and two others frozen to death. Captain William Washington, distinguished at a later period of the war as an officer of cavalry, and Lieutenant James Monroe, afterward president of the United States, were wounded in taking the enemy's artillery. The number of prisoners was nearly one thousand, and the trophies of victory were six brass field-pieces, a thousand stand of arms, and considerable ammunition. The British light-horse, and about five hundred Hessians, escaped at the beginning of the action and fled to Bordentown, where they joined the British and Hessian troops in that vicinity and all retreated to Princeton ; thus the whole line of the enemy's encampments on the Delaware was broken up. It was thought most prudent by Washington to recross the Delaware, with all his prisoners and military stores, on the same day, which he accomplished the same evening, and gained his encampment on the Pennsylvania side.

This brilliant exploit of Washington, and unexpected success of the continental troops under his command, electrified the American people, particularly those of the middle states, who were either desponding or disaffected at the aspect of affairs, before the tables were turned by this fortunate event. The British generals, Howe and Cornwallis, were astonished and bewildered at this display of vigor on the part of the American general. Previous to this affair at Trenton, New Jersey appeared to be subdued, Pennsylvania was supposed to be anxious for British pardon, and instead of offensive operations, the total dispersion of the small remnant of the American army was confidently anticipated. Finding that he was contending with an adversary who could never cease to be formidable, and that the conquest of America was more distant than had been supposed, Gen. Howe determined, in the depth of winter, to commence active operations. Lord Cornwallis, who had retired to New York, with the intention of embarking for England, returned to New Jersey in great force, for the purpose of recovering the ground which had been lost. The British army was assembled at Princeton, with the design of making an attack upon the Americans under Washington, who had again crossed the Delaware, and taken post at Trenton, determined to act on the offensive, after being joined by considerable reinforcements of regulars and militia.

Lord Cornwallis advanced on the morning of the second of January, 1777, and his van reached Trenton the same afternoon. On its approach, General Washington retired across the creek which runs through the town. The British finding the fords of the creek well guarded, desisted from attempts to cross, and kindled their fires. The Americans kindled their fires likewise, and a cannonade was kept up till dark.

The situation of General Washington was once more extremely critical. The passage of the Delaware was rendered difficult by the ice, and if he remained at Trenton, an attack on the following morning, by an overwhelming force seemed certain, which must render the destruction of his army inevitable. In this embarrassing state of things, he formed the bold design of abandoning the Delaware, and marching by a circuitous route along the left flank of the British army, into its rear at Princeton; and, after beating the troops at that place, to move rapidly on Brunswick, where the baggage, and principal magazines of the British army lay, under a weak guard.*

This plan being approved by a council of war, Washington silently withdrew his army from Trenton, favored by the darkness of the night, while the enemy were at rest; leaving a few of his men at work with pickaxes, and the camp-fires kindled, for the purpose of deceiving the British into the belief that the Americans were throwing up intrenchments. Before dawn these men left their work and hastened to join the American army who were then on a rapid march toward Princeton, where three British regiments had encamped the preceding night. Two of these regiments commencing their march toward Trenton, early in the morning to join the rear of their army, met the Americans, a mile and a half from Trenton. The morning being foggy, the enemy at first mistook the Americans for Hessians, but the mistake was soon discovered, and a smart skirmish ensued. The British commander sent to Princeton for the other regiment, which was soon on the spot, and after a battle of more than an hour, the American militia gave way in disorder. General Mercer, attempting to rally them, was mortally wounded. Washington pushed forward at the head of his division and rallied the flying troops, who encouraged by his example made a stand, and compelled the British to retreat in various directions. In the course of the engagement, one hundred of the

* Marshall.

enemy were killed and wounded, and about three hundred taken prisoners. The rest made their escape ; some by pushing on to Trenton, others by returning to Brunswick. The American loss was about one hundred.

At break of day, Lord Cornwallis perceived, to his great astonishment, that the Americans had deserted their camp at Trenton, and at once penetrating the designs of Washington upon New Brunswick, marched hastily toward that place to protect his stores there, and was close in the rear of the Americans, before they could leave Princeton. General Washington, finding his army exhausted with fatigue and closely pursued by a superior force, abandoned the remaining part of his original plan, and took the road leading up the country to the north. Lord Cornwallis continued his march to Brunswick, and Washington retired to Morristown, where he established his headquarters. Having given his army some repose, he entered the field again in an offensive attitude, and in a short time overran the whole country as far as the Raritan to the south. He also took possession of Newark, Elizabethtown, and Woodbridge. The British army, meanwhile, was restricting its operations to a small part of New Jersey.

The victories at Trenton and Princeton produced the most extensive effects, and had a decided influence on subsequent events. Philadelphia was saved for that winter, New Jersey was mostly recovered from the enemy, and the drooping spirits of the Americans were revived. Their gloomy apprehensions yielded to a confidence in their general and their army, and in the ultimate success of their struggles for liberty and independence.

.Gen. Washington had been invested by Congress a few days before the successful affair at Trenton, with additional and extraordinary powers as commander-in-chief, which additional powers were conferred on him for a period of six months, and the wisdom of the measure was soon seen and felt by the favorable turn of American affairs. After the recent successes he hoped that his country would have placed at his disposal a large and efficient army, to enable him to undertake decisive operations before reinforcements to the British army should arrive in the ensuing spring. Congress, at his instance passed the requisite resolutions ; but these could not be carried into effect, without the aid of the state legislatures. The recruiting service was therefore retarded by the delays consequent upon the action of thirteen legislative bodies, and Washington with infinite reluctance, was obliged to give up his favorite project of an early active campaign. The remainder of the winter season passed over in a light war of skirmishes. They were generally in favor of the Americans ; but Washington's views were much more extensive ; he cherished hopes of being enabled to strike a decisive blow against the British forces during the winter, but being disappointed, he went into winter-quarters with the main army, at Morristown. Cantonments were likewise established at various points from Princeton on the right, where General Putnam commanded, to the Highlands on the left, which post continued under the charge of General Heath.   The first care of General Washington, after putting the troops in winter-quarters, was drawn to the completion of the army for the next campaign ; and he wrote circular letters to the governors of the middle and eastern states, urging them to adopt prompt and effectual methods for raising recruits, and filling up their regiments.   To stimulate the activity of the states, by reiterated representations to their governors and legislatures, by argument, persuasion, and appeals to every motive of pride, honor, and patriotism, was the task which he was obliged to repeat every winter ; and this was a source of increasing anxiety, from the time the troops went into winter-quarters, till they again took the field to combat the enemy.   Congress, embarrassed by the indefinite nature of their powers deliberated with caution, and were seldom ready to act in military affairs, till incited by the counsels or earnest entreaties of the commander-in-chief.*

As the recruits for the American army were collected, the camp at Morristown was broken up, and the army assembled on the twenty-eighth of May, 1777, at Middlebrook, in New Jersey, ten miles from Brunswick. The exertions made during the winter by the commander-in-chief, to raise a powerful army for the ensuing campaign, had not been successful.   On the twentieth of May, the total of the army in New Jersey, excluding cavalry and artillery, amounted only to eight thousand, three hundred and seventy-eight men, of whom upward of two thousand were sick, and more than half were raw recruits.   Anticipating a movement of the British army toward Philadelphia, Washington had given orders for assembling an army of militia, with a few continental troops, on the western bank of the Delaware, to be commanded by General Arnold.   The primary objects to which Washington directed his attention in this campaign, were to endeavor to prevent the British from obtaining possession of Philadelphia, or the Highlands on the Hudson river, and he made such an arrangement of his troops as would enable him to oppose either.   The northern troops were divided between Ticonderoga, and Peekskill, while those from New Jersey, and other middle states, were encamped at Middlebrook.

On the twelfth of June, General Howe assembled the main body of his army at Brunswick, in New Jersey, and gave strong indications of an intention to reach Philadelphia by land.   The American army under Washington, was now swelled to about fourteen thousand.   Howe feigned a design to cross the Delaware by making toward that river, but failing to draw Washington into a general engagement, by his various manœuvres, he withdrew his forces to Amboy, and passed over to Staten island, leaving the Americans in quiet possession of New Jersey.   Having abandoned the idea of forming a junction with General Burgoyne, who, having

* Sparks.

arrived from England with a powerful army, was invading the northern states by way of Canada, General Howe turned his attention toward Philadelphia. He resolved to proceed to that city by way of the Chesapeake bay, and accordingly embarked at Staten island, with about eighteen thousand troops, on board of the British fleet under Lord Howe. He left General Sir Henry Clinton, with a large force to defend New York, and in the latter part of July appeared off the capes of Delaware ; but the fleet suddenly again put to sea, and its destination was for some time a matter of uncertainty to the Americans. In the meanwhile, Washington marched the main body of his army to Germantown, to await certain information respecting the movements of General Howe. During his suspense, he took an opportunity of conferring with committees of Congress, at Philadelphia, and it was at this time that he had his first interview with the Marquis de Lafayette, on his arrival from France, to offer his services to the Americans. Congress appointed the marquis a major-general in the army, and he was invited by General Washington to become a member of his military family, which position he maintained during the war.

The British fleet having sailed up the Chesapeake, reached Elk river on the twenty-fifth of August, where the troops, under Gen. Howe were landed, and commenced their march toward Philadelphia. The day before the landing of the British, the American army marched through Philadelphia, toward Wilmington, in Delaware. Advance parties from each army soon met, and several skirmishes took place.

As the British army approached, Washington took post on the river Brandywine, and awaited the attack of the enemy. A general action took place early on the eleventh of September, which continued all day, and terminated in favor of the British, who remained in possession of the field of battle, while the Americans retreated to Chester, and the following day to Philadelphia.

The British force in this engagement, was stated at about eighteen thousand ; that of the Americans a little over eleven thousand. The American loss in killed, wounded, and prisoners, was over a thousand ; that of the British was less than six hundred.

Washington made every exertion to repair the loss which had been sustained. The battle of Brandywine was represented as not being decisive. Congress and the people wished to hazard a second engagement, for the security of Philadelphia ; General Howe sought for it, and Washington did not decline it. He therefore advanced on the Lancaster road, with an intention of meeting the British army. Both armies were on the point of engaging, but were prevented by a violent storm. When the rain ceased, the Americans finding that their ammunition was ruined, withdrew to a place of safety. The British instead of urging an action, afterward began to march toward Reading. To save the stores at that place, Washington took a new position, and left the British in undisturbed possession of the roads which led to Philadelphia.   His troops were worn down with a succession of severe duties.   There were in his army above a thousand men who were barefooted, and who had performed all their late movements in that condition.

Though Washington had failed in his object of saving Philadelphia, yet he retained the confidence of Congress and the states.   With an army inferior in numbers, discipline, and equipments, he had delayed the British army thirty days in advancing sixty miles through an open country, without fortifications.

The British army entered Philadelphia, on the twenty-sixth of September, and pushed forward to Germantown.   Congress had previously adjourned to Lancaster.   While the British camp at Germantown was weakened by detachments sent against the American forts on the Delaware, Gen. Washington, having received considerable reinforcements to his army, resolved to attack the enemy in their encampment.   Accordingly, in the evening of the third of October, the Americans advanced in four divisions, and after a march of fourteen miles to Germantown, at daybreak the next morning took the British by surprise.   A battle commenced, and for a time victory seemed to incline to the Americans ; but finally, after a severe action, they were repulsed with great slaughter, losing about eleven hundred men, in killed, wounded, and prisoners.   The British loss was not more than half that number.   General Howe shortly after evacuated Germantown, and concentrated his forces at Philadelphia, where the British army under his command took up their winter-quarters.   Howe at first directed his attention to the opening of the navigation of the Delaware river, which had been obstructed by many ingenious contrivances placed there by the Americans.   This task employed the British for more than six weeks ; and after a great display of gallantry on both sides, it was finally accomplished.

When the Delaware was cleared, and there was a free inland communication for the British between Philadelphia and New York, Gen. Howe determined to close the campaign by an attack upon Washington, then stationed at Whitemarsh, about eleven miles from Philadelphia.   On the night of the fourth of December, Howe marched out of the city and took post upon Chestnut Hill, in front of the American army, which had been reinforced by detachments from the northern army.   Finding Washington's position too strong to risk a general attack, after a few days' skirmishing, Howe fell back upon Philadelphia.

While the British arms were successful on the banks of the Delaware, intelligence arrived that General Burgoyne and the British army of the north, had surrendered prisoners-of-war, to the American northern army under General Gates.   This event took place at Saratoga, in the state of New York, on the seventeenth of October.   On the receipt of this important information, General Washington took measures to obtain large reinforcements to the forces under his immediate command, from the victorious troops of the north. He therefore deputed one of his aids, Colonel Alexander Hamilton, to wait on General Gates, and communicate his wishes to that officer. In his letter of instructions to Hamilton, General Washington writes as follows, under date of October 30, 1777 :—

" It has been judged expedient by the members of a council of war held yesterday, that one of the gentlemen of my family should be sent to General Gates, in order to lay before him the state of this army, and the situation of the enemy, and to point out to him the many happy consequences that will accrue from an immediate reinforcement being sent from the northern army. I have thought proper to appoint you to that duty, and desire that you will immediately set out for Albany.

" What you are chiefly to attend to is, to point out to General Gates the absolute necessity that there is for his detaching a very considerable part of the army, at present under his command, to the reinforcement of this ; a measure that will, in all probability, reduce General Howe to the same situation in which General Burgoyne now is, should he attempt to remain in Philadelphia.

" I have understood that General Gates has already detached Nixon's and Glover's brigades to join General Putnam.* If this be a fact, you are to desire General Putnam, to send the two brigades forward with the greatest expedition, as there can be no occasion for them there."

To the president of Congress, Washington also wrote on the first of November as follows : " I can not conceive that there is any object, now remaining, that demands our attention and most vigorous efforts so much as the destruction of the [British] army in this quarter. Should we be able to effect this, we shall have little to fear in future." And on the seventeenth of November; he wrote to the same functionary thus : " I am anxiously waiting the arrival of the troops from the northward, who ought to have been here before this. The want of these troops has embarrassed all my measures exceedingly."

Instead of promptly seconding the desires of Washington, when communicated to them by Hamilton, Generals Gates and Putnam were unwilling to part with a sufficient number of the troops under their respective commands to effect the object designed. The former general was then contemplating an expedition to Ticonderoga, and the latter an attack on the British forces in New York. After considerable delay, those generals, at the urgent request of Colonel Hamilton, finally sent on about five thousand men to the aid of General Washington ; but in the meantime, Sir Henry Clinton, who commanded the British forces stationed at the city of New York, detached about six thousand men to the aid of General Howe in Philadelphia.

Thus, will it be seen, that the well-formed plans of General Washing-

* General Putnam then commanded the troops on the Hudson river, below the Highlands.

ton, to follow up the capture of the British army under Burgoyne, by that of the forces under Howe, were frustrated by the want of cordial co-operation on the part of Gates and Putnam. Had Washington succeeded by their prompt aid in effecting his purposes at Philadelphia, he would doubtless have moved upon New York, and by an attack upon that city, with the whole American forces, have either compelled the surrender of the forces under Sir Henry Clinton, or the evacuation by them of that point; and thus the campaign of 1777 would have been closed by a suc-cession of American victories and British reverses, from which the latter could not have recovered. Is it too much to say, that in that event, Great Britain would have sought for peace in 1778, as she did afterward in 1782, and that the American alliance with France, would have thus been ren-dered unnecessary? This view is confirmed by the correspondence of Washington, who evidently was of opinion that a protracted war for years was unnecessary. In a letter to John Parke Custis, dated, February 28, 1781, more than three years after the fall of Philadelphia, he says, "We have brought a cause, which might have been happily *terminated years ago* by the adoption of proper measures, to the very verge of ruin," &c.

The following extract of a letter from Washington to Patrick Henry, dated November 13, 1777, soon after the British had entered Philadelphia, throws farther light upon the state of affairs at this period; and shows particularly that Washington's army had been weakened by reinforcements sent to the aid of General Gates.

"I was left to fight two battles, in order if possible to save Philadel-phia, with less numbers than composed the army of my antagonist, while the world has given us double.

"How different is the case in the northern department. There the states of New York and New England, resolving to crush Burgoyne, continued pouring in their troops till the surrender of that army. Had the same spirit pervaded the people of this and the neighboring states, we might before this time have had General Howe nearly in the situation of General Burgoyne.

"My own difficulties in the course of the campaign have been not a little increased by the extra aid of continental troops which the gloomy prospect of our affairs, immediately after the reduction of Ticonderoga,* induced me to spare from this army."

The campaign of 1777 having closed, Washington communicated in general orders his intention of retiring with his army into winter-quar-ters. He expressed to his officers and soldiers his high approbation of their past conduct; gave an encouraging statement of the prospects of the country, and exhorted the men to bear the hardships inseparable from their condition. Valley Forge, about twenty miles northwest from Philadelphia, was selected by Washington for the winter-quarters of the

---

* Ticonderoga was taken by Burgoyne, on the 5th of July, 1777.

army. This position was preferred to distant and more comfortable villages, as being calculated to give security to the country from the enemy. In the latter end of December, the troops were compelled to build huts for their own accommodation, and during the winter, which was unusually severe, their sufferings were great, from want of both clothing and food, Washington was compelled to make seizures from the inhabitants, as he was authorized by Congress to do, for the sustenance of his army. The commander-in-chief and his principal officers sent for their wives, from the different states to which they belonged, to pass the winter with their husbands at headquarters.

To the other vexations and troubles which crowded on General Washington at this time, was added one of a peculiar nature. This was the formation of a cabal among members of Congress, and a few officers in the northern division of the army, the object of which was to supersede him in the command of the army, or to induce his resignation. This intrigue is known in American history under the name of *Conway's cabal.* Generals Gates, Mifflin, and Conway, are the only officers of note who were known to have been engaged in it. The former of these generals was proposed to supersede Washington. About the same time a board of war was created by Congress, of which General Gates was appointed president.

These machinations did not abate the ardor of Washington in the common cause. His patriotism was too solid to be shaken, either by envy or ingratitude. Nor was the smallest effect produced in diminishing his well-earned reputation. Zeal the most active, and services the most beneficial, and at the same time disinterested, had riveted him in the affections of his country and the army. Even the victorious troops under Gen. Gates, though comparisons highly flattering to their vanity, had been made between them and the army in Pennsylvania, clung to Washington as their political savior. The resentment of the people was generally excited against those who were supposed to be engaged in, or friendly to, the scheme of appointing a new commander-in-chief over the American army.*

The sufferings of the army while encamped at Valley Forge, are memmorable in the history of the war. They were not only greatly in want of the necessary supplies of food, but of blankets and clothing. " Naked and starving as they are," says Washington in one of his letters, " we can not enough admire the incomparable patience and fidelity of the soldiery; that they have not been ere this excited by their sufferings, to a general mutiny and desertion." Although the officers were better provided than the soldiers, yet none were exempt from privations and hardships.

When the encampment was begun at Valley Forge, the whole number of men in the field was 11,098, of whom 2,898, were unfit for duty, " being barefoot and otherwise naked." Much of the suffering of the army was

* Ramsay.

attributed to mismanagement in the quartermaster's department; while reforms on this subject were proposed in Congress, the distresses of the troops approached their acme.   General Washington found it necessary to interpose his personal exertions to procure provisions from a distance. In a few days the army was rescued from the famine with which it had been threatened.   It was perceived that the difficulties which had occurred, were occasioned more by the want of due exertion in the commissary department, and by the efforts of the people to save their stock for a better market, than by a real deficiency of food in the country.

The impression made on the British nation by the capitulation of Burgoyne, at length made its way into the cabinet, and Lord North brought into parliament two bills, which were adopted, having conciliation for their object.   The first surrendered the principle of taxation, and the second empowered the crown to appoint commissioners to treat for peace with the United States.   This movement was prompted by the apprehension that France would acknowledge the independence of America, and join in the war against England.

The terms held out by these bills were such as would have been accepted by the Americans in the early stages of the controversy, but they now came too late.   It was no part of the plan of the British ministers to treat with the American states as an independent power.   They were to go back to their old condition as colonies, favored with certain privileges ; but having declared their independence, and shed their blood, and expended their means to sustain it, these new offers of the British government were not likely to gain the confidence or change the sentiments of those who had taken the lead in the cause of American liberty.   Washington, in a letter to a member of Congress, after he had learned the purport of the conciliatory bills, expresses himself thus : " Nothing short of independence, it appears to me, can possibly do.   A peace on other terms would, if I may be allowed the expression, be a peace of war.   The injuries we have received from the British nation were so unprovoked, and have been so great and so many, that they can never be forgotten.   Our fidelity as a people, our gratitude, our character as men, are opposed to a coalition with them as subjects, but in case of the last extremity."   The subject appeared in the same light to Congress, and they unanimously resolved, that no advances on the part of the British government would be met, unless, as a preliminary step, they either withdrew their armies and fleets, or acknowledged, unequivocally, the independence of the United States.

On the second of May, 1778, ten days after Congress had passed their resolves respecting Lord North's bill of conciliation, a messenger arrived in the United States, bearing treaties of amity, commerce, and alliance, between France and America, signed at Paris, on the sixth of February, 1778, by which the independence of the United States was formally acknowledged by the former power. This intelligence was received with joy by the Americans, and the army participated in the rejoicings of the people on the occasion, and a day was set apart by the commander-in-chief for a public celebration in camp.

The British kept possession of Philadelphia through the winter and the spring following; and although Washington's camp was within twenty miles of the city, yet no enterprise was undertaken to molest him in his quarters. Foraging parties were sent out, and committed depredations on the inhabitants; but they were watched by the Americans, who sometimes met them in fierce and bloody rencontres. The British army in New York and Philadelphia, amounted to nearly thirty thousand, of which number 19,500 were in Philadelphia, and 10,400 in New York. There were besides 3,700 at Rhode Island. The American army on the eighth of May, 1778, did not exceed 15,000 men, including the detachments on the North river, and at other places. The number at Valley Forge was 11,800. The new establishment agreed upon by a committee of Congress at Valley Forge, was to consist of forty thousand continental troops, besides artillery and horse; but it was not supposed by a council of war, held on the eighth of May, that it could soon be raised higher than twenty thousand effective men, while the British army in the middle and eastern states, amounted, as above stated, to upward of thirty-three thousand.[*]

Sir William Howe, having at his own request been recalled, resigned the command of the British army to Sir Henry Clinton, and embarked for England. About the same time, orders were received for the evacuation of Philadelphia. The great naval force of France rendered that city a dangerous position, and determined the British cabinet to withdraw their army from the Delaware.

On the morning of the eighteenth of June, Philadelphia was evacuated by the British army, which crossed the Delaware, and landed on Gloucester point. Their line extended nearly twelve miles, and as they were encumbered with numerous wagons, and compelled to stop and build bridges over the streams in their route, their progress was slow. It was the first purpose of Sir Henry Clinton to proceed to the Raritan, and embark his troops at Brunswick, or South Amboy, for New York, but finding Washington with his army in motion in that direction, he turned to the right and took the road leading to Monmouth and Sandy Hook.

A council of war, called by Washington, to discuss the best mode of attacking the enemy on their march, was divided in opinion. Gen. Lee and others advising to avoid a general battle, but to harass the enemy upon flank and rear. Washington determined to act according to his own judgment, and sent forward a detachment to commence an attack, while he with the rest of the army followed to support the advance corps. Sir Henry Clinton, with the British army encamped near Monmouth court-

* Sparks.

house, whence they commenced their march on the twenty-eighth of June, and were attacked by the Americans. The battle became general, and lasted till night, when both armies remained on the field. The British troops withdrew during the night, and soon after proceeded to Sandy Hook, where they embarked on board a fleet for New York.

The battle of Monmouth, although favorable to the Americans, was not a decided victory; yet Congress viewed it somewhat in that light, and passed a vote of thanks to the commander-in-chief and the army. The American loss was sixty-nine killed, while the British loss was much greater, being nearly three hundred. On their march through New Jersey, the British army lost by battle, captured as prisoners, and desertion, more than twelve hundred men. The conduct of General Lee, at the battle of Monmouth, in ordering a hasty retreat of his detachment and otherwise, was severely censured by Washington; he was consequently tried by a court-martial, found guilty of the charges against him, and suspended from his command for one year. He left the service, and died four years afterward, in Philadelphia.

After the action at Monmouth, General Washington marched with his army to the Hudson river, which he crossed, and encamped at White Plains, about twenty-five miles north of the city of New York. Before crossing the river, he heard of the arrival on the coast of a French fleet, under Count d'Estaing, consisting of twelve ships-of-the-line and four frigates. No time was lost by the American general in sending a letter of congratulation to the French admiral, and proposing to co-operate with him, in plans for attacking the enemy. It was at first proposed to attack New York, by land and water; but the scheme was abandoned, and the French squadron sailed for Rhode Island, to attack the British forces there, chiefly in garrison at Newport. Various causes conspired to the failure of this expedition, by defeating the combined action of the land and naval forces. After leaving Newport, the French fleet was crippled by a storm and engagement at sea, and put into the harbor of Boston to refit, where they remained until November.

The American army was employed in various operations in the northern and eastern states, during the campaign of 1778, to guard against an apprehended attack by the British on Boston, or some other point at the eastward; but it was finally ascertained that the enemy had no design in that direction. Washington established his headquarters at Fredericksburg, thirty miles from West Point, on the borders of Connecticut, and at the close of the campaign put his army in winter-quarters at West Point and at several other places, his headquarters being at Middlebrook, in New Jersey.

Notwithstanding the flattering prospects which the alliance with France held out for the American cause, General Washington at this time had many causes of anxiety which oppressed him, and filled his mind with the most gloomy feelings. Among the most prominent subjects of anxiety and apprehension, he viewed that of the apathy and dissensions among members of Congress with alarm. The men of talent who had taken the lead in Congress, in the early period of the war, had gradually withdrawn from that body, until it had become small in numbers and comparatively feeble in counsels and resources. At no time were private jealousies and party feuds more rife or mischievous in their effects.

To those in whom he had confidence, Washington laid open his fears, and endeavored to awaken a sense of the public danger. To Benjamin Harrison, of Virginia, he thus writes, on the 30th of December, 1778 : " I confess to you that I feel more real distress on account of the present appearances of things, than I have done at any one time since the commencement of the dispute. But Providence has heretofore taken us up, when all other means and hope seemed to be departing from us. In this I will confide."

A project for conquering Canada was at this time entertained in Congress ; but Washington, being requested to communicate his sentiments on the subject, replied in a long letter to Congress, showing that the plan was impracticable, requiring resources in troops and money which were not to be had ; also, that there were political reasons why it would be against the future interests of the United States for Canada to be restored to France, as would probably be the case if conquered by the allied forces of France and America. He afterward, in December, 1777, visited Philadelphia ; and on a more full discussion of the subject with a committee of Congress, the Canada scheme was given up. The French government was also decidedly opposed to it, and it was the policy of that court that Canada and Nova Scotia should remain in the power of Great Britain.[*]

The winter and spring of 1779 passed away without the occurrence of any remarkable event. The British remained within their lines at New York, apparently making no preparation for any enterprise of magnitude. General Washington, in the meantime, turned his attention to the fitting out of an expedition against the hostile Indians in the state of New York. General Sullivan was despatched with a large force to the Susquehannah river, and was completely successful in subduing the Indians.

Washington removed his headquarters to New Windsor, a few miles above West Point, distributing his army chiefly in and near the highlands of the Hudson river, but stationing a force below, to check any sudden incursion of the enemy. Washington at this time resolved upon an attack on the strong British post at Stony Point, on the Hudson river, and intrusted the enterprise to General Wayne. That officer stormed the works on the night of the 15th of July, with a body of picked men, and the assault was successful in all its parts. The number of prisoners captured

* Sparks.

5

by the Americans was 543, and the number killed on the side of the British was 63 ; while the American loss was 15 killed, and 83 wounded.

The campaign of 1779 having terminated, the American army went into winter-quarters ; the main body in the neighborhood of Morristown, in New Jersey, and various detachments on the Hudson river and in, Connecticut. The headquarters of Washington were at Morristown.   A descent upon Staten island by a party of Americans under Lord Stirling, a retaliatory incursion of the enemy into New Jersey, and a skirmish near White Plains, were the only military events during the winter.

In April, 1780, the marquis de Lafayette arrived at Boston from France, with the cheering intelligence that the French government had fitted out an armament of naval and land forces, which might soon be expected in the United States.   On the 10th of July, the French fleet arrived at Newport, in Rhode Island.   The armament consisted of seven or eight ships-of-the-line, two frigates, two bombs, and upward of five thousand men. The fleet was commanded by De Ternay, and the army by Count de Rochambeau.   The general and troops were directed by the French government to be in all cases under the command of General Washington.

Having a decided naval superiority, the British fleet, under Admiral Arbuthnot, blockaded the French squadron in the harbor of Newport, and Rochambeau's army was obliged to remain there for its protection.   This state of things continued through the season, and no military enterprise was undertaken.   Both parties stood on the defensive, watching each other's motions, and depending on the operations of the British and French fleets.   General Washington encamped on the west side of the Hudson, below Orangetown, or Tappan, on the borders of New Jersey, which station he held till winter.

A conference was held between the commanders of the two allied armies, being suggested by Rochambeau, and readily assented to by Washington.   They met at Hartford, in Connecticut, on the 21st of September.   During the absence of General Washington, the army was left under the command of General Greene.   No definite plan of operations could be agreed upon between the American and French commanders, as a naval superiority was essential to any effectual enterprise by land, and the French fleet was inferior to that of the British naval force on the American station.

At this time, General Arnold held the command at West Point, and other fortified posts on the Hudson river, in the highlands.   On Washington's return to West Point from the conference with the French commander at Hartford, he was filled with astonishment at the discovery of a plot which had been formed between General Arnold and Sir Henry Clinton, to deliver up the American post to the enemy — the agent employed by the British general being Major John André, adjutant-general in the British army.   On the detection of his treachery, Arnold fled to a British sloopof-war in the Hudson river, immediately after the arrival of Washington at West Point, on the 25th of September. Major André had been taken by the Americans, and was soon after removed to the headquarters of the army at Tappan.

On discovering the treason of Arnold, Washington took immediate measures to secure the posts. Orders were despatched to all the principal officers, and every precaution was taken. It was soon ascertained by Washington that no other officer in the American army was implicated in the conspiracy of Arnold; and he forthwith ordered a court of inquiry, consisting of a board of general officers, for the trial of Major André. Various papers were laid before the board, which met on the twenty-ninth of September, and André himself was questioned and desired to make such statements and explanations as he chose. After a full investigation, the board reported the essential facts which had appeared, with their opinion that he was a spy and ought to suffer death. General Washington approved this decision, and Major André was executed at Tappan, on the second of October. He met his fate with composure and dignity.

While André's case was pending, Sir Henry Clinton used every effort in his power to rescue him from his fate. He wrote to General Washington, and endeavored to show that he could not be regarded as a spy, inasmuch as he came on shore at the request of an American general, and afterward acted by his direction. Connected with all the circumstances, this argument could have no weight. There was no stronger trait in the character of Washington than humanity; the misfortunes and sufferings of others touched him keenly; and his feelings were deeply moved at the part he was compelled to act, in consenting to the death of André; yet, justice to the office he held, and to the cause for which his countrymen were shedding their blood, left him no alternative.*

While these operations were going on at the north, all the intelligence from the southern states showed that the American cause was in a gloomy condition in that quarter. The British forces under Lord Cornwallis were overrunning the Carolinas, and preparations were making in New York to detach a squadron with troops to fall upon Virginia. The city of Charleston had been taken by the British in May, 1780, and the American army of six thousand, under General Lincoln, stationed there, surrendered prisoners-of-war. The defeat of General Gates near Camden, in South Carolina, in August, was a heavy blow to the Americans. Congress requested General Washington to appoint an officer to succeed Gates in the command of the southern army. With his usual discrimination and judgment, he selected General Greene, who repaired to the theatre of action, in which he was so eminently distinguished during the subsequent years of the war.

Congress at length adopted the important measures, in regard to the

* Sparks.

army which Washington had earnestly and repeatedly advised. They decreed that all the troops thenceforward to be raised, should be enlisted to serve during the war; and that all the officers who continued in the service to the end of the war, should be entitled to half-pay for life. Washington ever believed, that, if this system had been pursued from the beginning, it would have shortened the war, or at least have caused a great diminution of the expense. Unfortunately the states did not comply with the former part of the requisition, but adhered to the old method of filling up their quotas with men raised for three years, and for shorter terms. The extreme difficulty of procuring recruits, was the reason assigned for persevering in this practice.

The army went into winter-quarters at the end of November; the Pennsylvania line near Morristown, the New Jersey regiments at Pompton, and the eastern troops in the Highlands. The headquarters of the commander-in-chief were at New Windsor, on the Hudson river. The French army remained at Newport, Rhode Island, except the duke de Lauzun's legion, which was cantoned at Lebanon, in Connecticut.*

Washington felt with infinite regret, the succession of abortive projects throughout the campaign of 1780. In that year he had indulged the hope of terminating the war. In a letter to a friend, he wrote as follows : "We are now drawing to a close an inactive campaign, the beginning of which appeared pregnant with events of a very favorable complexion. I hoped, but I hoped in vain, that a prospect was opening which would enable me to fix a period to my military pursuits, and restore me to domestic life."

*   *   *   *   *   *   *   *   *   *   *   *

"But alas! these prospects, flattering as they were, have proved delusory ; and I see nothing before us but accumulating distress. We have been half of our time without provisions, and are likely to continue so. We have no magazines, nor money to form them. We have lived upon expedients until we can live no longer. In a word, the history of the war is a history of false hopes and temporary devices, instead of system and economy. It is in vain, however, to look back ; nor is it our business to do so. Our case is not desperate, if virtue exists in the people, and there is wisdom among our rulers. But to suppose that this great revolution can be accomplished by a temporary army, that this army will be subsisted by state supplies, and that taxation alone is adequate to our wants, is, in my opinion, absurd."

A dangerous mutiny broke out in January, 1781, among the Pennsylvania troops stationed near Morristown, which was suppressed by the prudence and good management of Gen. Wayne, acting under the advice of Washington, and aided by a committee of Congress. The latter proposed terms to the revolters, which were accepted. This mutiny was followed by a similar revolt of the New Jersey troops, which was promptly put down

* Sparks.

by an armed force under Gen. Howe, by direction of Washington. Two of the ringleaders were tried by a court-martial and shot. By this summary proceeding, the spirit of mutiny in the army was subdued

Colonel John Laurens, having been appointed on a mission to France, to obtain a loan and military supplies, Washington wrote a letter to that gentleman, in support of the application of Congress, which was first presented by the commissioner to Dr. Franklin, and afterward laid before the French king and cabinet. The French government having determined to grant the aid requested, previous to the arrival of Colonel Laurens, suggested that the money to be appropriated for the army, should be left at the disposal of General Washington.

On the first of May, 1781, Gen. Washington commenced a military journal, from which the following is an extract : "I begin at this epoch a concise journal of military transactions, &c. I lament not having attempted it from the commencement of the war, in aid of my memory ; and wish the multiplicity of matter which continually surrounds me, and the embarrassed state of our affairs, which is momentarily calling the attention to perplexities of one kind or another, may not defeat altogether, or so interrupt my present intention and plans, as to render it of little avail."

After briefly sketching the wants and condition of the army at the time, he adds : "In a word, instead of having anything in readiness to take the field, we have nothing ; and instead of having the prospect of a glorious and offensive campaign before us, we have a bewildered and gloomy prospect of a defensive one ; unless we should receive a powerful aid of ships, troops, and money, from our generous allies, and these at present are too contingent to build upon."

While the Americans were suffering the complicated calamities which introduced the year 1781, their adversaries were carrying on the most extensive plan of operations against them which had ever been attempted. The war raged in that year, not only in the vicinity of the British headquarters at New York, but in Georgia, South Carolina, North Carolina, and in Virginia.

While the war raged in Virginia, the governor thereof, its representatives in Congress, and other influential citizens, urged his return, in defence of his native state. But, considering America as his country, and the general safety as his object, he deemed it of more importance to remain on the Hudson. In Washington's disregard of property, when in competition with national objects, he was in no respect partial to his own. While the British were in the Potomac, they sent a flag on shore to his estate at Mount Vernon requiring a fresh supply of provisions. To save the buildings from destruction his agent granted the supply of provisions required by the enemy. For this he received a severe reprimand from the general, who in a letter to the agent observed, that " it would have been a less painful circumstance to me to have heard, that in consequence of your noncompliance with the request of the British, they had burnt my house, and laid my plantation in ruins.   You ought to have considered yourself as my representative, and should have reflected on the bad example of communicating with the enemy, and making a voluntary offer of refreshment to them, with a view to prevent a conflagration."

Though, in conducting the war, General Washington often acted on the Fabian system, by evacuating, retreating, and avoiding decisive engagements, yet this was much more the result of necessity than of choice. His uniform opinion was in favor of energetic offensive operations, as the most effectual means of bringing the war to a termination.   On this principle he planned attacks, in almost every year, on some one or other of the British armies or strong posts in the United States.   He endeavored, from year to year, to stimulate the public mind to some great operation, but was never properly supported.   In the years 1778, '79, and '80, the projected operations with the French, as has been related, entirely miscarried.   The idea of ending the war by some decisive military exploit, continually occupied his active mind.   To insure success, a naval superiority on the coast, and a loan of money, were indispensably necessary. To obtain these necessary aids, the French government were applied to, as already stated.   His most Christian majesty (Louis XVI.) gave his American allies a subsidy of six millions of livres, and became their security for ten millions more, borrowed in Holland.   A naval co-operation was promised, and a conjunct expedition against their common foes projected.*

To mature the plan for the campaign, and to communicate personally with the French commanders, General Washington made a journey to Newport.   He left headquarters on the second of March, and was absent nearly three weeks.   The citizens of Newport received him with a public address, expressive of their attachment and gratitude for his services.   A second meeting for consultation took place between the American and French commanders, at Wethersfield, in Connecticut, on the twenty-second of May.   The two principal objects considered were, first, a southern expedition to act against the enemy in Virginia; secondly, a combined attack on New York.   The French commander leaned to the former, but he yielded to the stronger reasons for the latter, which was decidedly preferred by General Washington.   It was believed that Sir Henry Clinton's force in New York had been so much weakened by detachments, that the British general would be compelled either to sacrifice that place and its dependencies, or recall part of his troops from the south to defend them.

It was therefore agreed that Count de Rochambeau should march with the French army, as soon as possible, from Newport, and form a junction with the American army near the Hudson river.

* Ramsay.

The attention of Washington was but partially taken up with the affairs under his own eye. He held a constant correspondence with Generals Greene and Lafayette, who kept him informed of the operations at the south, and asked his advice and directions. Other sections of the country, also, required and received his care and attention.

On the sixth of July, the French army formed a junction with the American forces on the Hudson, a few miles north of the city of New York. The French army, which had marched in four divisions from Providence, by way of Hartford, occupied the left, in a single line extending to the river Bronx. The Americans encamped in two lines, with their right resting on the Hudson.

Preparations were made for an attack on New York, and Washington pushed forward with the main army to within four miles of King's bridge, but finally fell back to Dobb's ferry, at which place the two armies continued six weeks. The American commander, observing how tardily his call on the respective states for troops was responded to, resolved not to make an attack until the arrival of the French fleet, under Count de Grasse, from the West Indies, then daily expected. At length, in August, he received a letter from De Grasse, informing him that he was about to sail with his whole fleet, and 3,200 land troops, for the Chesapeake. Washington at once resolved to abandon the project of an attack upon New York, and, with the cordial co-operation of Count de Rochambeau, proceeded without delay toward Virginia, with the whole of the French army, and as many Americans as could be spared from the posts on the Hudson. Washington and De Rochambeau preceded the army, and reached Lafayette's headquarters, at Williamsburg, Virginia, on the fourteenth of September, where, soon after, the whole army arrived. On his way, Washington made a flying visit to his seat at Mount Vernon, for the first time in six years, so completely had he devoted himself to the service of his country.

The French fleet under Count de Grasse, consisting of twenty-six ships-of-the-line and several frigates, entered the Chesapeake, where they were joined by the French squadron from Newport. Three thousand troops, under the marquis de St. Simon, disembarked from the French fleet, ascended the James river, and joined the allied armies at Williamsburg. The whole combined forces then took up their line of march for Yorktown, where the British army, under Lord Cornwallis, was entrenched; having erected strong fortifications at that place, and at Gloucester point, on the opposite shore.

On the thirtieth of September, the allied armies completely invested Yorktown, the Americans being on the right, and the French on the left, in a semicircular line, each wing resting on York river. The post at Gloucester was invested by part of the French army and marines, with some Virginia militia. On the ninth and tenth of October, the Americans and French opened their batteries, and destroyed an English frigate and transport in the harbor. The siege lasted seventeen days, and was vigorously kept up, when, on the seventeenth of October, Lord Cornwallis proposed a cessation of hostilities, and the appointment of a commission to conclude upon terms for surrendering the posts of Yorktown and Gloucester. The proposition was accepted by General Washington, commissioners appointed, terms of surrender settled; and the articles were signed on the nineteenth of October, 1781.

On the afternoon of the day on which the capitulation was signed, the garrison marched out, and laid down their arms. The soldiers were surrendered to Washington, and the shipping in the harbor to the count de Grasse. The number of prisoners was over seven thousand. The British lost, during the siege, between five and six hundred killed; the Americans about three hundred. The allied army consisted of about seven thousand American continental troops, five thousand French, and four thousand militia. The British force was only about half that of the allies; and doubtless Lord Cornwallis would have abandoned Yorktown before its investment, had he not confidently expected reinforcements from New York. On the very day of the surrender of Cornwallis, Sir Henry Clinton left New York with seven thousand men, on board of a fleet, to reinforce the former; but on reaching the capes of the Chesapeake, he heard of the capture of Yorktown, and returned to New York.

The surrender of the British army at Yorktown was the last important military operation of the war of the Revolution. It was generally considered throughout the country as decisive of the contest in favor of the American cause. The year 1781 (says Ramsay) terminated, in all parts of the United States, in favor of the Americans. It began with weakness in Carolina, mutiny in New Jersey, and devastation in Virginia; nevertheless, at its close, the British were confined in their strongholds in or near New York, Charleston, and Savannah, and their whole army in Virginia was captured.

Washington endeavored, but in vain, to induce the count de Grasse to remain and assist in the reduction of Charleston; he pleaded special engagements in the West Indies, whence he sailed immediately, leaving with Rochambeau the three thousand land-troops he brought with him. The French army cantoned during the winter at Williamsburg, in Virginia, whither the prisoners taken at Yorktown were marched: and the main body of the American army returned to its late position in New Jersey and upon the Hudson. A detachment, under General St. Clair, was sent to the south, to strengthen the army of General Greene. The French army remained in Virginia until the summer of 1782, when they joined the Americans on the Hudson. On the cessation of hostilities, they embarked from Boston for St. Domingo, in December, 1782.

Vigilant measures were adopted by Washington for the campaign of

1782 ; but fortunately they were unnecessary, for active hostilities soon after ceased.   In the southern states some skirmishes took place ; but these combats were chiefly partisan, carried on between whigs and tories.

General Washington left Yorktown on the fifth of November, and hastened to Eltham, where his wife was attending the death-bed of her only son, Mr. Custis.   He remained there a few days, to mingle his grief with the relatives of Mr. Custis, who died at the age of twenty-eight, leaving four young children, the two youngest of whom, a son and daughter, were adopted by the general, and they resided in his family till the end of his life.   From Eltham he proceeded, by the way of Mount Vernon, to Philadelphia, receiving and answering various public addresses while on his journey.   He attended Congress the day after his arrival, and was greeted with a congratulatory address by the president of that body.   By request, he remained some time in Philadelphia, to confer with Congress, and that he might enjoy some respite from the fatigues of war ; and joined the army in the following month of April, establishing his headquarters at Newburgh, on the Hudson river.

Sir Guy Carleton, who was appointed to succeed Sir Henry Clinton in command of the British forces in America, arrived at New York early in May, 1782, bearing instructions to use all honorable means to bring about an accommodation with the United States.   Both parties, therefore, ceased offensive warfare, and preparations were made to conclude terms of peace. On the twentieth of January, 1783, the preliminary treaty was signed between France, Spain, and Great Britain, and on the third of September, of the same year, definitive treaties of all the powers were signed at one time.   Congress ratified the one with America on the fourteenth of January, 1784.

On the anniversary of the battle of Lexington (April 19, 1783), a cessation of hostilities was proclaimed in the American army.   On the third of November following, the army was disbanded by the orders of Congress, and the three cities occupied by British troops were evacuated — Savannah in July, New York in November, and Charleston in December, of the same year.

The conclusion of peace, and the disbanding of the army, were events that reflecting men looked forward to with feelings of mingled joy and fear.   Although the struggle had been brought to a triumphant issue by the United States, the country was impoverished.   Much of the territory had been laid waste, commerce was nearly annihilated, a heavy burden of debt incurred by the war was weighing upon the people, and the circulating medium of paper-money had become so utterly worthless, that, by a decree of Congress, its functions were terminated.   Added to this, an army of about ten thousand men were large creditors to Congress, their pay being greatly in arrears.   It was manifest that Congress was unable to meet the claims of the soldiers, and could only recommend their case to their respective states.

In the month of December, 1782, the officers in the army resolved to memorialize Congress upon the subject of their grievances, proposing that the half-pay for life should be commuted for a specific sum, and requesting government to give security for the fulfilment of its engagements. Congress had a stormy debate upon the subject; but as nine states could not be obtained to vote the commutation proposition, the whole matter was dropped. This neglect of Congress to provide for their wants, produced a violent ferment among the officers, and through them the whole army became excited, and many minds among them determined upon coercive measures. In the midst of this ferment, an anonymous notice for a meeting of the general and field-officers, and a commissioned officer from each company, was circulated in the camp, accompanied with a letter, or address, complaining of their great hardships, and asserting that their country, instead of relieving them, " trampled upon their rights, disdained their cries, and insulted their distresses."

Fortunately, Washington was in the camp, and, with his usual promptness and wisdom, called a general meeting of all the officers, in place of the irregular one. He condemned the tone of the letter, as implying a proposal either to desert their country or turn their arms against her, and then gave them the strongest pledges that he would use his utmost power to induce Congress to grant their demands. His address was a feeling one, and appealed directly to their patriotism and the nobler sentiments of the heart. When he had concluded, he immediately retired from the meeting. The deliberations of the officers were exceedingly brief, and resulted in the adoption of resolutions, thanking the commander-in-chief for the course he had pursued, and expressing their unabated attachment to him, and confidence in the justice and good faith of Congress. They then separated, and, with hearts glowing with warmer patriotism, resolved still longer to endure privations for their beloved country. Congress soon after made arrangements for granting the officers full pay for five years, instead of half-pay for life, and four months full pay for the army, in part payment of arrearages. But as there were no funds to make this payment immediately, it required all the address of Washington to induce the soldiers to quietly return to their homes.

On the 24th of March, 1783, a letter was received from Lafayette, announcing the signing of the preliminary treaty; and Sir Guy Carleton gave official notice of the same soon after. In June, Washington wrote a circular letter to the governors of the states, having for its theme the general welfare of the country, in which he exhibited great ability, and the most truthful features of genuine patriotism. During the summer, many of the troops went home on furlough, and the commander-in-chief was employed, with Congress, in arranging a peace-establishment, and making preparations for the evacuation of New York by the British troops. On the eighteenth of October, Congress issued a proclamation, discharging the troops from further service; and thus, in effect, the continental army was disbanded. This proclamation was soon followed by General Washington's Farewell Address to the Army, November 2, 1783; an address replete with sound wisdom and evidences of a virtuous attachment to the men and the cause with whom, and for which, he had labored for eight years.

A small body of troops, who had enlisted for a definite period, were retained in the service, and assembled at West Point, under General Knox. Arrangements having been made with Carleton for the evacuation and surrender of New York on the twenty-fifth of November, these troops proceeded to the city, and, as soon as the British were embarked, they entered in triumphal procession, with Governor Clinton and other civil officers of the state. The ceremonies of the day were ended by a public entertainment given by Governor Clinton, and, throughout the whole transaction, perfect order prevailed.

On the fourth of December, Washington bade a final adieu to his companions in arms. "At noon," says Marshall, "the principal officers of the army assembled at Francis's tavern, in New York, soon after which their beloved commander entered the room. His emotions were too strong to be concealed. Filling a glass, he turned to them and said: 'With a heart full of love and gratitude, I now take leave of you. I most devoutly wish that your latter days may be as prosperous and happy, as your former ones have been glorious and honorable.' Having drunk, he added: 'I can not come to each of you to take my leave, but shall be obliged if each of you will come and take me by the hand.' General Knox, being nearest, turned to him. Washington, incapable of utterance, grasped his hand and embraced him. In the same affectionate manner, he took leave of each succeeding officer. The tear of manly sensibility was in every eye, and not a word was articulated to interrupt the dignified silence, and the tenderness of the scene. Leaving the room, he passed through the corps of light-infantry, and walked to Whitehall, where a barge waited to convey him to Paulus's Hook. The whole company followed in mute and solemn procession, with dejected countenances, testifying feelings of delicious melancholy, which no language can describe. Having entered the barge, he turned to the company, and, waving his hat, bade them a silent adieu. They paid him the same affectionate compliment; and, after the barge had left them, returned in the same solemn manner to the place where they had assembled."

Washington then repaired to Annapolis, where Congress was in session, and, on the twenty-third of December, resigned into their hands the commission he had received from that body more than eight years before, appointing him commander-in-chief of the continental armies. In all the towns and villages through which he passed, public and private demonstrations of joy and gratitude met him on every side; and Congress resolved that the resignation of his commission should be in a public audience.   A large concourse of distinguished persons were present; and, at the close of a brief address,* Washington stepped forward and handed his commission to the president (General Mifflin), who made an affectionate and appropriate reply.   He then "hastened with ineffable delight" (to use his own words) to his seat at Mount Vernon, resolved there to pass the remainder of his days amid the pure and quiet pleasures of his domestic circle, enhanced a thousand-fold by the consideration that his country was free and independent, and had taken a place among the nations of the earth.†

The conclusion of the revolutionary war permitted Washington to return to those domestic scenes in which he delighted, and from which no views of ambition seem to have had the power to draw his affections.   One of the greatest proofs of his patriotism was his refusal to receive any pecuniary compensation for his services as commander-in-chief during the eight years in which he had served his country in that capacity.   When he accepted the appointment, he announced to Congress his determination to decline payment for his services.   He simply asked the reimbursement of his expenses, an exact account of which he kept and presented to the government, drawn up by his own hand at the close of the war.‡

In the month of September, 1784, Washington made a tour to the western country, for the purpose of inspecting the lands he possessed beyond the Allegany mountains, and also of ascertaining the practicability of opening a canal between the head-waters of the rivers running eastward into the Atlantic, and those that flow westward to the Ohio.   The extent of this journey was six hundred and eighty miles, which he travelled on horseback.   He crossed the mountains, and examined the waters of the Monongahela river, with the special view of deciding the question in his own mind, whether the Potomac and James rivers could be connected by internal navigation with the western waters.   He conversed on the subject with such intelligent persons as he met, and kept a journal in which he recorded the results of his observations and inquiries.   His thoughts had been turned to this enterprise before the Revolution; and soon after returning from this western tour, in October, 1784, he communicated to

* Washington closed his address with the following words : " I consider it an indispensable duty to close this last solemn act of my official life by commending the interests of our dearest country to the protection of Almighty God, and those who have the superintendence of them into his holy keeping. Having now finished the work assigned me, I retire from the great theatre of action ; and bidding an affectionate farewell to this august body, under whose orders I have long acted, I here offer my commission, and take my leave of all employment of public life."

† Lossing's War of Independence.

‡ A fac-simile of this account of Washington's public expenditures has been published in a handsome volume, by Mr. Franklin Knight, of Washington city.

the governor of Virginia the fruits of his investigations in a letter, one of the ablest, most sagacious, and most important productions of his pen. The governor laid this letter before the legislature. It was the first suggestion of the great system of internal improvements which has since been pursued in the United States.

The legislature of Virginia, after duly considering this letter of Washington to the governor, appointed a commission for surveys, and organized two companies called the Potomac company, and the James river company, for the purpose of carrying the plan into effect.

It may here be added, that Washington was a zealous advocate for schools and literary institutions of every kind, and sought to promote them by his public addresses and by private benefactions. In this spirit he accepted the chancellorship of William and Mary college, being earnestly solicited by the trustees.*

Washington was not long allowed to remain in retirement. To remedy the distress into which the country had been thrown by the war, and to organize a permanent plan of national government, a national convention of delegates from the several states was called, and met at Philadelphia in 1787. Having been chosen one of the delegates from Virginia, Washington was appointed to preside over the deliberations of the convention, and used his influence to cause the adoption of the constitution of the United States.

By the unanimous voice of his fellow-citizens and of the electoral colleges, he was called, in 1789, to act as president of the United States, and cheerfully lent his aid in organizing the new government. Amid all the difficulties which occurred at that period from differences of opinion among the people, many of whom were opposed to the measures proposed and adopted, the national government would probably have perished in its infancy, if it had not been for the wisdom and firmness of Washington. During his first term the French revolution commenced, which convulsed the whole political world, and which tried most severely his moderation and prudence. His conduct was a model of firm and dignified moderation. Insults were offered to his authority by the minister of the French republic (Mr. Genet) and his adherents, in official papers, in anonymous libels, and by tumultuous meetings. The law of nations was trampled under foot. No vexation could disturb the tranquillity of his mind, or make him deviate from the policy which his situation prescribed. During the whole course of that arduous struggle, his personal character gave that strength to a new magistracy which in other countries arises from ancient habits of obedience and respect. The authority of his virtue was more efficacious for the preservation of America, than the legal powers of his office. During this turbulent period he was unanimously re-elected to the presidency, in 1793, for another term, although he had expressed a

* Sparks.

wish to retire. The nation was then nearly equally divided into two great political parties, who united only on the name of Washington. Throughout the whole course of his second presidency the danger of the United States was great and imminent. The spirit of change, indeed, shook all nations. But in other countries it had to encounter ancient and strong established power; in America the government was new and weak; the people had scarcely time to recover from the effects of a recent civil war. Washington employed the horror excited by the atrocities of the French revolution for the best purposes; to preserve the internal quiet of his country; to assert the dignity and to maintain the rights of the commonwealth which he governed, against foreign enemies. He avoided war, without incurring the imputation of pusillanimity. He cherished the detestation of the best portion of his countrymen for anarchy, without weakening the spirit of liberty; and he maintained the authority of the government without infringing on the rights of the states, or abridging the privileges of the people. He raised no hopes that he did not gratify; he made no promises that he did not fulfil; he exacted proper respect due to the high office he held, and rendered to others every courtesy belonging to his high station.

Having determined to retire from the presidency at the expiration of his second term, in March, 1797, he issued in September, 1796, a farewell address to the people of the United States, which will be found in this volume, and which will remain as a permanent legacy to his countrymen through future generations, for its sentiments of patriotism, and sound maxims of political sagacity. He remained at the seat of government until the inauguration of his successor, Mr. Adams, which occasion he honored with his presence, and immediately retired to Mount Vernon to pass the remainder of his days in quiet retirement; but when, in 1798, the United States armed by sea and land, in consequence of their difficulties with France, he consented to act as lieutenant-general of the army; but was never afterward called upon to take the field, although he bore the commission until his death. On Thursday, the twelfth of December, 1799, he was seized with an inflammation in his throat, which became considerably worse the next day, and which terminated his life on Saturday, the fourteenth of the same month, in the sixty-eighth year of his age.

" No man," says Colonel Knapp, in his biographical sketch, " was ever mourned so widely and sincerely as Washington. Throughout the United States, eulogies were pronounced upon his character, sermons were preached, or some mark of respect paid to his memory. It was not speaking extravagantly to say that a nation was in tears at his death. There have been popular men, who were great in their day and generation, but whose fame soon passed away. It is not so with the fame of Washington, it grows brighter by years. The writings of Washington (a portion only of which comprise eleven octavo volumes) show that he had a clear, lucid mind, and will be read with pleasure for ages to come."

" General Washington," says Judge Marshall, " was rather above the common size ; his frame was robust, and his constitution vigorous — capable of enduring great fatigue, and requiring a considerable degree of exercise for the preservation of his health. His exterior created in the beholder the idea of strength united with manly gracefulness.

" His manners were rather reserved than free, though they partook nothing of that dryness and sternness which accompany reserve when carried to an extreme ; and on all proper occasions he could relax sufficiently to show how highly he was gratified by the charms of conversation, and the pleasures of society. His person and whole deportment exhibited an unaffected and indescribable dignity, unmingled with haughtiness, of which all who approached him were sensible ; and the attachment of those who possessed his friendship, and enjoyed his intimacy, was ardent, but always respectful.

" His temper was humane, benevolent, and conciliatory ; but there was a quickness in his sensibility to anything apparently offensive, which experience had taught him to watch and to correct.

" In the management of his private affairs he exhibited an exact yet liberal economy. His funds were not prodigally wasted on capricious and ill-examined schemes, nor refused to beneficial though costly improvements. They remained, therefore, competent to that extensive establishment which his reputation, added to an hospitable temper, had in some measure imposed upon him, and to those donations which real distress has a right to claim from opulence.

" In his civil administration, as in his military career, were exhibited ample and repeated proofs of that practical good sense, of that sound judgment which is perhaps the most rare, and is certainly the most valuable quality of the human mind.

" In speculation he was a real republican, devoted to the constitution of his country, and to that system of equal political rights on which it is founded. But between a balanced republic and a democracy, the difference is like that between order and chaos. Real liberty, he thought, was to be preserved only by preserving the authority of the laws, and maintaining the energy of government."

FAREWELL ADDRESS.

SEPTEMBER 17, 1796.

Friends and Fellow-Citizens :—

THE period for a new election of a citizen to administer the executive government of the United States being not far distant, and the time actually arrived when your thoughts must be employed in designating the person who is to be clothed with that important trust, it appears to me proper, especially as it may conduce to a more distinct expression of the public voice, that I should now apprize you of the resolution I have formed, to decline being considered among the number of those out of whom the choice is to be made.

I beg you, at the same time, to do me the justice to be assured that this resolution has not been taken without a strict regard to all the considerations appertaining to the relation which binds a dutiful citizen to his country ; and that, in withdrawing the tender of service, which silence in my situation might imply, I am influenced by no diminution of zeal for your future interest, no deficiency of respect for your past kindness, but am supported by a full conviction that the step is compatible with both.

The acceptance of, and continuance hitherto in, the office to which your suffrages have twice called me, have been a uniform sacrifice of inclination to the opinion of duty and to a deference for what appeared to be your desire. I constantly hoped that it would have been much earlier in my power, consistently with motives which I was not at liberty to disregard, to return to that retirement from which I had been reluctantly drawn. The strength of my inclination to do this, previous to the last election, had even led to the preparation of an address to declare it to you ; but mature reflection on the then perplexed and critical posture of affairs with foreign nations, and the unanimous advice of persons entitled to my confidence, impelled me to abandon the idea. I rejoice that the state of your concerns, external as well as internal, no longer renders the pursuit of inclination incompatible with the sentiment of duty or propriety ; and am persuaded, whatever partiality may be retained for my services, that in the present circumstances of our country, you will not disapprove of my determination to retire.

The impressions with which I first undertook the arduous trust were explained on the proper occasion. In the discharge of this trust, I will only say that I have, with good intentions, contributed toward the organization and administration of the government the best exertions of which a very fallible judgment was capable. Not unconscious, in the outset, of the inferiority of my qualifications, experience in my own eyes, perhaps still more in the eyes of others, has strengthened the motives to diffidence of myself ; and every day the increasing weight of years admonishes me more and more that the shade of retirement is as necessary to me as it will be welcome. Satisfied that, if any circumstances have given peculiar value to my services, they were temporary, I have the consolation to believe that, while choice and prudence invite me to quit the political scene, patriotism does not forbid it.

In looking forward to the moment which is to terminate the career of my political life, my feelings do not permit me to suspend the deep acknowledgment of that debt of gratitude which I owe to my beloved coun-

try for the many honors it has conferred upon me ; still more for the stead-
fast confidence with which it has supported me, and for the opportunities I
have thence enjoyed of manifesting my inviolable attachment by services
faithful and persevering, though in usefulness unequal to my zeal.   If
benefits have resulted to our country from these services, let it always be
remembered to your praise, and as an instructive example in our annals,
that under circumstances in which the passions, agitated in every direction, were liable to mislead—amid appearances sometimes dubious—vicissitudes of fortune often discouraging—in situations in which not unfrequently want of success has countenanced the spirit of criticism—the
constancy of your support was the essential prop of the efforts and a guaranty of the plans by which they were effected.   Profoundly penetrated
with this idea, I shall carry it with me to my grave as a strong incitement
to unceasing wishes that Heaven may continue to you the choicest tokens
of its beneficence—that your union and brotherly affection may be perpetual
—that the free constitution which is the work of your hands may be sacredly maintained—that its administration in every department may be
stamped with wisdom and virtue—that, in fine, the happiness of the people of these states, under the auspices of liberty, may be made complete
by so careful a preservation and so prudent a use of this blessing as will
acquire to them the glory of recommending it to the applause, the affection, and adoption, of every nation which is yet a stranger to it.

Here, perhaps, I ought to stop.   But a solicitude for your welfare which
can not end but with my life, and the apprehension of danger natural to
that solicitude, urge me, on an occasion like the present, to offer to your
solemn contemplation, and to recommend to your frequent review, some
sentiments which are the result of much reflection, of no inconsiderable
observation, and which appear to me all-important to the permanency of
your felicity as a people.   These will be offered to you with the more
freedom, as you can only see in them the disinterested warnings of a
parting friend, who can possibly have no personal motive to bias his counsel.   Nor can I forget, as an encouragement to it, your indulgent reception of my sentiments on a former and not dissimilar occasion.

Interwoven as is the love of liberty with every ligament of our hearts,
no recommendation of mine is necessary to fortify or confirm the attachment.

The unity of government which constitutes you one people, is also now
dear to you.   It is justly so ; for it is a main pillar in the edifice of your
real independence, the support of your tranquillity at home, your peace
abroad, of your safety, of your prosperity, of that very liberty which you
so highly prize.   But as it is easy to foresee that from different causes,
and from different quarters, much pains will be taken, many artifices employed, to weaken in your minds the conviction of this truth—as this is
the point in your political fortress against which the batteries of internal
and external enemies will be most constantly and actively (though often
covertly and insidiously) directed—it is of infinite moment that you should
properly estimate the immense value of your national union to your collective and individual happiness ; that you should cherish a cordial, habitual, and immovable attachment to it ; accustoming yourselves to think and to
speak of it as a palladium of your political safety and prosperity ; watching for its preservation with jealous anxiety ; discountenancing whatever
may suggest even a suspicion that it can in any event be abandoned ; and
indignantly frowning upon the first dawning of every attempt to alienate

any portion of our country from the rest, or to enfeeble the sacred ties which now link together the various parts.

For this you have every inducement of sympathy and interest. Citizens by birth or choice of a common country, that country has a right to concentrate your affections. The name of AMERICAN, which belongs to you in your national capacity, must always exalt the just pride of patriotism more than any appellation derived from local discriminations. With slight shades of difference, you have the same religion, manners, habits, and political principles. You have, in a common cause, fought and triumphed together. The independence and liberty you possess are the work of joint councils and joint efforts, of common dangers, sufferings, and success.

But these considerations, however powerfully they address themselves to your sensibility, are greatly outweighed by those which apply more immediately to your interest. Here, every portion of our country finds the most commanding motives for carefully guarding and preserving the union of the whole.

The *north*, in an unrestrained intercourse with the *south*, protected by the equal laws of a common government, finds in the productions of the latter great additional resources of maritime and commercial enterprise, and precious materials of manufacturing industry. The *south*, in the same intercourse, benefiting by the same agency of the *north*, sees its agriculture grow and its commerce expand. Turning partly into its own channels the seamen of the *north*, it finds its particular navigation invigorated; and while it contributes in different ways to nourish and increase the general mass of the national navigation, it looks forward to the protection of a maritime strength to which itself is unequally adapted. The *east*, in like intercourse with the *west*, in the progressive improvement of interior communications by land and water, will more and more find a valuable vent for the commodities which it brings from abroad or manufactures at home. The *west* derives from the *east* supplies requisite to its growth and comfort; and what is perhaps of still greater consequence, it must of necessity owe the secure enjoyment of the indispensable outlets for its own productions to the weight, influence, and future maritime strength of the Atlantic side of the Union, directed by an indissoluble community of interest, as one nation. Any other tenure by which the *west* can hold this essential advantage, whether derived from its own separate strength, or from an apostate and unnatural connexion with any foreign power, must be intrinsically precarious.

While, then, every part of our country thus feels an immediate and particular interest in union, all the parts combined can not fail to find in the united mass of means and efforts greater strength, greater resource, proportionably greater security from external danger, a less frequent interruption of their peace by foreign nations, and, what is of inestimable value, they must derive from union an exemption from those broils and wars between themselves which so frequently afflict neighboring countries not tied together by the same government, which their own rivalships alone would be sufficient to produce, but which opposite foreign alliances, attachments, and intrigues, would stimulate and embitter. Hence, likewise, they will avoid the necessity of those overgrown military establishments which, under any form of government, are inauspicious to liberty, and which are to be regarded as particularly hostile to republican liberty. In this sense it is that your union ought to be considered as a main prop of your liberty, and that the love of the one ought to endear to you the preservation of the other.

These considerations speak a persuasive language to every reflecting and virtuous mind, and exhibit the continuance of the union as a primary object of patriotic desire. Is there a doubt whether a common government can embrace so large a sphere? Let experience solve it. To listen to mere speculation in such a case were criminal. We are authorized to hope that a proper organization of the whole, with the auxiliary agency of governments for the respective subdivisions, will afford a happy issue of the experiment. It is well worth a fair and full experiment. With such powerful and obvious motives to union, affecting all parts of our country, while experience shall not have demonstrated its impracticability, there will always be reason to distrust the patriotism of those who in any quarter may endeavor to weaken its bands.

In contemplating the causes which may disturb our union, it occurs as matter of serious concern that any ground should have been furnished for characterizing parties by geographical discriminations—*northern* and *southern*, *Atlantic* and *western*; whence designing men may endeavor to excite a belief that there is a real difference of local interests and views. One of the expedients of party to acquire influence within particular districts is, to misrepresent the opinions and aims of other districts. You can not shield yourselves too much against the jealousies and heart-burnings which spring from these misrepresentations. They tend to render alien to each other those who ought to be bound together by fraternal affection. The inhabitants of our western country have lately had a useful lesson on this head. They have seen in the negotiation by the executive, and in the unanimous ratification by the senate, of the treaty with Spain, and in the universal satisfaction at that event throughout the United States, a decisive proof how unfounded were the suspicions propagated among them of a policy in the general government and in the Atlantic states unfriendly to their interests in regard to the Mississippi. They have been witnesses to the formation of two treaties—that with Great Britain and that with Spain—which secure to them everything they could desire, in respect to our foreign relations, toward confirming their prosperity. Will it not be their wisdom to rely for the preservation of these advantages on the union by which they were procured? Will they not henceforth be deaf to those advisers, if such there are, who would sever them from their brethren and connect them with aliens?

To the efficacy and permanency of your union, a government for the whole is indispensable. No alliances, however strict, between the parts can be an adequate substitute. They must inevitably experience the infractions and interruptions which alliances in all times have experienced. Sensible of this momentous truth, you have improved upon your first essay by the adoption of a constitution of government better calculated than your former for an intimate union and for the efficacious management of your common concerns. This government, the offspring of your own choice, uninfluenced and unawed, adopted upon full investigation and mature deliberation, completely free in its principles, in the distribution of its powers, uniting security with energy, and containing within itself provision for its own amendment, has a just claim to your confidence and your support. Respect for its authority, compliance with its laws, acquiescence in its measures, are duties enjoined by the fundamental maxims of true liberty. The basis of our political system is, the right of the people to make and to alter their constitutions of government. But the constitution which at any time exists, until changed by an explicit and authentic act of the whole people, is sacredly obligatory upon all. The very idea of the power and the right of the people to establish government, presupposes the duty of every individual to obey the established government.

All obstructions to the execution of the laws, all combinations and associations, under whatever plausible character, with the real design to direct, control, counteract, or awe the regular deliberations and action of the constituted authorities, are destructive of this fundamental principle, and of fatal tendency. They serve to organize faction; to give it an artificial and extraordinary force; to put in the place of the delegated will of the nation the will of party, often a small but artful and enterprising minority of the community; and according to the alternate triumphs of different parties, to make the public administration the mirror of the ill-concerted and incongruous projects of faction, rather than the organ of consistent and wholesome plans, digested by common councils, and modified by mutual interests.

However combinations or associations of the above description may now and then answer popular ends, they are likely, in the course of time and things, to become potent engines by which cunning, ambitious, and unprincipled men will be enabled to subvert the power of the people, and to usurp for themselves the reins of government, destroying afterward the very engines which have lifted them to unjust dominion.

Toward the preservation of your government and the permanency of your present happy state, it is requisite not only that you steadily discountenance irregular opposition to its acknowledged authority, but also that you resist with care the spirit of innovation upon its principles, however specious the pretext. One method of assault may be to effect in the forms of the constitution alterations which will impair the energy of the system, and thus to undermine what can not be directly overthrown. In all the changes to which you may be invited, remember that time and habit are at least as necessary to fix the true character of governments as of other human institutions; that experience is the surest standard by which to test the real tendency of the existing constitutions of a country; that facility in changes upon the credit of mere hypothesis and opinion exposes to perpetual change, from the endless variety of hypothesis and opinion; and remember especially, that from the efficient management of your common interests, in a country so extensive as ours, a government of as much vigor as is consistent with the perfect security of liberty is indispensable. Liberty itself will find in such a government, with powers properly distributed and adjusted, its surest guardian. It is, indeed, little else than a name, where the government is too feeble to withstand the enterprises of faction, to confine each member of society within the limits prescribed by the laws, and to maintain all in the secure and tranquil enjoyment of the rights of person and property.

I have already intimated to you the danger of parties in the state, with particular reference to the founding of them upon geographical discriminations. Let me now take a more comprehensive view, and warn you in the most solemn manner against the baneful effects of the spirit of party generally.

This spirit, unfortunately, is inseparable from our nature, having its root in the strongest passions of the human mind. It exists under different shapes in all governments, more or less stifled, controlled, or repressed;

but in those of the popular form, it is seen in its greatest rankness, and is truly their worst enemy.

The alternate domination of one faction over another, sharpened by the spirit of revenge natural to party dissension, which in different ages and countries has perpetrated the most horrid enormities, is itself a frightful despotism. But this leads at length to a more formal and permanent despotism. The disorders and miseries which result, gradually incline the minds of men to seek security and repose in the absolute power of an individual; and sooner or later, the chief of some prevailing faction, more able or more fortunate than his competitors, turns this disposition to the purposes of his own elevation on the ruins of the public liberty.

Without looking forward to an extremity of this kind, which nevertheless ought not to be entirely out of sight, the common and continual mischiefs of the spirit of party are sufficient to make it the interest and duty of a wise people to discourage and restrain it.

It serves always to distract the public councils and enfeeble the public administration. It agitates the community with ill-founded jealousies and false alarms; kindles the animosity of one part against another; foments occasional riot and insurrection. It opens the door to foreign influence and corruption, which finds a facilitated access to the government itself through the channels of party passion. Thus the policy and will of one country are subjected to the policy and will of another.

There is an opinion that parties in free countries are useful checks upon the administration of the government, and serve to keep alive the spirit of liberty. This, within certain limits, is probably true; and in governments of a monarchical cast, patriotism may look with indulgence, if not with favor, upon the spirit of party. But in those of popular character, in governments purely elective, it is a spirit not to be encouraged. From the natural tendency, it is certain there will always be enough of that spirit for every salutary purpose; and there being constant danger of excess, the effort ought to be by force of public opinion to mitigate and assuage it. A fire not to be quenched, it demands a uniform vigilance to prevent its bursting into a flame, lest, instead of warming, it should consume.

It is important, likewise, that the habits of thinking in a free country should inspire caution in those intrusted with its administration to confine themselves within their respective constitutional spheres, avoiding, in the exercise of the powers of one department, to encroach upon another. The spirit of encroachment tends to consolidate the powers of all the departments in one, and thus to create, whatever the form of government, a real despotism. A just estimate of that love of power and proneness to abuse it which predominate in the human heart, is sufficient to satisfy us of the truth of this position. The necessity of reciprocal checks in the exercise of political power, by dividing and distributing it into different depositories, and constituting each the guardian of the public weal against invasions of the other, has been evinced by experiments ancient and modern—some of them in our country, and under our own eyes. To preserve them must be as necessary as to institute them. If, in the opinion of the people, the distribution or modification of the constitutional powers be in any particular wrong, let it be corrected by an amendment in the way in which the constitution designates. But let there be no change by usurpation; for though this in one instance may be the instrument of good, it is the customary weapon by which free governments are destroyed.

The precedent must always greatly overbalance in permanent evil any partial or transient benefit which the use can at any time yield.

Of all the dispositions and habits which lead to political prosperity, religion and morality are indispensable supports. In vain would that man claim the tribute of patriotism who should labor to subvert these great pillars of human happiness—these firmest props of the duties of men and citizens. The mere politician, equally with the pious man, ought to respect and to cherish them. A volume could not trace all their connexion with private and public felicity. Let it be simply asked, where is the security for property, for reputation, for life, if the sense of religious obligation desert the oaths which are the instruments of investigation in courts of justice? And let us with caution indulge the supposition that morality can be maintained without religion. Whatever may be conceded to the influence of refined education on minds of peculiar structure, reason and experience both forbid us to expect that national morality can prevail in exclusion of religious principles.

It is substantially true that virtue or morality is a necessary spring of popular government. The rule indeed extends with more or less force to every species of free government. Who that is a sincere friend to it can look with indifference upon attempts to shake the foundation of the fabric? Promote, then, as an object of primary importance, institutions for the general diffusion of knowledge. In proportion as the structure of a government gives force to public opinion, it is essential that public opinion should be enlightened.

As a very important source of strength and security, cherish public credit. One method of preserving it is to use it as sparingly as possible, avoiding occasions of expense by cultivating peace, but remembering, also, that timely disbursements to prepare for danger frequently prevent much greater disbursements to repel it; avoiding likewise the accumulation of debt, not only by shunning occasions of expense, but by vigorous exertions in time of peace to discharge the debts which unavoidable wars have occasioned, not ungenerously throwing upon posterity the burden which we ourselves ought to bear. The execution of these maxims belongs to your representatives; but it is necessary that public opinion should co-operate. To facilitate to them the performance of their duty, it is essential you should practically bear in mind that toward the payment of debts there must be revenue; that to have revenue there must be taxes; that no taxes can be devised which are not more or less inconvenient and unpleasant; that the intrinsic embarrassment inseparable from the selection of the proper objects, which is always a choice of difficulties, ought to be a decisive motive for a candid construction of the conduct of the government in making it, and for a spirit of acquiescence in the measures for obtaining revenue which the public exigencies may at any time dictate.

Observe good faith and justice toward all nations. Cultivate peace and harmony with all. Religion and morality enjoin this conduct; and can it be that good policy does not equally enjoin it? It will be worthy of a free, enlightened, and, at no distant period, a great nation, to give to mankind the magnanimous and too novel example of a people always guided by an exalted justice and benevolence. Who can doubt that in the course of time and things the fruits of such a plan would richly repay any temporary advantages that might be lost by a steady adherence to it? Can it be that Providence has connected the permanent felicity of a nation with its virtue? The experiment, at least, is recommended by every sentiment which ennobles human nature. Alas! it is rendered impossible by its vices.

In the execution of such a plan, nothing is more essential than that permanent, inveterate antipathies against particular nations, and passionate attachments for others, should be excluded; and that in the place of them, just and amicable feelings toward all should be cultivated. The nation which indulges toward another an habitual hatred or an habitual fondness, is in some degree a slave. It is a slave to its animosity or to its affection, either of which is sufficient to lead it astray from its duty and its interest. Antipathy in one nation against another disposes each more readily to offer insult and injury, to lay hold of slight causes of umbrage, and to be haughty and intractable when accidental or trifling occasions of dispute occur.

Hence, frequent collisions and obstinate, envenomed, and bloody contests. The nation, prompted by ill-will and resentment, sometimes impels to war the government contrary to the best calculations of policy. The government sometimes participates in the national propensity, and adopts through passion what reason would reject. At other times, it makes the animosity of the nation subservient to the projects of hostility, instigated by pride, ambition, and other sinister and pernicious motives. The peace often, sometimes perhaps the liberty, of nations has been the victim.

So, likewise, a passionate attachment of one nation for another produces a variety of evils. Sympathy for the favorite nation, facilitating the illusion of an imaginary common interest in cases where no real common interest exists, and infusing into one the enmities of the other, betrays the former into a participation in the quarrels and the wars of the latter without adequate inducements or justification. It leads, also, to concessions to the favorite nation of privileges denied to others, which are apt doubly to injure the nation making the concessions, by unnecessarily parting with what ought to have been retained, and by exciting jealousy, ill-will, and a disposition to retaliate, in the parties from whom equal privileges are withheld; and it gives to ambitious, corrupt, or deluded citizens, who devote themselves to the favorite nation, facility to betray or sacrifice the interests of their own country without odium, sometimes even with popularity, gilding with the appearances of a virtuous sense of obligation to a commendable deference for public opinion, or a laudable zeal for public good, the base or foolish compliances of ambition, corruption, or infatuation.

As avenues to foreign influence in innumerable ways, such attachments are particularly alarming to the truly enlightened and independent patriot. How many opportunities do they afford to tamper with domestic factions, to practise the arts of seduction, to mislead public opinion, to influence or awe the public councils! Such an attachment of a small or weak nation toward a great and powerful one, dooms the former to be the satellite of the latter. Against the insidious wiles of foreign influence, I conjure you to believe me, fellow-citizens, the jealousy of a free people ought to be constantly awake, since history and experience prove that foreign influence is one of the most baneful foes of republican government. But that jealousy, to be useful, must be impartial, else it becomes the instrument of the very influence to be avoided, instead of a defence against it. Excessive partiality for one foreign nation, and excessive dislike for another, cause those whom they actuate to see danger only on one side, and serve to veil and even second the arts of influence on the other. Real patriots, who may resist the intrigues of the favorite, are liable to become suspected and odious, while its tools and dupes usurp the applause and confidence of the people to surrender their interests.

The great rule of conduct for us in regard to foreign nations is, in extending our commercial relations, to have with them as little political connexion as possible. So far as we have already formed engagements, let them be fulfilled with perfect good faith. Here let us stop.

Europe has a set of primary interests which to us have none or a very remote relation. Hence, she must be engaged in frequent controversies, the causes of which are essentially foreign to our concerns. Hence, therefore, it must be unwise in us to implicate ourselves by artificial ties in the ordinary vicissitudes of her politics, or the ordinary combinations and collisions of her friendships or enmities.

Our detached and distant situation invites and enables us to pursue a different course. If we remain one people, under an efficient government, the period is not far off when we may defy material injury from external annoyance; when we may take such an attitude as will cause the neutrality we may at any time resolve upon to be scrupulously respected; when belligerent nations, under the impossibility of making acquisitions upon us, will not lightly hazard the giving us provocation; when we may choose peace or war as our interests, guided by justice, shall counsel.

Why forego the advantages of so peculiar a situation? Why quit our own to stand on foreign ground? Why, by interweaving our destiny with that of any part of Europe, entangle our peace and prosperity in the toils of European ambition, rivalship, interest, humor, or caprice?

It is our true policy to steer clear of permanent alliances with any portion of the foreign world, so far, I mean, as we are now at liberty to do it; for let me not be understood as capable of patronising infidelity to existing engagements. I hold the maxim no less applicable to public than to private affairs, that honesty is always the best policy. I repeat, therefore, let those engagements be observed in their genuine sense. But in my opinion, it is unnecessary and would be unwise to extend them.

Taking care always to keep ourselves by suitable establishments on a respectable defensive posture, we may safely trust to temporary alliances for extraordinary emergencies.

Harmony and a liberal intercourse with all nations are recommended by policy, humanity, and interest. But even our commercial policy should hold an equal and impartial hand; neither seeking nor granting exclusive favors or preferences; consulting the natural course of things; diffusing and diversifying by gentle means the stream of commerce, but forcing nothing; establishing with powers so disposed (in order to give trade a stable course, to define the rights of our merchants, to enable the government to support them) conventional rules of intercourse, the best that present circumstances and natural opinion will permit, but temporary and liable to be from time to time abandoned or varied as experience and circumstances shall dictate; constantly keeping in view that it is folly in one nation to look for disinterested favors from another—that it must pay with a portion of its independence for whatever it may accept under that character—that by such acceptance it may place itself in the condition of having given equivalents for nominal favors, and yet of being reproached with ingratitude for not having given more. There can be no greater error than to expect or calculate upon real favors from nation to nation. It is an illusion which experience must cure, which a just pride ought to discard.

In offering to you, my countrymen, these counsels of an old affectionate friend, I dare not hope they will make the strong and lasting impression I could wish—that they will control the usual current of the passions, or prevent our nation from running the course which has hitherto marked the destiny of nations. But if I may even flatter myself that they may be productive of some partial benefit, some occasional good—that they may now and then recur to moderate the fury of party spirit, to warn against the mischiefs of foreign intrigue, to guard against the impostures of pretended patriotism—this hope will be a full recompense for the solicitude for your welfare by which they have been dictated.

How far in the discharge of my official duties I have been guided by the principles which have been delineated, the public records and the other evidences of my conduct must witness to you and to the world. To myself, the assurance of my own conscience is, that I have at least believed myself to be guided by them.

In relation to the still subsisting war in Europe, my proclamation of the 22d of April, 1793, is the index to my plan. Sanctioned by your approving voice, and by that of your representatives in both houses of Congress, the spirit of that measure has continually governed me, uninfluenced by any attempts to deter or divert me from it.

After deliberate examination, with the aid of the best lights I could obtain, I was well satisfied that our country, under all the circumstances of the case, had a right to take, and was bound in duty and interest to take, a neutral position. Having taken it, I determined, as far as should depend upon me, to maintain it with moderation, perseverance, and firmness.

The considerations which respect the right to hold this conduct, it is not necessary on this occasion to detail. I will only observe, that according to my understanding of the matter, that right, so far from being denied by any of the belligerent powers, has been virtually admitted by all.

The duty of holding a neutral conduct may be inferred, without anything more, from the obligation which justice and humanity impose on every nation, in cases in which it is free to act, to maintain inviolate the relations of peace and amity toward other nations.

The inducements of interest for observing that conduct will best be referred to your own reflections and experience. With me, a predominant motive has been to endeavor to gain time to our country to settle and mature its yet recent institutions, and to progress without interruption to that degree of strength and constancy which it is necessary to give it, humanly speaking, the command of its own fortune.

Though in reviewing the incidents of my administration I am unconscious of intentional error, I am nevertheless too sensible of my defects not to think it probable that I may have committed many errors. Whatever they may be, I fervently beseech the Almighty to avert or mitigate the evils to which they may tend. I shall also carry with me the hope that my country will never cease to view them with indulgence, and that, after forty-five years of my life dedicated to its service with an upright zeal, the faults of incompetent abilities will be consigned[1] to oblivion, as myself must soon be to the mansions of rest.

Relying on its kindness in this as in other things, and actuated by that fervent love toward it which is so natural to a man who views in it the native soil of himself and his progenitors for several generations, I anticipate with pleasing expectations that retreat in which I promise myself to realize without alloy the sweet enjoyment of partaking in the midst of my fellow-citizens the benign influence of good laws under a free government—the ever favorite object of my heart, and the happy reward, as I trust, of our mutual cares, labors, and dangers.

John Adams

BIOGRAPHICAL SKETCH

OF

JOHN ADAMS.

JOHN ADAMS, the second president of the United States, was born on the 19th of October (old style), 1735, in that part of the town of Braintree, in Massachusetts (near Boston) which has since been incorporated by the name of Quincy.   He was the fourth in descent from Henry Adams, who fled from persecution in Devonshire, England, and settled in Massachusetts, about the year 1630.   Another of the ancestors of Mr. Adams was John Alden, one of the pilgrim founders of the Plymouth colony in 1620.   Receiving his early education in his native town, John Adams, in 1751, was admitted a member of Harvard college, at Cambridge, where he graduated in regular course, four years afterward.   On leaving college he went to Worcester, for the purpose of studying law, and at the same time to support himself, according to the usage at that time in New England, by teaching in the grammar-school of that town.   He studied law with James Putnam, a barrister of eminence, by whom he was afterward introduced to the acquaintance of Jeremy Gridley, then attorney-general of the province, who proposed him to the court for admission to the bar of Suffolk county, in 1758, and gave him access to his library, which was then one of the best in America.

Mr. Adams commenced the practice of his profession in his native town, and, by travelling the circuits with the court, became well known in that part of the country.   In 1766, by the advice of Mr. Gridley, he removed to Boston, where he soon distinguished himself at the bar, by his superior talents as counsel and advocate.   At an earlier period of his life, his thoughts had begun to turn on general politics, and the prospects of his country engaged his attention.   Soon after leaving college, he wrote a letter to a friend, dated at Worcester, the 12th of October, 1755, which evinces so remarkable a foresight that it is fortunate it has been preserved.   We make the following extracts: "Soon after the reformation, a few people came over into this new world, for conscience' sake.

Perhaps this apparently trivial incident may transfer the great seat of empire into America. It looks likely to me, if we can remove the turbulent Gallics, our people, according to the exactest computation, will, in another century, become more numerous than England herself. The only way to keep us from setting up for ourselves, is to disunite us. *Divide et impera.* Keep us in distinct colonies, and then some great men in each colony, desiring the monarchy of the whole, will destroy each other's influence, and keep the country in equilibrio. Be not surprised that I am turned politician ; the whole town is immersed in politics. I sit and hear, and, after being led through a maze of sage observations, I sometimes retire and, by laying things together, form some reflections pleasing to myself. The produce of one of these reveries you have read above." Mr. Webster observes : " It is remarkable that the author of this prognostication should live to see fulfilled to the letter what could have seemed to others, at the time, but the extravagance of youthful fancy. His earliest political feelings were thus strongly American, and from this ardent attachment to his native soil he never departed."

In 1764, he married Abigail Smith, daughter of Rev. William Smith, of Weymouth, and grand-daughter of Colonel Quincy, a lady of uncommon endowments and excellent education. He had previously imbibed a prejudice against the prevailing religious opinions of New England, and became attached to speculations hostile to those opinions. Nor were his views afterward changed. In his religious sentiments he accorded with Doctor Bancroft, a unitarian minister of Worcester, of whose printed sermons he expressed his high approbation. In 1765, Mr. Adams published an essay on canon and feudal law, the object of which was to show the conspiracy between church and state for the purpose of oppressing the people.

In 1770, he was chosen a representative, from the town of Boston, in the legislature of Massachusetts. The same year he was one of the counsel who defended Captain Preston, and the British soldiers who fired at his order, upon the inhabitants of Boston. Captain Preston was acquitted, and Mr. Adams lost no favor with his fellow-citizens by engaging in this trial. As a member of the legislature, he opposed the royal governor, Hutchinson, in his measures, and also wrote against the British government in the newspapers. In 1774, he was elected a member of the Massachusetts council, and negatived by Governor Gage. In this and the next year, he wrote on the whig side the numbers called " Nov Anglus," in reply to essays, signed " Massachusitensis," in favor of the British government, by Sewall, the attorney-general. The same year he was appointed a member of the continental congress, from Massachusetts, and in that body, which met at Philadelphia, he became one of the most efficient and able advocates of liberty. In the Congress which met in May, 1775, he again took his seat, having been reappointed as a delegate. In 1775 he seconded the nomination of Washington as commander-in-chief of the army, and in July, 1776, he was the adviser and great supporter of the declaration of independence. It was reported by a committee composed of Thomas Jefferson, John Adams, Benjamin Franklin, Roger Sherman, and Robert R. Livingston. During the same year, he, with Doctor Franklin and Edward Rutledge, was deputed to treat with Lord Howe for the pacification of the colonies. He declined, at this time, the offer of the office of chief justice of the supreme court of Massachusetts.

In December, 1777, Mr. Adams was appointed a commissioner to the court of France, in place of Silas Deane, who was recalled. He embarked in the frigate Boston, in February, 1778. On his arrival in France he found a treaty of amity and commerce, also a treaty of alliance, had been already signed, and, after Doctor Franklin received from Congress the appointment of minister plenipotentiary, Mr. Adams returned to the United States, in the summer of 1779.

Immediately after his return he was chosen a member of the Massachusetts convention for framing the new state constitution. He accepted a seat in that body, and his plan for a constitution being reported by a committee of which he was a member, was, in most of its important features, adopted by the convention.

During the time when he was attending to the business of the Massachusetts convention, Congress resolved to appoint a minister plenipotentiary for negotiating a treaty of peace with Great Britain. On the 29th of September, 1779, Mr. Adams received this appointment, and sailed in the French frigate La Sensible, in November. He landed at Ferrol, in Spain, and arrived in Paris in February, 1780. In August he repaired to Amsterdam, having previously been instructed to procure loans in Holland, and soon afterward receiving power to negotiate a treaty of amity and commerce. In 1782 he effected a loan for eight millions of guilders, also negotiated a very favorable treaty with Holland, which nation recognised the United States as free, sovereign, and independent.

In 1781 Mr. Adams was associated by Congress with Franklin, Jay, Laurens, and Jefferson, in a commission for concluding treaties of peace with the several European powers; and in 1783 he was associated with Franklin and Jay for the purpose of negotiating a commercial treaty with Great Britain. The definitive treaty of peace with Great Britain was signed on the 3d of September, 1783, by Messrs. Adams, Franklin, and Jay; the provisional treaty had been signed by the same commissioners, with Mr. Laurens, on the 30th of November, 1782.

During part of the year 1784, Mr. Adams remained in Holland, and returned to France, where he joined his associates appointed by Congress to negotiate commercial treaties with foreign nations. An extensive plan of operations for commercial conventions was formed, but not carried out.

In January, 1785, Congress appointed Mr. Adams minister to represent the United States at the court of Great Britain, an office at that time deemed peculiarly delicate and interesting. Although his reception by the king was favorable and courteous, Mr. Adams found the British ministry cold and unfriendly toward the United States, and he was, therefore, unable to negotiate a commercial treaty with that nation. In other respects, however, he rendered valuable services to his country, and, besides assisting in forming treaties with Prussia and Morocco, he wrote, while in Europe, an elaborate and eloquent defence of the forms of government established in the United States, in reply to strictures advanced by Mr. Turgot, the Abbé de Mably, Dr. Price, and other European writers. Immediately after the publication of this work, Mr. Adams asked permission to resign and return, and in June, 1788, he arrived in his native land, after an absence of between eight and nine years.

The services of Mr. Adams in the cause of his country, at home and abroad, during the period to which we have referred, it is believed, were not excelled by those of any other of the patriots of the revolution. In the language of one of his eulogists (Mr. J. E. Sprague, of Massachusetts): " Not a hundred men in the country could have been acquainted with any part of the labors of Mr. Adams—they appeared anonymously, or under assumed titles ; they were concealed in the secret conclaves of Congress, or the more secret cabinets of princes. Such services are never known to the public ; or, if known, only in history, when the actors of the day have passed from the stage, and the motives for longer concealment cease to exist. As we ascend the mount of history, and rise above the vapors of party prejudice, we shall all acknowledge that we owe our independence more to John Adams than to any other created being, and that he was the GREAT LEADER of the American Revolution."

When permission was given him to return from Europe, the continental Congress adopted the following resolution : " Resolved, that Congress entertain a high sense of the services which Mr. Adams has rendered to the United States, in the execution of the various important trusts which they have from time to time committed to him ; and that the thanks of Congress be presented to him for the patriotism, perseverance, integrity, and diligence. with which he has ably and faithfully served his country." Such was the testimonial of his country, expressed through the national councils, at the termination of his revolutionary and diplomatic career.

During the absence of Mr. Adams in Europe, the constitution of the United States had been formed and adopted. He highly approved of its provisions, and on his return, when it was about to go into operation, he was selected by the friends of the constitution to be placed on the ticket with Washington as a candidate for one of the two highest offices in the gift of the people. He was consequently elected vice-president, and on the assembling of the senate, he took his seat as president of that body, at New York, in April, 1789. Having been re-elected to that office in 1792.

he held it, and presided in the senate, with great dignity, during the entire period of Washington's administration, whose confidence he enjoyed, and by whom he was consulted on important questions. In his valedictory address to the senate, he remarks : " It is a recollection of which nothing can ever deprive me, and it will be a source of comfort to me through the remainder of my life, that on the one hand, I have for eight years held the second situation under our constitution, in perfect and uninterrupted harmony with the first, without envy in the one, or jealousy in the other, so, on the other hand, I have never had the smallest misunderstanding with any member of the senate."

In 1790, Mr. Adams wrote his celebrated " Discourses on Davila ;" they were anonymously published, at first, in the Gazette of the United States, of Philadelphia, in a series of numbers ; they may be considered as a sequel to his " Defence of the American Constitutions." He was a decided friend and patron of literature and the arts, and while in Europe, having obtained much information on the subject of public institutions, he contributed largely to the advancement of establishments in his native state, for the encouragement of arts, sciences, and letters.

On the retirement of General Washington from the presidency of the United States, Mr. Adams was elected his successor, after a close and spirited contest with two rivals for that high office ; Mr. Jefferson being supported by the democratic or republican party, while a portion of the federal party preferred Mr. Thomas Pinckney, of South Carolina, who was placed on the ticket with Mr. Adams. The result, as we have stated, in our notice of Washington's administration, was the election of Mr. Adams as president, and Mr. Jefferson as vice-president, and in March, 1797, they entered upon their duties in those offices.

On meeting the senate, as their presiding officer, Mr. Jefferson remarked, that the duties of the chief magistracy had been " justly confided to the eminent character who preceded him, whose talents and integrity," he added, " have been known and revered by me through a long term of years ; have been the foundation of a cordial and uninterrupted friendship between us ; and I devoutly pray that he may be long preserved for the government, the happiness, and prosperity of our country." The senate adopted an address taking leave of Mr. Adams, after he had presided over them for eight years, with the strongest expressions of respect and attachment.

The administration of Mr. Adams we shall have occasion to notice in another place. He came to the presidency in a stormy time. In the language of Colonel Knapp, " the French revolution had just reached its highest point of settled delirium, after some of the paroxysms of its fury had passed away. The people of the United States took sides, some approving, others deprecating, the course pursued by France. Mr. Adams wished to preserve a neutrality, but found this quite impossible. A navy was raised, with surprising promptitude, to prevent insolence, and to chastise aggression. It had the desired effect, and France was taught that the Americans were friends in peace, but were not fearful of war when it could not be averted. When the historian shall come to this page of our history, he will do justice to the sagacity, to the spirit, and to the integrity of Mr. Adams, and will find that he had more reasons, and good ones, for his conduct, than his friends or enemies ever gave him."

In his course of public policy, when war with France was expected, he was encouraged by addresses from all quarters, and by the approving voice of Washington. He, however, gave dissatisfaction to many of his own political party, in his final attempts to conciliate France, and in his removal of two members of his cabinet, toward the close of his administration. Under these circumstances, notwithstanding Mr. Adams was the candidate of the federal party for re-election as president, and received their faithful support, it is not strange that his opponents, with the advantage in their favor of the superior popularity of Mr. Jefferson, succeeded in defeating him. For this event, the correspondence of Mr. Adams shows that he was prepared, and he left the arduous duties of chief magistrate probably with less of disappointment than his enemies had expected.

Immediately after Mr. Jefferson had succeeded to the presidency, in 1801, Mr. Adams retired to his estate at Quincy, in Massachusetts, and passed the remainder of his days in literary and scientific leisure, though occasionally addressing various communications to the public. He gave his support generally to the administration of Mr. Jefferson, and the friendship between these distinguished men was revived by a correspondence, and continued for several years previous to their death. When the disputes with Great Britain eventuated in war, Mr. Adams avowed his approbation of that measure, and in 1815 he saw the second treaty of peace concluded with that nation, by a commission of which his son was at the head, as he had been himself in that commission which formed the treaty of 1783.

In 1816, the republican party in Massachusetts, which had once vehemently opposed him as president of the United States, paid him the compliment of placing his name at the head of their list of presidential electors. In 1820, he was chosen a member of the state convention to revise the constitution of Massachusetts, which body unanimously solicited him to act as their president. This he declined, on account of his age, but he was complimented by a vote of the convention acknowledging his great services, for a period of more than half a century, in the cause of his country and of mankind.

In 1818, he had lost, by her death, his amiable and faithful consort, who had for so many years shared his anxieties and fortunes. His only daughter, Mrs. Smith, died in 1813. These ladies were distinguished through life as among the most excellent and talented of American females. The heroic spirit of Mrs. Adams is shown in a striking light in a letter from her to a friend in London, dated in 1777; we give the following extract: " Heaven is our witness, that we do not rejoice in the effusion of blood; but having forced us to draw the sword, we are determined never to sheathe it slaves of Britain. Our cause is, I trust, the cause of truth and justice, and will finally prevail, though the combined force of earth and hell shall rise against them. To this cause I have sacrificed much of my own personal happiness, by giving up to the councils of America one of my nearest connexions, and living for more than three years in a state of widowhood."

The last years of the long life of Mr. Adams were peaceful and tranquil. His mansion was always the abode of elegant hospitality, and he was occasionally enlivened by visits from his distinguished son, who, in 1825, he had the singular felicity of seeing elevated to the office of president of the United States. At length, having lived to a good old age, he expired, surrounded by his affectionate relatives, on the fourth of July, 1826, the fiftieth anniversary of that independence which he had done so much to achieve. A short time before his death, being asked to suggest a toast for the customary celebration, he replied, " I will give you—Independence for ever." It is known that Mr. Jefferson died on the same day—a most remarkable dispensation of Providence. A similar coincidence occurred five years afterward, in the death of President Monroe, July 4, 1831.

Mr. Adams was of middle stature, and full person, and when elected president, he was bald on the top of his head. His countenance beamed with intelligence, and moral as well as physical courage. His walk was firm and dignified, to a late period of his life. His manner was slow and deliberate, unless he was excited, and when this happened, he expressed himself with great energy. He was ever a man of purest morals, and is said to have been a firm believer in Christianity, not from habit and example, but from diligent investigation of its proofs.

To use the words of a political friend of his (Mr. Sullivan): " He had an uncompromising regard for his own opinion; and seemed to have supposed that his opinions could not be corrected by those of other men, nor bettered by any comparison. It is not improbable that Mr. Adams was impatient in finding how much the more easily understood services of military men were appreciated, than were the secluded, though no less important ones, of diplomatic agency and cabinet council. So made up, from natural propensities, and from the circumstances of his life, Mr. Adams came to the presidency at the time when more forbearance and discretion were required than he is supposed to have had. He seems to have been deficient in the rare excellence of attempting to see himself as others saw him; and he ventured to act as though everybody

7

saw as he saw himself. He considered only what was right in his own view ; and that was to be carried by main force, whatever were the obstacles."

But whatever may be the judgment of posterity as to his merits as a ruler, there can be no question on the subject of his general character— nor of his penetrating mind—his patriotism, and his devotion to what he considered the true interests of his country.

Eng.d by V.Balch from a Painting by G. Stuart

BIOGRAPHICAL SKETCH

OF

THOMAS JEFFERSON.

THE life of Thomas Jefferson, the third president of the United States, is one of the most interesting and instructive among those of the distinguished persons whose names are identified with American history. In the character of this extraordinary man, as well as in the events of his life, we are presented with a combination of philosophical attainments and political talents, of benevolent feelings, and ambitious aspirations, rarely found united in the same individual, and still more rarely resulting in the popular veneration bestowed upon his name by a large portion of his countrymen; while by others he has been regarded in an unfavorable light as a statesman and a ruler, particularly in the effect of his political principles upon the American people, over whom he acquired such an astonishing ascendency.

The family of Jefferson were among the early emigrants from Great Britain to Virginia. "The tradition in my father's family," the subject of this sketch says, in his own memoirs, "was, that their ancestor came to this country from Wales, and from near the mountain of Snowdon; but the first particular information I have of any ancestor, was of my grandfather, who lived at the place in Chesterfield called Osborne's, and owned the lands, afterward the glebe of the parish. He had three sons: Thomas, who died young; Field, who settled on the waters of the Roanoke, and left numerous descendants; and Peter, my father, who settled on the lands I still own, called Shadwell, adjoining my present residence. He was born February 29, 1707–'8, and intermarried, 1739, with Jane Randolph, of the age of 19, daughter of Isham Randolph, one of the seven sons of that name and family settled in Goochland. They traced their pedigree far back in England and Scotland, to which let every one ascribe the faith and merit he chooses."

At the above-named place, Shadwell, in Albemarle county, Virginia, Thomas Jefferson was born, on the 2d of April (old style), 1743. His father, Peter Jefferson, a man of some distinction in the colony, died in 1757, leaving a widow (who lived until 1776) with two sons and six daughters. These children inherited a handsome estate from their father: Thomas, the eldest, received the lands which he called Monticello, on which he resided, when not in public life and when he died.

At the age of five, his father placed him at an English school, and at nine years of age he commenced the study of Latin and Greek, with Mr. Douglass, a Scotch clergyman, who also instructed him in French. On the death of his father, he was placed under the tuition of another clergyman, Mr. Maury, a classical scholar, with whom he pursued his studies two years. In the spring of 1760, he entered William and Mary College, where he continued two years. Dr. William Small, of Scotland, was then professor of mathematics, and is described by Mr. Jefferson as " a man profound in most of the useful branches of science, with a happy talent of communication, correct and gentlemanly manners, and an enlarged and liberal mind. He, most happily for me," he adds, " became soon attached to me, and made me his daily companion when not engaged in the school; and from his conversation I got my first views of the expansion of science, and of the system of things in which we are placed. He returned to Europe in 1762, having previously filled up the measure of his goodness to me, by procuring for me, from his most intimate friend, George Wythe, a reception as a student at law under his direction, and introducing me to the acquaintance and familiar table of Governor Fauquier, the ablest man who had ever filled that office. Mr. Wythe continued to be my faithful and beloved mentor in youth, and my most affectionate friend through life. In 1767, he led me into the practice of the law, at the bar of the general court, at which I continued until the revolution shut up the courts of justice."

" It has been thought," says Mr. Wirt, " that Mr. Jefferson made no figure at the bar; but the case was far otherwise. There are still extant, in his own fair and neat hand, in the manner of his master, a number of arguments which were delivered by him at the bar, upon some of the most intricate questions of the law; which, if they shall ever see the light, will vindicate his claim to the first honors of his profession. It is true, he was not distinguished in popular debate; why he was not so, has often been matter of surprise to those who have not seen his eloquence on paper, and heard it in conversation. He had all the attributes of the mind, and the heart, and the soul, which are essential to eloquence of the highest order. The only defect was a physical one: he wanted volume and compass of voice for a large, deliberative assembly; and his voice, from the excess of his sensibility, instead of rising with his feelings and conceptions, sank under their pressure, and became guttural and inarticulate. The consciousness of this infirmity repressed any attempt in a large body in which he knew he must fail. But his voice was all-sufficient for the purposes of judicial debate; and there is no reason to doubt that, if the service of his country had not called him away so soon from his profession, his fame as a lawyer would now have stood upon the same distinguished ground which he confessedly occupies as a statesman, an author, and a scholar.

" At the time of Mr. Jefferson's appearance," the same writer remarks, " the society of Virginia was much diversified, and reflected pretty distinctly an image of that of England. There was, first, the landed aristocracy, shadowing forth the order of English nobility; then the sturdy yeomanry, common to them both; and last, a *fæculum* of beings, as they were called by Mr. Jefferson, corresponding with the mass of the English plebeians.

" Mr. Jefferson, by birth, belonged to the aristocracy: but the idle and voluptuous life which marked that order had no charms for a mind like his. He relished better the strong, unsophisticated, and racy character of the yeomanry, and attached himself, of choice, to that body. He was a republican and a philanthropist, from the earliest dawn of his character. He read with a sort of poetic illusion, which identified him with every scene that his author spread before him. Enraptured with the brighter ages of republican Greece and Rome, he had followed with an aching heart the march of history which had told him of the desolation of those fairest portions of the earth; and had read, with dismay and indignation, of that swarm of monarchies, the progeny of the Scandinavian hive, under which genius and liberty were now everywhere crushed. He loved his own country with a passion not less intense, deep, and holy, than that of his great compatriot (John Adams): and with this love he combined an expanded philanthropy which encircled the globe. From the working of the strong energies within him, there arose an early vision, too, which cheered his youth and accompanied him through life—the vision of emancipated man throughout the world."*

While he was a student of law at Williamsburg, in 1765, Mr. Jefferson heard the celebrated speech of Patrick Henry, in the Virginia house of delegates, against the stamp-act; animated by the eloquence of Henry, he from that time stood forward as a champion for his country.

In 1769, he was chosen by the people of his county to represent them in the legislature of the colony, a station that he continued to fill up to the period of the revolution. In that capacity he made an effort, which was not successful, for the emancipation of slaves in Virginia.

In January, 1772, Mr. Jefferson married Mrs. Martha Skelton, a widow of twenty-three years of age, daughter of Mr. John Wayles, an eminent lawyer of Virginia, who left her a considerable fortune.

On the 12th of March, 1773, Mr. Jefferson was chosen a member of the first committee of correspondence established by the colonial legisla-

* Wirt's Eulogy on Adams and Jefferson.

tures. In 1774, he published his "Summary View of the Rights of British America," a powerful pamphlet, addressed to the king of Great Britain, in which he set forth the true relations between the mother-country and colonies, as claimed by the people of this country. This pamphlet was republished in England, under the auspices of Edmund Burke.

In 1775, he was elected one of the delegates to represent Virginia in the continental Congress, of which body he was for several years one of the most active members. The Virginia delegates having, in pursuance of instructions from their provincial convention, moved a resolution in favor of the independence of the colonies, that question was taken up in Congress, and, after debate, referred to a committee of five, of whom Mr. Jefferson was chosen chairman. The committee, whose names are given in our biography of Mr. Adams, requested Mr. Jefferson to prepare the *Declaration of Independence*. To this he consented, although then one of the youngest members of Congress, and his draught of that paper, which is the principal monument of his fame, was accepted by the committee and by Congress, with few amendments, and finally adopted on the 4th of July, 1776.

The new state government of Virginia having been organized the same year, while Mr. Jefferson was in Congress, and he having been elected a member of the legislature, where he thought he could be useful in framing the laws required under a republican form of government, he resigned his place in Congress, and took his seat in the Virginia legislature, in October. In this station he acted as one of a commission for revising the laws of the commonwealth.

Among the laws proposed by him, and adopted, were those prohibiting the future importation of slaves ; for abolishing the law of primogeniture, and providing for the equal partition of inheritances ; for establishing religious freedom ; and for a system of general education ; which last measure was never carried into practice in the state.

The benevolence of Mr. Jefferson's character is shown in a transaction which took place in 1779. Congress had deemed it prudent to retain in this country the British troops who were captured at Saratoga on the surrender of Burgoyne, until the British government ratified the agreement of their commanding officer. These troops were removed into the interior of the county, and Charlottesville, in Virginia, in the immediate vicinity of Mr. Jefferson's residence, was selected for their residence. There they were sent in the early part of 1779, although the barracks were in an unfinished state, the provisions for their sustenance insufficient, and the roads in a bad condition. Mr. Jefferson and some of his neighbors did all in their power to alleviate the distresses of the troops, and the circumstances of their captivity. After arrangements were made for their accommodation, the governor and council, in consequence of the representations of persons who apprehended a scarcity of provisions, determined, as they were authorized to do by Congress, to remove the prisoners to another state, or to some other part of Virginia. This intention was heard by the officers and men with distress, and with regret by Mr. Jefferson and his neighbors. He therefore addressed a letter to Governor Henry, in which he stated, in earnest and feeling language, the inhumanity and impolicy of the proposed measure. This appeal was successful, and the troops were suffered to remain at Charlottesville. From the British officers Mr. Jefferson received many letters of thanks for his kindness and hospitality, which they did not forget in his subsequent visit to Europe. When the time arrived for their leaving Virginia to return to England, the officers united in a letter of renewed thanks and respectful farewell to him. In his reply Mr. Jefferson said: " The little attentions you are pleased to magnify so much, never deserved a mention or thought. Opposed as we happen to be, in our sentiments of duty and honor, and anxious for contrary events, I shall, nevertheless, sincerely rejoice in every circumstance of happiness and safety which may attend you personally."

On the first of June, 1779, Mr. Jefferson was elected by the legislature to succeed Patrick Henry, the first republican governor of Virginia. After holding the office two years, he retired to private life, and soon afterward he narrowly escaped capture by a company of 250 British cavalry, who were sent into the interior for the purpose of surprising and making prisoners the members of assembly at Charlottesville. No one was taken, and Mr. Jefferson, when pursued, escaped on his horse, through the woods at Carter's mountain. He was the same year elected a member of the legislature.

In 1781, Mr. Jefferson wrote his " Notes on Virginia," in reply to certain questions addressed to him by M. de Marbois, the secretary of legation from France in the United States, embracing a general view of its geography, natural productions, statistics, government, history, and laws. This little work, which has been very generally admired for its style and variety of information, was soon after published, both in French and English.

He had, in 1776, declined the appointment of commissioner, with Franklin and Deane, to negotiate treaties with France. In 1782, Congress appointed him a minister plenipotentiary, to join those who were in Europe, to negotiate a treaty of peace with Great Britain, but intelligence having been received that preliminaries had been signed, Congress dispensed with his leaving the United States.

Having been again elected a delegate to Congress, in 1783, he was chairman of the committee to whom the treaty of peace with Great Britain was referred; and on the report of this committee the treaty was unanimously ratified. In 1784, he wrote notes on the establishment of a coinage for the United States, and proposed a different money unit from that suggested by Robert Morris, the continental financier, and of his assistant, Gouverneur Morris.   To Mr. Jefferson we are indebted for the dollar as the unit, and our present system of coins and decimals.

As a member of Congress, Mr. Jefferson made but few speeches.   He remarks : " I served with General Washington in the legislature of Virginia, before the revolution, and during it, with Dr. Franklin in Congress. I never heard either of them speak ten minutes at a time, nor to any but the main point which was to decide the question."

He was appointed by Congress, in May, 1784, with Adams and Franklin, a minister plenipotentiary to negotiate treaties of commerce with foreign nations.   In July he sailed from Boston for Europe, with his eldest daughter, and joined the other commissioners, at Paris, in August.   Negotiations were only successful with Prussia and Morocco.   In March, 1785, Mr. Jefferson was appointed by Congress to succeed Dr. Franklin as minister at the French court, and remained in France until October, 1789.

During his residence in Paris, his society was courted by Condorcet, D'Alembert, Morrellet, and other distinguished literary and scientific men of France ; and in the gayety, learning, taste, elegance, and hospitality of Paris, he found the pleasures most congenial to his disposition.   In the month of October, 1789, he obtained leave of absence for a short time, and returned to the United States.   He arrived at Norfolk on the 23d of November, and on his way home received from President Washington a letter offering him the appointment of secretary of state, at the organization of the federal government under the constitution, which had then recently been adopted.   His inclinations were to return to France, as minister, which was left at his option by the president, but he finally concluded to accede to the wishes of Washington that he should accept the seat in his cabinet offered to him.   His reports, while secretary of state, on the currency, on weights and measures, on the fisheries, and on commercial restrictions, as well as his correspondence with foreign ministers, gave ample proofs of his ability as a statesman.   In 1790, Mr. Jefferson accompanied President Washington on a visit to Rhode Island, after that state had accepted the federal constitution.   In 1791, being called on by the president for his opinion on the act passed by Congress establishing a national bank, he made a written communication, objecting to the institution as unconstitutional.   The bill was, however, approved by President Washington.   On the 31st of December, 1793, Mr. Jefferson resigned his seat in the cabinet, and retired to private life, at Monticello.   While holding office under Washington, he had disapproved of many of the measures of his administration, particularly in those which originated with the secretary of the treasury, Hamilton.   Between that gentleman and Mr. Jefferson there were irreconcilable differences of opinion on political matters, which caused constant bickerings in the cabinet first formed by General Washington. The opposition to the federal administration assumed an organized form under the auspices of Mr. Jefferson. By his advice, the opposition party, which had been called *anti-federalists*, claimed the name of *republicans*, while their federal opponents called them *democrats*, after that name was introduced here from France. The term democrat was seldom used or countenanced by Mr. Jefferson.

In 1796, the political friends of Mr. Jefferson brought him forward as a candidate for president, but as Mr. Adams received the highest number of votes, that gentleman was elected president, and Mr. Jefferson vice-president, for four years from March 4, 1797. During that period, when not presiding in the senate, his time was passed in his favorite retreat at Monticello. He wrote a manual for the senate, which has ever since been the standard guide of Congress, as well as other political bodies, in the rules for transacting business.

In 1800, Mr. Jefferson was again nominated by his party, for president, and received a majority of votes over Mr. Adams. The votes for Mr. Jefferson and Colonel Burr, the republican candidates for president and vice-president, being equal, the house of representatives, as then required by the constitution, were called upon to decide which should be president. When the election came on in the house, the political opponents of Mr. Jefferson voted for Burr; but on the 36th ballot, the opposition being partially withdrawn, Mr. Jefferson was elected president, and Colonel Burr became, of course, vice-president.

Of the events of Mr. Jefferson's administration we shall speak in another place. He was re-elected president in 1804, and retired finally from public life March 4, 1809. The remaining seventeen years of his life were passed in the tranquillity of Monticello. "Here," says Mr. Webster, "he lived as became a wise man. Surrounded by affectionate friends, his ardor in the pursuit of knowledge undiminished, with uncommon health, and unbroken spirits, he was able to enjoy largely the rational pleasures of life, and to partake in that public prosperity which he had so much contributed to produce. His kindness and hospitality, the charm of his conversation, the ease of his manners, the extent of his acquirements, and especially the full store of revolutionary incidents which he possessed, and which he knew when and how to dispense, rendered his abode in a high degree attractive to his admiring countrymen, while his public and scientific character drew toward him every intelligent and educated traveller from abroad."

The correspondence of Mr. Jefferson was extensive through life. In his latter years he renewed his intimacy with Mr. Adams, and the letters between the two ex-presidents which were published, are of the most friendly character.

The principal object in which Mr. Jefferson took an interest in his declining years, was that of a system of education in Virginia, especially in the superintendence of the university of Virginia, which was founded in 1818, through his instrumentality. This institution was located at Charlottesville, at the foot of the mountain on which Monticello is situated, and Mr. Jefferson acted as rector from the time of its foundation until his death.

The pecuniary circumstances of Mr. Jefferson became embarrassed in his old age. He was compelled to dispose of his library, which was purchased by Congress for $23,950, and in 1825 he applied to the legislature of Virginia for leave to dispose of his estate at Monticello by lottery, to prevent its being sacrificed in payment of his debts. His request was granted, but his earthly career was closed before his wishes could be carried into effect. After a short illness, he died the following 4th of July, 1826, the aniversary of that day which fifty years before had been rendered memorable by that declaration of independence which had emanated from his pen. We have mentioned in another place the remarkable coincidence that his compatriot, John Adams, died on the same day.

In a private memorandum left by Mr. Jefferson, he desired that a small granite obelisk might be erected over his remains, with the following inscription :—

Here was buried
THOMAS JEFFERSON,
Author of the Declaration of Independence,
Of the Statute of Virginia for Religious Freedom,
And Father of the University of Virginia.

The age of Mr. Jefferson at the time of his death, was a little over eighty-three years. His wife died in 1782, leaving three daughters, one of whom died young, one married John W. Eppes, and the other Thomas M. Randolph, both of Virginia, the latter afterward governor of the state. Mrs. Eppes died in 1804, while Mr. Jefferson was president; Mrs. Randolph survived him.

In person Mr. Jefferson was beyond the ordinary dimensions, being six feet two inches in height, thin, but well formed, erect in his carriage, and imposing in his appearance. His complexion was fair, his hair, originally red, became white and silvery in old age ; his eyes were light blue, sparkling with intelligence, and beaming with philanthropy ; his nose was large, his forehead broad, and his whole countenance indicated great sensibility and profound thought. His manners were simple and unpolished, yet dignified, and all who approached him were rendered perfectly at ease, both by his republican habits and his genuine politeness. His disposition being cheerful, his conversation was lively and enthusiastic, remarkable for the chastity of his colloquial diction and the correctness of his phraseology. He disliked form and parade, and his dress was remarkably plain, and often slovenly. Benevolence and liberality were prominent traits of his disposition. To his slaves he was an indulgent master. As a neighbor, he was much esteemed for his liberality and friendly offices. As a friend, he was ardent and unchangeable ; and as a host, the munificence of his hospitality was carried to the excess of self-impoverishment. He possessed great fortitude of mind, and his command of temper was such that he was never seen in a passion.

As a man of letters, and a votary of science, he acquired high distinction. In the classics, and in several European languages, as well as in mathematics, he attained a proficiency not common to American students.

With regard to his political opinions, and his character as a statesman, his countrymen have widely differed in their estimates. By some persons he has been considered as one of the most pure, amiable, dignified, wise, and patriotic of men. By others he has been considered as remarkably defective in the qualities which dignify and adorn human life, and as one of the most wrong-headed statesmen that ever lived. Posterity will judge which of these opinions is right, and which is wrong. His writings which, agreeably to directions left by him, have been published since his death, afford ample materials for judging of his character. They consist of four volumes, octavo, of correspondence, *anas*, &c.

The religious opinions of Mr. Jefferson were peculiar and eccentric. His writings show that he was a free-thinker, with a preference for some of the doctrines of unitarianism. In a letter to a friend he says : " I have to thank you for your pamphlets on the subjects of unitarianism, and to express my gratification with your efforts for the revival of *primitive Christianity* in your quarter. And a strong proof of the solidity of the primitive faith is its restoration, as soon as a nation arises which vindicates to itself the freedom of religious opinion, and its external divorce from civil authority. I confidently expect that the present generation will see unitarianism become the general religion of the United States."

In a letter to William Short, dated April, 1820, when alluding to the subject of religion, Mr. Jefferson remarks : " But it is not to be understood that I am with him [Jesus] in all his doctrines. I am a materialist ; he takes the side of spiritualism ; he preaches the efficacy of repentance toward forgiveness of sin ; I require a counterpoise of good works to redeem it, &c., &c. It is the innocence of his character, the purity and sublimity of his moral precepts, the eloquence of his inculcations, the beauty of the apologues in which he conveys them, that I so much admire ; sometimes, indeed, needing indulgence to eastern hyperbolism. My eulogies, too, may be founded on a postulate which all may not be ready to grant. Among the sayings and discourses imputed to him by his biographers, I find many passages of fine imagination, correct morality, and of the most lovely benevolence ; and others, again, of so much ignorance, so much absurdity, so much untruth, charlatanism, and imposture, as to pronounce it impossible that such contradictions should have proceeded from the same being. I separate, therefore, the gold from the dross; restore to him the former, and leave the latter to the stupidity of some, and roguery of others of his disciples. Of this band of dupes and impostors, Paul was the great Coryphæus, and first corrupter of the doctrines of Jesus. These palpable interpolations and falsification of his doctrines led me to try to sift them apart. I found the work obvious and easy, and that his part composed the most beautiful morsel of morality which has been given to us by man."

The following is an extract from the last letter of Mr. Jefferson, written only ten days previous to his death :—

"MONTICELLO, *June* 24, 1826.

"RESPECTED SIR: The kind invitation I received from you, on the part of the citizens of Washington, to be present with them at their celebration on the fiftieth anniversary of American independence, as one of the surviving signers of an instrument pregnant with our own, and the fate of the world, is most flattering to myself, and heightened by the honorable accompaniment proposed for the comfort of such a journey. It adds sensibly to the sufferings of sickness, to be deprived by it of a personal participation in the rejoicings of that day. But acquiescence is a duty, under circumstances not placed among those we are permitted to control. May that day be to the world, what I believe it will be (to some parts sooner, to others later, but finally to all) the signal of arousing men to burst the chains under which monkish ignorance and superstition had persuaded them to bind themselves, and to assume the blessings and security of self-government. For ourselves, let the annual return of this day for ever refresh our recollections of these rights, and an undiminished devotion to them.   "TH. JEFFERSON.

"To Mr. WEIGHTMAN."

Eng'd by Thomas Kelly from a Painting by Stuart

James Madison

BIOGRAPHICAL SKETCH

OF

JAMES MADISON.

JAMES MADISON, the fourth president of the United States, was born in Orange county, Virginia, on the 16th of March, 1751. His father was James Madison, the family being of Welsh descent, and among the early emigrants to Virginia. The subject of the present sketch studied the English, Latin, Greek, French, and Italian languages, and was fitted for college under the tuition of Mr. Robertson, a native of Scotland, and the Rev. Mr. Martin, a Jerseyman. He graduated at Princeton, New Jersey, in 1771 ; and afterward remained a year at college, pursuing his studies under the superintendence of Doctor Witherspoon, president of the institution. His constitution was impaired by close application to his studies, and his health was, for many years, feeble. Returning to Virginia, he commenced the practice of the law, but the scenes of the revolution left but little opportunity for the quiet pursuits of private life, and his talents being soon appreciated by his neighbors, he was called into the public service at an early age. In 1776 he was elected a member of the general assembly of Virginia, and in 1778 he was appointed one of the executive councillors. In the winter of 1779–'80 he was chosen a delegate to the continental Congress, of which body he continued an active and prominent member till 1784. In January, 1786, the legislature of Virginia appointed Mr. Madison one of their delegates to a convention of commissioners, or delegates, from the several states, to meet at Annapolis, Maryland, the ensuing September, to devise a uniform system of commercial regulations which should be binding on the whole confederacy, when ratified by all the states. Only five states were represented in this convention, but the members present took a step which led to important results. They recommended a convention of delegates from all the states, to be held at Philadelphia, in May, 1787, to take into consideration the situation of the United States, to devise such further provisions as should appear to them necessary to render the constitution of the federal government adequate to the exigencies of the Union. Of that convention, which framed the constitution of the United States, Mr. Madison was one of the most distinguished members. He took a leading part in the debates on the various plans of a constitution submitted to the convention, and to his efforts in maturing the constitution as finally adopted, the country is greatly indebted. He took notes of the proceedings and debates of the convention, which, since his death, have been published, forming a valuable text-book for American statesmen.

In the convention, Mr. Madison generally coincided with General Washington and other members in their views in favor of a strong national government. A paper in the handwriting of General Washington, and found among the documents left by him, contains a summary of Mr. Madison's opinions on the subject of a form of constitution to be proposed. It is the substance of a letter received by Washington from Mr. Madison, a short time previous to the assembling of the convention at Philadelphia, and has been published in the North American Review, volume xxxv., as follows :—

" Mr. Madison thinks an individual independence of the states utterly irreconcilable with their aggregate sovereignty, and that a consolidation of the whole into one simple republic would be as inexpedient as it is unattainable. He therefore proposes a middle ground, which may at once support a due supremacy of the national authority, and not exclude the local authorities whenever they can be subordinately useful.

" As the groundwork, he proposes that a change be made in the principle of representation, and thinks there would be no great difficulty in effecting it.

" Next, that, in addition to the present federal powers, the national government should be armed with positive and complete authority in all cases which require uniformity; such as regulation of trade, including the right of taxing both exports and imports, the fixing the terms and forms of naturalization, &c.

" Over and above this positive power, a negative *in all cases* whatever on the legislative acts of the states, as heretofore exercised by the kingly prerogative, appears to him absolutely necessary, and to be the least possible encroachment on the state jurisdictions. Without this defensive power he conceives that every positive law which can be given on paper, will be evaded.

" This control over the laws would prevent the internal vicissitudes of state policy, and the aggressions of interested majorities.

" The national supremacy ought also to be extended, he thinks, to the judiciary departments ; the oaths of the judges should at least include a fidelity to the general as well as local constitution ; and that an appeal should be to some national tribunals in all cases to which foreigners or inhabitants of other states may be parties. The admiralty jurisdictions to fall entirely within the purview of the national government.

" The national supremacy in the executive departments is liable to some difficulty, unless the officers administering them could be made appointable by the supreme government. The militia ought entirely to be placed, in some form or other, under the authority which is intrusted with the general protection and defence.

" A government composed of such extensive powers should be well organized and balanced.

" The legislative department might be divided into two branches, one of them chosen every — years, by the people at large, or by the legislatures ; the other to consist of fewer members, to hold their places for a longer term, and to go out in such rotation as always to leave in office a large majority of old members.

" Perhaps the negative on the laws might be most conveniently exercised by this branch.

" As a further check, a council of revision, including the great ministerial officers, might be superadded.

" A national executive must also be provided. He has scarcely ventured as yet to form his own opinion, either of the manner in which it ought to be constituted, or of the authorities with which it ought to be clothed.

" An article should be inserted, expressly guarantying the tranquillity of the states against internal as well as external dangers.

" In like manner, the right of coercion should be expressly declared. With the resources of commerce in hand, the national administration might always find means of exerting it either by sea or land ; but the difficulty and awkwardness of operating by force on the collective will of a state, render it particularly desirable that the necessity of it might be precluded. Perhaps the negative on the laws might create such a mutual dependence between the general and particular authorities as to answer ; or perhaps some defined objects of taxation might be submitted along with commerce, to the general authority.

" To give a new system its proper validity and energy, a ratification must be obtained from the people, and not merely from the ordinary authority of the legislature. This will be the more essential, as inroads on the existing constitutions of the states will be unavoidable."

The foregoing views of Mr. Madison, expressed by him before the constitution was formed, are highly interesting, as evincing a remarkable degree of foresight and political wisdom, and forming the basis of the principal features of the constitution as finally adopted by the convention.

The constitution having passed the ordeal of the national convention, in September, 1787, was next, by the recommendation of that body, submitted to conventions elected by the people of the several states, for their consideration.   Mr. Madison was elected a member of the convention of Virginia, chosen for that purpose, and here his best efforts were again called into requisition, to secure the sanction of his native state to a measure which he deemed of the most vital importance to the interests of the whole Union.   In this state convention of Virginia were assembled some of the most able and talented of her sons, including many of the patriots of the revolution, and others renowned for wisdom and eloquence ; but with widely discordant views on the subject of a form of national government.   Among those who acted with Mr. Madison in advocating the adoption of the constitution, were John Marshall, Edmund Pendleton, George Wythe, and Edmund Randolph ; while Patrick Henry, James Monroe, William Grayson, and George Mason, were among the opponents.   The question was finally carried in favor of adoption by 89 votes to 79.

Notwithstanding the triumph of the federalists, as the friends of the constitution were then called, in the convention of Virginia, the anti-federalists held the majority in the legislature.   An attempt to elect Mr. Madison to the senate of the United States was, therefore, unsuccessful, Messrs. Grayson and R. H. Lee being preferred.   Mr. Madison was, however, elected by the people of one of the congressional districts, a member of the house of representatives, and took his seat in the new Congress, at New York, in April, 1789.   In that body he bore an active and leading part in the adoption of measures for the organization of the government.   He continued a distinguished member of Congress during the eight years of General Washington's administration, which terminated in March, 1797. He opposed the funding system, the national bank, and other measures of the administration which originated with Hamilton, secretary of the treasury ; acting generally with the anti-federalists, who sustained the views of Mr. Jefferson, then secretary of state ; notwithstanding Madison had been one of the most distinguished champions of the constitution previous to its adoption, and was associated with Hamilton and Jay in the production of the celebrated essays called " The Federalist," which had an important influence with the people, in favor of the constitution.

In 1794, being then in his forty-third year, Mr. Madison married Mrs. Dolly Paine Todd, of Philadelphia, the widow of a lawyer of Pennsylvania, who died in less than three years after her first marriage.   This lady's maiden name was Paine ; and her father, who belonged to the society of Friends, had removed from Virginia to Philadelphia.   She was about twenty years younger than Mr. Madison; she died in 1849.   She was always admired for her agreeable manners, her fine person, and talents in conversation.   With an amiable disposition, a mild and dignified deportment, few American ladies have been more distinguished than Mrs. Madison, in the various and high stations she has been called to occupy and adorn through life.

In January, 1794, Mr. Madison introduced into the house of representatives a series of resolutions on the subject of the commerce of the United States with foreign nations. They were based on a previous report made to Congress by Mr. Jefferson, secretary of state, on the subject of foreign relations, and were probably prepared with the concurrence of Mr. Jefferson, as a manuscript copy was found among his papers. They were retaliatory in their character toward Great Britain, and considered favorable to the interests of France. They gave rise to a warm debate, parties being nearly balanced in the house, but the subject was finally postponed, without definite action.

Mr. Madison continued to act with the democratic, or republican party, for the remainder of his political career, co-operating with Mr. Jefferson in his views of national policy, and between these two gentlemen there existed through their lives the warmest personal friendship. In 1797, Mr. Madison retired from Congress, and in order to oppose the administration of Mr. Adams in a new form, he accepted a seat in the Virginia legislature, in 1798, where he made a report on the subject of the alien and sedition laws which had been passed by the federal party in Congress, concluding with a series of resolutions against those laws; which resolutions have since formed a text for the doctrine of state-rights, as held by the democratic party of Virginia and some other states.

On the accession of Mr. Jefferson to the presidency, in 1801, he appointed Mr. Madison secretary of state, which office he held during the eight years of Mr. Jefferson's administration; and in 1809, having received the nomination and support of the democratic party, he succeeded his friend and coadjutor, as president of the United States. During his administration, in 1812, war was declared by Congress against Great Britain, to which measure he reluctantly consented, and the same year he was re-elected to the presidency. In his selection of commissioners to negotiate a treaty of peace, Mr. Madison showed his anxiety for a termination of the war, by the appointment of able men, sincerely desirous of peace, which was concluded at Ghent, in December, 1814.

The anxious and exciting scenes of war were not congenial to a person of the peaceful disposition of Mr. Madison, yet the duties of his high office were performed with firmness and ability. Among the events of the war which were calculated to disturb his equanimity, was the capture of the city of Washington, and the destruction of the public buildings, by the British, in 1814. The president and some other principal officers of the government narrowly escaped from being made prisoners by the British troops; they, however, were saved by a rapid flight.

After the return of peace, the remainder of Mr. Madison's administration was prosperous and tranquil. The interests of agriculture and commerce revived among the people, and the national revenue was rapidly replenished from the fruits of returning prosperity. The manufacturing

8

interests, however, languished for want of adequate protection. The president was favorable to their encouragement. He changed his views on the subject of a national bank, and signed the bill for incorporating the bank of the United States, in 1816. He had, in 1791, opposed the bank then incorporated, as unconstitutional, and in 1815 he had returned to Congress a bill incorporating a bank, as he disapproved of some of its provisions; but in the following year he waived his objections, and approved of an act of incorporation, somewhat modified.

On the 3d of March, 1817, Mr. Madison's administration was brought to a close, and he retired from public life, being then sixty-six years of age, to his seat at Montpelier, in Orange county, Virginia, where he passed the remainder of his days. In 1829 he was chosen a member of the state convention to revise the constitution of Virginia, and for several years he acted as visiter and rector of the University of Virginia. He was also chosen president of an agricultural society in the county where he resided, and before this society he delivered an address, admirable for its classical beauty and practical knowledge.

Having arrived at a good old age, and numbered eighty-five years, the mortal career of Mr. Madison was closed on the 28th of June, 1836. Congress and other public bodies adopted testimonials of respect for his memory. He left no children.

In his personal appearance, Mr. Madison was of small stature, and rather protuberant in front. He had a calm expression, penetrating blue eyes, and was slow and grave in his speech. At the close of his presidency he seemed to be care-worn, with an appearance of more advanced age than was the fact. He was bald on the top of his head, wore his hair powdered, and generally dressed in black. His manner was modest and retiring, but in conversation he was pleasing and instructive, having a mind well stored with the treasures of learning, and being particularly familiar with the political world. On his accession to the presidency he restored the custom of levees at the presidential mansion, which had been abolished by Mr. Jefferson. It was on the occasion of these levees, that his accomplished lady, by her polite and attractive attentions and manners, shone with peculiar lustre. Mr. Madison was fond of society, although he had travelled but little; never having visited foreign countries, or seen much of the people and country over which he presided.

When a member of deliberative bodies, Mr. Madison was an able debater, having acquired self-confidence by slow degrees. As a writer, he has few equals among American statesmen, and the style of his public documents and his correspondence has always been much admired. He was at the time of his death, the last surviving signer of the constitution, and the part he bore in framing that instrument, his subsequent advocacy of it, by his writings, with his adherence to its provisions, obtained for him the title of "Father of the Constitution."

James Monroe

‑‑ ‑ part of this sketch we are indebted to the American Annual Register, vol. vi., published in 1832.

BIOGRAPHICAL SKETCH

OF

JAMES MONROE.

THE family of Monroe is one of the most ancient and honorable among the early settlers of Virginia. It is remarkable that the tide water section of that state has produced four of the first five presidents of the United States ; Washington, Jefferson, Madison, and Monroe, having been born in that part of Virginia, and within a few miles of each other. The same section of country, it may be added, was honored also as the birthplace of the biographer of Washington, who for many years was the ornament of the supreme court of the United States—Chief-Justice Marshall.

The fifth president of the United States, James Monroe, was born on the 2d of April, 1759, in the county of Westmoreland, Virginia. His parents were Spence Monroe and Elizabeth Jones, both members of old and highly respectable families in the ancient dominion. His early youth was passed in the midst of that exciting contest which led to the American revolution ; the stamp act being passed in the sixth year of his age. He was thus educated in the detestation of tyranny, and prompted by a patriotism which went beyond his years, he left the college of William and Mary, where he was pursuing collegiate studies, to join the standard of his country, in the 18th year of his age. The declaration of independence had just been issued, and at that disastrous moment when Washington was preparing to defend New York, against the increasing armies of England ; when the timid and wavering were sinking from the side of their country's chief, James Monroe arrived at headquarters, with a firm determination to share her fate, whether for good or for evil.*

During the gloomy year of 1776, he shared with the army their defeats and their privations ; was present at the disastrous battles of Harlem

---

* For a part of this sketch we are indebted to the American Annual Register, vol. vi., published in 1832.

heights and Whiteplains; and in the battle of Trenton, while leading the vanguard, he received a wound, the scar of which he carried to his grave. After recovering from his wound, he was promoted for his gallantry, to the rank of a captain of infantry, and returned to active service. During the campaigns of 1777 and 1778, he acted as aid to Lord Stirling, and by accepting this place in the staff of that general, he receded from the line of promotion; but in that capacity he distinguished himself in the actions of Brandywine, Germantown, and Monmouth. Becoming desirous to regain his position in the line of the army, he endeavored to raise a regiment of Virginia troops, under the recommendation of General Washington, and the authority of the legislature. In this he failed, owing to the exhausted state of the country. He therefore devoted himself to the study of the law, under the direction of Mr. Jefferson, who was then governor of the state. He occasionally acted as a volunteer in repelling the invasions with which Virginia was afterward visited; and after the fall of Charleston, in 1780, he repaired to the southern army, as a military commissioner, to collect information as to its ability to rescue that portion of the Union from the enemy. This duty was performed to the satisfaction of the governor, by whom he was appointed.

He now commenced his career in the legislative councils of his country, being elected in 1782, by the county of King George, a member of the legislature of Virginia, and by that body shortly after chosen a member of the executive council. He was then only in his twenty-fourth year, but appears to have evinced sufficient tact in legislation to induce the legislature to elect him the following year one of the delegates to represent the state in the continental Congress. He took his seat in that body on the 13th of December, just in time to be present at Annapolis when Washington surrendered his commission into the hands of the authority by whom he had been appointed. From that time until 1786, Mr. Monroe continued to represent his native state in Congress, and became entirely convinced of the inefficiency of that body to govern the country under the articles of confederation. He accordingly sought an extension of its powers, and in 1785 moved to invest Congress with the power of regulating trade. This resolution, together with another in favor of investing it with the power of levying an impost duty of five per cent., were referred to a committee, of which Mr. Monroe was chairman.

A report was made, which combined both the objects, and proposed such alterations in the articles of confederation as were necessary to vest in Congress the powers required. These were among the steps which led to the convention at Annapolis, and consequently to the formation and adoption of the federal constitution. Mr. Monroe was also active and influential in devising a system for disposing of and settling the public lands, and warmly opposed the plan of selling each range of townships separately, before any other should be offered for sale.

On the 24th of December, 1784, Mr. Monroe was appointed, with eight other highly distinguished men of that period, members of a federal court, to decide the long pending controversy between Massachusetts and New York. He accepted of the appointment, but on the 15th of May, 1786, he resigned his commission, and the two states having, during the same year adjusted the matter by mutual agreement, the court never met.

Mr. Monroe differed from both New York and Massachusetts on the question of relinquishing our right to navigate the Mississippi river, as demanded by Spain and assented to by the northern states. The southern states opposed the relinquishment of this right, and Mr. Monroe took a leading part against any concession to Spain.

While attending the continental Congress, as a member, at New York, Mr. Monroe married Miss Kortright, daughter of Mr. L. Kortright, of that city. This lady had been celebrated in the fashionable circles of London and Paris for her beauty and accomplishments, and in married life she was exemplary, as well as an ornament to the society in which she was called to act during the scenes of her husband's subsequent career.

Toward the conclusion of the year 1786, Mr. Monroe's term of service in Congress expired, and, by the rule then adopted, being ineligible for a second term, he established himself at Fredericksburg, with the view of practising law. He was soon, however, again called from the pursuits of private life, by being elected a member of the legislature, and the following year, 1788, he was chosen a delegate to the state convention, assembled to decide upon the adoption of the federal constitution.

Notwithstanding Mr. Monroe was convinced of the inefficiency of the articles of confederation, and of the necessity of a radical change in the government of the Union, he was not altogether prepared to adopt the federal constitution, as framed by the convention of 1787. He thought that certain amendments ought to be made previous to its adoption, and decidedly advocated that course in the convention. We have already stated, in the memoir of Mr. Madison, that the leading men of Virginia in the state convention, were much divided on the question of the adoption of the constitution. Among those who opposed it in that body, besides Mr. Monroe, were Patrick Henry, George Mason, and William Grayson, while its most powerful advocates were James Madison, John Marshall, Edmund Randolph, and Edmund Pendleton. The convention finally adopted the constitution as it was, by a vote of 89 to 79, Mr. Monroe being among the negatives; certain amendments were at the same time recommended for the adoption of the states, instead of being insisted on previous to the acceptance of the constitution.

The course which Mr. Monroe pursued on this occasion was acceptable to the state of Virginia, as was proved by the election of a majority of anti-federalists to Congress, including the two senators; and on the death of Mr. Grayson, one of the latter, Mr. Monroe was chosen to the senate of the United States in his place, and took his seat in that body in 1790.   In this station he continued until 1794, acting with the anti-federal party in opposition to Washington's administration, as did Mr. Madison and most of the Virginia delegation in Congress.   The French republican government having requested the recall of Gouverneur Morris, American minister to France, General Washington complied with their wishes, as also those of the democratic party in Congress, and appointed Mr. Monroe the successor of Mr. Morris, in May, 1794.   He was received with distinguished favor in France by the government and people, but the course he pursued during his residence at the capital of that republic was not conformable to the views of neutrality entertained by General Washington, who therefore recalled him in 1796, and sent Charles Cotesworth Pinckney in his place.

On his return to the United States, Mr. Monroe published a volume in explanation of his views and proceedings relative to his mission to France, vindicating his own course, and censuring the policy of the administration toward the French republic.

He, however, did not cherish any animosity toward General Washington, but at a subsequent period he joined with his countrymen in acknowledging the merits and perfect integrity of that great man.   He also did ample justice to the character of John Jay, who negotiated his celebrated treaty with Great Britain about the same time that Mr. Monroe visited France.   Although opposed to the treaty made by Mr. Jay, and to his political views generally, Mr. Monroe left on record in his own handwriting, an unqualified testimonial to the pure patriotism, the pre-eminent ability, and the spotless integrity of John Jay.

Shortly after his return from France, Mr. Monroe was chosen to the legislature, and in 1799 he was elected by that body governor of Virginia, where he served for the term of three years, then limited by the constitution of the state.

In 1803, President Jefferson appointed Mr. Monroe envoy extraordinary to France, to act jointly with Mr. Livingston, then resident minister at Paris, to negotiate the purchase of New Orleans, or a right of depot for the United States on the Mississippi.   He was also associated with Mr. Charles Pinckney, then resident minister at Madrid, to negotiate terms also with Spain relative to Louisiana.

We have, in our notice of Mr. Jefferson's administration, given an account of the purchase of Louisiana by the United States, of France. That country had been ceded by Spain to France, and Mr. Monroe, upon his arrival in France, found a most favorable conjuncture for the accomplishment of the mission, in being enabled to obtain for his country the possession, not only of New Orleans, but of the whole province of Louisiana.   The treaty was concluded within a fortnight after the arrival of Mr. Monroe at Paris, and after the conclusion of the negotiation he proceeded to London, where he was also commissioned to act as successor to Mr. Rufus King, who had resigned.

Here he sought to obtain a conventional arrangement for the protection of American seamen against impressment, and for the protection of neutral rights ; but in the midst of these discussions he was called away to the discharge of his mission to Spain.

In the transfer of Louisiana to France by Spain, and to the United States by France, the boundaries of the province were not defined. Spain was encouraged to dispute the extent of the province, and she sought to reduce it to a territory of small dimensions. A controversy arose between the United States and Spain, at one time threatening war, and for the purpose of attempting an adjustment of these difficulties Mr. Monroe proceeded to Madrid. His efforts, joined with those of Mr. Pinckney, were unsuccessful, and the controversy was left unsettled.

Mr. Monroe was then recalled to London to maintain our rights as neutrals, against the systematic encroachment of Great Britain. He was there joined by Mr. William Pinkney, who had then been recently sent from the United States, as minister to England. A whig ministry being then in power in Great Britain, with the friendly feelings of that party toward the United States, Messrs. Monroe and Pinkney were enabled to negotiate a treaty, in 1807, which, although not as favorable as they would have wished, was considered by those envoys as advantageous to the United States. As the treaty was clogged with certain conditions which were deemed by President Jefferson inadmissible, it was not submitted by him to the senate, but sent back to England for revisal. The British cabinet, however, had been changed, and Mr. Canning, the secretary for foreign affairs, refused to resume the negotiation. The mission of Messrs. Monroe and Pinkney was now at an end. Mr. Monroe, after a short detention, in consequence of the difficulty which grew out of the affair of the Chesapeake frigate, returned to the United States in 1807.

For a considerable time Mr. Monroe felt dissatisfied with his friend, President Jefferson, in consequence of his rejection of the treaty with Great Britain without consulting the senate, and also from an impression that the president's influence was exerted in favor of Mr. Madison as his successor to the presidency. Mr. Jefferson, in his correspondence with Mr. Monroe, explained his course with regard to the rejection of the treaty, and declared his intention to remain perfectly neutral between his two friends who were named to succeed him. The Virginia legislature settled their respective claims to the presidency, by deciding in favor of Mr. Madison, in which decision Mr. Monroe and his friends acquiesced.

In 1811 he was again elected governor of Virginia, but continued but a short time in that station, for upon the resignation of Robert Smith, he was appointed by Mr. Madison secretary of state. This office he continued to hold during the remainder of Mr. Madison's administration.

After the capture of Washington city, and the resignation of General Armstrong, Mr. Monroe was appointed to the war department, without, however, resigning as secretary of state.   In this station he exhibited a remarkable energy and boldness of character.   He found the treasury exhausted, and the public credit prostrated ; while the enemy, relieved from his war with France, was preparing to turn his numerous armies, flushed with victory over the legions of Napoleon, against the United States.   The first duty of the secretary of war was to prepare for the new campaign, and this he was enabled to do by the now excited spirit of the country.   The army already authorized by acts of Congress, if the regiments were full, numbered 60,000 men, which Mr. Monroe proposed to increase by the addition of 40,000, and to levy new recruits by draughting from the whole mass of able-bodied men in the United States.   This proposition, which was considered an imitation of the French mode of conscription long practised by Napoleon, and would inevitably have lost him the favor of the people, he felt it to be his duty to make, and had intended, in case of the continuance of the war, to withdraw his name from the presidential canvass.   To two or three friends he disclosed his feelings on this occasion, in confidence, and had authorized them to publish his intention of declining a nomination as successor to Mr. Madison, when the conclusion of peace rendered the increase of the army unnecessary, and therefore removed the objections to his being a candidate for president.

Toward the end of the year 1814, Mr. Monroe's attention, as secretary of war, was most urgently called to the defence of New Orleans, against which a powerful fleet and army had been despatched.   To raise the funds for the defence of this important point, Mr. Monroe was compelled to pledge his private credit, as subsidiary to that of the government, which then was at a low ebb.   By this act of devotion he was enabled to furnish the necessary supplies ; New Orleans was successfully defended, and the entire defeat of the British army under General Packenham terminated the war in a manner honorable to the American arms.

A new series of duties now awaited Mr. Monroe.   Upon the conclusion of peace he resumed his station in the department of state, and as the long-tried friend and confidential adviser of Mr. Madison, he was called to the arduous task of deciding upon those measures which aimed at the re-establishment of the public credit, and to place the country in a better state of preparation, in case she should be called upon again to assert her rights by an appeal to arms.   Our foreign relations, which had been partially suspended during the war, were to be renewed, and the domestic policy of the United States required to be modified so as to adapt it to the great changes which had been produced by the general pacification of Europe. In the performance of the arduous duties imposed upon him at this period, Mr. Monroe had the good fortune to be sustained by public opinion, and with that auxiliary he lent his zealous co-operation to Mr. Madison in establishing the system of internal policy, adopted after the close of the war, and continued it with new and enlarged features after his election as president of the United States, in 1817.

In 1816, Mr. Monroe received the nomination of the democratic party, through their representatives in Congress, for president of the United States. With that party he had uniformly acted, under the various names of anti-federal, democratic, and republican, and by them was he elected, in 1816, chief magistrate of the nation, to succeed Mr. Madison, on the 4th of March, 1817. Previous to entering on the duties of his high office, he was advised by General Jackson, with whom he was on the most friendly terms, to disregard former party divisions in the formation of his cabinet, and to use his influence and power to destroy party spirit, by appointing the best men to office, without regard to their political preferences. This course Mr. Monroe declined to pursue, confining his appointments generally, as did his predecessors Jefferson and Madison, to those who professed his own political faith, and excluding federalists from office, with but few exceptions.

In other respects the policy of Mr. Monroe was liberal and satisfactory to men of all parties, excepting, perhaps, the ardent supporters of a system of internal improvements, who regretted the adherence of the president to a strict construction of the constitution on that subject. On many points the policy of Mr. Monroe's administration resembled that of the federal school established in the early stages of the government under the auspices of Washington and Hamilton. The perfecting of the establishment of a national bank, of the plan for the gradual discharge of the public debt, of the system of fortifying the coast and increasing the navy, and of encouraging by adequate protection the manufactures and arts of the country, formed essential parts of the policy referred to, adopted at the close of Mr. Madison's administration, and continued by that of Mr. Monroe. To these measures Mr. Monroe, finally, after long deliberation, and with the entire concurrence of his whole cabinet, sanctioned by repeated demonstrations of Congress, determined to add a system of internal improvement, thus yielding his own scruples to advance the interests of the nation. This was done on the 30th of April, 1824, when the act appropriating $30,000 for the survey of such routes for canals and public roads as the president might direct, received his sanction.

Among the measures which distinguished the administration of Mr. Monroe, was the negotiation of the treaty which added Florida to the Uniten States. This cession secured to the nation all the territory north of Mexico; and it was negotiated with great propriety by one who had borne so conspicuous a part in the acquisition of Louisiana.

In 1817 the president made a tour through a large portion of the northern and middle states, which elicited a general expression of kindness, respect, and courtesy from the people.

Mr. Monroe was re-elected president in 1820, with more unanimity than any one since Washington, receiving every vote of the electoral colleges of the United States, except one, and ended his career in the service of the federal government on the 3d of March, 1825.   He then retired to his residence in Loudon county, Virginia, where he was shortly after appointed a county magistrate, the duties of which office he continued to discharge until his departure for the city of New York.   He was also appointed curator of the university of Virginia ; and in 1830, having been elected a member of the convention called to revise the constitution of that state, he was unanimously chosen to preside over its deliberations. Before the close of its labors, however, he was compelled by severe indisposition to retire, and in the succeeding summer removed to New York, to take up his abode with his son-in-law, Mr. Samuel L. Gouverneur. There he remained, surrounded by filial solicitude and tenderness, until, on the fifty-fifth anniversary of the nation's birth (July 4, 1831), he terminated his earthly career, in the 72d year of his age ; furnishing another striking coincidence, which, as in the instance of the simultaneous deaths of Adams and Jefferson, on the same day, five years previous, afforded occasion for grave reflection, and seemed pregnant with some mysterious moral lesson to a nation whose attention was thus forcibly directed to the act which, while it gave it birth as an independent community, also served to mark the commencement of a new era in the history of the world.

Mr. Monroe left only two children, both daughters, one the widow of George Hay, Esq., of Richmond, the other the wife of Samuel L. Gouverneur, Esq., of New York.   Mrs. Monroe died but a short time before her venerable husband.

Though in the course of his life he had received from the public treasury, for his services, $358,000, he retired from office deeply in debt.   He was, however, relieved at last by the adjustment by Congress of his claims, founded chiefly on the disbursements made during the war.

In his personal appearance Mr. Monroe was tall and well formed, being about six feet in stature, with light complexion, and blue eyes.   His countenance had no indications of superior intellect, but an honesty and firmness of purpose which commanded respect, and gained favor and friendship.   He was laborious and industrious, and doubtless compensated in some degree by diligence, for slowness of thought and want of imagination.   His talents, however, were respectable, and he was a fine specimen of the old school of Virginia gentlemen, generous, hospitable, and devoted to his country, which he did not hesitate to serve to the utmost of his ability, through a long life, and his career was highly honorable, useful, and worthy of admiration.

Eng^d by V Balch from a Painting by Durand

J. Q. Adams

BIOGRAPHICAL SKETCH

OF

JOHN QUINCY ADAMS

BIOGRAPHICAL SKETCH

OF

JOHN QUINCY ADAMS.

WHEN the constitution of the United States was formed, in 1787, and the question of its adoption was before the people, the opponents of a consolidated government, and those who preferred the old confederation, represented the executive established by the constitution, as the chief of an elective monarchy. Mr. Jefferson considered him a bad edition of a Polish king, as he expressed it. But no one apprehended any danger of the office of president ever becoming hereditary. It is, however, a curious circumstance, that the only one of the first five presidents of the United States who had a son, should have lived to see his eldest son elected to the presidency. It must not from this be supposed that the circumstances of the birth and family of John Quincy Adams had any influence in contributing to his elevation to the same high office which his father had previously filled. On the contrary, the jealousy of the American people on the subject of any supposed preference in consequence of family or rank, probably operated to the prejudice of Mr. Adams, and diminished the popular support which he would otherwise have received; for no American was ever more fully qualified by talents and education for the various important stations which he has been called to fill, than the distinguished statesman who is the subject of the present memoir.

Born in the year 1767, on the 11th day of July, at the mansion of his father, John Adams, who then resided in Boston, although the family-seat was in the present town of Quincy, Massachusetts, John Quincy Adams (who afterward became the sixth president of the United States) took the name of John Quincy, his great grandfather, who bore a distinguished part in the councils of the province, at the commencement of the eighteenth century.*

In the very dawn of his existence the principles of American independence and freedom were instilled into the mind of the younger Adams.

* A part of this sketch is an abstract of a memoir of Mr. Adams published in 1828.

Both his father and mother were the most zealous promoters of the cause of their country in the struggle with Great Britain. When the father of Mr. Adams repaired to France as joint commissioner with Franklin and Lee, he was accompanied by his son John Quincy, then in his eleventh year. In that country he passed a year and a half with his father, and enjoyed the privilege of the daily intercourse and parental attentions of Doctor Franklin, whose kind notice of the young was a peculiar trait in his character, and whose primitive simplicity of manners and methodical habits left a lasting impression on the mind of his youthful countryman.

After a residence of about eighteen months in France, young Adams returned to America with his father, who assisted in forming a constitution for Massachusetts, but was soon called upon again by Congress to repair to Europe, as a commissioner for negotiating treaties with Holland and other powers, but particularly with Great Britain, as soon as she was disposed to put an end to the war.

He again took his son with him, and sailed in a French frigate, which in consequence of springing a dangerous leak, was compelled to put into Ferrol, in Spain. From that place Mr. Adams and his son travelled by land to Paris, where they arrived in January, 1780. For a few months Mr. Adams sent his son to school in Paris; but in July, the same year, he took him with him to Holland, where he was called to negotiate a loan for the United States. He placed his son first in the public school of the city of Amsterdam, and afterward in the city university of Leyden. In July, 1781, Mr. Francis Dana (afterward chief-justice of the state of Massachusetts), who had gone out with Mr. Adams as secretary of legation, received from the continental Congress the appointment of minister to the court of the empress of Russia, and John Quincy Adams was selected by Mr. Dana as a private secretary of this mission. After spending fourteen months with Mr. Dana, he left him to return through Sweden, Denmark, Hamburg, and Bremen, to Holland, where his father had been publicly received as minister from the United States, and had concluded a commercial treaty with the republic of the Netherlands. He performed this journey during the winter of 1782–'3, being only sixteen years of age, without a companion. He reached the Hague in April, 1783, his father being at that time engaged at Paris in the negotiation of peace. From April to July his son remained at the Hague, under the care of Mr. Dumas, a native of Switzerland, who then filled the office of an agent of the United States. The negotiations for peace being suspended in July, Mr. Adams's father repaired on business to Amsterdam; and on his return to Paris he took his son with him. The definitive treaty of peace was signed in September, 1783, from which time till May, 1785, he was chiefly with his father in England, Holland, and France.

It was at this period that he formed an acquaintance with Mr. Jefferson, then residing in France as American minister. The intercourse of Mr.

Jefferson with his former colleague in Congress, the father of Mr. Adams was of an intimate and confidential kind, and led to a friendship for his son which, formed in early life, scarcely suffered an interruption from subsequent political dissensions, and revived with original strength during the last years of the life of this venerable statesman.

Mr. Adams was, at the period last mentioned, about eighteen years of age. Born in the crisis of his country's fortunes, he had led a life of wandering and vicissitude, unusual at any age. His education, in everything but the school of liberty, had been interrupted and irregular. He had seen much of the world—much of men—and had enjoyed but little leisure for books. Anxious to complete his education, and still more anxious to return to his native land, when his father was, in 1785, appointed minister to the court of St. James, his son, at that period of life when the pleasures and splendor of a city like London are most calculated to fascinate and mislead, asked permission of his father to go back to his native shores. This he accordingly did. On his return to America he became a member of the ancient college of Harvard, at Cambridge, Massachusetts, where he graduated in July, 1787.

On leaving college, Mr. Adams entered the office of Theophilus Parsons, afterward chief justice of the state, as a student of law, at Newburyport. On a visit of General Washington to that town, in 1789, Mr. Parsons, being chosen by his fellow-citizens to be the medium of expressing their sentiments to the general, called upon his pupils each to prepare an address. This call was obeyed by Mr. Adams, and his address was delivered by Mr. Parsons.

After completing his law studies, at Newburyport, Mr. Adams removed to Boston, with view of commencing the practice of his profession at the bar. His time not being fully occupied, Mr. Adams employed his leisure hours in speculations upon the great political questions of the day.

In April, 1793, on the first intimation that war between Great Britain and France had been declared, Mr. Adams published a short series of papers, the object of which was, to prove that the duty and interest of the United States required them to remain neutral in the contest. These papers were published before General Washington's proclamation of neutrality, and without any knowledge that a proclamation would be issued. The opinions they expressed were in opposition to the views generally prevailing, that the treaty of alliance of 1778 obliged us to take part in the wars of France. But the proclamation of neutrality by General Washington, sanctioned by all his cabinet, including Mr. Jefferson, was shortly made public, and confirmed the justice of the views which Mr. Adams had been (it is believed) the first to express before the public on this new and difficult topic of national law.

In the winter of 1793 and 1794, the inflammatory appeals of the French minister to the United States, Mr. Genet, caused much excitement in the public mind. Among those who co-operated in support of the administration of Washington in resisting Mr. Genet, none was more conspicuous than Mr. Adams, whose essays in favor of neutrality were read and admired throughout the country.

His reputation was soon established, as an American statesman and political writer. Before his retirement from the department of state, Mr. Jefferson recommended him to General Washington, as a proper person to be introduced into the public service of the country. The acquaintance between Mr. Jefferson and Mr. Adams which had been formed in France, had lately been renewed, on occasion of a visit to Philadelphia in 1792 ; and the promptitude and ability with which he had seconded the efforts of the secretary of state in enforcing neutrality, no doubt led Mr. Jefferson thus to recommend him to General Washington.

The publications of Mr. Adams above alluded to, had attracted the attention of General Washington. He had in private expressed the highest opinion of them, and had made particular inquiries with respect to their author. Thus honorably identified, at the early age of twenty-seven, with the first great and decisive step of the foreign policy of the United States, and thus early attracting the notice, and enjoying the confidence of Washington, Mr. Adams was, in May, 1794, appointed minister resident to the Netherlands, an office corresponding in rank and salary with that of a chargé d'affaires at the present day. The father of Mr. Adams was at this time vice-president of the United States ; but the appointment of his son was made by General Washington, unexpectedly to the vice-president, and without any previous intimation that it would take place.

Mr. Adams remained at his post in Holland about two years. He was an attentive observer of the great events then occurring in Europe, and his official correspondence with the government was regarded by General Washington as of the highest importance.

Toward the close of General Washington's administration, he appointed Mr. Adams minister plenipotentiary to Portugal. On his way from the Hague to Lisbon, he received a new commission, changing his destination to Berlin. This latter appointment was made by Mr. Adams's father, then president of the United States, and in a manner highly honorable to the restraint of his parental feelings, in the discharge of an act of public duty. Although Mr. Adams's appointment to Portugal was made by General Washington, and President Adams did no more than propose his transfer to Berlin, yet feelings of delicacy led him to hesitate, before he took even this step. He consulted his predecessor and friend, then retired from office, and placed in a situation beyond the reach of any of the motives which can possibly prejudice the minds of men in power. The following letter from General Washington, is the reply to President Adams's inquiry, and will ever remain an honorable testimony to the character of Mr. Adams :—

"MONDAY, *February* 20, 1797.

"DEAR SIR : I thank you for giving me a perusal of the enclosed. The sentiments do honor to the head and heart of the writer ; and if my wishes would be of any avail, they should go to you in a strong hope that you will not withhold merited promotion from John Q. Adams because he is your son. For, without intending to compliment the father or the mother, or to censure any others, I give it as my decided opinion, that Mr. Adams is the most valuable public character we have abroad ; and that there remains no doubt in my mind, that he will prove himself to be the ablest of all our diplomatic corps. If he was now to be brought into that line, or into any other public walk, I could not, upon the principle which has regulated my own conduct, disapprove of the caution which is hinted at in the letter. But he is already entered ; the public, more and more, as he is known, are appreciating his talents and worth ; and his country would sustain a loss, if these were to be checked by over-delicacy on your part.

"With sincere esteem, and affectionate regard,

"I am ever yours,

"GEORGE WASHINGTON."

The principal object of Mr. Adams's mission to Berlin was effected by the conclusion of a treaty of commerce with Prussia. He remained at that court till the spring of 1801, when he was recalled by his father, and returned to America. During the last year of his residence in Prussia, he made an excursion into the province of Silesia, which he described in a series of letters that were afterward collected and published in a volume, and have been translated into French and German, and extensively circulated in Europe. In March, 1798, while he was at Berlin, he was appointed by the president and senate, commissioner to renew the treaty with Sweden.

The advantages enjoyed by Mr. Adams, during his residence on the continent of Europe, from 1794 to 1801, he did not fail to improve, and they were of great importance in extending his political knowledge, and in their influence upon his character and feelings. He contemplated with the eye of a careful observer the great movements in the political world which were then taking place, and which included many of the most important events of the French revolution. A combination of peculiar circumstances enabled him to hold an important and truly American course between the violent extremes to which public opinion in America ran, on the great question of our foreign relations. It was also fortunate that he was absent from the country during the period when domestic parties were organized and arrayed against each other. His situation secured him from the necessity of taking part in those political contentions in which he must either have been placed in the painful position of acting with the party opposed to his father, or he would have been obliged to encounter the natural imputation of being biased in support of him by filial attachment.   From this alternative Mr. Adams was spared by his residence abroad during the whole period in which our domestic parties were acquiring their organization; and he returned to his native land a stranger to local parties, and a friend to his country.

In 1802, Mr. Adams was elected to the senate of Massachusetts from the district of Boston; and signalized that fearless independence which has ever characterized his political course, by his strong, though ineffectual opposition to a powerful combination of banking interests, of which the centre was placed among his immediate constituents.

In 1803, he was elected by the legislature of Massachusetts, a senator of the United States. There was a federal majority in that body, but Mr. Adams was not elected by a party vote. He was considered a moderate federalist, but, when elected, was unpledged, either as to opposition or support, to any men or measures other than those which his own sense of duty should dictate to him to be supported or opposed.

His conduct in the United States senate was such as might have been expected from his position. He neither had principles to permit, nor passions to drive him into indiscriminate opposition or blind support. He supported the administration of Mr. Jefferson in every measure which his judgment approved. With the democratic party in the senate he voted for the embargo recommended by Mr. Jefferson, believing that the hostile decrees of France and England against American commerce called for retaliatory or restrictive measures. For his course in this particular, Mr. Adams was censured by the legislature of Massachusetts, in a series of resolutions passed by that body, which also, in May, 1808, elected Mr. Lloyd as senator from the period of the expiration of Mr. Adams's term. Not choosing to represent constituents who had lost their confidence in him, Mr. Adams resigned his place in the senate of the United States.

The support of a man holding the position and possessing the talents of Mr. Adams, was peculiarly acceptable to the administration of Mr. Jefferson, at a crisis when a defection in the ranks of the democratic party wore an alarming aspect to those in power. His course was, however, severely censured by his former political friends, the federalists of Massachusetts, who considered his support of the embargo, and other measures of Mr. Jefferson's administration, as an act of separation from the federal party. His father had previously indicated similar views to those of his son, and finally became a zealous supporter of democratic men and measures.

Previous to retiring from the senate of the United States, namely, in 1806, Mr. Adams was called to the chair of rhetoric and oratory in Harvard college, and delivered a course of lectures on the *art of speaking well;* an important art to the youth of a free country.

But Mr. Adams was not destined to remain long in retirement. Soon after the accession of Mr. Madison to the presidency, he appointed Mr.

Adams, with the senate's concurrence, in June, 1809, minister plenipotentiary to the court of the emperor of Russia. He was the first minister from the United States to that country. Mr. Jefferson, perceiving the importance to the United States of both political amity and commercial intercourse with the great Russian empire, sent Levett Harris as American consul to St. Petersburg, through whom a correspondence ensued between the Russian emperor and the American president, which began the good relations that have subsisted without interruption between the two countries. One of the last acts of Mr. Jefferson's administration was to nominate an envoy extraordinary and minister plenipotentiary to Russia, whom the senate rejected.

The emperor Alexander, who was then on the throne of Russia, was one of the most remarkable men of the age ; well educated, well informed, liberal, and generous, he regarded the United States with such kindness that, on the most despotic throne in the old world, he freely expressed his admiration of the republican institutions of the new.*

The intelligence of the declaration of war by the United States against Great Britain, was known in Russia in September, 1812. Mr. Adams had the good fortune to acquire the confidence of the emperor, who admitted him to a degree of intimacy rarely enjoyed with despotic monarchs, even by their own ministers. On the 20th of September, 1812, the Russian minister Romanzoff informed Mr. Adams that, having made peace with Great Britain, the emperor was much concerned and disappointed to find the commercial benefits which he expected his subjects would derive from that event, defeated and lost by the war between the United States and Great Britain. He therefore suggested a settlement of the difficulties by mediation, offering himself to act as mediator, in terms of great good-will, which Mr. Adams met and answered with corresponding cordiality. In the course of his conversation with the Russian minister, the American envoy stated that he knew his government engaged in the war with reluctance ; that it would be highly injurious, both to the United States and to England ; that he could see no good result as likely to arise from it to any one. The minister from Russia to the United States was directed to proffer the mediation to the American government, which was formally accepted in March, 1813, by the latter, but it was declined by the British government. It was unquestionably owing to the confidential relation between Mr. Adams and the emperor, that the mediation of Russia was tendered ; and though it was declined by England, the mediation produced an offer from that country to treat directly with the United States, and thus led to peace.

It was for this reason that Mr. Adams was placed at the head of the five commissioners by whom the treaty of peace was negotiated at Ghent,.

9   * Ingersoll.

in 1814; his associates on that commission being James A. Bayard, Henry Clay, Jonathan Russell and Albert Gallatin.

The skill with which that negotiation was conducted, is well known. Mr. Adams bore a full part in its counsels and labors; and a proportionate share of the credit is due to him for that cogency and skill which drew from the marquis of Wellesley, in the British house of lords, the declaration, that "in his opinion the American commissioners had shown the most astonishing superiority over the British, during the whole of the correspondence."

This tribute is the more honorable to Mr. Adams and his colleagues, from the circumstance that, on every important point, the British commissioners received special instructions from the ministry at London, directing the terms in which the American envoys were to be answered.

Having borne this distinguished part, in bringing the war to a close by an honorable peace, Mr. Adams was employed, in conjunction with Messrs. Clay and Gallatin, in negotiating a convention of commerce with Great Britain, on the basis of which our commercial intercourse with that country has since been conducted.

On the 28th of February, 1815, Mr. Madison gave a further proof of his confidence in Mr. Adams, by appointing him (with the consent of the senate) minister to Great Britain, and he continued to represent the United States at that court until the accession of Mr. Monroe to the presidency, in March, 1817.

In the formation of his cabinet, Mr. Monroe consulted with several of the most distinguished of his friends, among others with General Jackson, to whom he wrote as follows : " I shall take a person for the department of state from the eastward; and Mr. Adams's long service in our diplomatic concerns appearing to entitle him to the preference, supported by his acknowledged talents and integrity, his nomination will go to the senate."   To this General Jackson replied : " I have no hesitation in saying, you have made the best selection to fill the department of state that could be made.   Mr. Adams in the hour of difficulty will be an able helpmate, and I am convinced his appointment will afford general satisfaction."

In pursuance of the above intimation of Mr. Monroe, Mr. Adams was called home from England, and appointed secretary of state in March, 1817.   On this arduous office he entered with the general approbation of the people.   During the eight years of Mr. Monroe's administration, Mr. Adams remained in the department of state, retaining the entire confidence of Mr. Monroe, and acquiring that of his colleagues in the cabinet. In reference to all questions of the foreign relations of the country, he was the influential member of the government; and is, consequently, more than any other individual connected with the executive, entitled to the credit of the measures which, during Mr. Monroe's administration, were adopted in reference to the foreign policy of the government. One of the most important of these measures was the recognition of the independence of the new republics of Spanish America. The credit of first effectually proposing that measure in the house of representatives is due to Mr. Clay, while speaker of that body ; that of choosing the propitious moment when it could be proposed with the unanimous consent of Congress, and the nation, belongs to Mr. Adams. Nor is he entitled to less credit for the successful termination of our differences with Spain. A controversy of thirty years' standing, which had resisted the skill of every preceding administration of the government, was brought to an honorable close. Indemnity was procured for our merchants, and East and West Florida added to our republic. Next to the purchase of Louisiana, the acquisition of Florida may be viewed as one of the most important measures in our history as a nation. Among his reports while secretary of state, may be mentioned that on weights and measures, made to the United States senate in 1821, in conformity with a resolution of that body, passed in 1817. This report is distinguished for its ability and research.

On every important occasion and question that arose during Mr. Monroe's administration, the voice of Mr. Adams was for his country, for mild councils, and for union. In the agitation of the Missouri question, his influence was exerted for conciliation. He believed that by the constitution and the treaty of cession of 1803, Congress was barred from adopting the proposed restrictions on the admission of Missouri. Of internal improvement by roads and canals, he was ever the friend, and moved in the senate of the United States the first project of their systematic construction.

When the question of a successor to Mr. Monroe in the presidency became the subject of agitation, the claims of Mr. Adams to that high office were admitted to be strong and decided, by a large portion of his countrymen. His elevation was desired by a numerous body of calm, reflecting men, throughout the Union, who desired to see the government administered with the ability and integrity which belonged, as they knew, to the character of Mr. Adams. The other rival candidates for the presidency, Andrew Jackson, William H. Crawford, and Henry Clay, also presented severally strong claims for the support of the people. Of these several candidates, Mr. Adams was the only one who represented the non-slaveholding interest, and he was the second choice of an immense proportion of the people, who, for various causes, preferred one of the other candidates.

In consequence of the number in nomination for president, no choice was effected by the electoral colleges, and neither candidate approached nearer than within thirty-two votes of a majority. General Jackson received 99 votes, Mr. Adams 84, Mr. Crawford 41, and Mr. Clay 37. For the vice-presidency, John C. Calhoun, of South Carolina, received 182

votes, and was consequently elected. The choice of the president, according to constitutional provisions, was referred to the house of representatives, and, contrary to general expectation, an election was made on
the first ballot; Mr. Adams having received the votes of thirteen states,
General Jackson seven states, and Mr. Crawford four states. In this
election by the house, Mr. Clay and his friends having voted for Mr. Adams, great indignation was expressed by the supporters of General Jackson, but the friends of Mr. Crawford, generally, at first appeared satisfied
with the result, as they preferred Mr. Adams to General Jackson, and the
health of Mr. Crawford was then so precarious as to render him nearly, if
not quite, incompetent for the office.

A committee of the house was appointed to wait on Mr. Adams and no-
tify him of his election to the presidency; to this notification he made the
following reply :—

"GENTLEMEN: In receiving this testimonial from the representatives
of the people, and states of this Union, I am deeply sensible to the circumstances under which it has been given. All my predecessors in the
high station to which the favor of the house now calls me, have been honored with majorities of the electoral voices in their primary colleges. It
has been my fortune to be placed, by the divisions of sentiment prevailing
among our countrymen on this occasion, in competition, friendly and honorable, with three of my fellow-citizens, all justly enjoying, in an eminent
degree, the public favor; and of whose worth, talents, and services, no
one entertains a higher and more respectful sense than myself. The
names of two of them were, in the fulfilment of the provisions of the
constitution, presented to the selection of the house, in concurrence with
my own; names closely associated with the glory of the nation, and one
of them further recommended by a larger majority of the primary electoral suffrages than mine.

"In this state of things, could my refusal to accept the trust thus delegated to me, give an immediate opportunity to the people to form and to
express with a nearer approach to unanimity, the object of their preference, I should not hesitate to decline the acceptance of this eminent
charge, and to submit the decision of this momentous question again to
their determination. But the constitution itself has not so disposed of the
contingency which would arise in the event of my refusal; I shall, therefore, repair to the post assigned me by the call of my country signified
through her constitutional organs; oppressed with the magnitude of the
task before me, but cheered with the hope of that generous support from
my fellow-citizens which, in the vicissitudes of a life devoted to their service, has never failed to sustain me—confident in the trust, that the wisdom of the legislative councils will guide and direct me in the path of my
official duty, and relying, above all, upon the superintending providence of
that Being, in whose hand our breath is, and whose are all our ways.

" Gentlemen, I pray you to make acceptable to the house the assurance of my profound gratitude for their confidence, and to accept yourselves my thanks for the friendly terms in which you have communicated to me their decision."

The administration of Mr. Adams as president of the United States, commenced on the 4th of March, 1825, and continued four years. A combination having taken place immediately after the election, of a majority of the friends of Mr. Crawford with those of General Jackson, it was soon apparent that the new administration was destined to meet with a systematic and violent opposition. Every effort on the part of Mr. Adams to conciliate his opponents, and to conduct the public affairs with integrity and usefulness, proved ineffectual to turn the torrent of popular opinion which set steadily against him. In the third year of his term the administration was in the minority in both branches of Congress, and the opposition being concentrated on General Jackson as a candidate for president, he was in 1828 elected, by a large majority, over Mr. Adams.

In March, 1829, Mr. Adams retired to private life, carrying with him the esteem of his political friends, and the respect of his opponents, who generally gave him the credit of good intentions, however they might have differed with him in his views of public policy. While holding the high office of president, he uniformly declined the exercise of a proscriptive spirit toward those of his political opponents whom he found in office ; magnanimously conceding to all the right of exercising their own free will in the choice of rulers, and in supporting or opposing the administration.

After the inauguration of his successor, General Jackson, Mr. Adams continued a short time at Washington city. He then repaired to his family mansion, and the scenes of his early youth, at Quincy, near Boston, Massachusetts, where, in the possession of a competent fortune, and in the enjoyment of the pleasures of domestic life with his family, he might have expected to pass the remainder of his days. But the people of his own immediate neighborhood were not willing to allow him to remain long in retirement. In 1830 he was elected to represent the district in which he resided, in the Congress of the United States, and the following year, namely, in December, 1831, he took his seat in the house of representatives at Washington city, being then in the 65th year of his age, and having already passed about forty years in the public service.

In the national legislature, he took and maintained the stand to which his eminent talents and distinguished services entitled him. The confidence of his constituents, was manifested by continued re-elections to the house of representatives, of which he was a constant member until his death, a period of more than sixteen years.

His reports as chairman of committees on various subjects, particularly on those of manufactures and finance, are among the ablest papers to be found among the national records. He distinguished himself especially on the organization of the twenty-sixth Congress, in December, 1839, when difficulties of a novel character occurred, in consequence of disputed seats from the state of New Jersey, which prevented for many days the choice of a speaker. On that occasion Mr. Adams was chosen, by unanimous consent, chairman of the house while it was in a state of confusion and disorder. By his skill and influence, he was enabled to calm the turbulent elements of a disorganized house, and to bring about a settlement of the difficulties which threatened the dissolution of the government.

Perhaps the most striking feature of Mr. Adams's career as a member of the house of representatives, was his firm adherence to the right of the people to petition Congress, and to be heard through their representatives, on any subject whatsoever. He took an active part in debate, on nearly every topic of public interest, and his speeches were frequently marked with the most fervid eloquence.

The private character of Mr. Adams was always above reproach, in his intercourse with his fellow-men, and in all the various duties of a long life. Without any uncommon professions, he uniformly evinced great respect for the Christian religion, and, like his father, gave a preference to the doctrines of the unitarian church.

In a biographical sketch of Mr. Adams, written for the STATESMAN'S MANUAL, and published in 1846, we made use of the following words : " The subject of this memoir is still found at his post in the public service, where, like the earl of Chatham, it may be expected his mortal career will finally close."

What was then a thought, in advance of a probable result, became an historical fact in 1848. On the twenty-second of February (the birthday of Washington), in that year Mr. Adams was prostrated by paralysis, while in his seat in the house of representatives, and yielded up his spirit to his Maker on the following day (February 23, 1848), being then in his eighty-first year. He died in the speaker's room in the capitol, and his last words were, " This is the last of earth." A committee of members of Congress accompanied his remains to the family burying-ground at Quincy, due honors being paid to his memory in the principal cities and towns, through which the corpse was carried to its final resting-place.

Mr. Adams was of middle stature, and full person, his eyes dark and piercing, and beaming with intelligence. He always led an active life, and enjoyed good health to an advanced age, his health being promoted, doubtless, by his early rising and bodily exercise. His mind was highly cultivated, and he was considered one of the most accomplished scholars and statesmen in America.

Mr. Adams, in May, 1797, was married to Louisa Catherine, daughter of Joshua Johnson, Esq., of Maryland, who then resided in London. By this lady, who survives him, he had four children, three sons and one daughter, of whom one only, Charles F. Adams of Boston, is now living.

Andrew Jackson

BIOGRAPHICAL SKETCH

OF

ANDREW JACKSON.

THE ancestors of Andrew Jackson, the seventh president of the United States, were among the emigrants from Scotland to the province of Ulster, in Ireland, at a period when it was the policy of the English government to promote the colonization of settlers from England and Scotland on the confiscated lands of the Irish. The family of Jackson was therefore of Scottish origin; and they were attached to the presbyterian church. Hugh Jackson, the grandfather of the subject of the present sketch, was a linen draper, near Carrickfergus, in Ireland. His four sons were respectable farmers; of whom Andrew, the youngest, married Elizabeth Hutchinson, and had in Ireland two sons, Hugh and Robert. The unfortunate condition of his native country induced him to dispose of his farm, and in 1765, with his wife and children, to emigrate to America, and settle in South Carolina. Samuel Jackson, a son of another of the brothers, at a subsequent period, emigrated to Pennsylvania, and became a citizen of Philadelphia.

Three of the neighbors of Andrew Jackson, named Crawford, emigrated to America with him, and the four emigrants purchased lands and settled in the Waxhaw settlement, South Carolina, near the line of North Carolina.

On this plantation of his father, at Waxhaw settlement, Andrew Jackson, the subject of this memoir, was born, on the 15th of March, 1767. His father died about the time of his birth, leaving his farm to his widow, and his name to his infant son.

Left with three young sons, and moderate means Mrs. Jackson gave her two oldest a common school education, while the youngest she desired to see prepared for the ministry, and, at a proper age, placed him under the tuition of Mr. Humphries, principal of the Waxhaw academy, where he made considerable progress in his studies, including latin and

Greek, until interrupted by the events of the war of the revolution.   Although but about eight years of age, when the first conflicts between the British and Americans took place, Andrew Jackson soon became accustomed to the stirring scenes around him, of the friends and neighbors of his mother training themselves for battle, and preparing to defend their homes from the attacks and ravages of the invading foe.

The British commanding officers in America having resolved to carry the war into the southern states ; Savannah, in Georgia, was taken in 1778, and South Carolina invaded in the spring of 1779.   The militia were summoned to the field to repel them, and Hugh Jackson, the oldest brother of Andrew, lost his life in the fatigues of the service.   A battle took place at the Waxhaw settlement, between the British and Americans, in May, 1780, when 113 Americans were killed, and 150 wounded.   Considerable ammunition and stores fell into the hands of the enemy.   In the Waxhaw meetinghouse, where the wounded were carried, Andrew Jackson, then thirteen years of age, first saw the horrors of war.   The mangled bodies of his countrymen confirmed the impression made upon his youthful mind by the tales of English oppression and cruelty which he had so often heard from his mother and kindred, while relating scenes of tyranny in Ireland, from which his father had fled to find a retreat in America.*

In the summer of 1780, Andrew Jackson, being then but little more than thirteen years of age, in company with his brother Robert, joined a corps of volunteers, under the command of Colonel Davie, to attempt the defence of that part of the country against a body of British troops and tories who had penetrated into the interior of the Carolinas.   Davie's corps was attached to General Sumter's brigade, and an action took place on the 6th of August, 1780, between the American troops and the British and tories, at a place called Hanging Rock.   The corps of Davie, in which the young Jacksons fought, particularly distinguished itself, and suffered heavy loss.

Not being regularly attached to any military corps, on account of their youth, Robert and Andrew Jackson did not participate in many of the numerous affairs in which the Americans were engaged with the British during their long campaign in the Carolinas.   They retired with their mother into North Carolina for some time, leaving their home on the approach of the British army in that quarter.   In 1781, both of the boys were taken prisoners by a party of dragoons.   While a prisoner, Andrew Jackson was ordered by a British officer to clean his muddy boots, which the young soldier refusing, he received a wound with a sword from the officer, and the wound left a scar which Jackson carried with him to his grave.   His brother Robert, for a similar offence, received a wound on his head, from the effects of which he never recovered.   The brothers were retained some time in

* For the facts in the first part of this memoir, we are indebted principally to Kendall's Life of Jackson.

captivity, at Camden, where their sufferings were great from their wounds, and the small-pox, then prevalent among the prisoners. Being finally released, by exchange, the Jacksons, accompanied by their mother, returned home to the Waxhaw settlement, where Robert died in two days afterward. By kind nursing and the care of a physician, Andrew finally recovered from a dangerous sickness. His mother died soon after this, from the effects of a fever taken on board the prison-ship at Charleston, whither she went on an adventure of kindness and mercy, for the relief of some of her relatives and friends confined on board of that vessel. Thus every member of the Jackson family which came from Ireland to America to escape British oppression, perished through the effects of the same oppression in America. The only remnant of the family was an American-born son, who, through many perils, lived to be the avenger of his race.

At the close of the war of the revolution, Andrew Jackson was left alone in the world, his own master, with some little property, but without the benefit of parental counsel or restraint. At first associating with idle young men, he imbibed loose and extravagant habits, which he suddenly determined to reform. Changing his course of life, he commenced the study of law, at Salisbury, North Carolina, with Spruce M'Cay, Esq., then an eminent counsellor, and subsequently a judge of distinction. This was in the winter of 1784, when he was in his eighteenth year. He finished his studies under Colonel Stokes, and in a little more than two years he was licensed to practise law. Soon after this, without solicitation on his part, he received from the governor of North Carolina the appointment of solicitor for the western district of that state, embracing the present state of Tennessee.

At the age of twenty-one, in 1788, Andrew Jackson, accompanied by Judge McNairy, crossed the mountains to take up his abode in Tennessee, then the western district of North Carolina. For several months he resided at Jonesborough, then the principal seat of justice in that district. In 1789, he first visited the infant settlements on the Cumberland river, near the present site of Nashville. The settlers had at this time many difficulties with the Indians, who were then numerous and hostile to the whites. During this perilous period, Jackson performed twenty-two journeys across the wilderness of two hundred miles, then intervening between Jonesborough and the Cumberland settlements. He was frequently under arms, with other settlers, to protect parties of emigrants from the attacks of the Indians. He was also engaged in several expeditions against the Indians, in one of which, in 1794, the native town of Nickajack, near the Tennessee river, was destroyed. By his gallantry in these affairs, Jackson became well known to the Indians, who gave him the names of "*Sharp Knife*" and "*Pointed Arrow*." He gained equally their respect and that of his companions, the hardy settlers of Tennessee.

Having determined to make the neighborhood of Nashville his permanent home, Jackson, with his friend Judge Overton, became boarders in the family of Mrs. Donelson, the widow of Colonel John Donelson, an emigrant from Virginia. Mrs. Rachel Robards, her daughter, who afterward became the wife of Jackson, was then living with her mother. This lady was celebrated for her beauty, affability, and other attractions. Her husband, Captain Robards, was a man of dissolute habits and jealous disposition. A separation took place, and Robards applied to the legislature of Virginia for a divorce ; soon after, intelligence was received that his petition had been granted. Mrs. Robards was then at Natchez, on the Mississippi, and Jackson, considering that she was free to form a new connexion, in the summer of 1791 went down to Natchez, paid her his addresses, and was accepted. In the fall they were married, and returned to the Cumberland, where they were cordially received by their mutual friends.

In December, 1793, Jackson learned, for the first time, that the act of the Virginia legislature did not grant a divorce, but only authorized a suit for divorce in a Kentucky court, which had just been brought to a successful issue. Surprised and mortified at this information, on his return to Nashville, in January, 1794, he took out a license, and was again regularly married. The conduct of Jackson in this affair was considered, by those familiar with the circumstances, correct and honorable, and perfectly consistent with true morality. His friend and confidential associate remarks : " In his singularly delicate sense of honor, and in what I thought his chivalrous conception of the female sex, it occurred to me that he was distinguished from every other person with whom I was acquainted."

Jackson, after his marriage, applied himself with renewed diligence to his profession in the practice of the law. Circumstances connected with his professional business required the exercise of his firmness of character and courage, in no ordinary degree. There had been a combination of debtors against him, as he was employed by creditors for the collection of claims, which he succeeded in breaking down, but not without making bitter enemies. Bullies were stimulated to attack and insult him, and thus brought him into several personal contests, which generally ended in a severe punishment of the aggressors, by the bold and fearless Jackson.

In 1795, the people of Tennessee elected delegates to a convention for the formation of a state constitution, preparatory to admission into the Union. Of that convention Jackson was chosen a member by his neighbors, and took an active part in the formation of the constitution. The convention sat at Knoxville from the 11th of January to the 6th of February, 1796, and Tennessee was admitted into the Union as a state, by act of Congress, on the 1st of June, the same year. Jackson was chosen the first representative from the new state in Congress, and took his seat in the house on the 5th of December, 1796. His term expired on the 3d of March following, and he was prevented from continuing longer in that body, being elected by the legislature of Tennessee to the senate of the United States, where he took his seat on the 22d of November, 1797, being then only a few months over thirty years of age. He appears not to have been ambitious or anxious for political distinction at that time, for, after serving one session, he resigned his seat in the senate. During his short career in Congress, it is believed that he made no speeches; but in his votes he acted with the democratic party, opposing the administration of Washington at its close, and subsequently that of John Adams. While a member of the house, he was one of a minority of twelve democrats, among whom were Edward Livingston, Nathaniel Macon, and William B. Giles, who voted against an answer to Washington's last speech to Congress; because that answer expressly approved of the measures of Washington's administration, some of which were condemned by the democratic party. The state gave her first vote for president to Mr. Jefferson in 1796, which vote she repeated in 1800. In the political revolution which elevated Mr. Jefferson to the presidency, Jackson participated, and acted with the friends of Mr. Jefferson; but little effort was required, however, to secure the vote for the democratic candidates, in a state so uniformly devoted to that party as Tennessee.

At this period, the popularity of Jackson in Tennessee was equal, if it did not exceed that of any other citizen of the state. Soon after his resignation as senator, the legislature again honored him by conferring upon him the appointment of judge of the supreme court of the state. This office he accepted, and for a time performed the duties of the station; but, owing to ill health, he determined to resign and retire to private life. This intention he was induced to defer for the present, in consequence of remonstrances from members of the legislature and others, who entreated him to remain upon the bench.

The circumstances in which Jackson was placed, and his course in several public affairs, occasioned a misunderstanding between him and other leading men in Tennessee. Among those who became his enemies, were Judge McNairy and Governor Sevier. A personal quarrel with the latter occasioned a challenge from Judge Jackson, which was accepted by the governor, and the parties, without any formal arrangement, met on horseback, each armed with a brace of pistols, the governor having also a sword, while Jackson had a cane, which he carried as a spear. Putting spurs to his horse, he charged upon his antagonist in a bold and unexpected manner, and the governor dismounted to avoid the shock. The interference of the governor's attendants prevented any serious mischief, and by the intercession of mutual friends further hostile intentions were abandoned. The affair, however, occasioned sundry angry publications by the friends of the respective parties, which show the peculiar state of society then existing in the frontier settlements, where men holding the highest public stations were engaged in personal rencounters.

Previous to his affair with Governor Sevier, Jackson was appointed major-general of the militia of the state, viz., in 1802. His competitor was John Sevier, who was then also a candidate for governor. The votes of the officers by whom the appointment of general was made being equally divided, the decision devolved on Governor Roane, who gave it in favor of Jackson.

On the purchase of Louisiana from France, in 1803, by the United States, there were apprehensions of a difficulty with Spain, when the Americans should take possession of the territory. The Tennessee militia were called upon for aid in case of need, and by request of the secretary of war, General Jackson caused boats to be prepared to transport the troops to New Orleans ; but neither the boats, nor his own proffered services, were required, as the Spaniards made no resistance to the peaceful transfer and occupation of Louisiana.

In 1804, General Jackson, having served six years on the bench, resigned his office of judge of the supreme court. His biographer and friend, Mr. Kendall, remarks, that he " was not made for what is usually called a first-rate lawyer. His mode of reasoning would not permit him to seek for justice through a labyrinth of technicalities and special pleading. Yet few, if any, exceeded him in seizing on the strong points of a case, and with vigor and clearness applying to them the great principles of law. As a lawyer, in criminal prosecutions, the case of his client always became his own, and he was considered one of the most eloquent and effective among his contemporaries. As a judge, his opinions were always clear, short, and to the point, aiming at justice, without the affectation of eloquence, or of superior learning. His retirement from the bench gratified only those who feared his justice, while it was deeply regretted by a large majority of the community."

After his resignation as judge, General Jackson found that retirement which he had long desired. Having acquired a moderate fortune, he took up his residence on his plantation on the banks of the Cumberland, near Nashville, and not far from that which he subsequently occupied under the name of the Hermitage. His time was now devoted to the pursuits of agriculture, in one of the finest districts of country in the United States, and his house was always the abode of hospitality, where his numerous friends and acquaintance were received by him with a cordial welcome.

In addition to other pursuits on his plantation, much of General Jackson's attention was given to the raising of fine horses, from the most improved breeds of the southern states. He consequently became a frequenter of race-courses at the west, to bring out his favorite horses, and occasionally lost and won in the sports of the turf. These affairs led to one of the most unfortunate events of his life. In consequence of a quarrel, which ended in blows, between Jackson and Charles Dickinson, on the subject of a bet made at a horse-race, followed by an abusive publication on the part of Dickinson, charging Jackson with cowardice ; the general sent Dickinson a challenge. The duel took place at Harrison's mills, on Red river, in Kentucky, on the 30th of May, 1806. The word being given, Dickinson fired first, his ball taking effect in Jackson's breast, and shattering two of his ribs ; the next instant Jackson fired, although thus severely wounded, and Dickinson fell ; he was taken to a neighboring house, and survived but a few hours. This melancholy affair caused much excitement in Tennessee at the time, and various publications on the subject appeared from the friends of the respective parties, and General Jackson himself ; but the certificates of the seconds declared that the duel had been fairly conducted, according to the previous understanding of the parties. The firmness of nerve displayed by General Jackson in this duel was remarkable, considering that he was wounded before discharging his pistol. Some weeks transpired before he recovered from the effects of his wounds.

During the short period while General Jackson was a member of Congress, he had formed the acquaintance of Colonel Aaron Burr, who, in 1805, visited the western country, and spent several days at the residence of Jackson. Burr, in his journal, describes the general as " once a lawyer, after a judge, now a planter ; a man of intelligence ; and one of those prompt, frank, ardent souls whom I love to meet." The general treated him with great kindness and hospitality, and understanding that his object was the settlement of a tract of land in Louisiana, and the making arrangements for the invasion of Mexico, in case of a war with Spain, he rendered him such assistance as he could afford, and procured for him a boat to descend the Cumberland river.

In 1806, Colonel Burr again returned to the western country, and commenced preparations for an expedition. General Jackson offered to accompany him to Mexico with a body of troops, in case of a war with Spain ; but declined holding communication with him if he had any hostile intentions against the United States. Burr assured him, in the most positive terms, that he had no such hostile design ; but Jackson having his suspicions, the previous intimacy between him and Burr ceased. He afterward received orders from the war department to call out the military, if necessary, to suppress Burr's projects, and arrest Burr himself. Twelve military companies of the militia under his command, were ordered out by General Jackson, but as Burr had descended the Cumberland and Mississippi rivers, with only a few unarmed men, the general dismissed the troops, and reported his proceedings to the government.

After Burr was arrested and taken to Richmond, Virginia, for trial, on a charge of treason against the United States, General Jackson was summoned as a witness, but was not examined. He knew nothing tending to criminate the accused, and his evidence, if given, would have been in favor of Burr.   It may be here remarked, that Colonel Burr's respect for General Jackson continued through life ; and he always spoke of him as a man of integrity and honor.   It is believed that he was the first to name him (though this was then unknown to the general himself), as early as 1815, in his private correspondence, as a suitable candidate for the presidency.

General Jackson continued in private life, attending to his agricultural employments, until the war of 1812 with Great Britain.   Having become interested in a mercantile establishment in Nashville, the management of which he intrusted to his partner in that business, he became seriously involved in the debts of the concern, which he was compelled to close ; and, for the payment of his debts, sold his residence and plantation.   He then retired into a log-cabin, near the place since called " the Hermitage," and commenced the world anew.   By a prudent and economical management of his affairs, he soon retrieved his pecuniary condition, and again became possessed of the means of comfort and enjoyment.

But a period approached when the pleasures and endearments of home were to be abandoned, for the duties of more active life.   War with Great Britain was declared by the Congress of the United States on the 12th of June, 1812.   General Jackson, ever devoted to the interests of his country, from the moment of the declaration knew no wish so strong as that of entering into her service against a power which, independent of public considerations, he had many private reasons for disliking.   In her he could trace sufferings and injuries received, and the efficient cause why, in early life, he had been left forlorn and wretched, without a single relation in the world.   His proud and inflexible mind, however, could not bend to solicit an appointment in the army which was about to be raised. He accordingly remained wholly unknown, until, at the head of the militia employed against the Creek Indians, his constant vigilance, and the splendor of his victories, apprized the general government of those great military talents which he so eminently possessed and conspicuously displayed, when opportunities for exerting them were afforded.

The acts of Congress on the 6th of February and July, 1812, afforded the means of bringing into view a display of those powers which, being unknown, unfortunately might have slumbered in inaction.   Under the authority of these acts, authorizing the president to accept the services of fifty thousand volunteers, he addressed the citizens of his division, and twenty-five hundred flocked to his standard.   A tender of them having been made, and the offer accepted, in November he received orders to place himself at their head and to descend the Mississippi, for the defence of the lower country, which was then supposed to be in danger. Accordingly, on the 10th of December, 1812, those troops rendezvoused at Nashville, prepared to advance to their place of destination ; and although the weather was then excessively severe, and the ground covered with snow, no troops could have displayed greater firmness. The general was everywhere with them, inspiring them with the ardor that animated his own bosom.*

Having procured supplies, and made the necessary arrangements for an active campaign, they proceeded, the 7th of January, 1813, on their journey, and descending the Ohio and Mississippi, through cold and ice, arrived and halted at Natchez. Here Jackson had been instructed to remain, until he should receive further orders. Having chosen a healthy site for the encampment of his troops, he devoted his time to training and preparing them for active service. The clouds of war, however, in that quarter having blown over, an order was received from the secretary of war, dated the fifth of January, directing him, on receipt thereof, to dismiss those under his command from service, and to take measures for delivering over every article of public property in his possession to General Wilkinson. When this order reached his camp, there were one hundred and fifty on the sick report, and almost the whole of them destitute of the means of defraying the expenses of their return. The consequence of a strict compliance with the secretary's order, would have been, that many of the sick must have perished, while most of the others, from their destitute condition, would, of necessity, have been compelled to enlist in the regular army, under General Wilkinson.†

General Jackson could not think of sacrificing or injuring an army that had shown such devotedness to their country ; and he determined to disregard the order, and march them again to their homes in Tennessee, where they had been embodied. This determination met with the disapprobation of his field-officers and of General Wilkinson ; but persisting in his design, General Jackson marched the whole of his division to the section of country whence they had been drawn, and dismissed them from service, as he had been instructed. The sick were transported in wagons, at the same time. It was at a time of the year when the roads were bad, and the swamps, lying in their passage, deep and full ; yet the general placed before his troops an example of patience under hardships that lulled to silence all complaints, and won to him, still stronger than before, the esteem and respect of every one. On arriving at Nashville, he communicated to the president of the United States the course he had pursued, and the reasons that had induced it. His conduct was in the end approved, and the expenses incurred directed to be paid by the government.

The volunteers who had descended the river having been discharged, early in May, 1813, there was little expectation that they would again be called for. Tennessee was too remotely situated in the interior, to expect their services would be required for the defence of the state ; and thus far, the British had discovered no serious intention of waging operations against any part of Louisiana. Their repose, however, was not of long

* Eaton's Life of Jackson.   † Ibid.

duration.   The Creek Indians, inhabiting the country lying between the Chattahoochee and Tombigbee rivers, and extending from the Tennessee river to the Florida line, had lately manifested strong symptoms of hostility toward the United States.   This disposition was greatly strengthened through means used by the northern Indians, who were then making preparations for a war against the United States, and who wished to engage the southern tribes in the same enterprise.

An artful impostor had, about this time, sprung up among the Shawnees, a northern tribe, who, by passing for a prophet, had acquired a most astonishing influence among his own and the neighboring Indian tribes.   He succeeded in a short time in kindling a phrensy and rage against the Anglo-Americans, which soon after burst forth in acts of destructive violence.   His brother, Tecumseh, who became so famous during the war, and who was killed subsequently at the battle of the Thames, in Canada, was despatched to the southern tribes, to excite in them the same temper.   To the Creeks, then the most numerous and powerful of the southern Indians, he directed his principal attention, and in the spring of 1812 he had repeated conferences with the chiefs of that nation.   Deriving his powers from his brother, the prophet, whose extraordinary commission and endowments were, previous to this, well understood by the tribes in the south, his authority was regarded with the highest veneration.   To afford additional weight to his councils, Tecumseh gave assurances of aid and support from Great Britain ; and having made other arrangements to carry out his plans, he returned to his own tribe.

From this time, a regular communication was kept up between the Creeks and the northern tribes ; while depredations were committed on the frontier settlers by parties of the allied Indians.   In the summer of 1812, several families were murdered near the mouth of the Ohio, and soon afterward similar outrages were committed in Tennessee and Georgia.   These acts were not sanctioned by the chiefs of the Creek nation, for, on application to them by the general government, the offenders were punished with death.   No sooner was this done, than the spirit of the greater part of the nation suddenly kindled into civil war.

They first attacked their own countrymen who were friendly to the United States, and compelled them to retire toward the white settlements for protection.   After this, they collected a supply of ammunition from the Spaniards at Pensacola, and, on the 30th of August, 1813, commenced an assault on Fort Mimms, in the Mississippi territory, which they succeeded in carrying, and put to death nearly three hundred persons, including women and children, with the most savage barbarity.   Only seventeen of the whole number in the fort escaped, to bring intelligence of the catastrophe.

This monstrous and unprovoked outrage was no sooner known in Tennessee, than the whole state was thrown into a ferment, and immediate measures were taken to inflict exemplary punishment on the hostile Indians. The legislature, by the advice of numerous citizens, among whom were the governor and General Jackson, authorized the executive to call into the field 3,500 men, to be marched against the Indians. The troops were placed under the command of General Jackson, notwithstanding he was at the time seriously indisposed, from the effects of a fractured arm, owing to a wound received by him from a pistol-shot, in a fight with Colonel Thomas H. Benton, at a public house in Nashville.

The army under General Jackson marched into the Indian country in October, 1813. Crossing the Tennessee river, and learning that a large body of the enemy had posted themselves at Tallushatchee, on the river Coosa; General Coffee was detached with nine hundred men to attack and disperse them. This was effected, with a small loss on the part of the Tennessee troops, while the Indians lost 186 killed, among whom were unfortunately, and through accident, a few women and children. Eighty-four Indian women and children were taken prisoners, and treated with the utmost humanity.

Another battle with over a thousand of the Creeks, took place shortly after, at Talladega, thirty miles below Tallushatchee; the Tennessee troops being commanded by General Jackson in person; when 300 Indians were left dead on the field, and about as many more slain in their flight.

This campaign was protracted much longer than would otherwise have been the case, in consequence of the want of supplies of provisions for the army, which caused large numbers of the troops to return to their homes. Having at length obtained supplies, and being joined by more troops, General Jackson advanced still further into the enemy's country. Several battles took place with the Indians, the most sanguinary of which was that of Tohopeka or the Horseshoe, at the bend of the Tallapoosa river. On that occasion, 557 warriors, of 1,000 in the engagement, were found dead on the field, besides many others who were killed and thrown into the river, while the battle raged, or shot in attempting to escape by swimming. Over 300 prisoners were taken, all, but three or four, women and children. In this and other battles, the whites were assisted by a considerable body of friendly Creek and Cherokee Indians, who engaged in pursuing and destroying their fugitive countrymen with the most unrelenting rigor; " a circumstance," says Eaton, in his life of Jackson, " which the patriot must ever view with abhorrence; and although, from necessity or policy, he may be compelled to avail himself of the advantages afforded by such a circumstance, he can never be induced either to approve or justify it."

The battle of the Horsehoe gave a deathblow to the hopes of the Indians; nor did they venture afterward to make a stand. The principal chiefs came in, made their submission to General Jackson, and sued for peace; the campaign was ended, and the troops were marched back to Tennessee and discharged.

10

In May, 1814, General Jackson received the appointment of major-general in the army of the United States, on the resignation of General Harrison. Previous to this appointment, a commission as brigadier and brevet major-general had been forwarded to General Jackson, but his commission for the higher office being received the day after the notification of the other, he had not sent his answer to the war department, and the appointment of major-general was accepted.

The contest with the Indians being ended, the first and principal object of the government was, to enter into some definite arrangement which should deprive of success any effort that might thereafter be made, by other powers, to enlist those savages in their wars. None was so well calculated to answer this end, as that of restricting their limits, so as to cut off their communication with British and Spanish agents, in East and West Florida.

No treaty of friendship or boundary had yet been entered into by the government with the Indians; they remained a conquered people, and within the limits, and subject to the regulations and restrictions which had been prescribed in March, 1814, by General Jackson, when he retired from the country. He was now, by the government, called upon to act in a new and different character, and to negotiate the terms upon which an amicable understanding should be restored between the United States and these conquered Indians. Colonel Hawkins, who for a considerable time past had been the agent to the Creek nation, was also associated in the mission.

On the 10th of July, 1814, General Jackson, with a small retinue, reached the Alabama; and on the 10th of August succeeded in procuring the execution of a treaty, in which the Indians pledged themselves no more to listen to foreign emissaries—to hold no communication with British or Spanish garrisons; guarantied to the United States the right of erecting military posts in their country, and a free navigation of all their waters. They stipulated also, that they would suffer no agent or trader to pass among them, or hold any kind of commerce or intercourse with the nation, unless specially deriving his authority from the president of the United States.*

The treaty also settled the boundary and defined the extent of territory secured to the Creeks, and that which they were required to surrender. Sufficient territory was acquired on the south by the United States, to give security to the Mobile settlements, and to the western borders of Georgia, effectually cutting off the communication of the Creeks with the Chickasaws and Choctaws, and separating them from the Seminole tribes and other unfriendly Indians in Florida.

The retreat of the savages in Florida had been always looked upon as a place whence the United States might apprehend serious difficulties to

* Eaton.

arise. General Jackson entertained the belief that the British, through this channel, with the aid of the Spanish governor, had protected the Indians, and supplied them with arms and ammunition. He received certain information, when on his way to negotiate the treaty with the Indians, that about three hundred English troops had landed ; were fortifying themselves at the mouth of the Apalachicola, and were endeavoring to excite the Indians to war. No time was lost in giving the government notice of what was passing, and of the course he deemed advisable to be pursued. The advantages to be secured from the possession of Pensacola he had frequently urged. But the government were unwilling to encounter the risk of a rupture with Spain, by authorizing the United States troops to enter her territory, while she occupied a neutral position, and Jackson was unable to obtain any answer to his repeated and pressing applications to be allowed to make a descent upon Pensacola, and reduce it, which, he gave it as his opinion, would bring the war in the south to a speedy termination. The secretary of war, General Armstrong, however, wrote him a letter on the 18th of July, 1814, which Jackson did not receive until the 17th of January, 1815, after the war was over, in which he remarked, that, " If the Spanish authorities admit, feed, arm, and co-operate with the British and hostile Indians, we must strike, on the broad principle of self-preservation ; under other and different circumstances we must forbear."

The general, afterward speaking of this transaction, remarked : " If this letter, or any hint that such a course would have been winked at by the government, had been received, it would have been in my power to have captured the British shipping in the bay. But acting on my own responsibility, against a neutral power, it became essential for me to proceed with more caution than my judgment or wishes approved, and consequently, important advantages were lost, which might have been secured."

Having ascertained, through some Indian spies, that a considerable English force had arrived in Florida, and that muskets and ammunition had been given to the Indians, General Jackson wrote to the Spanish governor of Pensacola, apprizing him of the information received, and demanding .the surrender to him of such chiefs of the hostile Indians as were with him. The governor, after some delay, replied to this letter, denying that any hostile Indians were with him at that time ; nor could he refuse those Indians assistance, on the ground of hospitality, when their distresses were so great, or surrender them without acting in open violation of the laws of nations. He also demanded to be informed, if the United States were ignorant that, at the conquest of Florida, there was a treaty between Great Britain and the Creek Indians, and whether they did not know that it still existed between Spain and those tribes. In the same letter, the governor accused the United States government of having harbored traitors from the

Mexican provinces, and of countenancing pirates who had committed robberies upon the merchant-vessels of Spain.

The general answered this letter by another equally high-toned, in which, among other things, he says : " Your excellency has been candid enough to admit your having supplied the Indians with arms. In addition to this, I have learned that a British flag has been seen flying on one of your forts. All this is done, while you are pretending to be neutral. You can not be surprised, then, but, on the contrary, will provide a fort in your town for my soldiers and Indians, should I take it in my head to pay you a visit.

" In future, I beg you to withhold your insulting charges against my government, for one more inclined to listen to slander than I am ; nor consider me any more as a diplomatic character, unless so proclaimed to you from the mouths of my cannon."

Captain Gordon, who had been despatched to Pensacola, on his return, reported to the general, that he had seen from one hundred and fifty to two hundred officers and soldiers, a park of artillery, and about five hundred Indians, under the drill of British officers, armed with new muskets, and dressed in the English uniform.

Jackson directly brought to the view of the government the information he had received, and again urged his favorite scheme, the reduction of Pensacola. Many difficulties were presented ; but, to have all things in a state of readiness for action, when the time should arrive to authorize it, he addressed the governors of Tennessee, Louisiana, and the Mississippi territory, informing them of the necessity of holding all the forces allotted for the defence of the southwestern military district, in a state of readiness to march at any notice, and to any point where they might be required. The warriors of the different Indian tribes were ordered to be marshalled, and taken into pay of the government.

On the day after completing his business at Fort Jackson, he departed for Mobile, to place the country in a state of defence. He had already despatched his adjutant-general, Colonel Butler, to Tennessee, with orders to raise volunteers ; and on the 28th September, 1814, two thousand ablebodied men, well supplied with rifles and muskets, assembled under the command of General Coffee, at Fayetteville, Tennessee, to march for Mobile, a distance of at least four hundred miles. The regular forces, lately enlisted, marched from Nashville to Mobile in about fourteen days.

As General Jackson kept his own determination a secret, the idea could scarcely be entertained, that at this time he intended to advance against Pensacola on his own responsibility. He was not long in doubt as to the course proper to be pursued. Colonel Nicholls had arrived in August at that place, with a squadron of British ships, and taken up his quarters with the Spanish governor, Manrequez. He issued a proclamation to the inhabitants of the southwest, inviting them to join the British standard.

After waiting two weeks, he made an unsuccessful attack on Fort Bowyer, which commanded the entrance to Mobile bay. The fort was defended by Major Lawrence in so gallant a manner, that the British were compelled to retire, with the loss of one of their ships and about two hundred men.

The British retired to Pensacola, and General Jackson determined, on his own responsibility, to enter Florida and take that town. General Coffee, with about twenty-eight hundred men, had arrived at Fort St. Stephens, on the Mobile river. General Jackson repaired to Coffee's camp, and made the necessary arrangement for marching into Florida. The quartermasters were destitute of funds, and the government credit was insufficient to procure supplies for the army. Thus situated, from his own limited funds, and loans effected on his credit and responsibility, he succeeded in carrying his plans into effect, and in hastening his army to the place of its destination.

The difficulty of subsisting cavalry on the route, rendered it necessary that part of the brigade should proceed on foot. Although they had volunteered in the service as mounted men, and expected that no different disposition would be made of them, yet they cheerfully acquiesced in the order; and one thousand, abandoning their horses, to subsist as they could, on the reeds that grew along the river-bottoms, prepared to commence their march. Being supplied with rations for the trip, on the 2d day of November the line of march was taken up, and Pensacola was reached on the 6th. The British and Spaniards had obtained intelligence of their approach and intended attack, and everything was in readiness to dispute their passage to the town. The forts were garrisoned, and prepared for resistance; batteries formed in the principal streets; and the British vessels moored within the bay, and so disposed as to command the main entrances which led to Pensacola.

The American army consisting of Coffee's brigade, the regulars, and a few Indians, in all about 3,000 men, had arrived within a mile and a half of the town, and formed their encampment. Before any final step was taken, General Jackson concluded to make a further application to the governor, and to learn of him what course, at the present moment, he would make it necessary for him to pursue. Major Piere was accordingly despatched with a flag, to disclose the object of the visit, and to require that the different forts, Barancas, St. Rose, and St. Michael, should be immediately surrendered, to be garrisoned and held by the United States, until Spain, by furnishing a sufficient force, might be able to protect the province, and preserve her neutral character.

This mission experienced no very favorable result. Major Piere, on approaching St. Michael's, was fired on, and compelled to return. The Spanish flag was displayed on the fort, and under it the outrage was committed, although the British flag had been associated with it until the day before.   Notwithstanding this unprovoked outrage, General Jackson acted with forbearance, and sent another letter to the governor, asking an explanation.   In answer, the governor stated that what had been done was not properly chargeable on him, but on the English; and he assured the general of his perfect willingness to receive any overtures he might be pleased to make.

Major Piere was again despatched to meet the offer of the governor. The surrender of the fortifications and munitions of war was demanded, to be receipted for, and become the subject of future arrangement by the respective governments.   The governor, after advising with his council, rejected the propositions; and as soon as the answer was received by Jackson, he resolved to urge his army forward, and, immediately commencing his march, proceeded to the accomplishment of his object, determined to effect it, in despite of danger and of consequences.

The American army was in motion early in the morning of the 7th of November.   Pushing forward, they were soon in the streets, and sheltered by the houses from the cannon of the British vessels in the harbor.   Captain Laval, who commanded the advance, fell severely wounded, while he was charging a Spanish battery.   From behind the houses and garden fences, constant volleys of musketry were discharged, until the regulars arriving, met the Spaniards, and drove them from their positions.

The governor, panic-struck, and trembling for the safety of the city, hastened, bearing a flag in his hand, to find the commander, and seek to stay the carnage, and promised to consent to whatever terms might be demanded of him.

No time was lost by General Jackson in procuring what was considered by him of vital importance—the surrender of the forts.   A capitulation was agreed on the next day; Pensacola and the different fortresses were to be retained by the United States, until Spain could better maintain her authority; while the rights and privileges of her citizens were to be regarded and respected.

Everything was in readiness the next day to take possession of Barancas fort, fourteen miles west of Pensacola.   The American troops were ready for marching, when a tremendous explosion gave notice that all was destroyed.   It was ascertained that the fort had been blown up, and that the British shipping had retired from the bay.   On their retreat from Pensacola, the British carried off with them three or four hundred slaves, in spite of the remonstrances of the owners.

The American loss in this expedition was quite inconsiderable.   The left column alone met resistance, and had fifteen or twenty wounded—none killed.   Captain Laval and Lieutenant Flournoy were among the number wounded.

Deeming it unnecessary to think of garrisoning and attempting to hold the forts in Florida, Jackson concluded to redeliver all that had been surrendered, and retire from the territory. Two days, therefore, after entering Pensacola, he abandoned it. He wrote to the Spanish governor, concluding as follows: "The enemy has retreated; the hostile Creeks have fled to the forest; and I now retire from your town, leaving you to occupy your forts and protect the rights of your citizens."

It had been for some time rumored and generally accredited, that a very considerable force might be expected from England, destined to act against some part of the United States, most probably New Orleans. The importance of this place was well known to the enemy; it was the key to the entire commerce of the western country. Had a descent been made upon it a few months before, it might have been taken with all imaginable ease; but the British had confidently indulged the belief that they could possess it at any time, without much difficulty.

There was nothing now so much desired by General Jackson, as to be able to depart for New Orleans, where he apprehended the greatest danger, and where he believed his presence was most material. He had already effected a partial security for Mobile, and the inhabitants in that vicinity. His health was still delicate, which almost wholly unfitted him for the duties he had to encounter; but his constant expectation of a large force appearing on the coast, impelled him to action. General Coffee and Colonel Hinds, with their mounted men, were ordered to march, and take a position convenient to New Orleans, where they could find forage for their horses. Everything being arranged, and the command at Mobile left with General Winchester, Jackson on the 22d of November, left Mobile for New Orleans, where he arrived on the 1st of December, and where his headquarters were for the present established.*

General Jackson was now on a new theatre, and soon to be brought in collision with an enemy different from any he had yet encountered; the time had arrived to call forth all the energies he possessed. His body worn down by sickness and exhaustion, with a mind constantly alive to the apprehension, that, with the means given him, it would not be in his power to satisfy his own wishes, and the expectations of his country, were circumstances well calculated to depress him.

Louisiana, he well knew, was ill supplied with arms, and contained a mixed population, of different tongues, and doubtful as to their attachment to the government of the United States. No troops, arms, or ammunition, had yet descended from the states of Kentucky and Tennessee. His only reliance for defence, if suddenly assailed, was on the few regulars he had, the volunteers of General Coffee, and such troops as the state itself could furnish. Although continually agitated by gloomy forebodings, he breathed his fears to none. He appeared constantly serene, endeavored to impress a general belief that the country could and would be successfully defended. This apparent tranquillity and avowed certainty

* Eaton.

of success in the general, excited strong hopes, dispelled everything like fear, and impressed all with additional confidence.

While engaged in his operations on the Mobile, he had kept up a correspondence with Governor Claiborne, of Louisiana, urging him to the adoption of measures for the defence of the state. He had also forwarded an address to the people of Louisiana, endeavoring to excite them to a defence of their rights and liberties. Preparations for collecting troops in sufficient strength to repel an invasion, had been actively carried forward. The secretary of war had called upon the governors of Kentucky and Tennessee for quotas of the militia of those states, which requisitions were promptly answered by the governors, and the troops embarked for New Orleans, in November.

While the troops from the upper country were expected, General Jackson was active in adopting such measures as could be earliest effected, and which were best calculated for resistance and defence. The volunteer corps of the city, and other militia, were reviewed, the forts in the vicinity visited, to ascertain their situation and capacity for defence, and new works were erected on the banks of the Mississippi, below the city. Having endeavored, without success, to induce the legislature of Louisiana promptly to suspend the writ of *habeas corpus*, and sensible that delay was dangerous, he assumed the responsibility, and superseded their deliberations, by declaring the city and environs of New Orleans under martial law.

The expected British force appeared off Pensacola, early in December, and on the 22d effected a landing of their troops, about fifteen miles southeast of New Orleans. The American gunboats on Lake Borgne, only five in number, were previously attacked by a force of forty-three British boats, and captured, after a gallant defence, on the 14th of December.

With the exception of the Kentucky troops, 2,250 in number, all the forces expected had arrived previous to the 21st of December. The Kentucky troops arrived on the 4th of January. The Tennessee troops, under General Carroll, were about 2,500 in number. The remaining portion of the American forces consisted of Coffee's brigade of mounted men, the Mississippi dragoons, the Louisiana militia, two regiments of United States regular troops, and a company of marines and artillery.

On the approach of the enemy being announced to General Jackson, on the 22d of December, he resolved to march, and that night give them battle. He therefore advanced, at the head of about 2,000 men, and the following day a battle took place with a detachment of about 2,500 of the British army, nine miles below New Orleans. The enemy's force was increased during the day to four or five thousand, with which the Americans maintained a severe conflict of more than an hour, and retired in safety from the ground; with the loss of but 24 killed, 115 wounded, and 74 made prisoners, while the British loss, in killed, wounded, and prisoners, was about 400.

General Jackson now withdrew his troops to his intrenchments. four miles below the city. On the 28th of December, and the 1st of January, these were vigorously cannonaded by the enemy, but without success.

On the morning of the 8th of January, General Pakenham, commander-in-chief of the British, advanced against the American intrenchments with the main body of his army, numbering more than twelve thousand men.

Behind their breastworks of cotton bales, which no balls could penetrate, six thousand Americans, mostly militia, but the best marksmen in the land, silently awaited the attack. When the advancing columns had approached within reach of the batteries, they were met by an incessant and destructive cannonade ; but, closing their ranks as fast as they were opened, they continued steadily to advance, until they came within reach of the American musketry and rifles. The extended American line now presented one vivid stream of fire, throwing the enemy into confusion, and covering the plain with the wounded and the dead.[*]

In an attempt to rally his troops, General Pakenham was killed ; General Gibbs, the second in command, was mortally wounded, and General Keene severely. The enemy now fled in dismay from the certain death which seemed to await them. General Lambert, on whom the command devolved, being unable to check the flight of the troops, retired to his encampment. On the 18th, the whole British army hastily withdrew, and retreated to their shipping.

The heartfelt joy at the glorious victory achieved on one side of the river was clouded by the disaster witnessed on the other. A small body of the American forces was stationed on the right bank of the river. They were attacked by eight hundred chosen British troops, under Colonel Thornton, and compelled to retreat.

The loss of the British in the main attack on the left bank has been variously stated. The killed, wounded, and prisoners, ascertained on the next day after the battle, by Colonel Hayne, the inspector-general, places it at 2,600 ; General Lambert's report to Lord Bathurst makes it 2,070. The loss of the Americans in killed and wounded was but thirteen.[†]

On the 20th of January, 1815, General Jackson, with his army, returned to New Orleans. The general glow excited at beholding his entrance into the city, at the head of a victorious army, was manifested by all those feelings which patriotism and sympathy inspire. All greeted his return, and hailed him as their deliverer. The 23d was appointed a day of thanksgiving. Jackson repaired to the cathedral, which was crowded to excess. Children, robed in white, strewed his way with flowers, and an ode was recited as he passed. A *Te Deum* was sung, and Bishop Dubourg delivered an address, which he concluded by presenting the general with a wreath of laurel.

Martial law still prevailed in New Orleans, and in February General

* Wilson's United States.   † Eaton.

Jackson arrested Mr Louallier, a member of the legislature, on a charge of exciting mutiny among his troops, by a publication, on the 10th of February, in the Louisiana Gazette, stating that a treaty of peace had been signed. Louallier applied to Judge Hall for a writ of habeas corpus, which was immediately granted. Instead of obeying the writ, the general arrested the judge, and sent him from the city on the 11th of February. On the 13th of the same month, an express reached headquarters, from the war department at Washington city, announcing the conclusion of peace between Great Britain and the United States, and directing a cessation of hostilities. The previous unofficial intelligence on the 10th had been received by Mr. Livingston, through Admiral Cochrane, of the British fleet.

On being restored to the exercise of his functions, Judge Hall ordered General Jackson to appear before him, to show cause why an attachment for contempt should not be awarded, on the ground that he had refused to obey a writ issued to him, detained an original paper belonging to the court, and imprisoned the judge. The general obeyed the summons, and appeared in court in the garb of a citizen, to receive the sentence of the court, having previously made a written defence. The judge sentenced the general to pay a fine of one thousand dollars, which he paid. A sum was soon raised by the people, to relieve him from the payment, but he declined to receive it. The amount, with interest, was subsequently refunded to Jackson, by act of Congress, in 1844.

The war being ended, and the militia having been discharged, and returned to their homes, General Jackson left New Orleans for Nashville, where he arrived in May, 1815, and was received by his fellow-citizens with the most cordial feelings. An address was delivered at the courthouse, in behalf of the citizens, welcoming his return. He then retired to his family residence, to repair a broken constitution, and to enjoy that repose to which, for eighteen months, he had been a stranger.

The annunciation of the triumphant defence of New Orleans was, in every section of the United States, hailed with acclamation. The legislatures of many of the states voted to him their approbation and thanks, for what he had done. The Congress of the United States did the same, and directed a gold medal to be presented to him, commemorative of the event.

The president, on the resignation of General Thomas Pinckney, in 1815, appointed General Jackson commander-in-chief of the southern division of the United States. Toward the close of the autumn of 1815, he visited Washington city, and on his way met with continued demonstrations of respect from the people. At this period, Colonel Burr wrote from New York, to his son-in-law, Ex-Governor Alston, of South Carolina, dated November 20, 1815, recommending the adoption of measures to bring forward the nomination of General Jackson, as a candidate for president of the United States, previous to the nomination of James Monroe by a congressional caucus. which was then anticipated to take place in December following, "Nothing is wanting," says Burr, "but a respectable nomination before the proclamation of the Virginia caucus, and Jackson's success is inevitable. Jackson is on his way to Washington. If you should have any confidential friend among the members of Congress from your state, charge him to caution Jackson against the perfidious caresses with which he will be overwhelmed at Washington." On the 11th of December, Colonel Burr wrote to Governor Alston, saying, that, since the date of his last, "things are wonderfully advanced. These will require a letter from yourself and others, advising Jackson what is doing—that communications have been had with the northern states, requiring him only to be passive, and asking from him a list of persons to whom you may address your letters." To this letter Governor Alston replied, on the 16th February, 1816, informing Colonel Burr, that his letter was received in January, "too late, of course, had circumstances been ever so favorable, to be acted upon in the manner proposed. I fully coincide with you in sentiment; but the spirit, the energy, the health, necessary to give practical effect to sentiment, are all gone. I feel too much alone, too entirely unconnected with the world, to take much interest in anything."*

It appears, from this correspondence, that accidental circumstances alone, prevented the public nomination of General Jackson by his native state, as a candidate for president, at a very early period after the war with Great Britain, and caused the bringing forward of his name to be deferred until the last term of Mr. Monroe's administration, viz., in 1822. In the spring of 1816, General Jackson again visited New Orleans. After stationing the army in the southern section of his division, he concluded a treaty with the Indians, the object of which was to obtain from them the relinquishment of all the claim they pretended to have to lands within the limits of the United States, and which had been previously ceded by them.

In the year 1818, the services of General Jackson, in his military capacity, were again called into requisition. The Seminole Indians, of Florida, had shown their hostility to the United States, by committing depredations on the southern frontiers. General Gaines had been ordered by the president, in October, 1817, to take the necessary measures for the defence of the inhabitants of that section of the Union. He accordingly built three forts, and proceeded to expel the Indians, who resisted him, as far as was in their power, and committed various outrages. At the mouth of Flint river, the Indians fell in with a party of forty men, under Lieutenant Scott, all of whom they killed but six, who escaped by swimming.

When the news of this massacre reached General Jackson, he raised an army of two thousand five hundred volunteers, and mustered them as in the service of the United States. After a rapid march, he arrived with his army, on the 1st of April, at the Mickasucky villages, which were de-

* Davis's Life of Burr.

serted on his approach. Having burnt the villages, he marched to St. Marks, then a Spanish post on the Appalachee bay, in Florida.

Two persons, who were traders with the Indians, namely, Arbuthnot, a Scotchman, and Ambrister, a British lieutenant of marines, were taken prisoners by Jackson, near St. Marks, and confined. They were both accused of exciting the Indians to hostility against the United States, and supplying them with arms and ammunition. They were tried by a court-martial, consisting of officers of the militia, and found guilty. One of them was sentenced to be shot, and the other to be hung, and their execution took place by order of General Jackson.

About the middle of May, General Jackson arrived at the Escambia, near Pensacola, having been informed that a body of hostile Indians had been harbored at that place. He took possession of Pensacola and Fort Barancas, notwithstanding a remonstrance from the governor of the territory. Two Indian chiefs, who were captured, were hung, by order of General Jackson, under circumstances which he deemed justifiable, but for which he was censured by many.

On the 2d June, 1818, General Jackson addressed a letter to the secretary of war, at the close of which he says : " The Seminole war may now be considered as at a close ; tranquillity is again restored to the southern frontier of the United States, and, as long as a cordon of military posts is maintained along the gulf of Mexico, America has nothing to apprehend from either foreign or Indian hostilities. The immutable principles of self-defence justified the occupancy of the Floridas, and the same principles will warrant the American government in holding it, until such time as Spain can guaranty, by an adequate military force, the maintaining of her authority within the colony."

After the campaign in Florida, General Jackson returned to Nashville, and shortly afterward he resigned his commission in the army. During the session of Congress, in January, 1819, he visited Washington, when his transactions in the Seminole war became the subject of investigation by Congress. After a long and exciting debate on the subject, resolutions of censure, for his proceedings in Florida, were rejected in the house of representatives, by a large majority, and his course was sustained by the president and a majority of the cabinet, although the Spanish posts in Florida were restored.

When the congressional investigation had terminated favorably to General Jackson, he visited the cities of Baltimore, Philadelphia, and New York, and various other parts of the United States, being received with enthusiasm by his friends in all quarters, and with distinguished attention by the public authorities and others.

In June, 1821, the president appointed him governor of Florida, which office he accepted, and in August he took possession of the territory, according to the treaty of cession. The Spanish governor, Callava, having refused to give up certain public documents, deemed of importance, he was taken into custody, by order of Governor Jackson, and committed to prison. The papers being found, under a search-warrant issued by Jackson, Callava was immediately set at liberty. Jackson remained but a few months in Florida ; for, disliking the situation, and disapproving of the extent of powers vested in him as governor, he resigned the office and again retired to Tennessee. President Monroe offered him the appointment of minister to Mexico, which he declined in 1823.

In July, 1822, General Jackson was nominated by the legislature of Tennessee as a candidate for president of the United States. This nomination was repeated by assemblages of the people in several other states. In the autumn of 1823, he was elected by the legislature a senator from Tennessee, and took his seat in the senate of the United States in December, 1823. He voted for the protective tariff of 1824.

The popularity of General Jackson with the people of the United States, was shown at the presidential election of 1824, when he received a greater number of electoral votes than either of his competitors, namely, ninety-nine. Mr. Adams received eighty-four, Mr. Crawford forty-one, and Mr. Clay thirty-seven. The election consequently devolved on the house of representatives, where, by the constitutional provision, the decision is made by states. Mr. Adams was elected by that body, receiving the votes of thirteen states ; General Jackson seven states ; and Mr. Crawford four states. The result caused much dissatisfaction among the friends of General Jackson, but a large proportion of those who had supported Mr. Crawford, as well as most of those who had supported Mr. Clay, preferred Mr. Adams to General Jackson.

During General La Fayette's visit to the United States in 1824–'5, he passed through Tennessee, and was received by General Jackson, at the Hermitage, with his accustomed hospitality.

After the election of Mr. Adams to the presidency, the opposition to his administration was soon concentrated upon General Jackson as a candidate to succeed him. In October, 1825, he was again nominated by the legislature of Tennessee for president, on which occasion he resigned his seat in the senate of the United States, in a speech delivered to the legislature, giving his views on public affairs. During the exciting canvass which resulted in his election to the presidency in 1828, by a majority of more than two to one, of the electoral votes, over Mr. Adams, he remained in private life.

In January, 1828, he was present, by invitation, at New Orleans, at the celebration of the anniversary of his victory. Before departing for Washington, in 1829, to take the reins of government, he met with a severe affliction in the death of Mrs. Jackson. This loss bore heavily upon him for some time, and he came into power with gloomy feelings. He reached the national capital early in February, in a plain carriage.

The events of his administration are given in the Statesman's Manual, to those pages the reader is referred for the history of eight years of his life. In 1832 he was re-elected to the presidency; and at the close of his second term, in March, 1837, having published a farewell address to the people of the United States, he retired to his favorite residence, at the Hermitage, in Tennessee, where he passed the remnant of his days, generally a quiet, but not disinterested spectator of public events. He was a member of the presbyterian church, and religious faith and confidence appear to have soothed and cheered all the latter period of his life. For the last year or two of his life he was infirm of body, but retained his mental faculties undiminished up to the hour of his decease, which took place on the 8th of June, 1845. His countrymen throughout the United States joined in testimonials of respect to his memory. He left no blood relatives, and his estate was bequeathed to members of the Donelson family, who were the relations of Mrs. Jackson.

The violence of political strife will long confuse men's judgment of the character and abilities of General Jackson; but all will accord to him the praise of great firmness, energy, decision, and disinterestedness; of remarkable military skill, and ardent patriotism. With regard to his qualifications and services as a statesman, his countrymen have been and are divided in opinion. It is, perhaps, not yet time to speak decisively on this point, but it must be left for the impartial verdict of posterity.

The personal appearance and private character of General Jackson are thus described by his friend and biographer, Mr. Eaton, previous to his election to the presidency: " In the person of General Jackson is perceived nothing of the robust and elegant. He is six feet and an inch high, remarkably straight and spare, and weighs not more than one hundred and forty-five pounds. His conformation appears to disqualify him for hardship; yet, accustomed to it from early life, few are capable of enduring fatigue to the same extent, or with less injury. His dark blue eyes, with brows arched and slightly projecting, possess a marked expression; but when from any cause excited, they sparkle with peculiar lustre and penetration. In his manners he is pleasing—in his address commanding; while his countenance, marked with firmness and decision, beams with a strength and intelligence that strikes at first sight. In his deportment there is nothing repulsive. Easy, affable, and familiar, he is open and accessible to all. Influenced by the belief that merit should constitute the only difference in men, his attention is equally bestowed on honest poverty as on titled consequence. His moral character is without reproach; and by those who know him most intimately he is most esteemed. Benevolence in him is a prominent virtue. He was never known to pass distress without seeking to assist and to relieve it."

M. Van Buren

a-
ed,
ial
om
pe-
on a
to
etch
e all
ed ;"

were
ther-
ed in
of the
was a
en an
disposi-
also of
me dis-
d ; first
f whom
able law-
offices,
ss at his

e family
er amia-

BIOGRAPHICAL SKETCH

OF

MARTIN VAN BUREN.

THE seven presidents of the United States whose lives and administrations we have noticed in the preceding pages, it will have been observed, were all descended from emigrants from the British isles ; their official terms occupy a space of forty-eight years, or nearly half a century from the adoption of the constitution ; and each of them had witnessed the period when the nation acquired her independence. We now enter upon a new era, and, leaving those whose early lives carry our memories back to the men and the times of our revolutionary struggle, we proceed to sketch the career of our eighth president, who, to use his own words, " unlike all who have preceded him, was born after the revolution was achieved ;" belonging, also, to another race by descent, as well as to a later age.

The ancestors of Mr. Van Buren, both paternal and maternal, were among the early emigrants from Holland to the colony of New Netherlands, now the state of New York. The family have always resided in the ancient town of Kinderhook, Columbia county, on the east bank of the Hudson river. The father of the president, Abraham Van Buren, was a farmer of moderate circumstances, who is represented to have been an upright and intelligent man, of strong common sense, and pacific disposition. The maiden name of the mother of the president was Hoes, also of Dutch descent. The name was originally Goes, and was one of some distinction in the history of the Netherlands. She was twice married ; first to Mr. Van Alen, by whom she had two sons and a daughter, all of whom have been many years deceased. James I. Van Alen was a respectable lawyer of Columbia county, who was honored with several important offices, and with whom his younger half-brother was connected in business at his entrance to the bar.

The mother of Mr. Van Buren was distantly connected with the family of his father before their marriage. She was distinguished for her amiable disposition, sagacity, and exemplary piety.   She survived until 1818, four years after the death of her second husband.

Martin Van Buren is the eldest son of these parents.   He was born at Kinderhook, December, 5, 1782.   At an early age he exhibited indications of a superior understanding.   His opportunities of instruction were limited, probably on account of the moderate property of his father, who had two other sons, and two daughters.[*]

After acquiring the rudiments of an English education, he became a student in the academy, in his native village.   He there made considerable progress in the various branches of English literature, and gained some knowledge of Latin.   It may be inferred, however, that all these acquisitions were not great in amount, as he left the academy, when but fourteen years of age, to begin the study of his profession.

At that early period he evinced a strong passion for extempore speaking and literary composition.   Even at that early age, too, he is represented, by those who knew him, to have had a spirit of observation, with regard to public events, and the personal dispositions and characters of those around him, which gave an earnest of his future proficiency in the science of politics and of the human heart.

In the year 1796, at the age of fourteen, Mr. Van Buren commenced the study of the law, in the office of Francis Sylvester, Esq., a respectable lawyer of Kinderhook.   The courts of law in the state of New York have adhered more closely to the English forms of practice than has been done in most of the other states.   The period of study preparatory to admission to the bar, was seven years, for candidates who, like the subject of this memoir, had not the benefit of a collegiate education.

The management of cases in courts held by justices of the peace, not unfrequently devolved upon students at law.   The early indications of ability as a speaker and reasoner, which were exhibited by Mr. Van Buren, occasioned his almost incessant employment in trials in these courts, from the earliest period of commencing the study of his profession.   His father was a firm whig in the revolution, and a democrat in the days of John Adams ; and the son was educated in the same principles, and of course formed his most intimate connexion with persons of the same political faith.   The democratic party was then a small minority in the town and county of his nativity.   His political opinions, as well as his talents, led to his employment by the members of his own party, in their controversies with regard to personal rights, and rights of property.   It often happened that, in the management of cases, he encountered men of age, talent, and high standing in the profession.

At this early period Mr. Van Buren was an ardent and active politician. It was his constant habit to attend all meetings of the democratic party, to study with attention the political intelligence of the day, and to yield his

* For part of this memoir we are indebted to Professor Holland's Life of Van Buren.

most zealous aid to the principles he held to be true. As early as 1800, when only in his eighteenth year, and still a student at law, he was deputed by the republicans in his native town, to attend a convention of delegates to nominate a candidate for the legislature. He had similar marks of the confidence of his political friends, on other occasions during his minority.

The last year of Mr. Van Buren's preparatory studies was passed in the city of New York, in the office of Mr. William P. Van Ness, and under his direction. This gentleman was a native of Columbia county, but at that time a distinguished member of the bar in the city of New York, and a very conspicuous leader of the democratic party. In this situation Mr. Van Buren had every possible advantage for improvement; and his thirst for knowledge, together with his aptitude in acquiring it, enabled him to make great advances.

Mr. Van Ness was a devoted and intimate friend of Colonel Aaron Burr at that time vice-president of the United States; and in the feud which sprung up after the presidential election, between the respective friends of the president and vice-president, Mr. Van Ness advocated the cause of Colonel Burr, through the public press, with signal ability. Through the medium of this gentleman, Mr. Van Buren was introduced to the notice of the vice-president, who was led, by his knowledge of the young lawyer's activity and influence in his native county, as well as by a quick-sighted observation of the future eminence promised by his early display of talent, to treat him with marked attention, and to make every reasonable effort to secure his favorable regard. The tact and ability displayed by Colonel Burr in the great political contest which resulted in elevating Mr. Jefferson and himself to the highest offices in the gift of the people, and the reputation he had acquired as a leader of the party, caused him to be looked upon as an oracle of political wisdom, particularly by young and ardent democrats, who were desirous of availing themselves of instruction from so experienced and influential a source. Among the maxims of Colonel Burr for the guidance of politicians, one of the most prominent was, that the people at elections were to be managed by the same rules of discipline as the soldiers of an army; that a few leaders were to think for the masses; and that the latter were to obey implicitly their leaders, and to move only at the word of command. He had, therefore, great confidence in the machinery of party, and that system of regular nominations in American politics of which he may perhaps be considered one of the founders. Educated as a military man, and imbibing his early views with regard to governing others, in the camp, it is not surprising that Colonel Burr should have applied the rules of military life to politics, and always inculcated the importance of discipline in the ranks of a party, to insure its ultimate success. In no part of the United States have these party rules been more constantly and rigidly enforced, than among the demo-

11

crats of the state of New York ; and to their steady adherence to them may be attributed the long succession of triumphs which have been achieved by the party with whom Mr. Van Buren has uniformly acted.

In November, 1803, in the twenty-first year of his age, Mr. Van Buren was admitted, as an attorney at law, to the bar of the supreme court in the state of New York, and immediately returned to his native village, to commence the practice of his profession.   He formed a partnership in business with the Hon. James I. Van Alen, a half-brother on his mother's side, and a gentleman who was considerably his senior.   The bar of Columbia county, at that time, embraced some of the most distinguished members of the legal profession in the state of New York, among whom were William W. Van Ness (afterward a judge of the supreme court of the state), Elisha Williams, Thomas P. Grosvenor, and Jacob R. Van Rensselaer.   Other names might be mentioned as then in the field of competition upon which the youthful subject of this sketch then entered. The state of political parties at the period shows the difficulties with which he contended.

At the time when Mr. Van Buren commenced his professional career, the violence of party spirit was extreme throughout the country.   The state of New York was fearfully agitated by its influence ; and in the county of Mr. Van Buren's residence, political dissensions were carried to the greatest extremities.   The administration of the federal government had then passed, after a violent struggle, into the hands of the democratic party , but it was considered by no means certain that their ascendency would be of long continuance.   In the state of New York generally, the democratic party triumphed in the elections after 1800 ; but in the county of Columbia the federal party long held the reins of power.   The landholders in Kinderhook and its vicinity had inherited large estates from a long line of wealthy ancestors, and had exercised, by proscription, an influence over their tenants and the more recent emigrants, analogous in its nature, and almost in its extent, to the baronial prerogatives of feudal lords.   The great mass of mercantile and professional men in the county were dependent upon these wealthy freeholders for patronage, as also were the laborers and mechanics, in a still greater degree.   The members of these families were generally federalists, and looked with anxious disapprobation upon any efforts to extend popular rights.   Toward the champions of the democracy they exhibited neither liberality nor toleration, but carried on a warfare against them, both in public and private, of the most obstinate and embittered character.

Mr. Van Buren's early exhibition of energy and talent attracted their attention, and no ordinary pains were taken to detach him from the connexion he had chosen with the democracy.   The gentleman with whom he had studied his profession, Mr. Sylvester, and his relative and partner in business, Mr. Van Alen, were federalists, and by their example and advice endeavored to withdraw him from a political connexion which they viewed as wrong, and injurious to his prospects in business. " Firmly fixed in the political faith of his father, who was a whig in the revolution, an anti-federalist in 1788, and an early supporter of Jefferson, the subject of this memoir," says his biographer, " shrunk not from the severe tests which were applied to the strength and integrity of his convictions. Without patronage, comparatively poor, a plebeian by birth, and not furnished with the advantages of a superior education, he refused to worship, either at the shrine of wealth or power, but followed the dictates of his native judgment, and hesitated not, in behalf of the cause which he thus adopted, to encounter the utmost violence of his political enemies."

Thus connected with the democratic party, he naturally became the vindicator, not only of their political faith, but of their legal rights. The conflicts in which he engaged, rapidly invigorated and enlarged his natural powers. It was soon seen that he was able to cope with the ablest of his opponents in the local courts. In 1807 he was admitted as a counsellor in the supreme court, where he was brought into more immediate collision with the most distinguished members of the profession. In 1808 he was appointed surrogate of Columbia county, soon after which he removed to the city of Hudson, where he resided during seven years, and rapidly advanced toward a high rank in his profession. In 1815 he was appointed attorney-general of the state, at which time his practice in the courts had become extensive and lucrative. His career as a lawyer occupies a period of twenty-five years, and was closed in the spring of 1828.

Mr. Van Buren was married in 1806, to Miss Hannah Hoes, who was distantly related to him before their marriage. The intimacy which resulted in this union, was formed in very early life. His ardent attachment to her was evinced on all occasions until the period of her decease, by consumption, in 1818. This lady left him a family of four sons, and Mr. Van Buren has since remained a widower.

Having thus noted the professional and private life of Mr. Van Buren, it remains briefly to sketch his career as a politician and statesman.

His first active participation in political affairs, was in the great contest which preceded the elevation of Mr. Jefferson to the presidency, in 1801. At the early age of eighteen years we find him intrusted with the expression of the political views of a portion of the democratic party, as we have already stated, in being chosen a delegate to a convention. His abilities were put in requisition on that occasion, in preparing an address to the electors of the district in which he resided.

In the spring of 1804, he made his first appearance at the polls as an elector. At that election Morgan Lewis and Aaron Burr (then vice-president of the United States) were the opposing candidates for governor of New York. Both belonged to the democratic party, but the former received the regular nomination of a majority of the democrats in the legislature, while the latter was supported by a smaller section of the party, and a portion of the federalists.   In Columbia county Colonel Burr was warmly sustained by many leading politicians, among whom were some of Mr. Van Buren's best friends.   During his own residence as a student at law in the city of New York, with Mr. William P. Van Ness, a friend of Burr, he had received many flattering marks of attention from the vice-president.   But true to his own principles and the spirit of his party, Mr. Van Buren gave his vigorous and unhesitating support to Mr. Lewis, at the hazard of a temporary estrangement from several valued democratic friends.

In 1807 the antagonist candidates for governor were Morgan Lewis and Daniel D. Tompkins.   The latter was then the candidate of a large majority of the democratic party ; Governor Lewis receiving the support of the federalists and a few democrats.   Tompkins was elected by a large majority of votes ; he received Mr. Van Buren's most zealous and decided support on this occasion, also in 1810 and 1813 ; the views of these two leaders of the democratic party generally agreeing on the prominent political questions of the period.

In 1808 Mr. Van Buren was appointed surrogate of Columbia county, and retained the office until February, 1813, when, the federalists having obtained the ascendency in the state, he was removed.   It may be here remarked, that the administration of Mr. Jefferson, during its whole course, received his constant support.   The non-intercourse act, the embargo, and other measures of Mr. Jefferson, received his hearty concurrence.   He warmly defended and justified the course of George Clinton, then vice-president of the United States, in giving his casting vote, in February, 1811, against the bill for renewing the charter of the first bank of the United States.   It is curious to notice in this place, that the renewal of the charter of the bank was recommended by Mr. Gallatin, then secretary of the treasury, and sustained in the senate by William H. Crawford, two gentlemen whom Mr. Van Buren joined with others in recommending for president and vice-president of the United States in 1824.

In 1812 Mr. Van Buren was, for the first time, a candidate for an elective office, having been nominated as a senator from the counties then comprising the middle district of the state.   His opponent was Edward P. Livingston, belonging also to the democracy ; a man of wealth and powerful family connexions, and supported by the bank democrats and the entire federal party of the district.   The contest was one of the most violent ever known in the state, and resulted in the election of Mr. Van Buren, by a majority of about 200, in an aggregate of twenty thousand votes Thus, in the thirtieth year of his age, he was placed in the highest branch of the legislature of his native state.

Previous to his election, the democratic members of the legislature of

New York had, in the spring of 1812, nominated De Witt Clinton for president of the United States, and in November, 1812, the succeeding legislature met for the purpose of choosing presidential electors. On this occasion Mr. Van Buren took his seat in the senate, and voted for the electoral ticket which was elected, and which gave Mr. Clinton the vote of the state. In supporting the nomination of Mr. Clinton, Mr. Van Buren consulted what he believed to be the wishes of the majority of the democratic party of the state. At the same time, he was an open and decided advocate of all the strong measures proposed against Great Britain during the session of Congress in 1811–'12, the war included. And, though in the choice of electors Mr. Clinton received the votes of some of the federal members of the legislature of New York, and was also supported by that party in other states, Mr. Van Buren's relations to it were entirely unaltered. At the same session he was placed upon the committee of the senate to answer the governor's speech, which answer he prepared and reported. It vindicated the justice of the war, and urged a vigorous prosecution of it. At the ensuing session of the legislature, which commenced in 1813, the political relations previously existing between Mr. Clinton and Mr. Van Buren were dissolved, and never again resumed. From the commencement of his legislative career, Mr. Van Buren gave to all war measures the most decided and vigorous support ; among which was a plan for raising troops by classification. He supported the re-election of Governor Tompkins, and, as chairman of the committee which made the nomination, he prepared the address to the republican electors of the state.

In 1815, Mr. Van Buren received the appointment of attorney-general of the state of New York. The same year he was appointed by the legislature a regent of the university. In the spring of 1816 he was re-elected to the senate for the further period of four years.

When the project of internal improvement in the state of New York, by canals from Lakes Erie and Champlain to the Hudson river, was brought before the legislature, in 1816, it was sustained with zeal and ability by Mr. Van Buren, who on this occasion received the personal thanks of Mr. Clinton, the great advocate of the measure, for his exertions in favor of the same.

In 1817 De Witt Clinton was nominated for governor of the state of New York, in place of Daniel D. Tompkins, who had been elected vice-president of the United States. Mr. Van Buren acquiesced in this nomination, though it was contrary to his individual wishes and opinions, and he had used his exertions to prevent it. The distinguished talents of Mr. Clinton, and his zealous efforts in promoting the great interests of the state, had so far won the respect and confidence of the people, that there was comparatively little opposition to his election, after his nomination. But, though he received nearly the unanimous vote of both the great political parties throughout the state, the result proved that it was a deceitful calm which followed the election, and that, as a large portion of the democratic party were deadly hostile to the newly-elected governor, the elements for bitter party strife were only temporarily concealed.

We must now revert to the presidential election of 1816, for the purpose of showing Mr. Van Buren's course in that affair, and the bearing that election had on the politics of New York.

During the war, Governor Tompkins and Mr. Van Buren were considered the leaders of the democratic party in the state of New York. The public services and great personal popularity of Governor Tompkins, induced President Madison to offer him a seat in his cabinet, as secretary of state, which office, however, he declined. As the secretary of state was then, according to established usage, heir apparent to the presidential chair, and the admitted favorite of the president for the time being, Governor Tompkins considered the offer of Mr. Madison as a commitment on the part of the administration to support him for the next president. It was therefore expected, in the state of New York, that Tompkins would succeed Madison as president; and at a celebration of the return of peace, at Albany, in February, 1815, a splendid transparency was displaced, with the names of Tompkins and Crawford inscribed thereon. This indicated that the latter was expected to be nominated for vice-president.

The democratic members of the New York legislature, in February, 1816, instructed the members of Congress from the state to sustain the claims of Tompkins, and Mr. Van Buren visited Washington to aid his friend in the nomination. But his claims were not pressed in the congressional caucus which met in March, 1816; the contest in that body was between Monroe and Crawford, and the former was nominated by a small majority over the latter. Governor Tompkins was nominated for vice-president, a result at which he was much disappointed. Finding Tompkins out of the question for president, a majority of the New York delegation was rather ardent in support of Crawford. Mr. Van Buren took no decided part in the matter. Mr. Hammond, who was one of the New York delegation, remarks, that "if at Albany Mr. Van Buren was ardent in the support of Tompkins, at Washington, to say the least, he was philosophically calm and cool."[*]

From this time forward Mr. Van Buren co-operated with the leading democratic politicians of Virginia; and when it was determined by them that Mr. Crawford should be the successor of Mr. Monroe as president, Mr. Van Buren gave him his most zealous, though unsuccessful support, in the political campaign of 1824.

Having determined to oppose the administration of Governor Clinton, Mr. Van Buren, being then a member of the senate of the state, commenced, in 1818, the organization of that portion of the democratic party

* Hammond's Political History of New York.

who were dissatisfied with the election of the governor. Hence arose the formation, under his auspices, of a small but formidable and secret association of politicians at the seat of the state government, which received from their political opponents the cognomen of "the Albany regency." It was composed of persons holding offices under the state and the general governments, and a few other influential citizens of the democratic party; and by skill, position, and party discipline, with the aid of a party press, this regency is supposed to have swayed the power and destinies of the state for more than a quarter of a century. It is proper to mention, however, that the existence of this Albany regency has been generally denied by the friends of Mr. Van Buren.

The difficulties in the democratic party between the respective friends of Mr. Van Buren and Governor Clinton, soon widened into an open rupture. A large majority of the democrats of the state followed Mr. Van Buren, while most of the friends of the canal policy, and the great body of the federal party, with few exceptions, sustained Governor Clinton. The council of appointment being devoted to the views of Governor Clinton, in July, 1819, removed Mr. Van Buren from the office of attorney-general, the duties of which he had discharged for more than four years, during which period he had also been a member of the senate.

The opposition to Governor Clinton constantly increased in violence, and in the senate of the state there was a majority against him during the whole period of his administration. The most strenuous exertions were made by his democratic opponents to prevent his re-election. Mr. Van Buren took the lead in their efforts, and the vice-president, Daniel D. Tompkins, was prevailed upon to become the opposing candidate for governor. The contest was close and animated, Mr. Clinton being successful by a majority of 1,457 out of 93,437 votes. The whole number of votes against him on his former election was but twenty-two more than his present majority. Both houses of the legislature, and the council of appointment, however, were decidedly anti-Clintonian. A restoration to the office of attorney-general was now tendered to Mr. Van Buren, but was declined by him.

The legislature having failed to elect a senator of the United States, in 1819, in place of Mr. Rufus King, whose term of service expired that year, a pamphlet was prepared by Mr. Van Buren, shortly before the meeting of the succeeding legislature, in 1820, in favor of the election by the democratic party of Mr. King to the senate for another term of six years. Mr. King, it will be remembered, was a federalist, and had been one of the most prominent leaders of that party in the United States, while they acted as an organized political body. Mr. Van Buren and his friends had refused to vote for Mr. King in the legislature of 1819, but his election was now urged on democrats, in consequence of his having supported the last war; his revolutionary services, and his present opposition to Mr.

Clinton, were assigned as further reasons for supporting him. The real object of the pamphlet was to draw in a portion of the federalists throughout the state, to the support of Mr. Tompkins in the then approaching election. The friends of Mr. Van Buren were in the minority in the legislature, and were, therefore, compelled to choose between Mr. King, or some other federalist, and a friend of Governor Clinton. The result was, the election of Mr. King, by the legislature, by a vote nearly unanimous, the Clintonians also supporting him.

At the same session of the legislature, a resolution was adopted, instructing their senators, and requesting the representatives of the state in Congress, to oppose the admission of Missouri, or any other territory into the Union, without making the prohibition of slavery therein an indispensable condition of admission. The senate concurred in this resolution from the assembly without division or debate, and among the senators Mr. Van Buren, though it was not brought before the legislature by his agency. Still, he must be regarded as having concurred, at that time, in the sentiment of the resolution thus adopted by the legislature.*

Mr. Van Buren was, in February, 1821, elected by the legislature of New York, a member of the senate of the United States, in place of Nathan Sanford, whose term of service expired in March, 1821. Mr. Sanford was a democrat and a candidate for re-election, but at the legislative caucus, which was attended by eighty-two democratic members, Mr. Van Buren received fifty-eight votes, and Mr. Sanford twenty-four. The Clintonians and federalists in the legislature voted for Mr. Sanford, who received sixty votes, and Mr. Van Buren eighty-six votes. Thus it will be observed, that Mr. Sanford was the preference of a large majority of the legislature, and without the agency of a caucus nomination Mr. Van Buren could not have been chosen.

A convention to revise the constitution of the state of New York, was chosen by the people in 1821, and assembled in August of that year. Mr. Van Buren, then United States senator elect, was elected a member of the convention, by the democrats of Otsego county, although he then resided in the city of Albany.

In this convention, which comprised many of the most able and influential men in the state, Mr. Van Buren took an active and leading part. There were three classes of politicians in that body : first, those opposed to any important changes in the old constitution of 1777, except the abolition of the council of appointment and the council of revision ; second, those in favor of moderate changes in the constitution, of the abolition of the freehold qualification for voters, and the reasonable extension of the elective franchise ; third, the radicals, or those in favor of universal suffrage, and an entire and radical change in the form of government. Mr. Van Buren belonged to the second of these classes, and his course in the

* Holland.

convention was generally conservative. He advocated an extension of the right of suffrage to citizens paying taxes, being householders, and working on the highways, or doing military duty; he expressed his fears that the extension of the elective franchise contemplated by some of the amendments proposed, would not be sanctioned by the public approbation, and would occasion the rejection of the whole by the people. He said, "he was disposed to go as far as any man in the extension of rational liberty; but he could not consent to undervalue this precious privilege so far as to confer it, with an indiscriminating hand, upon every one, black or white, who would be kind enough to condescend to accept it." By the first constitution of New York, no distinction was made with regard to *color*, in the qualifications of electors. In the convention, a proposition to restrict the right of voting to *white* citizens, was rejected by a majority of four votes. Mr. Van Buren voted with the majority, or in favor of continuing the right of voting to colored citizens; but subsequently supported a proposition, which was adopted, requiring colored voters to possess a freehold estate of the value of two hundred and fifty dollars. Mr. Van Buren opposed the election of justices of the peace by the people, and the convention adopted a plan proposed by him, by which the executive of the state, through the judges of the county courts, controlled those appointments. This plan only continued in operation about four years, when the constitution was amended, giving the choice of justices to the people. The proposition which was adopted by the convention to reorganize the judiciary of the state, and sanctioned by the party with which he acted, was opposed by Mr. Van Buren, the only effect of it being to displace the judges then in office. On the whole, it may be remarked, that his course in the convention to revise the constitution, was considered honorable to him as a stateman, and, with few exceptions, was approved by candid men of all parties.

In December, 1821, Mr. Van Buren took his seat in the senate of the United States, his colleague from New York at this time being the Honorable Rufus King. On his first appearance in the senate, he was placed on the committee of finance, and on the committee on the judiciary. He took an active part in debate on most of the important subjects which were agitated in that branch of Congress during his senatorial career. He supported Colonel Johnson's efforts to abolish imprisonment for debt on actions in the United States courts. He proposed amendments to the judiciary system of the United States, and advocated a bankrupt law, to include corporations as well as persons. With regard to the public lands, he was in favor of a proposition to vest the lands in the states in which they were situated on " some just and equitable terms."

When the question of a successor to Mr. Monroe for the presidency was agitated, Mr. Van Buren took an early and decided part in favor of Mr. Crawford, whose election he labored to bring about by the aid of party machinery and discipline, particularly the system of regular nominations, as established in the state of New York, and had been practised by the democratic party in previous nominations of president and vice-president, by a caucus of members of Congress.   The congressional caucus which nominated Mr. Crawford, in February, 1824, proved a signal failure, as it was attended by only about one fourth of the whole number of the members of Congress.   In the state of New York, where the friends of Mr. Van Buren had defeated a law proposed to provide for the choice of presidential electors by the people, and retained the choice in the legislature, Mr. Crawford only obtained five of the thirty-six electoral votes of the state.   The election of president devolved on the house of representatives, and Mr. Adams was elected on the first ballot, receiving the vote of New York, although the friends of Mr. Van Buren adhered to Mr. Crawford.

· In the gubernatorial election in the state of New York, in 1824, the party which acted with Mr. Van Buren met with a decisive defeat, and De Witt Clinton was elected governor.   The next year, however, the party recovered its power in the state ; but Mr. Clinton was re-elected in 1826, and continued in office until his death, in February, 1828.

Mr. Van Buren took an active part in the opposition which was organized against the administration of Mr. Adams immediately after his election to the presidency.   He opposed the mission to Panama, and most of the bills for internal improvement.   His personal feelings were adverse to a high tariff of duties for protection, but as his constituents were generally in favor of protective duties, he voted for the tariff laws of 1824 and 1828.

In February, 1827, Mr. Van Buren was re-elected to the United States senate for another term of six years, by the legislature of New York. Circumstances, however, soon occurred to cause his resignation.   He was zealous and active in sustaining General Jackson for the presidency in opposition to Mr. Adams, in 1828.   Governor Clinton, who was also favorable to the election of Jackson, died suddenly, in February, 1828.   This event induced the political friends of Mr. Van Buren to nominate him for governor of the state, to succeed Mr. Clinton, and he was elected to that office in November, 1828.

Having resigned his seat in the senate of the United States, Mr. Van Buren entered upon the duties of the office of governor, January 1, 1829. His message to the legislature was remarkable for the attention bestowed upon banks and the currency.   On the 20th of January, in a brief message, he introduced to the legislature the celebrated safety-fund system. This plan originated with the Hon. Joshua Forman, and was by him laid before Mr. Van Buren.   It was somewhat modified by the suggestion of the latter, and finally adopted by the legislature.   The safety-fund system combined the moneyed interests of the state in a league of mutual dependence, but the experience of a few years proved its inadequacy to answer public expectation.

Mr. Van Buren remained but a short time in the chief magistracy of his native state. On the 12th of March, 1829, he resigned the office of governor, in consequence of his appointment as secretary of state of the United States. Of this appointment, General Jackson (who was said to have intended to have offered it to Governor Clinton, had he lived) said, in his letter to the democratic members of the legislature of New York, in February, 1832 : " In calling him [Mr. Van Buren] to the department of state, from the exalted station he then occupied, I was not influenced more by his acknowledged talents and public services, than by the general wish of the republican party throughout the Union."

An account of Mr. Van Buren's course as secretary of state, together with the causes of the dissolution of the cabinet, will be found in the Statesman's Manual, Jackson's administration. In June, 1831, Mr. Van Buren retired from the office of secretary of state, and was immediately appointed by the president minister to Great Britain. He arrived in London in September, 1831, and was received with distinguished favor at the court of St. James.

Soon after the meeting of Congress, the president submitted the nomination of Mr. Van Buren to the senate. He was rejected by that body, in consequence of their disapproval of the instructions which he issued, while secretary of state, to Mr. M'Lane, our minister to England, in reference to the West India trade.

The democratic party condemned the rejection of Mr. Van Buren as an act of political persecution, and vindicated the propriety of his course. The democratic members of the legislature of New York addressed a letter to the president, expressing their indignation at what they deemed a proscriptive act of the senate, and their high respect for the public and private character of Mr. Van Buren. The president, in reply, assumed the entire responsibility of the instructions condemned by the senate ; declared they were " the result of his own deliberate investigation and reflection, and still appeared to him to be entirely proper and consonant to his public duty."

On the 22d of May, 1832, Mr. Van Buren was nominated as a candidate for vice-president, by a national democratic convention assembled at Baltimore, and at the same time with the renomination of General Jackson for president. The result was the triumphant election of both to the respective offices to which they were nominated, Mr. Van Buren receiving the same number of electoral votes as General Jackson, with the exception of those of Pennsylvania, the democracy of which state refused to give him their vote ; and it was given to William Wilkins, of that state.

Mr. Van Buren returned from England to triumph over his political opponents, by being elevated to the second office in the government. He was inaugurated as vice-president on the 4th of March, 1833, and presided over the senate for four years, when in session ; during which he had the good fortune to escape the censure of all parties.   In 1833 he accompanied General Jackson in his tour to the eastern states.

To secure the support of the democratic party as a candidate for the presidency, as successor to General Jackson, whose favor and good wishes he already possessed, Mr. Van Buren seems to have relied upon an avowal of hostility to a national bank, and on a national convention for the nomination of president and vice-president.   Accordingly, we find him giving as a sentiment, at a public entertainment, " Uncompromising hostility to the United States bank ; the honor and interest of the country require it ;" which toast was adopted as a motto, by the democratic party. We also find the most strenuous efforts made to reconcile Pennsylvania to a national nominating convention, which efforts were finally successful.

On the 20th of May, 1835, the Jackson democratic convention met at Baltimore, for the nomination of a candidate to succeed General Jackson as president, also a vice-president of the United States.   About 600 delegates were in attendance ; and as all were selected as friends of Mr. Van Buren, he received the unanimous vote of the convention, for president. Colonel Richard M. Johnson, of Kentucky, was nominated for vice-president.   These nominations, it was well understood, received the express approbation of General Jackson, and the influence of the administration was, of course, exercised in favor of the election of these candidates.

The result of the vote by the electoral colleges was 170 for Mr. Van Buren. including Michigan (3), which was informal, and 124 for all other candidates.   There was no choice of vice-president by the people, in consequence of the state of Virginia refusing to vote for Colonel Johnson.   He received 147 electoral votes, including Michigan, and there were 147 for all other candidates.   Colonel Johnson was, thereupon, elected by the senate, agreeably to the constitution.

Mr. Van Buren was inaugurated as president, on the fourth of March, 1837.   The history of the four years of his administration is given in the STATEMAN's MANUEL, to which we refer for this part of his life.   In May, 1840, he was nominated for re-election, by a convention of his political friends, but such was the unpopularity of his measures as chief magistrate of the nation, that the election of 1840 resulted in the total defeat of Mr. Van Buren and the party with which he was connected, and the triumphant success of the whig candidates, General Harrison and Mr. Tyler, to the presidency and vice-presidency.   The electoral votes for Harrison were 234—for Van Buren 60.

General Harrison succeeded Mr. Van Buren, as president, on the 4th of March, 1841 ; soon after which the ex-president left Washington for his seat at Kinderhook, Columbia county, New York, near the Hudson river, to which retreat he gave the name of " Lindenwold."   He attended on the occasion of the funeral honors which were paid to General Harrison in the city of New York, in 1841.

Having acquired, during an active professional and political life, a large fortune, Mr. Van Buren retired to his estate before mentioned, to enjoy the possession of his wealth, and retaining the confidence of the large and powerful party of his countrymen which had sustained him. His friends, however, were not willing that he should rest under the political sentence which had been pronounced against him, as they deemed, under fortuitous circumstances. It was argued that, as an act of justice to him, he should be elected for another term to the presidency, to place him in history along side of Jefferson, Madison, Monroe, and Jackson, who were considered as the four democratic presidents, each of whom had been honored with a second term in the presidential chair. The most strenuous efforts, therefore, were made to effect the nomination of Mr. Van Buren for the presidency, in 1844 ; and when the democratic national convention met to nominate a president, in May of that year, there was an apparent majority of his friends in that body. But a new element was introduced into the political canvass for the presidency, by the democratic party, namely, the annexation of Texas to the United States. To that measure Mr. Van Buren had expressed himself adverse, in some particulars, in a letter to a southern gentleman, which was published previous to the meeting of the convention. Some of his friends regretted that he had not inserted a clause in his letter which, looking to the certain extension of the limits of the republic, would have been satisfactory to the democrats of the south. After protracted ballottings, it was found that Mr. Van Buren could not obtain the vote of two thirds of the delegates to the convention, as required by their rules. His name was therefore withdrawn, and James K. Polk, of Tennessee, received the nomination for president.

In the nomination of Mr. Polk, Mr. Van Buren cordially acquiesced, and urged upon his political friends the propriety and importance of sustaining the same in good faith. By the efforts of the democrats of New York, the election of Mr. Polk was effected, the popular majority in that important state, which turned the scale in favor of the democratic candidates, being but about one per cent. on the whole number of votes.

We conclude this brief memoir of Mr. Van Buren with the following notice of his personal appearance and character, from his life, by Professor Holland, written, of course, with all the partiality of friendship :—

" In personal appearance, Mr. Van Buren is about the middle size ; his form is erect (and formerly slender, but now inclining to corpulence), and is said to be capable of great endurance. His hair and eyes are light, his features animated and expressive, especially the eye, which is indicative of quick apprehension and close observation ; his forehead exhibits in its depth and expansion, the marks of great intellectual power. The physiognomist would accord to him penetration, quickness of apprehension, and benevolence of disposition.   The phrenologist would add unusual reflective faculties, firmness, and caution.

" The private character of Mr. Van Buren is above all censure or suspicion.   In the relations of father and son, of husband, brother, and friend, he has always displayed those excellencies of character and feeling which adorn human nature.   Extending our view to the larger circle of his personal friends, rarely has any man won a stronger hold upon the confidence and affection of those with whom he has been connected.   The purity of his motives, his integrity of character, and the steadiness of his attachments, have always retained for him the warm affection of many, even among the ranks of his political opponents.

" The ease and frankness of his manners, his felicitous powers of conversation, and the general amiableness of his feelings, render him the ornament of the social circle.   Uniting in his character, firmness and forbearance ; habitual self-respect and a delicate regard for the feelings of others ; neither the perplexities of legal practice, nor the cares of public life, nor the annoyance of party strife, have ever been able to disturb the serenity of his temper, or to derange for a moment the equanimity of his deportment.   He has with equal propriety mingled in the free intercourse of private life, and sustained the dignity of official station."

W. H. Harrison

the Indians
throughout

BIOGRAPHICAL SKETCH

OF

WILLIAM HENRY HARRISON.

THE family of Harrison is one of the most ancient and honorable in the history of Virginia. Among the early settlers of the colony was a lineal descendant of that General Harrison who bore a distinguished part during the civil wars of England, in the army of the Commonwealth.

Benjamin Harrison (of the same stock), the father of the subject of this memoir, was one of the signers of the declaration of independence, and among the most prominent of the illustrious men of his eventful day, having filled the executive chair of the "Old Dominion" at a period when moral daring and personal fearlessness were essential to the incumbent of that station. He was previously an active and influential member, both of the house of burgesses in Virginia, and of the continental Congress. Of the former body he was repeatedly chosen speaker, and in the latter, in June, 1776, he introduced the resolution which declared the independence of the colonies, and on the following fourth of July, as chairman of the committee of the whole, he reported the more formal declaration to which his signature is affixed. Governor Harrison died in 1791, after the most eminent public services, and the expenditure of an ample fortune in the cause of his country.

William Henry Harrison, the third and youngest son of the preceding, and ninth president of the United States, was born on the 9th of February, 1773, at Berkeley, on the James river, in Charles city county, Virginia. On the death of his father, he was placed under the guardianship of his intimate friend, Robert Morris, of Pennsylvania, the great financier of the revolution. Young Harrison was educated at Hampden Sidney college, in his native state, and afterward applied himself to the study of medicine as a profession. But before he had completed his course of studies as a physician, the barbarities of the Indians upon the western frontiers excited a feeling of indignation throughout the country. Harrison resolved to give up his profession and join the army raised for the defence of the Ohio frontier. His guardian, Mr. Morris, attempted to dissuade him from his purpose, but his resolution was not to be shaken, and on communicating with General Washington, that distinguished man cordially approved of the patriotic determination of the son of his deceased friend and associate.

At the age of nineteen, Harrison received from President Washington the commission of ensign in a regiment of artillery, and joined his corps at Fort Washington, on the Ohio, in 1791. A reinforcement was ordered to march for Fort Hamilton, on the Miami, a task which it required no ordinary degree of courage to accomplish, as they had to pass through forests infested by hordes of the hostile tribes, and Harrison was chosen to the command of the body of men forming the escort. The dexterity and skill which he displayed in the prosecution of this arduous duty, gained for him the approbation of his commanding officer, General St. Clair. He rapidly gained the entire confidence of his officers, and in 1792 was promoted to the rank of lieutenant.

During the following year Harrison joined the new army under the command of General Anthony Wayne, an officer whose intrepidity and daring impetuosity, accompanied at the same time with consummate skill, during the war of the revolution, obtained for him the title of " Mad Anthony." It was a period, indeed, worthy of such a man, for the repeated successes and incursions of the savage enemy had not only infused among the people generally, but even throughout the army itself, such terror and dread of these merciless foes, as greatly to paralyze their energies, and to render the duties of the commander extremely arduous and difficult. The instructions, indeed, which were forwarded by Congress to General Wayne, contained the following ominous expression : " Another defeat would prove inexpressibly ruinous to the reputation of the government ;" and consequently, in such a critical juncture, every available facility was rendered him. On the 25th of May, 1792, he repaired to Pittsburg, which was selected as the place of rendezvous. The newly-organized army consisted of a major-general, four brigadier-generals, with their respective staffs, the commissioned officers, and over five thousand rank and file ; which was designated, " the legion of the United States." Although this collective force had the effect of partially restoring the spirit and energy of the soldiers, they continued to desert in considerable numbers. To remedy this evil, General Wayne applied himself at all intervals of leisure, to the disciplining of his troops, with unremitting assiduity. Thus it must be obvious, that the early military career of Harrison had but few attractions for those who were not, like him, actuated solely by the true spirit of generous patriotism.

Finding all amicable negotiations with the Indians unavailing, no alternative was left to General Wayne but to adopt the most rigid and decisive measures; accordingly we find him breaking up his winter quarters, about the end of April, 1793, and transporting his army in boats down the Ohio to Fort Washington, an outpost situated upon the site now occupied by the city of Cincinnati. Having at length received instructions from the secretary of war to commence active operations, he left Fort Washington in October, 1793, and advanced with his army along the southwestern branch of the Miami, where he took up his position, and erected fortifications. To this post he gave the name of Greenville, and here the army went into winter quarters. General Wayne sent a detachment to take possession of the ground on which General St. Clair and his army had been defeated by the Indians two years before. Harrison volunteered for the service, and was accepted by the commander.

The battle-ground was taken possession of by the troops, and a fortification erected, to which the name of Fort Recovery was given. The bones of the soldiers slain on the fatal 4th of November, 1791, were collected, and interred with military honors. The artillery lost on that occasion were recovered; and on the return of the troops from the expedition, the name of Lieutenant Harrison, among others, was mentioned by General Wayne, in his general order of thanks to the officers and men for their gallant conduct on the occasion.

On the 30th of June, 1794, a fierce attack was made by large numbers of the Indians, upon the newly-constructed works at Fort Recovery; they were, however, repeatedly repulsed, and the arrival of a body of militia from Kentucky enabled General Wayne to force them to retreat with great loss.

Being reinforced by a body of mounted volunteers from Kentucky, General Wayne advanced seventy miles to Grand Glaize, in the very heart of the Indian territory. Here he erected a fort which he called Defiance, at the confluence of the Maumee and Au Glaize rivers.

Agreeably with his instructions, General Wayne renewed his overtures of peace, which again being rejected by the Indians, he prepared to bring them to a decisive settlement. In the heroic engagement or battle of the Maumee rapids, which ensued, on the 20th of August, 1794, the consummate skill of the general, as well as the valor of his troops, were alike resplendent with the important consequences which resulted from the action. In the official account of this battle, we also find the name of Lieutenant Harrison complimented by the commander-in-chief as his "faithful and gallant aid-de-camp," in having "rendered the most essential service by communicating his orders in every direction, and for his conduct and bravery, in exciting the troops to press for victory." The Indians now proposed to capitulate with General Wayne, and the result was, a treaty of peace was concluded, by which the United States obtained cessions of considerable tracts of land, as well as secured tranquillity to the border settlements. The news of Wayne's victory had a favorable effect upon

12

our pending negotiations in London, and was supposed to have enabled the American special minister, Mr. Jay, to secure the assent of Lord Grenville to the surrender to the United States of all the forts held and occupied by the British in the northwest, within the jurisdiction of our government. Thus undisputed possession of the territory northwest of the Ohio was obtained, and emigration to that country received a new and favorable impulse.   •

Not long after the close of this campaign, Harrison was promoted to the rank of captain ; and as an additional proof of the confidence reposed in his discretion and ability, by General Wayne, he was placed in command of Fort Washington. While at this place (where Cincinnati now stands), being now about twenty-one years of age, he married the daughter of John Cleves Symmes, the founder of the Miami settlements. " She has been," says Mr. Hall in his memoir, " the faithful companion of this distinguished patriot during the various perils and vicissitudes of his eventful life, and still lives to witness the maturity of his fame, and the honors paid him by a grateful country."

He continued in the army till the close of the year 1797, when, soon after the death of General Wayne, as peace had been ratified with the Indians, and the opportunity to serve his country in the field appeared to exist no longer, he resigned his commission. Scarcely had this event transpired, than he was appointed, by President Adams, secretary and ex officio lieutenant-governor of the northwestern territory. While in this station, in October, 1799, he was elected, by the legislature of that territory, their first delegate to Congress. He was at this time about twenty-six years of age, and took his seat in the house of representatives, at the first session of the sixth Congress, in 1799. Previous to proceeding to the seat of government, he resigned his office of secretary of the territory. In 1798, the northwestern territory contained five thousand white male inhabitants, and was admitted as a matter of right to the second grade of government, provided for in the ordinance of 1787. At that time great unanimity prevailed in the territory on political questions ; though the states were rent, and almost torn asunder, by party strife. The election of the elder Adams had met with general approbation among the people of the territory, and resolutions had been passed at popular meetings to sustain his administration, against the encroachments of France. An address was adopted by the legislature of 1799, to John Adams, president of the United States, approving of his administration. But few individuals were to be found who then advocated the election of Mr. Jefferson against Mr. Adams. Harrison having early imbibed democratic opinions, was one of the few who preferred Jefferson. His election as delegate to Congress was not effected by a party vote ; the same legislature which adopted the address to Mr. Adams with only five dissenting votes, elected Harrison by eleven votes, against ten for Arthur St. Clair, Jr.

Though he represented the territory but one year in Congress, Harrison obtained some important advantages for his constituents. He introduced a joint resolution to subdivide the surveys of the public lands, and to offer them for sale in small tracts; he succeeded in getting that measure through both houses, in opposition to the interest of speculators who were, and who wished to be, the retailers of land to the poorer class of the community. His proposition became a law, and was hailed as the most beneficent act that Congress had ever done for the territory. It put it in the power of every industrious man, however poor, to become a freeholder, and to lay a foundation for the future support and comfort for his family. At the same session, he obtained a liberal extension of time for the pre-emptioners in the northern part of the Miami purchase, which enabled them to secure their farms, and eventually to become independent and even wealthy.*

Congress, at that session, divided the northwestern territory, by establishing the new territory of Indiana, of which Harrison was appointed governor. He also received the appointment of superintendent of Indian affairs, and resigned his seat in Congress.

The new territory of Indiana then included not only the present state of Indiana, but those of Illinois, Michigan, and Wisconsin. The seat of government was at Vincennes, a village on the Wabash. This large extent of territory, however, contained but a scanty population, and therefore according to the laws of the United States, the executive authority of the territorial government was very extensive. The governor possessed the power of negativing bills passed by the territorial legislature, of enforcing the laws, of the appointment of magistrates, of making townships, confirming grants of lands, and other equally onerous duties; which rendered the office one of peculiar and important responsibility. To one of less rigid integrity and scrupulous regard for the public interest, the opportunity was offered for much personal aggrandizement, and the acquisition of great wealth; but this, it is well known, was never dreamed of by the individual who then occupied the trust. He never availed himself of the opportunity to enhance his own private interests, directly or indirectly; and his honor and disinterested integrity were not even suspected.

Besides being superintendent of Indian affairs, he was made commander-in-chief of the militia, and all the officers below the rank of general received their commissions from him. In 1803, Mr. Jefferson appointed him sole commissioner for treating with the Indians. By virtue of this authority, Harrison negotiated, in 1804, a treaty with the Sacs and Foxes, establishing amicable relations with those tribes, and obtaining the cession of the largest tract of country ever yielded by the Indians at one time since the settlement of America, consisting of upward of fifty millions of acres of the valuable region between the river Illinois and the Mississippi, with

* Judge Burnet's Letters.

a northern boundary stretching from the head of Fox river to a point on the Wisconsin, thirty-six miles above its mouth. Considerable tracts of land between the Ohio and the Wabash, and extending from Vincennes westward to the Mississippi, were likewise purchased by annuities, from the Delaware and Miami Indians.

Such was the high estimation with which his conduct as governor was regarded, that for a period of thirteen years, at the termination of every successive term of office, he was reappointed at the earnest solicitation of the people of the territory, and with the public expression of the most flattering approbation on the part of the president of the United States ; and this, notwithstanding the changes in the administration—his first appointment having been made by Mr. Adams, his second and third by Mr. Jefferson, and the fourth by Mr. Madison.

During the year 1806, the plans of the general government for the civilizing and conciliating the Indian tribes, were entirely frustrated by the intrigues of the two celebrated chiefs of the Shawnee tribe, Tecumseh, and his brother, the Prophet. The aim of these chiefs was, to induce all the surrounding tribes to form a common league against the United States, for the purpose of preventing the settlements of the whites from being extended farther west, and by making a simultaneous attack on the frontier settlements, to expel the whites from the valley of the west. The American government was informed that British emissaries from Canada were employed in forming alliances with the most powerful chiefs, and fomenting their hostility against the people of the United States.

A variety of circumstances invested the Prophet with a prodigious influence over the tribes ; he is said, indeed, to have possessed the faculty of appealing to them more eloquently and gracefully than almost any other Indian. He resorted to every imposture and stratagem of which even an Indian is capable, for the furtherance of his project ; asserting, among other absurdities, that he possessed the power of preventing the bullets of the enemy from taking effect upon his adherents.

In the course of the subsequent year, Governor Harrison received intelligence of the hostile demonstration of the congregated tribes ; in consequence of which he sent a messenger to the Shawnees, strongly reprehending their conduct, and warning them to refrain from further listening to the fatal instructions of the Prophet. The deluded and superstitious Indians, however, disregarding the admonition, continued to collect in great numbers in the vicinity of Fort Wayne, and having entirely neglected their cornfields, they soon began to find themselves in a state bordering upon starvation. Again, in the hope of conciliating them, the governor, with his accustomed humanity and policy, ordered them supplies forthwith from the public stores.

The Prophet had now selected as his residence, a spot situated on the upper part of the Wabash, called Tippecanoe, where his infatuated followers soon rejoined him.   In July he visited the governor, when, with a cunning and duplicity common to his race, he loudly protested against the evils of war and the use of spirituous liquors, and affected the greatest desire for amity with the Americans.   Governor Harrison was, however, too shrewd to be thus imposed upon by these specious pretences, and in his reply told him, that he might come forward and exhibit any title he might have to the lands transferred by the treaty, and that if it was found to be just and equitable, they would be restored, or an ample equivalent given for them.   But the results of the interview proved anything but satisfactory to the absurd requirements of the Prophet, as he claimed all the lands that had formerly belonged to the several tribes, and insisted that their disposal could not have been valid but with the consent of all the tribes in common.   Accordingly, he redoubled his exertions for the concentration of the western tribes, studiously guarding his movements from the governor, lest he should become apprized of his intentions.   He had about him, at this time, one thousand warriors, and these continued to commit the most atrocious deeds of depredation along the frontier, till at length even the governor's house was scarcely considered secure from their hostile attacks.

In September, 1809, a council was convened at Fort Wayne, at which Governor Harrison negotiated with the Miamies, Delawares, Pottawatomies, and Kickapoos, for purchasing a large tract of country on both sides of the Wabash, extending along that river more than sixty miles above Vincennes.   Tecumseh, who was at this time absent on a visit to some distant tribes, expressed, on his return, great dissatisfaction, and threatened the lives of some of the chiefs who had concluded the treaty.   On hearing this, the governor invited him to come to Vincennes, with the direction that he should not be allowed to bring with him more than thirty warriors ; this restriction, however, he evaded, on the pretext of suspecting some treachery on the part of the Americans, and he, instead, brought with him four hundred men, armed.   This circumstance alone was sufficient to excite the suspicions of the governor, but when, added to this, the chief refused to hold the council at the appointed place, which was under the portico of the governor's house, and insisted on having it take place under some adjacent trees, his apprehensions were still greater.   At this council, held on the 12th of August, 1810, Tecumseh again complained of the alleged injustice of the sale of their lands ; to which the governor replied, that as the Miamies had found it to their interest to make the disposal, the Shawnees, from a distant part of the country, could have no just ground for remonstrance, or right to control them in their disposing of the property.   Tecumseh fiercely exclaimed, " It is false !" and giving a signal to his warriors, they sprang upon their feet, and seizing their war-clubs and tomahawks, they brandished them in the air, ferociously fixing their eyes upon the governor.   The military escort of Harrison on the occasion numbered only twelve, and they were not near his person, having been directed by him to retire for shelter from the heat, under some adjacent trees.

In this critical moment of excitement, the guard immediately advanced, and would have instantly fired upon the infuriated Indians, had it not been for the coolness and self-possession of Harrison, who, restraining them, and placing his hand upon his sword, said, in a calm, but authoritative tone, to Tecumseh: " You are a bad man : I will have no further talk with you. You must now take your departure from these settlements, and hasten immediately to your camp." On the following day, however, finding he had to deal with one so dauntless, Tecumseh solicited another interview, apologizing for his insolent affront. The precaution was now taken to defend the town, and place the governor in an attitude more likely to command their respect, by having two companies of militia in attendance. At this council the chiefs of five powerful tribes rose up, declaring their determination to stand by Tecumseh ; to which the governor replied, that " their decision should be reported to the president ;" but adding, that he would most certainly enforce the claims of the treaty. Still anxious, if possible, to conciliate, rather than coerce the haughty chief, he paid him a visit the next day at his camp, when, repeating in substance what has already been given, Tecumseh replied : " Well, as the great chief is to determine the matter, I hope the Great Spirit will put sense enough into his head to induce him to direct you to give up this land. It is true, he is so far off that he will not be injured by the war ; he may sit still in his town and drink his wine, while you and I will have to fight it out." Shortly after this, the Shawnee chief withdrew to Tippecanoe, the residence of the Prophet, where he is said to have formed a combination of several tribes.

In July, 1811, another messenger was sent, commissioned by the governor to demand the surrender of two Pottawatomie murderers who were at Tippecanoe, but without the desired effect. Indeed, such were the lawless and daring outrages which they now committed upon the more exposed settlements on the frontier, that at length, through the earnest solicitations of the people, directions were forwarded from the federal government to the governor to march forthwith against the Prophet's town with an armed force, with this injunction, however, " to avoid hostilities of any kind or degree not absolutely necessary." These instructions rendered the situation of Harrison one of great delicacy and responsibility, being equivalent to allowing the Indians the right of commencing the action.

The receipt of the governor's authority was hailed by the settlers with great enthusiasm, as they had long suffered severely from the incursions of these ruthless marauders, and, reposing unlimited confidence in the skill and courage of their commander, they viewed the measure as the only one which could insure to them the continued possession of their property. and even of life itself. Accordingly, a hastily-assembled force.

consisting of about nine hundred men, commenced its march from Fort Harrison, which was situated about sixty miles above Vincennes, on the 28th of October. After a protracted and somewhat difficult advance, through open prairies, thick woods, and deep ravines, constantly on their guard against surprise, they arrived within sight of the Indian town. Here the enemy began to appear in considerable numbers. Wearied with the fatigue of their expedition, after a brief conference, the troops encamped ; every precaution having been taken, however, to prevent surprise by the savages, as they apprehended an attack during the night.

In conformity to a general order, the troops rested in their clothes and accoutrements, their loaded muskets by their sides, and their bayonets fixed. The officers, of course, rested like the soldiers—the governor being ready to mount his horse in an instant. The night passed without a sound, and the governor and his aids rose a quarter before four, and were conversing around their fire. The new moon had risen, but afforded little light, the sky being obscured by ragged clouds, from which a drizzling rain fell at intervals. In a few minutes the signal would have been given to call the men to arms, when a blaze from Indian rifles lighted up the scene. The savage warriors had crept up as near the sentries as possible, in the darkness, intending to rush forward and despatch them without noise, and then fall upon their sleeping comrades in the camp. But one sentinel discovered what he rightly suspected to be an Indian creeping through the grass, and instantly gave him the contents of his musket. That discharge settled all doubts. Our men were started to their feet by a tremendous yell from a thousand savages, accompanied by a general volley from their rifles, and a desperate charge into the camp. But they found as warm a welcome. Every man rose on the post assigned him, with musket in hand, ready for thrust or rally. The attack centred on the sharp rear angle of the left flank, which was for some minutes exposed to a destructive fire. But this angle was promptly reinforced, and the enemy beaten back with loss, several being killed within the lines of the camp. The fires, which first served to direct the aim of the savage rifle, were promptly extinguished. But the enemy had still the advantage of shelter in the bushes and grass, and a knowledge of the ground, which rendered a charge upon them in the darkness almost certain destruction. An attempt was volunteered to rout them from their hiding-places, by a company headed by the gallant Jo. Daviess, but repulsed with loss, and among the slain was their lamented leader.

The battle still raged with desperation. The savages were bent on victory, and well organized for the contest, advancing and retreating by a rattling noise made with deers' hoofs. The governor was at every point of danger ; animating and encouraging the men where hardest pressed, ordering up companies to their support, and courting danger as if unaware of its existence. All of the troops were conducted and formed by himself. It need not be added that every man stood his ground like a hero.

The battle was fierce, but daylight at length broke on the combatants—a light most welcome to our harassed soldiers—fatal to their foes. The assailed left flank was fully strengthened, the dragoons were mounted, and, covered by them, a general charge was made upon the now baffled and dispirited enemy. The Indians gave way, and were driven into a swamp, through which the cavalry could not force their way. Repulsed in all quarters, the savages disappeared from the field, and the battle of Tippecanoe was at an end.

Such was the extraordinary influence that the Prophet retained over the minds of the infatuated savages, that they are said to have fought with desperate and unprecedented valor on the occasion, although he himself was snugly ensconced on some neighboring eminence, simply regaling his devotees with war-songs, and practising absurd incantations. Tecumseh also was, at the time, absent on a visit to some southern tribes.

The battle of Tippecanoe may unquestionably be regarded as one of the most memorable and decisive engagements ever fought with the Indians. The intrepidity and self-possession of the commander was also signally displayed on the occasion. "In the very heat of the action," says a contemporary record, "his voice was distinctly heard, giving orders in the same cool and collected manner with which he had been accustomed when on drill or parade ; nor was his personal bravery less conspicuous, as he was ever foremost in leading on his troops, regardless of the peculiar danger to which he was exposed, from the circumstance of his being known to most of the Indians, and being the marked object of their hostility." In the message of the president to Congress, of December 18th, 1811, the following allusion is made, which is as highly complimentary to the conduct of the governor as it is expressive of the importance attached to the action itself, and it must have been no mean achievement which could win from the federal government such decided terms of approbation and honor. "While it is to be lamented," says Mr. Madison, "that so many valuable lives have been lost in the action which took place on the 9th ult., Congress will see with satisfaction the dauntless spirit and fortitude victoriously displayed by every description of troops engaged, as well as the collected firmness which distinguished their commander on an occasion requiring the utmost exertion of valor and discipline."*

The decisive blow which Harrison had struck against the Indian

---

* The legislatures of Kentucky and Indiana also recorded their resolutions regarding the conduct of Harrison in this battle. The former is as follows : " *Resolved*, That in the late campaign against the Indians on the Wabash, Governor Harrison has, in the opinion of this legislature, behaved like a hero, a patriot, and a general ; and that, for his cool, deliberate, skilful, and gallant conduct in the late battle of Tippecanoe, he deserves the warmest thanks of the nation."

power had produced a more powerful effect than all the admonitory efforts of years had accomplished. Several of the tribes sent deputies to wait upon him with assurances of renewed amity, and a disavowal of further connexion with the hostile bands of Tecumseh. In February, 1812, intelligence that no less than eighty Indians, deputies from all the tribes who were engaged in the late hostilities, except the Shawnees, had arrived at Fort Harrison, on their way to Vincennes. Suspicion being again naturally aroused, from their numbers, that a new treachery was designed, the governor sent an expostulation, requiring them to come in less numbers and unarmed; they, however, not only delivered up their arms, but evinced the subdued deportment of men who had been taught to respect the authority of him with whom they had come to treat.

Meanwhile, Tecumseh had returned from the south, and notwithstanding the sad reverse which his cause had sustained during his absence, the commencement of hostilities with Great Britain found for him an ally both able and eager to second his plans, thus neutralizing in part the lasting advantages which otherwise might have accrued from the victory of Tippecanoe. He consequently again renewed his intrigues with greater activity than ever, and he caused the commencement of fresh depredations along the widely-extended borders of Ohio, Indiana, and Illinois, at points so distant from each other as to distract public attention and create an almost universal panic. The declaration of war with Great Britain, it will be remembered, took place on the 18th of June, 1812, and the western people suffered more than has been commonly supposed, from their almost defenceless exposure to the incursions and barbarities of the infuriated savages. Not that they were less energetic in the popular enthusiasm of the measure, for they are known never to have chosen the inane and timid counsel of preferring security to honor, while they emulated, by their deeds of noble daring, in this, the second great struggle for liberty, the stern republican virtues which their patriotic ancestors evinced in the first.

Here, again, are we called upon to notice the distinguishing preference which the whole people of the west bestowed upon General Harrison, in their nomination of him to the head of their armies at a time when the highest order of talents was, of necessity, put in requisition. Governor Harrison was repeatedly honored by consultations from the several parts of the country, and in consequence of a communication received from Governor Scott, of Kentucky, he repaired to Frankfort; and while here he suggested plans of operation which, had they been given some days earlier, would have proved of the most important service in the preservation of Detroit, but which, unhappily for the country, had not been anticipated by the government itself.

The surrender of this city, and with it the army of Hull, had exposed the vast region including western Pennsylvania, Ohio, and what are now

Michigan. Indiana, Illinois, and Missouri, to the enemy's ravages.   About this time Governor Harrison received a communication from the war department, which informed him that he had been appointed a brigadier-general in the army of the United States.   It is a matter of regret that this appointment had not been conferred upon him at an earlier period, as in that case it is more than probable that the melancholy tragedy of the massacre at the river Raisin would never have occurred.   His situation again, at this time, was one of peculiar difficulty, from the paucity in the provisions and clothing of the troops ; the demand for these in the Atlantic cities, from the constant failure of the contractors, causing a deficiency which often became alarming.   Having received advices informing him that Fort Wayne had become infested by a body of Indians, and in danger of being reduced, Harrison's first movement was to hasten to its relief.   Accordingly, on the 5th of September, he marched for that place, but finding his troops were deficient in a supply of flints—a trifling but indispensable article—he was subjected to some delay ; but he reached his destination on the 9th of the same month.   On the 17th he received a despatch from the president, investing him with the command of the northwestern army, which then nominally amounted to about ten thousand men, undisciplined, unprovided, and scattered over a wide region ; added to which he had authority to employ officers, and to draw from the public stores ; which reposed in him a trust more extensive and important than was ever deputed to any officer of the United States, if we except, perhaps, Washington and Greene.   The immediate objects of the campaign now committed to the sole direction of General Harrison, were the recapture of Detroit by a *coup de main*, the reduction of Malden, in Upper Canada, and the protection of the northwestern border.   The point from which the principal movement upon the enemy was to be made, was the rapids of the Miami.   The military arrangements extended from Upper Sandusky, on the right, to Fort Defiance, on the left.   As it comes not within our province to enumerate the details of this campaign, we shall strictly confine our remarks to the movements of General Harrison, and even our notice of these will necessarily be very brief.

Harrison had scarcely reached his intended theatre of action, when he received intelligence of General Winchester's contemplated movement against the enemy ; he immediately ordered a corps of three hundred men to the rapids, and on the following morning he proceeded himself to Lower Sandusky, and there found that General Perkins had also prepared to send a battalion and artillery ; but owing to the delay in their transmission, from the bad condition of the roads, they failed to reach the river Raisin before the fatal disaster had occurred.   Harrison now determined to proceed to the rapids, to learn personally the situation of General Winchester.   In the meantime, however, a reinforcement had been despatched by Colonel Lewis, for the purpose of occupying the village of Frenchtown, and while on his way thither, General Harrison received the intelligence of the victory which had been gained on the preceding day.

He was finally enabled, on the 20th of January, to reach the camp. Hearing of Proctor's attack, he hastened with all his disposable force to the river Raisin, but was soon met by fugitives from the field of battle, from whom he ascertained the total defeat of Winchester's forces. The temerity of Winchester was the sole cause of his fall; while all that could have been done to prevent the disaster, was done by General Harrison; for had he received timely notice of the exigency of the case, his reinforcement would doubtless have terminated the action in our favor. On the 1st of February, the army having been reorganized and reinforced, their numbers now amounted to eighteen hundred men. Entertaining the confident expectation of ultimately accomplishing his purpose, General Harrison continued to make preparations with unremitting assiduity. He encamped for the winter at a fortified place which, in honor of the governor of Ohio, was called "*Camp Meigs.*" About this period Harrison, who was appointed major-general in the service of the United States, returned to Cincinnati, with the view of procuring and forwarding supplies of provisions and military stores. While engaged in the arduous duties of this campaign, he organized several minor expeditions against the Indians, in order to keep them in proper check.

Early in the spring of 1813, intelligence having been received of a contemplated expedition against Fort Meigs, by the British, accompanied by Tecumseh and six hundred warriors, General Harrison hastened back to the frontier, and immediately summoned three thousand troops from Kentucky, who reached Defiance on the 3d of May, while he himself arrived just in time to receive the enemy's attack. For five days their batteries kept up a constant shower of balls against our defences, although, through the skilful disposition of the commander, with comparatively little effect. Harrison, with his augmented forces, now made a vigorous and simultaneous attack on the enemy's batteries, and, having reduced them, preparations followed for a sortie from the fort, which resulted in triumphant success. The impetuosity of the charge proved irresistible, and, after a severe struggle, our troops drove the enemy from their batteries, notwithstanding they, including their Indian allies, nearly doubled their numbers. This action was one of the most desperate and sanguinary ever fought during the whole border war: it lasted, however, but forty-five minutes, during which time no less than one hundred and eighty were either killed or wounded of the American troops. Thus terminated the glorious defence of Fort Meigs. Harrison soon after left General Green Clay in command of the post.

The unceasing efforts of the British, and the restless spirit of Tecumseh, allowed our troops but little time to recover from their severe fatigues; for in less than two months (being early in July, 1813) the Indians assembled a formidable body of no less than five thousand warriors, and again invested the fortress. In consequence of this, Harrison had a fortification erected at Seneca town, about nine miles up the river, as a reserve for the better protection of his principal depôt at Upper Sandusky. The enemy remained but two days before the fortification, changing their route for Lower Sandusky. On the evening of the 29th, the general received information that the siege of Fort Meigs had been raised; it was of the utmost importance, therefore, that all the troops within reach should be immediately concentrated for the protection of the principal point of defence at Upper Sandusky. The enemy demanded the surrender of the fort, which being refused by its commander, Colonel Crogan, a cannonade was opened, after which they attempted an assault, but being met by a galling fire of musketry, they were repulsed with great loss, and obliged to make a precipitate retreat. On the 18th of August, Commodore Perry, with his fleet, arrived off Sandusky bay, and shortly afterward his celebrated action was fought, which so gloriously resulted in the capture of the enemy's whole fleet. Harrison, meanwhile, collected together his troops, and while Colonel Johnson marched for his station by way of the river Raisin, the general embarked on the 20th of September, with two brigades, for Bass island.

On the 27th the army again embarked, and made a descent upon the Canada shore. Surrounded by his gallant troops, General Harrison now proudly stood upon the ruined breastworks of Malden, from which destruction had been poured upon the frontier, and whence the firebrand and tomahawk of the Indian had gone forth in the work of desolation. In his despatches to the war department, Harrison thus writes : "I will pursue the enemy to-morrow, although there is little probability of overtaking him, as he has upward of one thousand horses, and we have not one in the army." He proceeded, accordingly, on the following day, to Sandwich, but Proctor had fled. "At a convention of the general officers, Harrison informed them," says M'Affee, "that there were but two ways of accomplishing their object ; one of which was to follow him up the strait by land ; the other, to embark and sail down Lake Erie to Long Point, then march hastily across by land twelve miles to the road, and intercept him." The former plan was unanimously preferred, and consequently adopted. The army rapidly advanced in pursuit of the enemy up the Thames to the Moravian towns. On the 5th of October the enemy were overtaken ; Proctor's position was flanked on the left by the Thames, and his right by a swamp, which was occupied by a horde of Indians under the celebrated Tecumseh. General Harrison, on this occasion, adopted a movement which, while it insured an easy victory, evinced a high degree of military skill and promptitude of character—one division of his infantry extending in a double line from the river to the swamp, opposite to Proctor's troops, and the other placed at right angles to the first, facing the swamp, with the view of preventing the Indians from turning his left flank, and getting into the rear. Observing the enemy's troops to be in open order, that is, with intervals of three or four between the files, which can never successfully resist a charge of cavalry, Harrison instantly ordered Colonel Johnson's mounted regiment, which occupied the front, to dash through the enemy's line in column. This command was brilliantly executed, and the attempt was triumphant, for the British were at once thrown into confusion, and our men wisely taking advantage of their disorder by attacking their broken line in the rear, they were compelled to surrender their arms, and thus a splendid and almost bloodless victory was virtuously achieved, rather by the consummate skill of the general than by the energies of his troops.

The contest with the Indian allies, however, was more severe, as they advanced and poured in a continuous and galling fire, not only upon the cavalry, but also the infantry, which for some time made a great impression upon them. Suddenly, however, the voice of command which had hitherto inspired their courage was hushed: the haughty chief, Tecumseh, had fallen. The Indians, as soon as the event became known, hastily decamped, leaving about thirty of their number dead where the chief had fallen. Thus ended this decisive engagement, which, together with the brilliant victory on the adjacent lake, rescued the whole northwestern territory from the depredations of the savage, and all the accumulated horrors of war; for the Indians, finding themselves no longer sustained by the British, sued for peace, and the result was, an armistice was granted, and finally an amicable arrangement with them ratified by the general government at Washington. The loss on both sides, in the battle of the Thames, was about fifty killed and wounded, while the prisoners taken by the American troops amounted to six hundred.

This event, so important to the security and honor of the country, was hailed with universal rejoicing and gratulations, while all parties participated in the most enthusiastic encomiums upon the magnanimous and heroic conduct of him through whose talents and skill it was accomplished. In his message to Congress of the 7th of December, 1813, Mr. Madison spoke of the result as "signally honorable to Major-General Harrison, by whose military talents it was prepared." And in his speech in Congress, Mr. Cheves thus also alludes to the same subject: "The victory of Harrison was such as would have secured to a Roman general, in the best days of the republic, the honors of a triumph He put an end to the war in the uppermost Canada."—"The blessings," said Governor Snyder, of Pennsylvania, in his message to the legislature of that state, "of thousands of women and children, rescued from the scalping-knife of the ruthless savage of the wilderness, and from the still more savage Proctor, rest on Harrison and his gallant army." Numerous other contemporaneous records might also be referred to in testimony of the nation's gratitude all of which, however, with the exception of the resolution which was adopted by both houses of Congress, it is needless to notice. This is as follows :—

"*Resolved, by the Senate and House of Representatives of the United States of America in Congress assembled*, That the thanks of Congress be, and they are hereby, presented to Major-General William Henry Harrison, and Isaac Shelby, late governor of Kentucky, and through them to the officers and men under their command, for their gallant and good conduct in defeating the combined British and Indian forces under Major-General Proctor, on the Thames, in Upper Canada, on the fifth day of October, 1813, capturing the British army, with their baggage, camp equipage, and artillery ; and that the president of the United States be requested to cause two *gold medals* to be struck, emblematical of this triumph, and presented to General Harrison and Isaac Shelby, late governor of Kentucky."

The pacification of the northwestern border no longer requiring his services, General Harrison despatched his troops to the Niagara frontier, with the view of assisting in the operations then going on in that quarter, although this formed no part of the plan of the campaign he had to execute.   On his arrival at Fort Niagara, preparations were being made for an expedition against Burlington heights ; these were, however, summarily arrested by the receipt of an order from the war department, directing him to send his troops to Sackett's Harbor, for the defence of that place. He accompanied them thither, and, having no right to command in that district, proceeded at once to Washington.   In every city through which he passed he was received with the most enthusiastic demonstrations of respect.   He remained in Washington but a few days, being desired by the president to hasten to Ohio, as his presence there would be of important service, both as regarded the peace of the border, the filling up of the regiments intended to be raised in the western states, and other measures then in anticipation.

It will be remembered that the secretary of war at this time was General Armstrong, who, from some unknown cause, appears to have imbibed a strong prejudice against General Harrison, as, from the plan of the campaign for 1814, submitted by him to the president, it was evident that Harrison would no longer be employed in any active service.   He also is known to have interfered, on more than one occasion during the winter, with the internal arrangements of the district which Harrison commanded, in contravention to all military etiquette.   These circumstances, when contrasted with the almost unlimited powers confided to him by the government during the two previous campaigns, evidently prove them to have been intended as a source of mortification to Harrison ; accordingly, he rendered his resignation, which, unfortunately for the country, as Mr. Madison was absent on a visit to Virginia, was, without consulting the president, accepted at the war department.   The president himself, in his reply to an appeal from Governor Shelby, is said to have expressed his great regret that he had not received the intimation earlier, as in that case the valuable services of General Harrison would have been preserved to the nation in the ensuing campaign. Thus prematurely, were the efficient military services of General Harrison brought to a close.* Not the less, however, did he continue to receive fresh tokens of confidence and esteem from Mr. Madison, for in the summer of 1814 he was appointed, in conjunction with Governor Shelby and General Cass, to treat with the Indians in the northwest, at Greenville and the old headquarters of General Wayne ; and during the following year, when the treaty of Ghent provided for the pacification of several important tribes, he was placed at the head of the commission.

General Harrison was not permitted by the people to remain long in retirement. In 1816 he was elected to represent the congressional district of Ohio in which he resided, in the house of representatives of the United States. He was chosen to supply a vacancy, and also for the two succeeding years. As in almost every instance where an individual has rendered himself prominently an object of popular regard, we find his conduct at some period of his career the subject of malignity and slander, General Harrison had scarcely taken his seat at Washington when his conduct while in command of the northwestern army, was impugned ; this was done by one of the contractors of the army, whose profits, by the integrity of Harrison, had suffered considerable diminution. At the instance of the general, a committee for the full investigation of the charges was appointed, of which Colonel Johnson was chairman ; and after a full examination of numerous witnesses, they made a unanimous report, in which they exculpated General Harrison, in the fullest manner, from all the charges brought against him, and paid a high compliment to his patriotism, disinterestedness, and devotion to the public service. This unjust calumny produced serious injury to General Harrison, having caused the postponement of the resolution introduced into the senate for awarding to him the gold medal and the thanks of Congress ; it was speedily dissipated, however, as it ultimately was adopted by the senate, and concurred in by the house, with but one dissenting vote.

While a member of the house, General Harrison assiduously labored to accomplish two great political objects ; one was a reform in the militia, and the other for the relief of the veteran soldiers who had served in the revolutionary armies, as well as those who had been wounded, or otherwise disabled, in the last war with Great Britain. With respect to the former

---

* But although his brilliant and glorious career in the field was ended, during which, for nearly a quarter of a century, he had successfully led his countrymen through every vicissitude and peril to victory, when he could no longer serve them in his military capacity, he retired into private life, too high-minded and disinterested to sacrifice his sense of duty to pecuniary considerations, and disdaining to receive emoluments for services which he could not, consistently with justice to himself, any longer fulfil.

measure, he obtained the appointment of a committee, of which he was chairman, and subsequently brought in a bill; but the aversion which Congress has always displayed for any legislation upon the subject, caused its frequent postponement, till at length, on his retirement from Congress, it was finally dropped altogether, for the want of some one to sustain it. His other project, however, was crowned with success, and the numerous pensioners who received the nation's bounty always regarded General Harrison as their benefactor and friend.

He subsequently took a prominent part in supporting the affirmative of the question of acknowledging the independence of the South American republics, as proposed by Mr. Clay, then speaker of the house; in whose views of a liberal public policy he generally concurred. In the debate on the conduct of General Jackson during the Seminole war, Harrison participated, censuring such acts of General Jackson as he deemed wrong, although giving him credit for patriotic motives, and defending him in those points which he considered right.

In 1819 General Harrison was elected to the senate of Ohio; and in 1824 he was chosen by the people one of the presidential electors of that state, on the ticket formed by the friends of Mr. Clay, and gave his vote for that gentleman for president. The same year, viz., in 1824, he was elected by the legislature a member of the senate of the United States, and soon after taking his seat in that body, the following year, he was appointed chairman of the military committee, in place of General Jackson, who had resigned. He supported the administration of Mr. Adams, and in 1828 was appointed by that president, minister plenipotentiary to the republic of Colombia. Having proceeded immediately upon his mission, he arrived at Bogota in December, 1828. He found the country in a state of confusion, the government little better than a despotism, and the people as lawless as they were ignorant of their rights. His reception, however, was characterized by the most flattering tokens of respect. His plain republican simplicity ultimately caused him to be suspected of favoring the liberal or opposition party, and occasioned a series of petty annoyances, rendering his situation exceedingly irksome. But he was speedily released from his embarrassment on this account, as one of the very first acts of General Jackson's administration, in 1829, was to recall him from the mission. Before leaving Colombia, but after he had become a private citizen, Harrison addressed to General Bolivar his celebrated appeal in favor of constitutional liberty, a document which has often been quoted in North and South America, and which, for its manly vigor, pure principles of republicanism, and fervid eloquence, has always been considered highly honorable to its author, and an evidence of his superior literary attainments.

On his return from Colombia, General Harrison ceased to engage himself in any active pursuits of public life, living in retirement upon his farm at North Bend, on the Ohio river, a few miles below Cincinnati. Never having sought personal aggrandizement, nor availed himself of his public situation to acquire a fortune, he had not been wealthy; he was, therefore, induced as a means of contributing to his support, to accept the office of clerk to the court of Hamilton county, where he resided, and which station, up to the time of his election to the presidency, he continued to occupy. This circumstance alone exhibits a trait in the character of General Harrison, no less ennobling than it is rare; since he not only proved himself superior to the influence of the specious yet arbitrary forms of conventional life, but he also evinced the greatness of his mind in rising superior to false pride as to selfish ambition in the service of his country.

In 1835 General Harrison was brought forward as a candidate for the presidency of the United States, as successor to General Jackson, at a time when it was generally expected that Mr. Van Buren, then vice-president, would be supported as the democratic candidate for that high office, by the friends of Jackson. Harrison was nominated by meetings of the people in Pennsylvania, Ohio, New York, and other states. Anti-masonic and whig conventions, and those who had supported Jackson, but now refused to vote for Van Buren, joined in sustaining the nomination of Harrison. The opposition were not, however, united in their candidate; Judge Hugh L. White was nominated and supported for the presidency, in Tennessee, Georgia, and other southern and southwestern states, while Daniel Webster received the vote of Massachusetts, and Willie P. Mangum that of South Carolina. The result of the election, which took place in 1836, showed the great popularity of General Harrison. Without any general concert among his friends, he received 73 electoral votes, and in Pennsylvania, Connecticut, and Rhode Island, the majorities for the electoral tickets in favor of Mr. Van Buren were comparatively small.

The national convention of whig delegates which assembled at Harrisburg, the seat of government of Pennsylvania, on the 4th of December, 1839, after a careful and friendly interchange of views with regard to the respective claims and prospects of the three candidates named in the convention, viz., General Harrison, Mr. Clay, and General Scott, finally awarded the nomination to Harrison. The friends of the rival opposition candidates, and all desirous to effect a change in the national administration, cordially united in the nomination; and after a contest more animated and more general than any which ever before occurred in this country, General Harrison was elected to the presidency by an overwhelming vote. He received 234 electoral votes; Mr. Van Buren 60 only. Harrison attended several of the mass meetings of the people in Ohio during the contest, and addressed them in a powerful and eloquent manner.

The elevation of General Harrison to the presidency diffused a general feeling of joy and satisfaction throughout the nation; for many even of

13

those who had opposed his election, admitted his patriotism, and hoped
for a prosperous administration of the government in the hands of one who
had always proved faithful to the public trust. In February, 1841, the venerable chief left his peaceful residence at North Bend, Ohio, to proceed to the
seat of the national government and take the reins of power committed to
him by the voice of the people. He was received at the different cities, towns,
and villages, on the route to Washington, by immense concourses of people, anxious to tender him every demonstration of respect, and showing the
highest degree of enthusiasm. He arrived at Washington on the 9th of
February, and was received by the mayor, aldermen, and citizens of the
capital, with distinguished honor and cordial welcome. A few days afterward, he visited Richmond, Virginia, and mingled freely with the citizens;
after spending a few days with his relatives residing on James river,
in the vicinity of Richmond, he returned to Washington, preparatory to
assuming the responsible duties of his station.

The inauguration of General Harrison as president of the United States,
took place on the 4th of March, 1841. The city of Washington was
thronged with people, many of whom were from the most distant states
of the Union. A procession was formed, civic and military, from the
quarters of the president elect to the capitol. General Harrison was
mounted on a white charger, accompanied by several personal friends,
and his immediate escort were the officers and soldiers who had fought
under him. The scene, as described in the National Intelligencer, was
highly interesting and imposing. The ladies everywhere, from the windows on each side of the avenue, waved their handkerchiefs in token of
their kind feelings, and General Harrison returned their smiles and greet-
ings with repeated bows. The enthusiastic cheers of the citizens who
moved in the procession were, with equal enthusiasm, responded to by
thousands of citizen spectators who lined Pennsylvania avenue, or appeared at the side windows, in the numerous balconies, on the tops of
houses, or on other elevated stands.

At the capitol, the senate having been convened, by the late president,
in extra session, assembled at the appointed hour, and was organized by
the appointment of Mr. King, of Alabama, president pro tem.; after which
Mr. Tyler, the vice-president elect, took the oath of office, and, on taking
his seat as presiding officer, delivered a brief and appropriate address to
the senate. The judges of the supreme court, the diplomatic corps, and
several distinguished officers of the army and navy were present in the
senate-chamber.

At twenty minutes past twelve o'clock, General Harrison entered and
took the seat prepared for him in front of the secretary's table. He
looked cheerful, but composed; his bodily health was manifestly good;
there was an alertness in his movement which was quite astonishing
considering his advanced age, the multiplied hardships through which

his frame had passed, and the fatigues he had lately undergone. After he had retained his seat for a few minutes, preparations were made for forming the line of procession to the platform prepared for the ceremony of the inauguration, erected over the front steps of the portico of the east front of the capitol.

On the platform, seats had been provided for the president elect and the chief-justice, who were placed immediately in front. On their right, seats were assigned to the diplomatic corps. Behind sat members of both houses of Congress, officers of the army and navy, and many distinguished characters from different parts of the Union; intermingled with a great company of ladies who occupied, not only the steps in the rear of the platform, but both the broad abutments of stone which support the steps on either side.

But the sight which attracted and arrested and filled the eye of the observer, was the people. They stood for hours in a solid, dense mass, variously estimated to contain, in the space before the capitol, from thirty to sixty thousand.

While patiently waiting for the arrival of the president, the mass of heads resembled some placid lake; but the instant he was seen advancing from the capitol, it suddenly resembled that same lake when a blast from the mountain has descended upon it, thrown it into tumultuous agitation, and "lifted up its hands on high." A deafening shout went up from the hearts and voices of the people. It sung welcome to the man whom the people delighted to honor, and must have met, with overwhelming power, the throbbings of his own bosom.*

When the uproar had subsided, it was succeeded by the deep stillness of expectation, and the new president forthwith proceeded to read, in accents loud and clear, his address to the nation. In its delivery, the voice of General Harrison never flagged, but to the end retained its full and commanding tone. As he touched on successive topics lying near the hearts of the people, their sympathy with his sentiments was manifested by shouts which broke forth involuntarily from time to time; and when the reading of the address was concluded, they were renewed and prolonged without restraint.

Previous to delivering the closing sentences of the address, the oath of office, tendered by Chief-Justice Taney, was taken by the president, in tones loud, distinct, and solemn, manifesting a due and a deep impression of the importance of the act; after which the president pronounced the remaining passage of his address.

The pealing cannon then announced to the country that it had a new chief magistrate. The procession was again formed; and setting out from the capitol, proceeded along Pennsylvania avenue to the mansion of the president, cheered throughout the whole route as General Harrison passed,

* National Intelligencer.

by the immense crowds on foot, which lined the avenue and filled the doors and windows of the buildings.

Nearly the whole throng of visiters accompanied the president to his new abode, and as many as possible entered and paid their personal respects to him.   The close of the day was marked by the repetition of salutes from the artillery, the whole city being yet alive with a population of strangers and residents, whom the mildness of the season invited into the open air.

In the evening, the several ball-rooms and places of amusement were crowded with gentlemen and ladies attracted to Washington city by the novelty and interest of the occasion.   In the course of the evening the president paid a short visit to each of the assemblies held in honor of the inauguration, and was received with the warmest demonstrations of attachment and respect.

The president immediately nominated to the senate the members of his cabinet, as follows : Daniel Webster, of Massachusetts, secretary of state ; Thomas Ewing, of Ohio, secretary of the treasury ; John Bell, of Tennessee, secretary of war ; George E. Badger, of North Carolina, secretary of the navy ; Francis Granger, of New York, postmaster-general ; John J. Crittenden, of Kentucky, attorney-general.   These nominations were all confirmed by the senate.   That body also confirmed a number of other nominations by the president, chiefly to fill vacancies ; and, after electing a sergeant-at-arms, and dismissing Messrs. Blair and Rives as printers to the senate, also having elected Samuel L. Southard, of New Jersey, president *pro tem.*, the senate adjourned on the 15th of March.

The members of the diplomatic body, or foreign ministers in Washington accredited to the government of the United States, waited on the president on the 9th of March, and through Mr. Fox, the British minister, being presented by the secretary of state, made to him an appropriate address, congratulating him upon his accession to the presidency.   To this address the president of the United States made the following reply :—

" Sir : I receive with great pleasure the congratulations you have been pleased to offer me, in the name of the distinguished diplomatic body now present, the representatives of the most powerful and polished nations with whom the republic which has honored me with the office of its chief magistrate has the most intimate relations—relations which I trust no sinister event will, for ages, interrupt.

" The sentiments contained in my late address to my fellow-citizens, and to which you have been pleased to advert, are those which will continue to govern my conduct through the whole course of my administration.   Lately one of the people, the undisputed sovereigns of the country, and coming immediately from among them, I am enabled, with confidence, to say, that in thus acting I shall be sustained by their undivided approbation.

" I beg leave to add, sir, that, both from duty and inclination, I shall omit nothing in my power to contribute to your own personal happiness and that of the friends whom, on this occasion, you represent, as long as you may continue among us."

The other ministers, with their secretaries, and the persons attached to their respective missions, were then successively presented to the president. The Russian minister was prevented from being present, by indisposition; but on the 12th of March he was presented to the president, by the secretary of state, and to his address on the occasion, the president replied as follows :—

" I receive, sir, the congratulations which you offer me in your capacity of envoy extraordinary and minister plenipotentiary of the emperor of all the Russias, upon my election to the presidency of the United States, with great pleasure.

" From the epoch which introduced the United States to the world as an independent nation, the most amicable relations have existed between them and the powerful and distinguished monarchs who have successively swayed the sceptre of Russia. The presidents, my predecessors, acting in behalf and under the authority of the people, their constituents, have never failed to use every proper occasion to confirm and strengthen the friendship so auspiciously commenced, and which a mutuality of interests, render so desirable to be continued. I assure you, sir, that none of them felt the obligations of this duty more powerfully than I do; and you can not in language too strong communicate to your august monarch my sentiments on this subject. And permit me to add, that no more acceptable medium of communicating them could have been offered than that of a personage who has rendered himself so acceptable, as well to the people as to the government of the United States."

On the 17th of March, President Harrison issued his proclamation, calling an extra session of Congress, principally on account of the condition of the revenue and finances of the country, to be held on the last Monday, being the 31st day, of May ensuing.

The extra sessions of Congress called by the predecessors of General Harrison, since the organization of the government, were as follows : John Adams convened Congress on the 16th of May, 1797; Thomas Jefferson called the eighth Congress on the 17th of October, 1803, to provide for carrying the Louisiana treaty into effect, but that day was only about three weeks earlier than had been fixed by the preceding Congress; James Madison convened Congress on the 23d of May, 1809; also on the 25th of May, 1813; Martin Van Buren convened Congress on the 4th of September, 1837.

Mrs. Harrison did not accompany her husband to Washington, but remained at the homestead at North Bend, superintending the care of her numerous family, and intending to join the president at the seat of government in the course of the spring; but the family and the nation were destined soon to receive a mournful lesson upon the mutability of human affairs.

From the moment General Harrison was elected president, his heart was filled with gratitude to the people, to whom indeed he had always been devoted. Anxious to fulfil the wishes of his political friends, he received with kindness and attention the numerous applicants for office who thronged the seat of government; and although he would doubtless have been better pleased to have deferred many appointments for a time, yet a considerable number of removals were made by him, and appointments made, in compliance with the views of the cabinet, during the month of March. In the generosity of his heart, he invariably opened the doors of the president's mansion wide to the reception of his friends, and that house was the abode of hospitality and kindness. He indulged his friends to his own destruction. From sunrise till midnight, he indulgently devoted himself to his fellow-citizens who visited him, with the exception of an hour each day spent in cabinet council. It was his habit, after rising, first to peruse his bible, and then to take a walk before breakfast. And afterward, the whole day would be spent in receiving company and transacting business.

On Saturday, March 27, President Harrison, after several days previous indisposition from the effects of a cold, was seized with a chill and other symptoms of fever. These were followed by pneumonia, or bilious pleurisy, which ultimately baffled all medical skill, and terminated his virtuous, useful, and illustrious life, on Sunday morning, the 4th of April, after an illness of eight days, being a little over 68 years of age.

The last time the president spoke was at nine o'clock on Saturday night, a little more than three hours before he expired. While Doctor Worthington and one or two other attendants were standing over him, having just administered something to his comfort, he cleared his throat, as if desiring to speak audibly, and, as though he fancied himself addressing his successor, or some official associate in the government, said: "SIR, I WISH YOU TO UNDERSTAND THE PRINCIPLES OF THE GOVERNMENT. I WISH THEM CARRIED OUT. I ASK NOTHING MORE."

He expired a little after midnight, surrounded by those members of his family who were in the city, the members of his cabinet and many personal friends, among whom were Colonels Chambers and Todd, who were the aids of General Harrison at the battle of the Thames, in 1813. The connexions of the president who were present in the executive mansion at the time of his decease, were the following: Mrs. William Harrison (son's widow); Mrs. Taylor, of Richmond (niece); Mr. D. O. Coupeland (nephew); Henry Harrison, of Virginia (grand nephew), and Findlay Harrison, of Ohio (grandson).

The general feeling throughout the country was thus eloquently portrayed in the National Intelligencer of April 9, 1841, which contained an account of the funeral :—

"Never, since the time of Washington, has any one man so concentrated upon himself the love and confidence of the American people ; and never, since the melancholy day which shrouded a nation in mourning for his sudden death, has any event produced so general and so profound a sensation of surprise and sorrow.

"So brief had been the late president's illness, that now, as in the case of Washington, there had scarce been time for us to begin to fear, when the stunning blow of the reality fell upon us like the stroke of thunder from a cloudless sky. Men looked aghast, and staggered, as if amazed by something they could scarce believe. But it was true. He who, with beaming countenance, passed along our streets in the joy of his heart— he, the welcome, the long-expected, the desired, on whom all eyes were fastened, to whom all hearts went out ; who had within him more stirring subjects of exhilarating consciousness than have met in any single bosom since Washington was crowned with wreaths as he came back from Yorktown, was, on Wednesday last, within one month, 'one little month,' borne along that same crowded avenue—crowded, not as before, with a jubilant people gathered from every quarter of the country, but with sincerely sorrowing multitudes following his bier. When the words, ' the president is dead,' met the ear, the man of business dropped his pen, the artisan dropped his tools—children looked into the faces of their parents, and wives into the countenances of their husbands—and the wail of sorrow arose as if each had lost a parent, or some near and dear friend. Could General Harrison now look down on the land he loved, he might, indeed, ' read his history in a nation's eyes ;' and those whose bosoms glow and struggle with high purposes and strong desires for their country's good, may learn in what they now behold, wherever they turn their eyes, how glorious a reward awaits the memory of those who faithfully serve their country !"

On Wednesday, the 7th of April, the funeral of President Harrison took place at Washington, and was attended by an immense concourse of citizens, who thronged to the city from Baltimore, Philadelphia, Alexandria, and other places, anxious to join in the honors and solemnities paid to the memory of the illustrious deceased. The civic and military procession was large and imposing, occupying two miles in length. The funeral service of the episcopal church was recited by the Rev. Mr. Hawley. The body was interred in the congressional burying ground, but afterward removed to North Bend, Ohio, at the request of the family of General Harrison.

All party distinctions were merged in the feeling of respect due to the memory of the honored dead ; and throughout the Union, funeral honors and other testimonials of public feeling, similar to those which took place on the death of General Washington, were awarded to the memory of Harrison. At every city, town, and village, in the Union, as the unwelcome tidings of the death of the president arrived, it was received with every demonstration of mourning and regret, and followed immediately by such marks of respect as the several communities had it in their power to offer. Such legislative bodies as happened to be in session, were among the foremost to demonstrate their sympathy with the general impulse. That exhibited by the legislature of Maryland, in leaving the seat of the state government, and attending the funeral as an organized body, was among the most touching evidences of the kind. The Pennsylvania legislature deputed a number of members from each branch of that body, to proceed from Harrisburg to Washington, to attend the funeral. The legislature of New York adopted such measures as the occasion enabled them to do, to testify their feelings. The respective courts, wherever they were in session, officially united in the general expression, as did also the municipalities of all the principal cities and towns in the Union. The occasion was also appropriately noticed by the clergy of the different denominations.

General Harrison left one son and three daughters, all living at or near North Bend, Ohio. Four sons and a daughter died before their father. All of the sons left children.

In person, General Harrison was tall and slender. Although he never had the appearance of possessing a robust constitution, yet such had been the effects of habitual activity and temperance, that few men at his age enjoyed so much bodily vigor. He had a fine dark eye, remarkable for its keenness, fire, and intelligence, and his face was strongly expressive of the vivacity of his mind, and the benevolence of his character.

The most remarkable traits of General Harrison's character, and those by which he was distinguished throughout his whole career, were his disinterestedness, his regard for the rights and comforts of others, his generous disposition, his mild and forbearing temper, and his plain, easy, and unostentatious manner.

He had a most intimate knowledge of the history, and foreign and domestic polity of the United States ; and from the moderation of his political views and feelings as a party man, although firm, frank, and consistent, he was well calculated for the high station to which he was elected, and which it is believed he would have filled with ability, and to the satisfaction of the public, during his presidential term, had his life been spared. His talents, although, perhaps, not of the highest order, were very respectable, and, united with an accurate knowledge of mankind, enabled him to acquit himself well in the various public stations to which he was called. He was a bold and eloquent orator; and he has left on record numerous evidences of his literary acquirements, among which, besides his correspondence and public papers, we may mention his discourse before the Historical Society of Ohio (on the aborigines of the valley of the Ohio), published at Cincinnati, in 1839, which can not fail to please and instruct either the scholar, the lover of history, or the antiquary.

John Tyler

BIOGRAPHICAL SKETCH

OF

JOHN TYLER.

THE ancestors of John Tyler, the tenth president of the United States, and the sixth chief magistrate of the nation whose birthplace was Virginia, were among the early English settlers of the Old Dominion. This family of Tyler, it is understood, traced their lineage back to Walter, or Wat Tyler, who, in the fourteenth century, headed an insurrection in England, and, while demanding of the king (Richard II.) a recognition of the rights of the people, lost his life in their cause.

The father of the subject of this sketch, bearing the same name, was the second son of John Tyler, who was marshal of the colony, under the royal government, up to the period of his death, which occurred after the remonstrances against the stamp act, and whose patrimonial estate covered a large tract of country in and about Williamsburg. The son early entered with warmth and spirit into the discussion of those grievances which afterward kindled the flame of the revolution; and so earnestly were his sympathies enlisted in the cause of colonial rights, and so unhesitatingly were his opinions expressed, that his father, the marshal, often told him that he would some day be hung for a rebel. A rebel he did indeed prove, but his consequent exaltation was destined to be, not the scaffold, but the chair of state. Removing from James City, some time in 1775, to Charles City, he was, not long after, elected from that county a member of the house of delegates of Virginia, and in that capacity distinguished himself by the zeal and fearlessness with which he advocated the boldest measures of the revolution, and the devotion with which he lent all the energies of a powerful mind to its success.[*]

The intimate friend of Jefferson, Patrick Henry, and Edmund Randolph, he was scarcely less beloved by the entire people of Virginia.

* We are indebted to a life of President Tyler, written by one of his friends, and published by Harper and Brothers, in 1844, for a part of this sketch.

Throughout the revolution, Mr. Tyler devoted himself unceasingly and untiringly to its success. A bold, free, and elegant speaker, his voice was never silent when it could avail aught for the great cause in which he was enlisted; and possessing an ample fortune at the commencement of the revolution—partly the inheritance of his father, but more the result of his own industry as a distinguished lawyer of the colony—the liberality with which he lavished his wealth upon its progress, and the utter disregard of selfish considerations with which he sacrificed his whole time during its continuance, to aid in bringing it to a successful termination, left him almost utterly impoverished at its close. None appreciated better than the people of Virginia the great services he had rendered, and the patriotic sacrifices he had made to the cause of independence; and he was elevated by them successively to the offices of speaker of the house of delegates, governor of the state, and judge in one of her highest courts. At the breaking out of the last war, he was appointed, by Mr. Madison, a judge of the federal court of admiralty. In February, 1813, he died, full of years and honors. The legislature passed resolutions expressive of their sense of the bereavement, and went into mourning for the remainder of the session.

Judge Tyler left three sons, Wat, John, and William, the second of whom, the subject of this memoir, was born in Charles City county, Virginia, on the 29th of March, 1790. Passing over the period of his early youth, when he was noted for his love of books, and particularly of historical works, we find young Tyler, at the age of twelve years, entering William and Mary college. Here he soon attracted the notice of Bishop Madison, the venerable president of that institution; and during his whole collegiate course, Mr. Tyler was, in an especial degree, a favorite of that distinguished man, as well as of his fellow-students. He passed through the courses at the age of seventeen, and on that occasion delivered an address on the subject of " female education," which was pronounced by the faculty to have been the best commencement oration delivered there within their recollection.

After leaving college, Mr. Tyler devoted himself to the study of law, already commenced during his collegiate studies, and passed the next two years in reading, partly with his father, and partly with Edmund Randolph, formerly governor of Virginia, and one of the most eminent lawyers in the state. At nineteen years of age, he appeared at the bar of his native county as a practising lawyer, a certificate having been given him without inquiry as to his age; and such was his success, that ere three months had elapsed there was scarcely a disputable case on the docket of the court in which he was not retained upon the one side or the other. The year after his appearance at the bar, he was offered a nomination as member of the legislature from his own county, but he declined the proffered honor, until the following year, when, having reached the age of twenty-one but a few days before the election took place, he was chosen nearly unanimously, a member of the house of delegates.

He took his seat in that branch of the Virginia legislature in December, 1811. The breaking out of the war soon after, afforded fine scope for his oratorical abilities. Attached to the democratic party, and an advocate of the course of policy which had been pursued by Jefferson and Madison, in the limited sphere he then occupied, his voice was ever heard urging, so far as lay in the power of the government, the most energetic measures in carrying on the war. He spoke often, with the view of improving his powers of oratory; and the youthful debater had the gratification to find, that even in the forum of Virginia, the country of eloquence, his speeches commanded universal attention.

The senators in Congress from Virginia at that time, were Messrs. Giles and Brent, who had been instructed by the legislature to vote against the renewal of the charter of the bank of the United States. This instruction was disobeyed by Mr. Brent, in his vote on the question, in February, 1811, and Mr. Tyler introduced a resolution of censure into the house of delegates, animadverting severely upon the course of the senator, and laying it down as a principle to be established thereafter, that any person accepting the office of senator of the United States from the state of Virginia, by such acceptance tacitly bound himself to obey, during the period he should serve, the instructions he might receive from its legislature. Twenty-five years afterward he had not forgotten the ideas of senatorial duty he then inculcated, when, himself a senator, he was called upon to record a vote not less repugnant to his judgment than to his conscience. Mr. Tyler was elected to the legislature for five successive years; and, as an instance of his popularity in his native county, it may be mentioned, that on one occasion he received all the votes polled except five. Some years later, when a candidate for Congress, of the two hundred votes given in the same county, he received all but one, over a distinguished competitor.

At the time the British forces were in the Chesapeake bay, and threatened an attack on Norfolk and Richmond, Mr. Tyler evinced a disposition to serve his country in the field as well as in the halls of legislation, by raising a volunteer company, and devoting himself assiduously to effecting an efficient organization of the militia in his neighborhood. Hence the title of " Captain Tyler," which was applied to him, in ridicule, when president of the United States. In the sequel, the troops under his command were not brought into action, and his military career was, consequently, short and bloodless.

During the session of 1815–'16, while he was still a member of the house of delegates, Mr. Tyler was elected one of the executive council, in which capacity he acted until November, 1816, when, by the death of the Hon. John Clopton, a vacancy occurred in the representation in

Congress, from the Richmond district. Two candidates were presented, Mr. Andrew Stevenson, afterward distinguished in the national councils, and then speaker of the house of delegates, and Mr. Tyler. The contest was severe, and enlisted to a great extent the public feeling, though it produced no cessation of the friendly relations which had always existed between the two opposing candidates. Mr. Stevenson was a most popular man in Richmond, his place of residence, but Mr. Tyler's popularity was not less great in his own and the neighboring counties; and, after a closely contested canvass, Mr. Tyler was elected, by a majority of only about thirty votes. It was a mere trial of personal popularity, as they were both of the same political principle; and when Mr. Tyler retired from Congress, in 1821, he warmly advocated the election of Mr. Stevenson as his successor.

Mr. Tyler took his seat in the house of representatives in December, 1816, having reached the twenty-sixth year of his age the previous month of March. As a new member, custom, not less than the modesty which is ever the accompaniment of merit, prohibited him from taking a very active part in the proceedings of the house. Yet even during this period he was not idle, but occasionally participated in the discussions which occupied the short portion of time for which he had been elected.

Having witnessed the inauguration of President Monroe, Mr. Tyler returned home to his constituents, in March, 1817, and the following month he received a testimonial of their approbation, in his re-election to Congress by an overwhelming majority over his former rival, Mr. Stevenson.

In the fifteenth Congress many subjects of magnitude were brought forward and discussed. Among them were the Seminole war and the South American question. Mr. Clay, the speaker, introduced a proposition to acknowledge the independence of the provinces of Rio de la Plata, against which Mr. Tyler voted. He supported the resolutions of censure on the conduct of General Jackson in the Seminole war, taking the same view as some of his colleagues and Mr. Clay on that subject. The question of internal improvements by the general government was agitated at this session, as it had been by the previous Congress; on both occasions Mr. Tyler voted against all the propositions offered in the house which countenanced the doctrine of the possession of the power by the general government, under the constitution, to make internal improvements. Thus he avowed on all occasions, the state-rights or strict construction doctrines of the dominant party in Virginia, on constitutional points. The conduct of the directors of the bank of the United States, which institution was chartered in 1816, was the subject of investigation at this session of Congress, and Mr. Tyler was placed on the committee appointed to inspect the concerns of the bank. When the report of the committee was made, Mr. Tyler supported a resolution offered by Mr. Trimble of Kentucky, requiring that a *scire facias* should be issued immediately against the bank.

In his speech on this occasion, Mr. Tyler avowed his belief that the creation of this corporation was unconstitutional.

In 1819, Mr. Tyler was re-elected to Congress, there being no opposing candidate. He took an active part in the debates on the Missouri question, and on the proposed revision of the tariff. He opposed any restrictions upon Missouri, on the admission of that state into the Union; and also made an elaborate argument against the policy of a protective tariff. Ere the close of this Congress, increasing ill health compelled Mr. Tyler to resign his seat in that body. Placed on the committee of ways and means, at a time when the financial affairs of the country were in a most disordered condition, his whole time and energies were devoted to the fulfilment of his duties, and constant labor and confinement made fearful inroads upon a constitution not strong by nature. He left the house of representatives, carrying with him the reputation of an eloquent speaker, a constant advocate of popular rights, and a democrat of the school of Jefferson. He retired to his farm in Charles City county, among constituents who approved of his course in Congress, and were conscious that naught but physical inability had compelled him to leave their service.

Mr. Tyler now returned to the practice of his profession, but he was not suffered long to remain in private life. In the spring of 1823, after much urgent solicitation, he consented to become again a candidate for the legislature, and was elected with little or no opposition, and, in December, took his seat in that body which had been so early familiar to him. He soon took the lead in the debates of the house of delegates, and during the two years which followed, he having been twice re-elected, performed a most conspicuous part in all the proceedings. There was little of the legislation of Virginia at that period that did not bear the impress of his hands. He was an ardent advocate of a comprehensive system of public improvement by the state. He regretted to see Virginia gradually falling from the high estate she had occupied in the Union; and he put forth his utmost efforts to arrest the downward progress of the commonwealth, and to arouse her dormant energies to a display of her vast resources. He was not wholly unsuccessful. The construction of roads and canals was liberally encouraged by the legislature, and many of the finest works in the state are monuments to the indefatigable exertions of John Tyler.

In December, 1825, Mr. Pleasants's term of office having expired, Mr. Tyler was elected governor of Virginia. The office, unsolicited and unexpected, was conferred upon him by a large vote, there being, on joint ballot of the two houses of the legislature, for Tyler 131, for Floyd 81, scattering 2. During his administration of Virginia, Mr. Tyler promoted the cause of internal improvement, and devoted himself also to the healing of sectional disputes among the people. In July, 1825, he delivered, at the capitol square, in Richmond, an eloquent eulogy on the death of Mr. Jefferson.

During the next session of the legislature, Mr. Tyler was re-elected governor of Virginia by a unanimous vote. He was not, however, permitted to serve out his term. A senator of the United States was to be elected, for six years from the expiration of the term of John Randolph on the ensuing 4th of March. Mr. Randolph was the candidate of the democratic party for a re-election; but the strange vagaries and singular conduct which had so far marked his career in the senate, had excited discontent with very many of that party, and, convinced that he was no longer a proper representative of the state of Virginia, they began to look about for some man who, professing the same principles as themselves, had the firmness and ability to set them forth, and the dignity and strength of character to cause them to be respected. The friends of Mr. Adams's administration being in the minority in the legislature, united with a few of their political opponents in the support of Governor Tyler, in justice to whom, it must be said, that he sought not the nomination. "On the contrary," he remarked, in a letter written before the election, "I have constantly opposed myself to all solicitations. I desire, most earnestly, to be left at peace. There is no motive which could induce me to seek to change my present station for a seat in the senate at this time. I can not admit that to be *one* in a body of forty-eight members is to occupy a more elevated station than that presented in the chief magistracy of Virginia. My private interests, intimately connected with the good of my family, are more highly sustained by remaining where I am, than by the talked-of change." He also declared, in the same letter, that his political preferences on the fundamental principles of the government were the same with those espoused by Mr. Randolph.

Notwithstanding the positive manner in which he disclaimed any desire to be invested with the senatorial dignity, and the consequent loss of votes, Mr. Tyler was elected senator on the first ballot, the vote being for Tyler 115, Randolph 110.

The committee of the legislature appointed to wait on Governor Tyler and announce to him his election as senator, used the following, among other remarks: "Allow us, sir, to express to you the satisfaction which we feel in this new proof of the confidence which Virginia places in your known integrity, talents, and patriotism, believing that, as in your past, so in your future public life, you will never disappoint her confidence, and ever study to promote her true happiness; and while always faithfully representing, will ably and effectually vindicate her interests."

Mr. Tyler, in his reply, said, "A sense of what is due to the legislative will denies to me the privilege of giving longer audience to the suggestion of my feelings. That voice which called me to the chief magistracy, now makes upon me a new demand. I have opposed to it my wishes and inclinations up to that period when acquiescence becomes a duty, and resistance would be censurable by all. I shall, then, in due season, accept the appointment with which I have been honored. Be pleased, gentlemen, to bear to your respective houses my most profound acknowledgments for this distinguished testimonial of their confidence; convey to them, renewed assurances of my unshaken allegiance to the constitution, as received and expounded by our fathers; say to them, that if I carry with me into the national councils less of talent than many of my predecessors, yet that, in singleness of purpose, and in ardent devotion to the principles of civil liberty, I yield to none. ' If Virginia has changed her representative, her principles remain unaltered. Be assured, that the only and highest aspiration of my ambition consists in the desire of promoting the happiness of my native state, and that it shall be the untiring effort of my life to advance and vindicate her interests."

This election, though regretted by the immediate friends of Mr. Randolph and the most zealous of the democratic party in Virginia, who were desirous to retain Mr. Randolph in the senate, in consequence of his violent hostility to the administration of Mr. Adams, was generally popular with the people of Virginia. Even the Richmond Enquirer, devoted as it was to Mr. Randolph's interests, in a paragraph regretting his failure, after enumerating a long list of causes which, it asserted, led to that result, said, " Yet even this combination could not have succeeded in favor of *any other* man in the commonwealth than John Tyler, because he carried with him personal friends who would have voted for John Randolph in preference to any other man than himself;" thus giving the highest possible evidence of the esteem in which Mr. Tyler was then held by the people of his native state.

At the presidential election of 1824–'5, Mr. Tyler acted with a large majority of the politicians in the state, in giving a preference to William H. Crawford for the presidency, and that gentleman received the electoral vote of the state, and a decided expression of the popular will in his favor. When, however, the election was determined by the house of representatives, in Congress, in favor of Mr. Adams, the Crawford party in Virginia were generally satisfied, as Mr. Adams was their second choice; and Mr. Tyler wrote a letter to Mr. Clay, of Kentucky, approving of his vote for Mr. Adams, in preference to General Jackson; but soon after the election of the former to the presidency, Mr. Tyler changed his views, and with most of the friends of Mr. Crawford, became an opponent of the administration.

A few days after his election as senator, Mr. Tyler sent to the legislature his resignation of the office of governor. The following is an extract from his message on that occasion: " The principles on which I have acted, without abandonment, in any one instance, for the last sixteen years, in Congress and in the legislative hall of this state, will be the principles

by which I will regulate my future political life. Keeping them constantly in view, yielding them neither to the force of circumstances nor to
the suggestions of expediency, and thereby seeking to promote the lasting interests of my beloved country, if I do not acquire the individual confidence of Virginia, I shall at least have preserved my own consistency, and
secured my peace of mind through the days of my increasing years, and
in the hour of my final dissolution."

Upon the occasion of his retirement from the chief magistracy of the
state, he was invited to a public dinner, by a large number of the members of the legislature, and of the citizens of Richmond. In answer to
the following toast—"John Tyler, our friend and guest—a republican too
firm to be driven from his principles—too upright to be swerved by the
laws of ambition or power"—Mr. Tyler, among other remarks, said :—

"I can be at no loss to ascribe this manifestation of public respect to its
proper source. It flows from the late senatorial election, and the incidents connected with it. I place upon it, therefore, the highest possible
value. The recesses of my heart have been attempted to be scanned
with the view of detecting some lurking wish at variance with my public
declarations. Had I desired a change, what was there to have prevented
me from openly seeking it ? Are not the offices of the republic equally
open to all its citizens ? When was an exclusive monopoly established ?
or when was it before that 'Rome contained but one man' ? Virginia,
thank Heaven, depends upon no one of her citizens, however distinguished
by talents, for her character or standing. She has been compared to the
mother of the Gracchii, and I trust that she may still be permitted to be
proud of her sons. For one who had been taught from early infancy that
golden rule, that, next to his Creator, his first duty belonged to his country, and his last to himself, how could I have stood acquitted, had I
permitted private considerations to have controlled the obligations of public duty ? By accepting the appointment, while I interfered with the pretensions of no other citizen, I have acquitted myself of a sacred obligation."

After speaking at large upon the administration, and what he had hoped
would have been the policy of Mr. Adams, he said :—

"Candor requires me here publicly to say, that his first splendid message to Congress long since withered all my hopes. I saw in it an almost
total disregard of the federative principle—a more latitudinous construction
of the constitution than has ever before been insisted on ; lying not so
much in the particular measures recommended—which, though bad enough,
had some excuse in precedent—as in the broad and general principles
there laid down as the basis of governmental duty. From the moment of
seeing that message, all who have known anything of me have known
that I stood distinctly opposed to this administration ; not from a factious
spirit, not with a view to elevate a favorite, or to advance myself, but on

the great principles which have regulated my past life. I honestly believe the preservation of the federative principles of our government to be inseparably connected with the perpetuation of liberty."

This public compliment was given him on the 3d of March 1827, the last day of the period during which he occupied the office of governor. On the 3d of December, 1827, Mr. Tyler took his seat in the senate of the United States, and at once arrayed himself with the opposition, which, arising from the circumstances attending Mr. Adams's election, and combining the supporters of Jackson, Crawford, and Calhoun, finally overthrew the administration. There were many minor points upon which the opposition acted with little or no unity; consisting of men who had but a short time before held conflicting political relations—they were, nevertheless, firmly united against the administration, and resolute in combating its policy and doctrines; and at the time of Mr. Tyler's entering the senate, the entire opposition had rallied in the support of General Jackson.

In accordance with the Virginia doctrines respecting the powers of the general government, and the policy of the country respecting trade and commerce, which also coincided with the views entertained by Mr. Tyler himself, he voted against the tariff bill of 1828, and the various projects for internal improvement which were introduced. In the debate concerning the powers of the vice-president, Mr. Tyler participated, supporting the positions assumed by Mr. Calhoun, who then occupied the chair of the senate.

On the accession of General Jackson to the presidency, Mr. Tyler supported his administration, concurring, in this respect, with a large majority of the people of Virginia. He, however, pursued an independent course in the senate, disapproving of some of the nominations of the president, and holding, as he did, to a strict construction of the constitution, in 1831 he opposed the appropriation to pay the negotiators of the treaty with Turkey, as that mission had not been authorized by Congress. Though a sincere friend of the administration, he regarded this act of General Jackson, in appointing commissioners, as a dangerous stretch of the presidential power; and while he by no means withdrew his support from the general policy of the party then in power, he felt bound to declare his opinion of acts which all his ideas of constitutional authority led him to reprobate.

To projects of internal improvement by the general government, Mr. Tyler was uniformly opposed, believing them unconstitutional, as we have already stated. He therefore highly approved of General Jackson's veto on the Maysville road bill, the passage of which he had previously opposed in the senate, in a speech of considerable length. The subject of the tariff being brought before the senate at the session of 1831–'2, by Mr. Clay, in a resolution proposing certain changes in the existing duties, a long and able debate arose thereon, in which Mr. Tyler participated.

14

His speech on this occasion was continued for three days, and evinced an extensive knowledge of the subject ; and it was characterized by a warmth, earnestness, and depth of eloquence, which gave ample evidence of the intensity of his feeling on a topic which then excited much of the public attention at the south.   He was opposed to a tariff specially for the protection of home industry, but in favor of a tariff for revenue which might incidentally afford such protection, and he expressed an anxiety for such an adjustment of the question as would restore peace and harmony to the Union.

The question of renewing the charter of the bank of the United States came up at the same session.   Mr. Tyler steadily opposed the bill to modify and continue in force that institution, at every step of its progress through the senate, and voted against it on its final passage.   After receiving the sanction of the house of representatives, the bill renewing the charter of the bank was defeated by the veto of President Jackson.

For the confirmation of Mr. Van Buren, who was nominated at this session for minister to England, Mr. Tyler gave his vote ; and viewing the tariff of 1832 as a continuance of the system of protection, he voted against that measure, although the duties on imports were much reduced thereby, on many articles.   With the nullifiers of South Carolina Mr. Tyler sympathized ; and when the president took decided ground against the anti-tariff and nullifying proceedings of that state, the Virginia senator did not hesitate to withdraw his support from the administration, on the ground that they had abandoned the principles of state-rights, as he understood them, on which General Jackson had been supported in the southern states, and to which he owed his election as president.   A bill called the force bill being introduced into the senate, to provide for the collection of the revenue, and vesting extraordinary powers in the president, Mr. Tyler opposed it in an animated speech.   After a lengthened debate, the bill, was passed, Mr. Tyler's being the only name in the negative.   The other opponents of the bill, Mr. Calhoun at their head, left the senate-chamber when the vote was taken, considering further opposition useless. During the progress of the bill, however, efforts were made in both houses to terminate the controversy peaceably.   Mr. Clay finally introduced a bill in the senate, in February, 1833, which, conceived in the spirit of concession inculcated in the speech of Mr. Tyler, united the opposing parties in its favor, and passed the senate, with few dissenting voices. For this Mr. Tyler voted, and the bill, so celebrated since as Mr. Clay's compromise act, having previously passed the house, received the signature of the president.

During the preceding session of Congress, Mr. Tyler was re-elected to the senate for six years from the 4th of March, 1833.   The most prominent among the proceedings of Congress, at the session of 1833—'4, was the action of the two houses upon the removal of the deposites.   In the interim between the last adjournment and the commencement of that session, the president determined upon removing the public moneys from the bank of the United States. Mr. Duane, the secretary of the treasury, having refused to comply with the wishes of the president, was dismissed from office, and Mr. Taney was appointed in his place, after which the will of the president was accomplished. Early in the session the subject was taken up in the senate, and resolutions of censure against the president, introduced by Mr. Clay, were adopted. For these resolutions Mr. Tyler voted, as did the senators from the south and west who held state-rights doctrines, and who now acted with Mr. Calhoun, in opposition to the administration of General Jackson. These, joined with the original opponents of the administration, formed a decided majority in the senate.

Mr. Tyler took an active part in the debate on the removal of the deposites. However unconstitutional he thought the establishment of the bank of the United States, it had been established by law, and by the same law it was made the depository of the public money ; and any act by a public officer in derogation of that law, was as much deserving of, and as quickly received his censure, as if he had been the most ardent supporter of the institution. In his views he was sustained by instructions from Virginia, which state he said was exactly where she always had been —against the assumption of power by the Congress or by the president. " Her instructions to me," he continued, " convey the information, that she is against the bank, as she has always been ; can any man find his apology for ratifying the late proceedings of the executive department, in the mere fact that the bank of the United States is a great evil ; that it ought never to have been created ; and that it should not be rechartered ? For one, I say, if it is to die, let it die by law. It is a corporate existence created by law, and while it exists, entitled to the protection which the law throws around private rights. This, sir, is the aspect in which I regard this question ; and this, I am instructed to say, is the light in which Virginia regards it."

The call was often made upon the committee of finance, of which Mr. Tyler was a member, to report a scheme of treasury agency. Mr. Tyler answered that he could see no propriety for that call, until the sense of the senate should be expressed upon the resolutions then under their consideration. If the executive were sustained in the power it had exerted over the subject, then Congress had nothing to do with it. The great question before the country was, whether Congress or the president was to be charged with the keeping of the treasury. The latter had already decided to establish a treasury agency himself, and if Congress affirmed that he had done so with full power and authority, that would be decisive of the question as to legislative cognizance. The executive authority was, in such case, coextensive with the whole subject, and the legislature would encroach upon his rights if it acted at all.

At this session, Mr. Tyler, from the committee on finance, which had been directed to inquire into the condition and affairs of the United States bank, made an able and voluminous report thereon. The report was assailed by Mr. Benton, immediately upon its introduction into the senate, and in reply to him, Mr. Tyler entered into a defence of the document, and from his remarks we make the following extracts :—

"Nothing," said he, "would please me more than to have the report which has been so furiously attacked by the senator from Missouri, referred to another committee for their most rigid examination ; and I would be well pleased that he be one of the committee. Let him summon his witnesses, and take depositions without number ; let him then return with his budget to the house, and lay them, with or without an air of triumph, on the table. He would find himself mistaken. All his witnesses combined would not be able to overthrow the testimony upon which the report of the committee is based. There is not a single declaration in the report which is not founded upon testimony which cannot lie—written documentary evidence which no party testimony can overcome."

"The honorable senator has denominated the report 'an elaborate defence of the bank.' If he had paid more attention to the reading, or had waited to have it in print, he would not have hazarded such a declaration. The committee have presented both sides of the question ; the view most favorable, and that most unfavorable to the institution."

"He has loudly talked of the committee having been made an instrument of by the bank. For myself, I renounce the ascription. I must tell the senator that I can no more be made an instrument of by the bank, than by the still greater and more formidable power, the administration. I stand upon this floor to accomplish the purposes for which I am sent. In the consciousness of my own honesty, I stand firm and erect. I worship alone at the shrine of truth and honor. It is a precious thing in the eyes of some, to bask in the sunshine of power. I rest only upon the support which has *never* failed me—the high and lofty feeling of my constituents. I would not be an instrument even in their hands, if it were possible for them to require it of me, to gratify an unrighteous motive."

"The committee, in their investigations, have sought for nothing but the truth. I am opposed—have always been opposed—to the bank. In its creation I regard the constitution as having been violated, and I desire to see it expire. But the senate appointed me, with others, to inquire whether it was guilty of certain charges, and I should regard myself as the basest of mankind were I to charge it falsely. The report is founded on unquestionable documentary evidence. I shall hold myself ready to answer all the objections which can be raised against it, and to prove, from the documents themselves, that the report is made with the utmost fairness, and the most scrupulous regard to truth."

The extracts from Mr. Tyler's speeches and other productions, which we have given, serve to elucidate his political character and modes of thinking, as well as to exhibit the uniformity of his course, in adhering with singular tenacity to the doctrines of state-rights and strict construction of the Virginia school of democracy. His course in the senate effected a separation between him and that portion of the democratic party in Virginia, who still adhered to General Jackson, and who, in the sequel, supported Mr. Van Buren for the presidency. But there was still a wide difference between the principles and views entertained by Mr. Tyler, and those of the original opponents of General Jackson, who formed the largest proportion of the party which took the name of whigs, previous to the presidential election of 1836.

Near the close of the session, in March, 1835, Mr. Tyler was elected president of the senate *pro tempore*, by the united votes of the whig and state-rights senators. On taking the chair, he made a brief and eloquent address, in the course of which he said : "You are the representatives of sovereign states, deputed by them to uphold and maintain their rights and interests. You may severally, in your turn, have become the objects of attack and denunciation before the public ; but there is not, and can not be an American who does not turn his eyes on the senate of the United States, as to the great conservative body of our federal system, and to this chamber as the ark in which the covenant is deposited. To have received, therefore, at your hands, this station, furnishes to me abundant cause for self-gratulation."

One of the last acts of Mr. Tyler, at this session, was to vote against the amendment made by the house of representatives to the fortification bill, placing three millions of dollars at the disposal of the president, to provide for anticipated difficulties with France. This was a proposition to place the war-making power, belonging solely to Congress, in the hands of the president. The amendment was disagreed to by the senate, and Congress adjourned without passing the bill.

At the next session, that of 1835—'6, during the brief period he remained in the senate, Mr. Tyler took an active part in behalf of the sufferers by the great fire in New York, and supported the bill introduced into Congress for their relief. In February, 1836, the legislature of Virginia passed resolutions instructing the senators from that state to vote for a resolution directing the resolution of March 28, 1834, to be expunged from the journal of the senate. These resolutions were then, by direction of the general assembly, forwarded, by the speakers of the respective houses, to the senators from Virginia.

Mr. Leigh, the colleague of Mr. Tyler, in answer to the resolutions, wrote a long and able letter, in which, while he acknowledged the right of instruction in all cases where no constitutional point was involved, or where any doubt existed as to the constitutionality of any particular measure, he denied that he was bound to obey any instruction commanding him to do an act which, in his conscientious opinion, would be, in itself, a plain violation of the instrument he was sworn to support, and in its consequences dangerous and mischievous in the extreme.   He concluded his letter by declaring, that he would neither obey the instructions given him, nor resign his seat, and expressed the determination to vindicate the resolutions of the 28th of March, 1834, at any time when they should be brought under consideration.   Mr. Leigh, however, resigned his seat in 1836.

Mr. Tyler took a somewhat different course from his colleague ; and his conduct on the occasion greatly elevated him in the estimation of the public, particularly among the advocates of the doctrine of instruction. He might well have been held excusable, even by them, if he had refused to obey the instructions, and had retained his seat, for he was supported by the fact that the very vote he was now called upon to expunge was given under instructions, if not as explicit, at least quite as decisive of the opinion of the legislature as those now presented.   But he was not willing then to overthrow or mar in the least degree the consistency of his previous life, with regard to the right of instruction.   As his first act in the legislature of his own state had been the advocacy of that principle, so the first speech he had ever made in the Congress of the United States was declaratory of what he considered the same truth—the right of the constituent to instruct—the duty of the representative to obey.   He could not obey the instructions he had received without falsifying his own judgment, and violating his conscience by a breach of that constitution he had sworn to support, a clause of which requires that the senate shall " keep a journal of its proceedings, and publish it from time to time ;" and in such circumstances he was not long in deciding to surrender into the hands of those who gave it, or rather their successors, the honorable place with which he had been intrusted.   He could not silently submit, however, to be instructed out of his seat, and he took the opportunity to lay before the people of the state and the public generally, in his letter of resignation to the legislature of Virginia, an exhibition of the principles by which his public life had thus far been guided, and of the motives by which his present conduct was ruled.   The following are extracts from this letter, dated Washington, February 20, 1836 :—

" I now reaffirm the opinion at all times heretofore expressed by me, that instructions are mandatory, provided they do not require a violation of the constitution, or the commission of an act of moral turpitude.   In the course of a somewhat long political life, it must have occurred that my opinions have been variant from the opinions of those I represent ; but in presenting to me the alternative of resignation in this instance, you give me to be distinctly informed that the accomplishment of your object is regarded as of such primary importance that my resignation is desired if compliance can not be yielded.   I am bound to consider you as in this fairly representing the sentiments of our common constituents, the people of Virginia, to whom alone you are amenable if you have mistaken their wishes.

"In voting for the resolution of the senate, against which you are now so indignant, I did no more than carry out the people's declared views of the legislature, as expressed in their resolutions of that day, and which were passed by overwhelming majorities of more than two to one in both houses. The terms employed by the legislature were strong and decided. The conduct of the president was represented as dangerous and alarming I was told that it could not be too strongly condemned; that he had mani· fested a disposition greatly to extend his official influence; and because, with these declarations before me, I voted for a resolution which declares 'that the president, in the late executive proceedings, has assumed upon himself authority and power not conferred by the constitution and laws, but in derogation of both,' I am now ostracized by your fiat, which requires obedience or resignation. Compare the resolutions of the general assembly of that day with the above resolution, and its mildness will be entirely obvious. I submit, with all due deference, to yourselves, what is to be the condition of the senator in future, if, for yielding obedience to the wishes of one legislature, he is to be called upon to resign by another? If he disobeys the first, he is contemned; if he obeys the last, he violates his oath, and becomes an object of scorn and contempt. I respectfully ask, if this be the mode by which the great right of instructions is to be sustained, may it not degenerate into an engine of faction—an instrument to be employed by the outs to get in, instead of being directed to noble purposes—to the advancement of the cause of civil liberty? May it not be converted into a political guillotine, devoted to the worst of purposes? Nor are these anticipations at all weakened by the fact, as it existed in the case now under consideration, that several of those who constitute the present majority in the general assembly, and who now call upon me to expunge the journal or to resign my seat, actually voted for the very resolutions of a previous session, to which I have referred.

"I dare not touch the journal of the senate. The constitution forbids it. In the midst of all the agitations of party, I have heretofore stood by that sacred instrument. It is the only post of honor and of safety. A seat in the senate is sufficiently elevated to fill the measure of any man's ambition; and as an evidence of the sincerity of my convictions that your resolutions can not be executed, without violating my oath, I surrender into your hands three unexpired years of my term. I shall carry with me into retirement, the principles which I brought with me into public life, and by the surrender of the high station to which I was called by the voice of the people of Virginia, I shall set an example to my children which shall teach them to regard as nothing place and office, when to be either obtained or held at the sacrifice of honor."

At the same time, Mr. Tyler placed in the hands of the president of the senate, Mr. Van Buren, a letter informing the senate that he had resigned into the hands of the general assembly of Virginia his seat as a senator from that state.   Mr. Rives was elected, by the legislature of Virginia, to fill the vacancy occasioned by Mr. Tyler's resignation, and the latter retired once more to his home and the practice of his profession.   His course was highly commended, not only in Virginia, but throughout the Union.   Soon after his retirement, a public dinner was given to Mr. Leigh and himself, and the following was among the toasts expressing similar feelings : " Our honored guest, John Tyler—' Expunged' from a post that he adorned, and the functions of which he ever faithfully and ably discharged, by the complying tools of an unprincipled aspirant, he is but the more endeared to the hearts of his countrymen."

Some time in 1830, Mr. Tyler had removed from Charles City county to Gloucester, where his family had resided until the present year.   He now again removed to Williamsburg, the ancient dwelling-place of his fathers ; and though his name was, in 1836, placed upon the electoral ticket of some of the states, as a candidate for the vice-presidency, he mingled very little, for a time, in political matters, devoting himself exclusively to his private pursuits.

He was first nominated for vice-president in Maryland, in December, 1835, and in that state placed on the ticket with General Harrison, the whig candidate for president.   He also received, in 1836, the support of the friends of Judge White in the states where that gentleman was the candidate for president against Mr. Van Buren ; but Maryland was the only state that voted for Harrison which gave its electoral vote to Mr. Tyler.   He, however, received the votes of South Carolina (which state gave its vote to Mr. Mangum, of North Carolina, for president), Georgia, and Tennessee, for vice-president, in addition to the votes of Maryland, making 47 in all, Francis Granger receiving the votes of the other states in the opposition, including Kentucky.   It thus appears that Mr. Tyler was not in 1836 considered the whig candidate for vice-president, his principal support for that office being derived from the state-rights party of the south and west, who in some respects co-operated with the whigs in opposition to Jackson and Van Buren.   Virginia refused to vote for Richard M. Johnson for vice-president, but as the friends of Jackson and Van Buren controlled the electoral vote of the state, it was not given to Mr. Tyler, but to William Smith, of Alabama.

In the spring of 1838, Mr. Tyler was elected by the whigs of James City county, a member of the house of delegates of Virginia ; and during the subsequent session of the legislature he acted with the whig party, under which name the different sections of the opposition to Mr. Van Buren's administration gradually became amalgamated in Virginia.

In 1839, Mr. Tyler was elected one of the delegates from Virginia to the whig national convention which met at Harrisburg, Pennsylvania, to nominate candidates for president and vice-president of the United States. It is well known that Mr. Clay, of Kentucky, was the favorite candidate of the delegates from the southern states, in that convention. The course of Mr. Clay in the senate, on many occasions, particularly in bringing about a settlement of the controversy respecting the tariff and South Carolina nullification, had rendered him popular with the state-rights section of the whigs, and they were anxious for his nomination to the presidency. In this feeling Mr. Tyler warmly participated, with all the Virginia delegation. He was chosen one of the vice-presidents of the convention, and exerted his influence in favor of Mr. Clay. General Harrison, however, was nominated for president, and Mr. Tyler was among those who expressed their deep regrets at the defeat of Mr. Clay as a candidate.

The question of a candidate for president had so much absorbed the attention of the whigs, that the subject of a candidate for vice-president had attracted but little attention. When General Harrison was nominated for the first office, it became necessary, in the judgment of the delegates, to take a candidate for vice-president from the south, and, after a brief consultation, the nomination was offered to Mr. Tyler, and accepted. As he was an ardent friend of Mr. Clay, it was supposed that this nomination would be popular with the friends of that gentleman, under the feelings of disappointment with which it was anticipated they would receive the nomination of General Harrison. Had the event of Mr. Tyler's succession to the presidency been contemplated, it can not be doubted that a scrutiny of his principles, and the remembrance of his course and action on cherished whig measures, would have caused more hesitancy in placing him on the presidential ticket, if not his prompt rejection, by the whig convention.

The speeches, letters, and declarations of Mr. Tyler, during the canvass of 1840, were generally satisfactory to the whigs, and gave reasonable expectation that he would co-operate with General Harrison and Mr. Clay in carrying out the wishes of the whig party, if successful in the election.

The triumph of the whig party, elevated General Harrison to the presidency, Mr. Tyler to the vice-presidency, and secured a whig majority in both houses of Congress.

It remains to mention, in this place, that the sudden and lamented death of President Harrison, in one month after his inauguration, devolved upon Mr. Tyler, in April, 1841, the high and responsible duties of president of the United States.

There can be no doubt that Mr. Tyler mistook his position in attempting to act with the whig party, and in accepting their nomination for one of the highest offices in the nation, which, by the dispensation of Providence, placed him in the presidential chair, clothed with the power and patronage of that high station.   That the whigs also acted without due reflection, in his nomination, is alike evident; and from these two causes flowed the consequences which resulted in the embarrassment, difficulties, and total loss of popularity with both the great parties of the country, on the one side, of the president, and bitter disappointment and chagrin on the part of the whigs.

In person, Mr. Tyler is rather tall and thin, with light complexion, blue eyes, and prominent features.   His manners are plain and affable, and in private life he is amiable, hospitable, and courteous.   His errors as a politician are ascribed, by some, to a want of judgment, to an inordinate vanity, and the influence of bad advice; to which may be added, extreme obstinacy in persisting in opinions once formed, without regard to consequences.

In 1813, at the age of twenty-three, Mr. Tyler married a lady about his own age, Miss Letitia Christian, daughter of Robert Christian, Esq., of New Kent county, Virginia.   She was a lady much esteemed by her acquaintances, as a wife, a mother, a friend, and a Christian, being for many years a member of the episcopal church.   She died at Washington, September 10, 1842, leaving three sons and three daughters.   While president of the United States, Mr. Tyler was again married, to Miss Julia Gardiner, of New York, daughter of the late David Gardiner, Esq., of that city, who was killed by an explosion on board the steamship Princeton, in February, 1844.   The marriage of the president took place at New York, on the 26th of June, 1844.   Since his retirement from the presidency, Mr. Tyler has resided at his seat near Williamsburg, Virginia.

Eng.{1} by V Balch from a Daguerreotype

James K Polk

g---- ---- --- --- prosident ,
and the family is also connected with the Alexanders, chairman and sec-

BIOGRAPHICAL SKETCH

OF

JAMES KNOX POLK.

JAMES KNOX POLK, the eleventh president of the United States, is the oldest of ten children, and was born on the second of November, 1795, in Mecklenburg county, North Carolina. His ancestors, whose original name, Pollock, has, by obvious transition, assumed its present form, emigrated in the early part of the eighteenth century, from Ireland. The family traces their descent from Robert Polk, who was born and married in Ireland; his wife, Magdalen Tusker, was the heiress of Mowning hill. They had six sons and two daughters; Robert Polk, the progenitor of James Knox Polk, was the fifth son; he married a Miss Gullet, and removed to America. Ezekiel Polk, the grandfather of James K. Polk, was one of his sons.

The Polk family settled in Somerset county, on the eastern shore of Maryland, where some of their descendants still sojourn. Being the only democrats of note in that county, they were called the democratic family. The branch of the family from which the president is descended, removed to the neighborhood of Carlisle, in Pennsylvania, and thence to the western frontier of North Carolina, sometime before the commencement of the revolutionary war. Some of the Polk family were honorably distinguished in that eventful struggle. On the twentieth of May, 1775, consequently more than twelve months anterior to the declaration of independence of the fourth of July, 1776, the assembled inhabitants of Mecklenburg county publicly absolved themselves from their allegiance to the British crown, and issued a formal manifesto of independence, in terms of manly eloquence, similar to some of the expressions in the declaration of the American Congress adopted more than a year afterward. Colonel Thomas Polk, the prime mover in this act of noble daring, and one of the signers of this first declaration of independence, was the great uncle of the president; and the family is also connected with the Alexanders, chairman and secretary of the meeting which adopted the declaration, as well as with Dr. Ephraim Brevard, the author of the declaration itself.

The father of James K. Polk was a farmer of unassuming pretensions, but enterprising character. Thrown upon his own resources in early life, he became the architect of his own fortunes. He was a warm supporter of Mr. Jefferson, and through life a firm and undeviating democrat. In the autumn of 1806 he removed, with his family of ten children, from the homestead in North Carolina, to Tennessee, where he was one of the pioneers of the fertile valley of Duck river, a branch of the Cumberland, then a wilderness, but now the most flourishing and populous portion of the state. In this region the subject of this sketch resided, until his election to the presidency, so that he may be said, literally, to have grown with its growth, and strengthened with its strength. Of course, in the infancy of its settlement, the opportunities for instruction could not be great. Notwithstanding this disadvantage—and the still more formidable one of a painful affection from which, after years of suffering, he was finally relieved by a surgical operation—he acquired the elements of a good English education. Apprehending that his constitution had been too much impaired to permit the confinement of study, his father determined, much, however, against the will of the son, to make him a commercial man ; and with this view placed him with a merchant.

He remained a few weeks in a situation adverse to his wishes, and incompatible with his taste. Finally, his earnest appeals succeeded in overcoming the resistance of his father, and in July, 1813, he was placed, first under the care of the Rev. Dr. Henderson, and subsequently at the academy of Murfreesborough, Tennessee, then under the direction of Mr. Samuel P. Black, justly celebrated in that region as a classical teacher. In the autumn of 1815 he entered the university of North Carolina, having, in less than two years and a half, thoroughly prepared himself to commence his collegiate course, being then in the twentieth year of his age.

Mr. Polk's career at the university was distinguished. At each semiannual examination, he bore away the first honor, and finally graduated in 1818, with the highest distinction of his class, and with the reputation of being the first scholar in both the mathematics and classics. Of the former science he was passionately fond, though equally distinguished as a linguist. His course at college was marked by the same assiduity and studious application which have since distinguished him. His ambition to excel was equalled by his perseverance alone ; in proof of which, it is said that he never missed a recitation, nor omitted the punctilious performance of any duty. Habits of close application at college are apt to be despised by those who pride themselves on brilliancy of mind, as if they were incompatible. This is a melancholy mistake. Genius has ever been defined the faculty of appreciation. The latter is, at least, something better, and more available. So carefully has Mr. Polk avoided the pedantry of classical display, which is the false taste of our day and country, as almost to hide the acquisitions which distinguished his early career. His preference for the useful and substantial, indicated by his youthful passion for the mathematics, has made him select a style of elocution which would perhaps be deemed too plain by the admirers of flashy declamation.*

From the university he returned to Tennessee, with health impaired by application, and, in the beginning of the year 1819, commenced the study of the law (that profession which has furnished nine of the eleven presidents of the United States), in the office of the late Felix Grundy, for many years a representative and senator of Tennessee in Congress ; under whose auspices he was admitted to the bar, at the close of 1820. He commenced his professional career in the county of Maury, with great advantages, derived from the connexion of his family with its early settlement. His warmest friends were the sharers of his father's early privations and difficulties, and the associates of his own youth. But his success was due to his personal qualities still more than to extrinsic advantages. A republican in habits as well as in principles, depending for the maintenance of his dignity upon the esteem of others, and not upon his own assumption, his manners conciliated the general good will. The confidence of his friends was justified by the result. His thorough academical education, his accurate knowledge of the law, his readiness and resources in debate, his unwearied application to business, secured him, at once, full employment, and in less than a year he was already a leading practitioner.

Mr. Polk continued to devote some years exclusively to the prosecution of his profession, with a progressive augmentation of reputation, and the more solid rewards by which it is accompanied. In 1823, he entered upon the stormy career of politics, being chosen to represent his county in the state legislature, by a heavy majority over the former incumbent, but not without formidable opposition. He was for two successive years a member of that body, where his ability in debate, and talent for business, at once gave him reputation. The early personal and political friend of General Jackson, he was one of those who, in the session of 1823–'24, called that distinguished man from his retirement, by electing him to the senate of the United States.

In August, 1825, being then in his thirtieth year, Mr. Polk was chosen to represent his district in Congress, and took his seat in the national councils in December following. He brought with him those fundamental principles to which he has adhered through all the mutations of party. From his early youth he was a democratic republican of the strictest sect. He has ever regarded the constitution of the United States as an instrument of specific and limited powers, and he was found in opposition to

* For a part of this sketch we are indebted to the Democratic Review of May, 1838.

every measure that aimed to consolidate federal power, or to detract from the dignity and legitimate functions of the state governments. He signalized his hostility to the doctrines of those who held to a more liberal construction of the constitution, in all their modes. He always refused his assent to the appropriation of money by the federal government for what he deemed the unconstitutional purpose of constructing works of internal improvement within the states. He took ground early against the constitutionality as well as expediency of a national bank ; and in August, 1829, consequently several months before the appearance of General Jackson's first message, announced then his opinions in a published letter to his constituents. He has ever been opposed to a tariff for protection, and was, at all times, the strenuous advocate of a reduction of the revenue to the economical wants of the government. Entertaining these opinions, and entering Congress, as he did, at the first session after the election of John Quincy Adams to the presidency, he promptly took his stand against the doctrines developed in the message of that chief magistrate, and was, during the continuance of his administration, resolutely opposed to its leading measures.

When Mr. Polk entered Congress, he was, with one or two exceptions, the junior member of that body. His first speech was in favor of a proposition to amend the constitution in such manner as to prevent the choice of president of the United States from devolving on Congress in any event. This speech at once attracted public attention by the force of its reasoning, the copiousness of its research, and the spirit of indignation, with reference to the then recent election by Congress, by which it was animated. At the same session the subject of the Panama mission was brought before Congress, and the project was opposed by Mr. Polk, who strenuously protested against the doctrine of the friends of the administration, that as the president and senate are the treaty-making power, the house of representatives can not deliberate upon, nor refuse the appropriations necessary to carry them into effect. The views of Mr. Polk he embodied in a series of resolutions, which reproduced in a tangible shape, the doctrines, on this question, of the republican party of 1798. The first of these resolutions declares, " that it is the constitutional right and duty of the house of representatives, when called upon for appropriations to defray the expenses of foreign missions, to deliberate on the expediency of such missions, and to determine and act thereon, as in their judgment may seem most conducive to the public good."

From this time Mr. Polk's history became inseparably interwoven with that of the house. He was prominently connected with every important question, and upon every one took the boldest democratic ground. He continued to oppose the administration of Mr. Adams until its termination, and during the whole period of General Jackson's terms he was one of its leading supporters, and at times, and on certain questions of paramount importance its chief reliance. In December, 1827, Mr. Polk was placed on the committee of foreign affairs, and sometime after, as chairman of a select committee, he made a report on the surplus revenue, denying the constitutional power of Congress to collect from the people, for distribution, a surplus beyond the wants of the government, and maintaining that the revenue should be reduced to the exigencies of the public service. In 1830, he defended the act of General Jackson in placing his veto on the Maysville road bill, and thus checking the system of internal improvement by the general government, which had been entered upon by Congress.

In December, 1832, Mr. Polk was transferred to the committee of ways and means, and at that session presented the report of the minority of that committee, with regard to certain charges against the United States bank; this minority report presenting conclusions utterly adverse to the institution which had been the subject of inquiry.

The course of Mr. Polk arrayed against him the friends of the bank, and they held a meeting at Nashville to denounce his report. His re-election to Congress was opposed, but, after a violent contest, Mr. Polk was re-elected by a majority of more than three thousand. In September, 1833, President Jackson determined upon the removal of the public deposites from the bank of the United States. This measure, which caused great excitement throughout the country, was carried into effect in October following, and at the subsequent session of Congress it was the leading subject of discussion. In the senate the president was censured for the measure, but he was sustained in the house of representatives. On this occasion Mr. Polk, as chairman of the committee of ways and means, vindicated the president's measure, and by his coolness, promptitude, and skill, carried through the resolutions of the committee relating to the bank and the deposites, and sustaining the administration, after which the cause of the bank was abandoned in Congress.

Toward the close of the memorable session of 1834, Mr. Speaker Stevenson resigned the chair, as well as his seat in the house. The majority of the democratic party preferred Mr. Polk as his successor, but in consequence of a division in its ranks, the opposition united with the democratic friends of John Bell, of Tennessee, and thereby succeeded in electing that gentleman, then a professed friend, but since a decided opponent, of the president and his measures. Mr. Polk's defeat produced no change in his course. He remained faithful to his party, and assiduous in the performance of his arduous duties.

In December, 1835, Mr. Polk was elected speaker of the house of representatives, and again chosen to that station in 1837, at the extra session held in the first year of Mr. Van Buren's administration. The duties of speaker were discharged by him during five sessions, with ability, at a time when party feelings ran high in the house, and in the beginning unusual difficulties were thrown in his way by the animosity of his political opponents. During the first session in which he presided, more appeals were taken from his decision than had occurred in the whole period since the origin of the government; but he was uniformly sustained by the house, including many of his political adversaries. Notwithstanding the violence with which he had been assailed, Congress passed, at the close of the session, in March, 1837, a unanimous vote of thanks to its presiding officer, from whom it separated with the kindest feelings. In the twenty-fifth Congress, over which he presided as speaker at three sessions, commencing in September, 1837, and ending in March, 1839, parties were more nearly balanced (Mr. Polk's majority as speaker being only eight), and the most exciting questions were agitated during the whole period. At the close of the term, Mr. Elmore, of South Carolina, moved " that the thanks of the house be presented to the Hon. James K. Polk, for the able, impartial, and dignified manner in which he has presided over its deliberations, and performed the arduous and important duties of the chair." On this resolution, a long and excited debate arose, which was terminated by the previous question; when the resolution was adopted by 94 in the affirmative to 57 in the negative. But few of the members of the opposition concurred in the vote of approval. The speaker, in adjourning the house, made a reply of more than ordinary length, and showing, on his part, deep feeling. Among other remarks, he said: " When I look back to the period when I first took my seat in this house, and then look around me for those who were at that time my associates here, I find but few, very few, remaining. But five members who were here with me fourteen years ago, continue to be members of this body. My service here has been constant and laborious. I can perhaps say what but few others, if any, can, that I have not failed to attend the daily sittings of this house a single day since I have been a member of it, save on a single occasion, when prevented for a short time by indisposition. In my intercourse with the members of this body, when I occupied a place upon the floor, though occasionally engaged in debates upon interesting public questions, and of an exciting character, it is a source of unmingled gratification to me to recur to the fact, that on no occasion was there the slightest personal or unpleasant collision with any of its members. Maintaining, and at all times expressing, my own opinions firmly, the same right was fully conceded to others. For four years past, the station I have occupied, and a sense of propriety, in the divided and unusually-excited state of public opinion and feeling, which has existed both in this house and the country, have precluded me from participating in your debates. Other duties were assigned me.

" The high office of speaker, to which it has been twice the pleasure of this house to elevate me, has been at all times one of labor and high responsibility. It has been made my duty to decide more questions of parliamentary law and order, many of them of a complex and difficult character, arising often in the midst of high excitement, in the course of our proceedings, than had been decided, it is believed, by all my predecessors, from the foundation of the government. This house has uniformly sustained me, without distinction of the political parties of which it has been composed. I return them my thanks for their constant support in the discharge of the duties I have had to perform.

" But, gentlemen, my acknowledgments are especially due to the majority of this house, for the high and flattering evidence they have given me of their approbation of my conduct as the presiding officer of the house, by the resolution you have been pleased to pass. I regard it as of infinitely more value than if it had been the common, matter-of-course, and customary resolution which, in the courtesy usually prevailing between the presiding officer and the members of any deliberative assembly, is always passed, at the close of their deliberations. I regard this as the highest and most valued testimonial I have ever received from this house, because I know that the circumstances under which it has passed, have made it matter of substance, and not of mere form. I shall bear it in grateful remembrance to the latest hour of my life.

"I trust this high office may in future times be filled, as doubtless it will be, by abler men. It can not, I know, be filled by any one who will devote himself with more zeal and untiring industry to do his whole duty, than I have done."

Few public men have pursued a firmer or more consistent course than Mr. Polk, in adhering to the democratic party, in every vicissitude. In 1835, when all of his colleagues of the Tennessee delegation, in the house of representatives, determined to support Judge White, of that state, as the successor to General Jackson, for the presidency, he incurred the hazard of losing his popularity throughout the state, by avowing his unalterable purpose not to separate from the great body of the democratic party, in the presidential election. He therefore became identified with the friends of Mr. Van Buren, in Tennessee, in 1836, when Judge White received the vote of the state by a popular majority of over nine thousand.

After a service of fourteen years in Congress, Mr. Polk in 1839 declined a re-election from the district which had so long sustained him. He was then taken up by the friends of the administration in Tennessee, as a candidate for governor, to oppose Newton Cannon, who was then governor of the state, and supported by the Whig party for re-election. After an animated canvass, during which Mr. Polk visited the different counties of that extensive state, and addressed the people on the political topics of the day, the election took place in August, 1839, and resulted in a majority for Mr. Polk, of more than 2,500 over Governor Cannon. At the ensuing session of the legislature, Governor Polk was nominated by that body for vice-president of the United States, to be placed on the ticket with Mr. Van Buren. He was afterward nominated

15

for the same office in several other states, but at the election of 1840 he received one electoral vote only for vice-president, which was given by one of the electors in Virginia.

Having served as governor of Tennessee for the constitutional term of two years, Mr. Polk was a candidate for re-election in August, 1841. His prospect was unpromising, as the state in 1840 showed a Whig majority of twelve thousand at the presidential election. The result was the defeat of Mr. Polk, and the election of James C. Jones, the whig candidate, as governor, by a majority of 3,224. Mr. Polk therefore retired from public life, at the expiration of his executive term. Two years after, in 1843, he was again a candidate for the executive chair, in opposition to Governor Jones, but he was the second time defeated, and the whig candidate re-elected, by a majority of 3,833.

From October, 1841, until his elevation to the highest office in the Union, Mr. Polk remained in private life, not, however, an inert spectator of the wild and troubled drama of politics. Happy in the confidence of his immediate neighbors, and his numerous political friends throughout the state, in the affections of a charming family, and in the ardent friendship of Andrew Jackson; he had determined to withdraw himself from the anxieties and labors of public life. But the voice of the democracy of Tennessee forbade the gratification of his wishes; as we have seen, he was repeatedly summoned to stand forward as its representative for governor of the state, and he yielded to the summons, whatever might have been the prospects of success.

Mr. Polk did not conceal his opinions on political subjects, when called upon by his fellow-citizens to express them. Those who differed from him had no difficulty in ascertaining the fact of the difference. A proof of this was found in the circumstance which developed his opinions on the subject of Texas. The citizens of Cincinnati had, early in 1844, expressed their " settled opposition" to the annexation of that republic to the United States, and invited him to announce his concurrence in their judgment. In his reply, he said : " Let Texas be re-annexed, and the authority and laws of the United States be established and maintained within her limits, as also in the Oregon territory, and let the fixed policy of our government be, not to permit Great Britain to plant a colony or hold dominion over any portion of the people or territory of either. These are my opinions ; and without deeming it necessary to extend this letter, by assigning the many reasons which influence me in the conclusions to which I come, I regret to be compelled to differ so widely from the views expressed by yourselves, and the meeting of citizens of Cincinnati, whom you represent."

On the 29th of May, 1844, Mr. Polk received the nomination of the democratic national convention, assembled at Baltimore, for president of the United States. To this high office he was elected in the fall of the same year, by the people of the United States, and his majority over Mr. Clay, the Whig candidate, as expressed through the electoral colleges, in December, 1844, was 65. The votes of the presidential electors were— for James K. Polk 170, for Henry Clay 105. George M. Dallas was elected vice-president by the same majority, over Theodore Frelinghuysen. The votes were counted in the house of representatives, on the 10th of February, 1845. The president elect, having repaired to the seat of government, informed the joint committee of Congress, who waited on him, that, " in signifying his acceptance of the office to which he had been chosen by the people, he expressed his deep sense of gratitude to them, for the confidence which they had reposed in him, and requested the committee to convey to their respective houses of Congress, assurances, that, in executing the responsible duties which would devolve upon him, it would be his anxious desire to maintain the honor and promote the welfare of the country."

In person, President Polk is of middle stature, with a full angular brow, and a quick, penetrating eye. The expression of his countenance is grave, but its serious cast is often relieved by a peculiarly pleasant smile, indicative of the amenity of his disposition. The amiable character of his private life, which has ever been upright and pure, secures to him the esteem and friendship of all who have the advantage of his acquaintance. He married a lady of Tennessee, who is a member of the presbyterian church, and well qualified, by her virtues and accomplishments, equally to adorn the circles of private life, or the station to which she has been called. They have no children.

THE LAST DAYS AND DEATH OF MR. POLK.

Immediately after the inauguration of his successor, Gen. Taylor, to the presidency, in March, 1849, Mr. Polk, accompanied by his lady and a few friends, set out on his journey to Tennessee, intending to pass the remainder of his days in retirement, at Nashville, on the Cumberland river, where he had purchased an elegant seat for his future residence. He passed through several of the southern and southwestern states on his journey, and was everywhere received with demonstrations of respect by the people.

After his arrival at Nashville, he devoted his time principally to the improvement and embellishment of his estate ; but it pleased Providence that the days of his retirement should be few in number. In the month of June, he was seized with a chronic diarrhœa, to which disease he had before been subject, which after a few days of suffering, terminated his mortal career on the 15th of June, 1849, in the 54th year of his age, having on his death-bed, received the ordinance of baptism from a methodist clergyman. Public honors to his memory were paid throughout the United States.

Z Taylor

BIOGRAPHICAL SKETCH

OF

ZACHARY TAYLOR.

VIRGINIA, the "Ancient Dominion" of the British American colonies, has obtained also the name of the "Mother of Presidents," among the states; it being the native state of no less than seven of the presidents of the United States, including ZACHARY TAYLOR, the twelfth on the list of those who have filled that high station. It is worthy of remark, that three of these Virginians have been elected without the aid of the electoral votes of their native state.

The family of the Taylors of Virginia, to which the twelfth president belongs, is honorably distinguished in the annals of the colony and the state. Its ancestors of the same name emigrated from England, with other friends of liberty, and settled in the southeastern part of the colony of Virginia in the year 1692. Among the different branches and connexions of the family are the Madisons, Lees, Barbours, Pendletons, Conways, Taliaferos, Hunts, Gaineses, and others, whose public services and patriotism, during more than a century, are commemorated in colonial and national history.

Richard Taylor, the father of General Zachary Taylor, was born in Virginia, on the 22d of March, 1744. He received a plain but solid education, and in boyhood evinced the bold and adventurous spirit which afterward led him to seek a home in the western wilderness. When still a youth, he made a journey to Kentucky, and thence to the banks of the Mississippi, surveying the country as far as Natchez, and returning on foot, without guide or companion, through pathless woods, inhabited only by savages and wild beasts, to his father's house in Virginia.*

At the age of thirty-five, on the 20th of August, 1779, Richard Taylor married Sarah Strother, a young lady of highly respectable connexions, then in her twentieth year. At this time he held a colonel's commission

* For part of the facts mentioned in this sketch, we are indebted to Fry's Life of General Taylor; also to Montgomery's memoir of the same.

in the Virginia line, and served with zeal and valor throughout the revolutionary war.   He was engaged in several of the most important battles of that war, particularly in the brilliant achievement of Trenton, where he rendered distinguished and valuable aid to General Washington.

Five sons and three daughters were the offspring of the marriage of Colonel Richard Taylor — the first child born in 1781.   His third son, ZACHARY TAYLOR, the subject of this memoir, was born in Orange county, Virginia, on the 24th of November, 1784.   In the following summer his father fulfilled his long-cherished intention of emigrating to Kentucky, only ten years after the first habitation of a white man had been erected in the vast region between the western boundary of Virginia and the Mississippi.   In the emigration of Colonel Richard Taylor to this country, he had been preceded by his brother Hancock Taylor, a brave and intelligent man, who lost his life by the Indians while engaged in surveying lands in the Ohio valley.   He is said to have selected for his farm the site of the present city of Louisville.

The early years of Zachary Taylor were passed under the guidance of such men, and under such circumstances for the development of a bold spirit and active intellect.   His father had settled in Jefferson county, near Louisville, where he acquired a large estate by his industry and thrift, and honorable consideration by his intelligence, bravery, and patriotism.   As Louisville rose into importance, his own fortune and local distinction increased.   He received from President Washington a commission as collector of that port, New Orleans being then a Spanish possession.   Richard Taylor was also one of the framers of the constitution of Kentucky; represented Jefferson county for many years in both branches of the legislature, and was a member of the electoral colleges which voted for Jefferson, Madison, Monroe, and Clay.   Among the politicians of Kentucky he is remembered as one of the few men of the " Old Court party" who could be elected from Jefferson county during the excitement of the old and new court question.   He died on his plantation, near Louisville, leaving to survive him three sons and three daughters, of whom one son and two daughters have since died.   His two surviving sons, Zachary and Joseph, have both chosen a military profession, as did their brother Hancock, who died in 1808.

One of the chief cares of Colonel Taylor was the education of his children ; but during the first ten or fifteen years of his residence in Kentucky, the sparseness of the population, and the exposure of the inhabitants to Indian hostilities, made the accomplishment of his purpose very difficult.   A school for the rudiments of English merely was established in his neighborhood by Elisha Ayres, a native of Connecticut, who afterward returned to that state, and now resides, at the advanced age of fourscore years, at Preston, near Norwich.   To Mr. Ayres, as his teacher, was Zachary Taylor sent in his early years, to receive such instruction as was practicable under the circumstances, while constant care and watchfulness were necessary on the part of his father and other guardians of his youth, for protection against savage foes.

After the Indians were subdued by the decisive victory of General Wayne, in 1794, a general peace was concluded with them, in the following year, and from that period the prosperity of Kentucky advanced rapidly with the increase of population. Zachary Taylor was reared by his father to his own profession, that of a farmer; and, until he attained the age of twenty-one, was practically engaged in that laborious occupation, laying the foundation of the robust health, hardy habits, and persevering industry, which have been the test of various climates, rude fare, and severe duty, during a military life of more than forty years. The military service very early engaged his affections and excited his ambition. When Aaron Burr's movements in the west began to arouse suspicion, the patriotic young men of Kentucky formed volunteer companies to oppose his designs by arms, if occasion should demand such a result. The brothers Taylor were enrolled in a troop raised for this purpose. Their services were not required by the events, and after the alarm had subsided, Zachary returned to his farm.

On the death of his brother, Lieutenant Hancock Taylor, who held a commission in the United States army, an opportunity was afforded Zachary of obtaining the vacancy. Through the influence of his relative, James Madison, then secretary of state, and of his uncle, Major Edmund Taylor, he received from President Jefferson, on the 3d of May, 1808, his commission as first lieutenant in the seventh regiment of United States infantry. At this time, when he was in the twenty-fourth year of his age, he was in the enjoyment of a competency from his occupation as a farmer. But the activity of his mind, and his taste for a military profession, led him to prefer the care and privations of a soldier's life to the quiet and comforts of a landed proprietor at home. His first experience in his new vocation had nearly proved fatal. He was ordered to report himself to General Wilkinson, in New Orleans; and being seized there with the yellow fever, was obliged to return home for the recovery of his health. He appears to have employed his time sedulously in the study of his profession, as we find him, three years from this time, fulfilling with honor a dangerous and important post.

In 1810, Lieutenant Taylor was married to Miss Margaret Smith, a lady of Maryland, of a highly respectable family in that state. She was sister of the late Major R. S. Smith, of the marine corps.

The Indian tribes on the northwestern frontier of the United States having been excited to feelings of hostilities against the Americans, as was supposed and believed through the agency of British emissaries sent among them, and a general league of the tribes being on the point of formation, by the influence of the noted chief Tecumseh and his brother the Prophet, the American government took early steps to counteract their operations. General Harrison, then governor of the northwestern territory, was ordered to march a competent force into the Indian country.

After the declaration of war, in 1812, Taylor was placed in command of Fort Harrison, a block-house and stockade, which had been erected by order of General Harrison, on the Wabash river, about fifty miles above Vincennes. Congress declared war against Great Britain on the 19th of June, 1812, and at no previous period was the spirit of those Indians who were allies of England, and led on by Tecumseh and the Prophet, so fully aroused to the determination of exterminating the Americans on the northwestern frontier as at this time. Their first object of attack was Fort Harrison, and three months after war with England had been formally declared, they were banded for the purpose of this and other acts of hostility. Captain Taylor had some intimations of their intentions, which were confirmed on the 3d of September, by the report of guns in the vicinity of the fort. On the following day it was discovered that two men had been murdered and scalped by the Indians. Captain Taylor, therefore, made every effort in his power for defence. The whole force under his command was about fifty men, of whom nearly two thirds were invalids, and he himself was just recovering from a fever. The Indians were aware of his weakness, but preferred the exercise of their native cunning to the hazard of an open attack. A deputation of the Prophet's party came to the fort with a white flag, and affecting peaceable intentions. Captain Taylor was not deceived by this stratagem, and he made preparations for an assault from the enemy. At night a watch was set, and the remaining few retired to rest. An hour before midnight the report of a musket was heard, and Taylor, springing from his brief sleep, found his savage foes were making an attack upon the fort. On their approach, the sentinels had retreated within, and it was discovered that the lower building was already fired by the Indians, rendering the situation of the garrison one of extreme peril. The young captain, however, retained his composure, and while he directed a part of his small force to carry buckets of water to extinguish the flames, the other soldiers returned the fire of the Indians by a steady discharge of musketry, the assailants, during seven hours, abating no effort to carry the fort, and being for some time under the cover of a very dark night. In this protracted attack only three of the garrison were killed and three wounded, while the Indians suffered severely from their exposed situation. At six o'clock on the morning of the 5th, dispirited by their loss, they abandoned the attempt to carry the fort, and retired from the spot, after destroying all the provisions of the post, and killing or driving off all the horses and cattle.

The account of this affair by Captain Taylor, in a letter to General Harrison, dated the 10th of September, 1812, is his first official despatch, and has the unaffected spirit, without the experienced style, of his more mature productions.

The failure of their enterprise against Fort Harrison disheartened the Indians, and they abandoned for a time any further attempts against it; yet the garrison expected another attack, and Captain Taylor sent to General Harrison an account of his situation, and an application for assistance. A large force, under General Hopkins, was immediately sent to the relief of the garrison, then reduced to want by sickness, fatigue, and the loss of provisions.

The conduct of Taylor at Fort Harrison was not overlooked by his superior officers, by the public, or by the government. General Hopkins, in a letter to the governor of Kentucky, said of him: " The firm and almost unparalleled defence of Fort Harrison by Captain Zachary Taylor, has raised for him a fabric of character not to be effaced by eulogy." The president afforded a satisfactory proof of his favorable opinion, by conferring upon Taylor the rank of major by brevet—the oldest instance in the service of this species of promotion.

The Indians, notwithstanding their defeat, continued their depredations upon the inhabitants on the frontier, and to arrest their atrocities General Hopkins planned an expedition against the Indian villages on the Illinois, and commenced his march about the middle of October. But the volunteers under his command evinced insubordination, and the general resolved to abandon the expedition. The villages, however, were attacked by a detachment under Colonel Russell, and destroyed. In the following month, General Hopkins undertook a second expedition, directed against the Prophet's and Winebago town, in which Major Taylor took part, and received the commendations of the general. Several skirmishes occurred, in some of which our troops suffered severely. They succeeded in achieving their main objects, devastating the enemy's country and destroying their settlements. The winter forced both parties into a cessation of active hostilities. From this time to the close of the war with Great Britain, Major Taylor was engaged on the northwest frontier, accomplishing the purposes of the government with unremitting vigilance.

In 1814, Major Taylor commanded an expedition against the British and Indians on Rock river, a branch of the Mississippi. By order of General Howard, Major Taylor left Fort Independence, on the 2d August, at the head of a detachment of about three hundred and fifty men, and proceeded in boats up the Mississippi to Rock river, where they arrived on the 4th of September. The British and Indians being strongly posted near the mouth of the river, and well provided with artillery, commenced firing upon the Americans before they had an opportunity to land, and the boats were exposed to the fire of the artillery and musketry for a considerable time, which was returned by Taylor's troops, from small arms and the cannon on board the boats. The Americans then dropped down the river about three miles, and landed ; being followed by the enemy, Taylor halted on a small prairie and prepared his troops for action, when the British and Indians hastily retired. The Americans in this affair had eleven men killed and wounded.

Taylor then called a council of his officers, and as the enemy was at least three to one in number to the Americans, it was decided that it would be madness to attack them in their position, without a prospect of success. Major Taylor therefore determined to drop down the river to the Des Moines rapids, and execute one of the principal objects of the expedition, namely, to erect a fort to command the river ; which was done, and the same was called Fort Madison. The details of this expedition, Major Taylor communicated to General Howard, in an official despatch, dated September 6, 1814.

On the restoration of peace with Great Britain, in 1815, Congress adopted the policy of reducing the army and of annulling promotions made during the war. Among other officers who suffered from this policy was Major Taylor, who was reduced to the rank of captain ; in consequence of which he resigned his commission, and left the service, returning to his family, from whom he had so long been separated, and resuming his agricultural pursuits.

In consequence of the influence of his friends, who were not content to see him retire from the army, for such a cause, he was reinstated by President Madison, in the course of the year, and consented again to leave his home and its attractions for the monotonous service of the army in time of peace. In 1816, Major Taylor was ordered to Green Bay, on Lake Michigan, and remained in command of that post for two years. Returning to Kentucky, he passed a year with his family, and was then ordered to join Colonel Russell at New Orleans. Except during a temporary absence, when recalled by the illness of his wife, he continued in the south for several years, generally engaged in some active duty. One of his labors was the opening of a military road, and another, the erection of Fort Jesup——the latter in 1822. On the 20th of April, 1819, Taylor received the commission of a lieutenant-colonel. In 1824, he was engaged at Louisville in the recruiting service, and in the latter part of that year he was ordered to the city of Washington.

In 1826, he was member of a board of officers of the army and militia (of which General Scott was president), convened by Mr. Barbour, then secretary of war, to consider and propose a system for the organization and improvement of the militia of the United States. In this board, Taylor's opinions were in favor of maintaining the militia strictly as citizen-soldiery, instead of giving them the character of a regular army, as proposed by some. The report drawn by General Scott, and adopted on motion of Colonel Taylor, was approved in Congress, but was not carried into effect.

Resuming his duties on the northwestern frontier, Taylor continued for five years in that position, where he seems to have been unconsciously preparing himself in his profession for the splendid achievements of his latter years. A writer in the " Literary World" thus mentions him : " As plain Lieutenant-Colonel Taylor, I have often seen him putting his men through the battalion drill, on the northern banks of the Wisconsin, in the depth of February. This would seem only characteristic of the man who has since proved himself equally ' Rough and Ready' under the scorching sun of the tropics. But, looking back through long years to many a pleasant hour spent in the well-selected library of the post which Colonel Taylor then commanded, we recur now with singular interest to the agreeable conversations held in the room which was the colonel's favorite resort, amid the intervals of duty." And the same chronicler of his severe habits of discipline and study continues : " Nor will the reader think these personal reminiscences impertinent, when we add that our object in recurring to them here is simply to mention that, remembering alike the wintry drill and the snug book-room, Taylor's hardihood — the idea of which now so readily attaches to his soubriquet of ' Rough and Ready' — would certainly not then have struck a stranger as more characteristic than his liberal-minded intelligence."

In 1832, Taylor was promoted by President Jackson to the rank of colonel. During the previous year, the difficulties between the white settlers near Rock river, Illinois, and the Sac Indians under the celebrated chief Black Hawk, had been fomented, by bad and interested white men, to a point of open hostilities. Black Hawk and his brother the Prophet, at the head of a large party of Indians, having defeated an American volunteer force near Rock river, on the 14th of May, 1832, the people of Illinois became greatly alarmed, and the secretary of war ordered about a thousand regular troops, under the command of General Scott, to the scene of action, and active hostilities ensued, and continued for three months. In July, General Scott was reinforced by 2,500 men, under General Atkinson, including 400 regulars under Colonel Taylor. Toward the close of the month the Indians retreated into the wilderness, and General Atkinson, with a detachment of 1,300 men, including the regulars under Colonel Taylor, pursued them. By great perseverance, during a forced march, the Americans succeeded in overtaking the Indians near the junction of the Mississippi and Iowa rivers, where a desperate conflict ensued, which resulted in a total route of the Indians, many falling by our arms, others perishing in the river, and the rest dispersing or submitting themselves prisoners. The chief, Black Hawk, who then escaped, was in the course of the month surrendered by some of his faithless allies, and with his capture ended the war. The chief and his fellow-prisoners were confided to the charge of Colonel Taylor, who conveyed them to the Jefferson barracks, where they arrived about the middle of September.

After the Black Hawk war, Colonel Taylor was for a short time at

Louisville, with his family, and was thence ordered to Prairie du Chien, to the command of Fort Crawford, a work which had been erected under his superintendence.   Here he remained until 1836, when his services were required in Florida, to assist in reducing the Seminole Indians to submission.   To that field he immediately repaired, although he might with propriety have asked of the government a season of repose, having very rarely enjoyed the ease and tranquillity of home during a period of more than twenty-five years.

The Seminole Indians, the remnants of the aborigines of Florida, were required by the government of the United States to emigrate from that territory to lands appropriated for their occupation on the west of the Mississippi river.   A treaty with the Seminole chiefs for the removal of their tribe was concluded at Payne's landing, in Florida, in May, 1832, by which treaty they were allowed three years to depart.   The government was first advised in 1834 of their disinclination to leave their homes and those of their fathers.   But as late as the spring of 1835, there was among the whites in Florida a confidence in the calm disposition of the Seminoles, and their willingness to submit to the destiny of their race.   A daring chief, however, arose among this tribe, bearing the name of Osceola, destined to hold a place in history with other distinguished leaders of the aborigines who have resisted the progress of the Anglo-Saxons on this continent. By inheritance Osceola enjoyed no title or distinction among the Seminoles.   He derived his origin from the Creeks, and had affected, until over thirty years of age, pacific feelings toward the whites.   At length, throwing off disguise, he declared openly against the United States, supplanting himself the legitimate chiefs of the Seminoles ; and he even put to death those who were for peaceful measures.   He acquired perfect ascendency over his Indian brethren, and his signal war-cry met with a response from the remnants of the tribes who were still inhabitants of Florida.   Murders were committed on the frontiers, and at one time even St. Augustine was threatened by the hostile Indians.

The United States troops at this time in Florida numbered about 500 men, stationed at several posts, General Clinch being in command.   On the 23d of December, 1835, two companies under Major Dade, while marching to join the general, were surprised by a large body of Indians, and, after a protracted resistance, were all massacred, except three men, who, exhausted with wounds, escaped to tell the fate of their comrades. Open war now commenced.   Many Creeks joined the Seminoles, and the United States government found it necessary to send in succession its most able officers and best troops into the field.   On the part of the Indians, occasional success added vigor to their bold and cruel enterprises.

When Colonel Taylor reached Florida, the war with the Seminoles, began in 1835, had been prosecuted with indifferent success.   General Jesup then had command of the army in this territory, and had made fruitless attempts to bring the war to a close. All friendly conferences with the chiefs, aided by a delegation of Cherokees as mediators, having failed, it was determined, in the autumn of 1837, to take more active measures against the Indians. Colonel Taylor received orders to seek out any portion of the enemy wherever to be found, and to destroy or capture the hostile forces. Accordingly, in pursuance of instructions from General Jesup, Colonel Taylor, with about 1,100 men, left Fort Gardner on the 20th of December, 1837, and through dense thickets of cypress, palmetto, and other underwood, the troops made their way to the everglades, where the Indians were concealed.

After a march of five days, the troops, on the 25th of December, reached a cypress swamp where they had evidence that a large body of the enemy were near. Taylor disposed his army in order of battle, and crossing the swamp, reached a large prairie, on the farther side of which was an extensive hammock, in which the Indians were posted. The American troops had penetrated but a short distance, when they were suddenly attacked by several hundred warriors, with their rifles. The shock for a time was fearlessly sustained, although several officers and men fell at the first fire. Seeing their leaders fall, some of the volunteers gave way, but soon after rallied, and the regular troops eagerly pressed on through the morass. Thrice the enemy wavered and gave ground, and thrice returned to the most desperate conflict ever maintained by their arms. The battle lasted for more than two hours, when the savages were driven from the field to their camp on the borders of Lake Okeechobee, being closely pursued by the regulars and volunteers until night closed in.

This battle of Okeechobee is one of the most memorable in our annals of Indian wars, as one of the most remarkable for bravery and skill on both sides. The American loss was very severe, 26 being killed, and 112 wounded, among whom were some of the most valuable officers in the service, including Lieutenant-Colonel Thompson, Colonel Gentry, Adjutant Center, Captain Van Swaringen, and others, among the slain. The loss of the Indians could not be ascertained, but in the opinion of Colonel Taylor it was about equal to that of our troops.

The immediate consequence of the battle of Okeechobee was the surrender of a number of Seminoles to the forces under the command of Colonel Taylor. The decisive action and dearly-bought victory of the Americans gave a death-blow to the power and daring defiance of the hostile tribe. Although outrages were frequently committed by small parties of savages, for a year or two afterward, the Seminoles were never again completely organized, as a tribe or nation, in opposition to the whites.

If the triumph of Taylor failed to reduce the whole body of Indians immediately to terms of peace, it still demanded and received the grateful recognition of the nation and the government. The sentiments of the latter were expressed in a general order from the war department, through

Major-General Macomb, commander-in-chief of the army, dated February 20, 1838, tendering the thanks of the president of the United States to Colonel Taylor, and the officers and troops under his command, for their gallant conduct in the battle with the Seminole Indians on the 25th of December.

This official acknowledgment was soon after followed by Taylor's promotion to the rank of brigadier-general by brevet, "for distinguished services in the battle of Kissimmee (Okeechobee), in Florida."

In April, 1838, the command of the troops in Florida was assigned to General Taylor; relieving General Jesup, at the request of the latter. In this responsible position Taylor's energies were devoted to the protection of the inhabitants from the attacks of the Indians, and the reduction of the latter to the authority of the United States. The perfect accomplishment of these objects was impracticable with the means and forces placed at the disposal of the commander. From time to time skirmishes with the Indians took place, and small parties of them were occasionally captured, or voluntarily surrendered. But they never could be brought to a general action, and continued, at intervals, their outrages upon the white inhabitants.

The United States government, toward the close of the year 1839, abandoned the policy which it had pursued in Florida, and determined to leave the Indians in their strongholds, and to confine the operations of the troops to the protection of the border settlements. In the general orders of the war department in November, 1839, the conduct of the commander was thus approved:—

"General Taylor, by the zealous and intelligent discharge of his duties, having given satisfaction to the department, will continue in command."

General Taylor's skill and energies were faithfully exerted to fulfil the designs of the government, but the force at his disposal was never adequate. Having labored four years in this thankless field, he was anxious to retire from it; and, at his own request, was relieved from the command, and was succeeded by General Armistead, in April, 1840.

The distinguished talents which General Taylor had displayed throughout his career in the army, were too well known and appreciated by the government to allow him to remain idle, or to be stationed at a post of inactivity. He was, therefore, immediately after leaving Florida, appointed to the command of the first department of the army in the southwest. This department included the states of Alabama, Mississippi, Arkansas, and Louisiana, his headquarters being at Fort Jesup, in the latter state. In the summer of 1841, he was ordered to relieve General Arbuckle, at Fort Gibson, where he remained nearly five years, constantly engaged in disciplining his troops, and in other services pertaining to his command.

Having purchased an estate in Louisiana, General Taylor removed his family from Kentucky to Baton Rouge, on the banks of the Mississippi, where they continued to reside for some years. His constant occupation in the army gave him but few opportunities of enjoying the comforts of domestic retirement.

Soon after the annexation of Texas to the United States, General Taylor, who was then situated at Fort Jesup, Louisiana, received a confidential letter from the secretary of war, Mr. Marcy, dated May 28, 1845, instructing him to place his troops at such a position as would enable him to defend the territory of Texas in case of invasion from Mexico. The Congress of the United States, on the 1st of March, 1845, had passed a joint resolution giving its consent that the territory belonging to the republic of Texas might be erected into a new state, called the state of Texas; subject, however, to the adjustment by this government of "all questions of boundary that might arise with other governments."

The instructions of the war department to General Taylor, above referred to, implied clearly an apprehension that the consequence of the annexation of Texas might be a collision with Mexico. The secretary stated, that as soon as the Congress of Texas should assent to the act, and a convention should assemble and accept the terms offered in the joint annexation resolutions of the Congress of the United States, Texas would be regarded "as part of the United States, so far as to be entitled from this government to a defence from foreign invasion and Indian incursions." General Taylor was accordingly directed to keep his command in readiness for this duty. The anticipation of difficulty with Mexico was further indicated by instructions to General Taylor to open a correspondence with the authorities of Texas, or any diplomatic agent of the United States residing therein, with a view to information and advice in respect to the common Indian enemy, as well as to any foreign power; and also to employ his forces in defence of the Texan territory, if invaded by a foreign power, and to expel the invaders.

General Taylor was thus apprized of the service which might be expected of him. In July, 1845, he was informed by the war department, that the acceptance by Texas of the terms of annexation would probably be formally made by the Congress of that republic on the 4th of that month, and, in anticipation of that event, he was instructed to make an immediate forward movement with the troops under his command, and advance to the mouth of the Sabine, or to such other point on the gulf of Mexico, or its navigable waters, as might be most convenient for an embarkation at the proper time, for the western frontier of Texas.

The most expeditious route was recommended. The forces named for this duty were the 3d and 4th regiments of infantry, and seven companies of the 2d regiment of dragoons. The artillery was ordered from New Orleans.

In reply to inquiries by General Taylor of the war department, respecting the position he should take, he was directed, generally, to be governed by circumstances, to avoid all aggressive measures, and to hold his force ready to protect the territory of Texas " to the extent that it had been occupied by the people of Texas." The Rio Grande was indicated, by the secretary, as the boundary between Mexico and Texas, to which the army of occupation under Taylor was to approach, as nearly as prudence would permit. For this purpose it was necessary to pass the river Nueces.

On the 28th of June, Mr. Donelson, then United States minister to Texas, to whom General Taylor was referred for advice upon his movements, wrote him that he had best move his forces, " without delay, to the western frontier of Texas," and also informing him that Corpus Christi, on Aranzas bay (near the mouth of the Nueces), was the best point for the assembling of his troops. The same letter also admitted that the country between the Nueces and the Rio Grande was in dispute ; the Texans holding Corpus Christi, and the Mexicans Santiago, at the mouth of the Rio Grande.

General Taylor embarked at New Orleans in July, 1845, and proceeded immediately with the forces under his command, 1,500 in number, to Aranzas bay, and in the beginning of August, 1845, had taken the position assigned him by the government. All the troops in the west, the northwest, and on the Atlantic, which could be spared, were ordered to join him. In November, 1845, by the report of the adjutant-general, his army consisted, in the aggregate, of 4,049 officers and men.

To the terms of the joint resolution of annexation, by the Congress of the United States, Texas assented by her ordinance of July, 1845, and, having formed her constitution, became virtually a state in the American Union. Three days after this (July 7th) the same convention requested the president of the United States to occupy the ports of Texas, and send an army to their defence. This desire the president of the United States immediately complied with (or in fact had already, as has been seen, anticipated).*

At the same time that instructions were sent to General Taylor by the war department, a naval force was despatched to the gulf of Mexico to aid him in any hostile operations which might occur.

General Taylor established his headquarters at Corpus Christi, where the army of occupation under his command remained encamped over six months. On the 8th of March, 1846, agreeably to instructions from the president of the United States to General Taylor, the advance of the army commenced its march for the Rio Grande, and the fourth day thereafter the entire forces were moving in a southerly direction over the disputed territory — the wilderness lying between the Nueces and that river. At the Arroya Colorado the troops encountered a body of Mexicans, who seemed disposed to dispute their passage. This, however, was not attempted, and the Americans continued their march. While approaching

* Mansfield's History of the Mexican War.

Point Isabel, General Taylor was met by a deputation of citizens from Matamoras, on the Rio Grande, who handed him a protest, signed by the prefect of the district, against the occupation of the country by the American army. At this moment it was discovered that the buildings at Point Isabel were in flames, and believing that the place had been set on fire by the Mexican authorities, and considering the conflagration as a decided evidence of hostility, General Taylor dismissed the deputation, with the promise of an answer when he should arrive on the banks of the Rio Grande. Point Isabel, a small place with a few mean houses, had been selected as a depot for military stores for the American army, being the nearest port to Matamoras on the north. To preserve its buildings was therefore an object of moment, and the advance of the cavalry arrived in season to arrest the progress of the fire, after it had consumed but three or four houses. The Mexican port-captain who committed the act had made his escape.

The arrangements at this post being satisfactorily made, the general, with the cavalry, resumed the march toward Matamoras, and was joined by General Worth's command, which had encamped on the road. On the 28th of March, the army arrived on the banks of the Rio Grande, opposite Matamoras. Fortifications were immediately commenced, and soon a fort was erected, furnished with six bastions, and capable of containing two thousand men. It commanded the town of Matamoras, and was afterward called Fort Brown. On the other side the Mexicans also erected batteries and redoubts, both parties assuming the attitude of belligerents. An interview was held by direction of General Taylor, with the military authorities in Matamoras, but with no satisfactory result.

On the 10th of April the first American blood was shed by Mexican hands. Colonel Cross, deputy quartermaster-general, having rode out in the morning, for exercise, unattended, was killed as was supposed by some rancheros attached to the Mexican army; and his body was found on the 20th, when it was honored, by order of General Taylor, by a military funeral becoming the rank and character of the colonel.

A Mexican army having been concentrated on the Rio Grande, General Ampudia was placed in command, and arrived in Matamoras on the 11th of April. He had previously attempted to cause desertion among the soldiers of foreign birth in the American army, by issuing a circular addressed to them, in consequence of which some desertions, but unimportant as to numbers, took place. On the 12th of April, General Ampudia addressed a letter to General Taylor, concluding as follows:—

" By explicit and definite orders of my government, which neither can, will, nor should, receive new outrages, I require you in all form, and at latest in the peremptory term of twenty-four hours, to break up your camp, and retire to the other bank of the Nueces river, while our governments are regulating the pending question in relation to Texas. If you insist

16

on remaining upon the soil of the department of Tamaulipas, it will clearly result that arms, and arms alone, must decide the question; and in that case I advise you that we accept the war to which, with so much injustice on your part, you provoke us; and that, on our part, this war shall be conducted conformably to the principles established by the most civilized nations; that is to say, that the law of nations and of war shall be the guide of my operations; trusting that on your part the same will be observed."

In his reply to this letter from General Ampudia, General Taylor informed the Mexican commander that, charged as he was in only a military capacity with the performance of specific duties, he could not enter into a discussion of the international question involved in the advance of the American arms, but reminded him that the government of the United States had constantly sought a settlement by negotiation of the question of boundary. He concludes his letter as follows :—

" The instructions under which I am acting will not permit me to retrograde from the position I now occupy. In view of the relations between our respective governments, and the individual suffering which may result, I regret the alternative which you offer; but, at the same time, wish it understood, that I shall by no means avoid such alternative, leaving the responsibility with those who rashly commence hostilities. In conclusion, you will permit me to give the assurance that, on my part, the laws and customs of war among civilized nations, shall be carefully observed."

To confirm these declarations, General Taylor continued to fortify his camp, and to make every disposition to resist an attack. General Ampudia soon gave place, as commanding officer at Matamoras, to General Arista, commander-in-chief of the northern division of the Mexican army. The reported accession to its force also created new expectations in the American camp that a decisive demonstration would soon be made against it. On the 19th of April, it was reported to General Taylor that two vessels with supplies for the Mexicans in Matamoras, were at the mouth of the Rio Grande. He immediately ordered a blockade of the river and enforced it by placing the United States brig Lawrence and a revenue-cutter to guard its mouth. To this act the Mexican general took umbrage, and having sent a note of remonstrance to General Taylor, and the answer of the American commander being unsatisfactory, the Mexicans prepared to make an attack upon Fort Brown.

In the meantime it was evident that Point Isabel was marked out by the Mexican commander as a place of contemplated attack, and it was rumored that a large Mexican force was crossing the Rio Grande for that purpose. To ascertain the truth of these reports, General Taylor sent out a scouting party under Captain Thornton, up the river, and a squadron of dragoons under Captain Ker, down the river. The former were surprised by a party of Mexicans, sixteen were killed and wounded, and the remainder nearly all were taken prisoners. Lieutenant Mason was killed in the affray. Captain Thornton, at first escaping by an extraordinary leap of his horse over a hedge, was afterward captured and taken to Matamoras, where he remained for some time, but was finally given up. Captain Ker, with his detachment, after reconnoitring the country, returned, without having fallen in with the Mexicans. Three days after this affair, several of Captain Walker's Texan rangers were killed and wounded.

General Taylor, having received by the hands of Captain Walker of the Texan rangers information from Major Munroe, the commander at Point Isabel, of the attack of a party of Mexicans upon a wagon train, and from other causes being anxious for the safety of Point Isabel, where all the supplies for his army were deposited, resolved to march with his forces to the relief of that post. He left at Fort Brown a sufficient force of infantry and artillery to sustain a bombardment. He had previously sent a despatch to the governors of Louisiana and Texas, asking an immediate reinforcement of four regiments of militia from each state.

The plan of Arista, the Mexican general, it was believed, was to cross the Rio Grande, get in the rear of General Taylor's army, capture Point Isabel, and then fall on the American army. This plan was only prevented from being carried out by accidental information, brought to General Taylor by one of Thornton's party, sent in by the Mexican commander. The rapid return of the army under General Taylor to Point Isabel, was a consequence of this information, and the additional fact that the enemy was preparing to cross the river below. Either the Mexican army was dilatory in its movement, or the body detailed to cross below was unable to form a junction, for the forces of General Taylor, commencing their march from Fort Brown on the first of May, reached the depot at Point Isabel the following day, without encountering the enemy.

The Mexican general supposed that the movement of the Americans was a retreat, and at once ordered a large body of his troops across the Rio Grande. On the 3d of May, a heavy bombardment was commenced from the batteries in Matamoras on Fort Brown, where a garrison was left by General Taylor. During the night of the 4th, the Mexicans also erected a battery in the rear of Fort Brown, and the next morning opened a fire upon the fort simultaneously with the batteries on the opposite bank of the river. The bombardment was continued at intervals until the 10th, when the gallant defenders of the fort were relieved by the return of the main army under General Taylor, which had just fought the battles of Palo Alto and Resaca de la Palma. In the defence of the fort, Major Brown, Captain Hawkins, and Captain Mansfield, were greatly distinguished for skill and gallantry. The former was killed by a shell, and was succeeded in command by Captain Hawkins.

General Taylor, having garrisoned the depot at Point Isabel with new troops, commenced his return to Fort Brown on the 7th of May, at the head of two thousand, three hundred men, and a supply-train of three hundred wagons. The army encamped at night about seven miles from Point Isabel, and resumed their march on the following morning, the 8th of May. At noon, the Mexican forces were observed, drawn up in battle array, upon a prairie three miles from Palo Alto. General Taylor immediately prepared for action, and at two o'clock in the afternoon, gave orders to advance. The Mexican cannon opened upon them, when the American troops were deployed into line, and the light artillery under the command of Major Ringgold poured forth its rapid and deadly fire upon the enemy. The Mexican cavalry, mostly lancers, were on their left, and were forced back by the destructive discharges of artillery. On the left wing of the American army, attacks of the Mexicans were met by Duncan's battery, and by other troops of that division. The combat on the American side was chiefly carried on by artillery; and never was there a more complete demonstration of the superior skill and energy of that arm of service, as conducted by the accomplished graduates of West Point. He who was the life and leader of the light artillery — Major Ringgold — was in this engagement mortally wounded, and died in a few days.[*]

The battle, which lasted about five hours, terminated with the possession by the Americans of the field, and the retreat during the night of the Mexicans. The strength of the Mexicans was estimated by General Taylor at about six thousand men, with seven pieces of artillery and eight hundred cavalry. Their loss was at least two hundred killed and four hundred wounded; that of the Americans was nine killed and forty-four wounded.

General Taylor with his troops encamped on the field of battle, and resumed his march at two, P. M., the following day. In two hours the army came in sight of the Mexicans, who had taken a position on a ravine called Resaca de la Palma. They had formed a battery so as to sweep the road, and were otherwise strongly posted. The action commenced by the fire of the Mexican artillery, which the Americans returned by discharges from Ridgely's battery, and by the infantry on the wings. In this firing the Mexican cannon were well managed by Generals La Vega and Reguena, and the effect was severely felt in the American lines. It was necessary to dislodge them, and this duty was assigned by General Taylor to Captain May of the dragoons. It was here that this officer became so distinguished by his gallant charge upon the enemy's batteries. The artillerymen were dispersed and General La Vega taken prisoner. The regiments of infantry now charged the Mexican line and the battle was soon ended. Their columns were broken by successive charges and

[*] Mansfield's History of the War.

unable to bear the continued fire poured upon them by the American infantry and artillery. The Mexicans fled from the field, rapidly pursued by the Americans, and ceased not their flight till those who were not taken prisoners had either crossed the Rio Grande or were drowned in its waters. The enemy's loss in this engagement was very great ; nearly two hundred of their dead were buried by the Americans the day after the battle. Their loss in killed, wounded, and missing, in the two affairs of the 8th and 9th, was estimated by General Taylor at one thousand men. The loss of the Americans was thirty-nine killed and eighty-three wounded, in the last battle. The actual number of American troops engaged with the enemy, on the 9th, did not exceed seventeen hundred, while that of the Mexican army, which had been reinforced after the action of the 8th, was estimated at six thousand.

In a detailed report of these battles, General Taylor remarked : " Our victory has been decisive. A small force has overcome immense odds of the best troops that Mexico can furnish — veteran regiments, perfectly equipped and appointed. Eight pieces of artillery, several colors and standards, a great number of prisoners, including fourteen officers, and a large amount of baggage and public property, have fallen into our hands. The causes of victory are doubtless to be found in the superior quality of our officers and men."

In these engagements, General Taylor displayed the utmost coolness and bravery — exposing himself in the most dangerous positions, and encouraging the troops by his heroic example. After the battles, his attention to the wounded and the dying, whether friend or foe, evinced that sympathy with suffering humanity which is ever inseparable from true courage.*

The intelligence of hostilities on the Rio Grande, occasioned a powerful excitement in the United States. Congress was then in session, and the president, on the receipt of the news of the capture of Captain Thornton's party, immediately sent in his special message of May 11, 1846, in which he declared that the Mexican government, had " at last invaded our territory, and shed the blood of our fellow-citizens on our own soil." Congress with less than two days' deliberation, on the 13th of May, declared that " by the act of the republic of Mexico, war exists between that government and the United States ;" and at the same time passed a law authorizing the president to accept the services of fifty thousand volunteers, and appropriating ten millions of dollars toward carrying on the war. The intention was to put an end to the war by a vigorous effort, and decisive victories.

Four days before this declaration by Congress, as we have seen, the decisive battle of Resaca de la Palma had been fought, and the army of Arista pursued beyond the Rio Grande. The Mexican general saved

* Mansfield.

himself by flight, and quite unattended, he made his way across the river. General La Vega and a few other officers were sent on parole to New Orleans.

On the 11th of May, General Taylor leaving Colonel Twiggs in command of his army, repaired to Point Isabel, for the purpose of arranging with Commodore Connor of the gulf squadron, a combined attack on Matamoras. At Point Isabel a command of regulars and volunteers just arrived from Louisiana and Alabama, was organized under Colonel Wilson; and on the 15th, marched for Brazos, and with the aid of the squadron, crossed the river at its mouth, and marched upon the town, which the colonel occupied on the 17th of May; being the first landing of an American force on the right bank of the Rio Grande. The day before this expedition left Point Isabel, General Taylor also set out on his return to the camp on the river, where he speedily arrived, and at once commenced preparations for an attack on Matamoras. On the 17th of May, Arista sent a deputation to Taylor to ask for an armistice, until the two governments should settle the difficulties pending. This was refused by the American general, as it was apparent that time was only wanted to remove the munitions of war from Matamoras. But during the conference, Arista succeeded in taking away part of the military stores, and with the fragment of his army he abandoned Matamoras, and fled precipitately toward Monterey.

On the 18th of May, General Taylor with his army, crossed the Rio Grande, and entered Matamoras without opposition. Formal possession was taken of the city, and Colonel Twiggs appointed military governor. The day following, Lieutenant-Colonel Garland, with the cavalry of the army, was sent in pursuit of the Mexicans under Arista, but being ignorant of the country, which they found so barren as to afford insufficient support to the horses, the American troops were forced to return, after pursuing the flying enemy about sixty miles.

From May until September, General Taylor remained in camp with his army at Matamoras, awaiting the orders of his government, receiving reinforcements, and making preparations for marching into the interior. His operations were paralyzed during the summer, by the want of suitable boats to navigate the Rio Grande. In the meantime, the executive and Congress had highly approved of his course, and on the 30th of May, the president transmitted to him a commission as major-general by brevet, bearing the date of the battle of the 9th of May. On the 29th of June, he was promoted to the full rank of major-general.

On the day that General Taylor entered Matamoras, a United States squadron arrived off Vera Cruz, and commenced the blockade of that and other ports on the gulf of Mexico; and during the summer the towns of Mier, Camargo, Revilla, and Reynosa, submitted to the Americans, and became stations for different divisions of the army. Camargo, a town about one hundred and eighty miles above the mouth of the Rio Grande, was the point selected as the depot of supplies.   Here the various divisions which were to compose the particular army of General Taylor were gradually concentrated.

The reinforcements and supplies for the American army in Mexico which had been forwarded during the summer were at length sufficient to justify an advance into the interior.   The Rio Grande was assumed as the military base line of operations.   The entire army of General Taylor consisted of about nine thousand men.   A small portion was assigned to garrisons, while the main body, numbering six thousand, six hundred, was destined for Monterey, the capital city of New Leon, and of the northern division of Mexico.   The city contained about fifteen thousand inhabitants and is situated on a branch of the San Juan river, near the base of the Sierra Madre mountains.   Both the natural and artificial defences of Monterey were very strong ; but neither the extent of the defences, nor the number of the garrisons within them, seem to have been fully known to the American army previous to its arrival in front of the city.

The army under Taylor was in three divisions commanded respectively by Brigadier-Generals Twiggs (who had been promoted to that station) and Worth, and Major-General Butler.   On the 20th of August, General Worth began his march for Monterey ; and on the 5th of September, General Taylor left Camargo ; a garrison of two thousand men remaining behind.   Worth reached Ceralvo, about seventy miles, on the 25th of August, and at that point sent out reconnoitring parties who discovered strong bodies of the enemy in front.   He advanced to the village of Marin, where the entire army was in a few days concentrated, under the command of General Taylor.   On the 19th of September, the army arrived at Walnut Springs, three miles from Monterey, after a few skirmishes only with parties of Mexican cavalry.

Monterey was then under the command of General Ampudia, and the garrison under his command consisted of about seven thousand regular troops, and two or three thousand irregular troops.   Notwithstanding this strong garrison, superior in numbers to the American army, General Taylor thought it possible to carry the place by storm, with the bayonet and artillery.   Reconnoisances of the works were made on the evening of the 19th.*

Besides the numerous and well-constructed fortresses mounted with heavy cannon, which had been erected for the defence of Monterey ; the plan of the city itself is well adapted to defensive warfare.   The streets being straight, a few pieces of artillery can command their entire length. The stone walls of the houses rise above the roofs, thus forming regular parapets which afford thorough protection to the defenders.   Each dwelling is thus a separate castle, and the whole city one grand fortification, suggested by nature and consummated by art.

* Mansfield

On the night of the 20th of September, General Worth's advanced columns marched and occupied for the night a defensive position on the Saltillo road, just without the range of the enemy's batteries. The attack commenced on the 21st, by General Worth's forces, and continued, in connexion with other divisions of the army, all the next day. On the 23d, the assault became general, and a desperate conflict ensued in the streets of the city. From the strong stone houses, volleys of musketry dealt death in all directions among the American troops, but they steadily advanced from house to house, and from square to square, until the main body of the enemy had retired from the lower part of the city, to make a stand behind their barricades.

General Taylor then withdrew his troops to the works which had been evacuated by the Mexicans, and determined to concert with General Worth a combined attack upon the town the following day. But early in the morning of the 24th, General Ampudia sent a communication to the American commander, proposing to evacuate the town. General Taylor acceded to a personal interview with General Ampudia, as the latter had desired, and it was finally agreed that the city should be surrendered to General Taylor, and the material of war, with certain exceptions, and the Mexican troops were allowed to evacuate the following day. As soon as they had left, the division under General Worth was quartered in the city, and quiet reigned among the inhabitants. The American troops during the various contests at Monterey, had twelve officers and one hundred and eight men killed; thirty-one officers, and three hundred and thirty-seven wounded. The Mexican loss was not known, but believed considerably to exceed these numbers. The force under General Taylor at this siege was four hundred and twenty-five officers, and six thousand, two hundred and twenty men, accompanied with nineteen cannon. The town and works were armed with forty-two pieces of cannon well supplied with ammunition, and manned, as before stated, with a force of nearly ten thousand men.

In the transactions attending the capture of the city, General Taylor had hoped to secure the approbation of government. In this, however, he was disappointed. Not only were the terms of capitulation considered as entirely too lenient, but he was even blamed for not having carried the defences by assault, and thus making the garrison unconditional prisoners. Time, however, has shown, that by such a course, his little army would have endured appalling loss, without corresponding advantages; and that General Taylor's course, dictated as it was by humanity and honor, was the most advantageous to his troops and to the country that he could possibly have adopted.

General Taylor now established his headquarters at Monterey, despatching General Worth, on the 12th of November, with twelve hundred men and eight pieces of artillery, to Saltillo; and General Wool, who was on his march from Texas, toward Chihuahua, was directed by Taylor, in

November, to abandon the expedition, and advance with his column of two thousand and four hundred men to Parras, a place south of Saltillo. Here the army of General Wool remained for a short time until, in the month of December, it joined the division of Worth at Saltillo.

On the 13th of November, General Taylor followed General Worth's division to Saltillo, escorted by two squadrons of dragoons. This town is the capital of the state of Coahuila, and is distant sixty-five miles southwest from Monterey. It was considered by Taylor as an important point for occupation, for three reasons : first, as a necessary outpost of the main force at Monterey, covering as it does the defile which leads from the low country to the table land, and also the route to Monclova ; secondly, as controlling a region from which to obtain supplies of provisions, viz., the fertile country around Parras ; thirdly, as the capital of Coahuila, which renders it important in a political point of view.

General Taylor represented to the war department the difficulties to be encountered in a forward movement upon the city of San Luis Potosi, and with regard to a proposed expedition against Vera Cruz, he gave it as his opinion that twenty-five thousand troops would be properly required to take possession of Vera Cruz, and march thence against the city of Mexico. He proposed to proceed with the preparation for a movement on Tampico, if approved by the department, but his designs were not carried into effect. A movement against San Luis, he remarked, should not be undertaken except with a force so large as to render success certain. That force he considered should be at least 20,000 strong, as he supposed the Mexicans able to concentrate a force of 40,000 to 50,000 men at San Luis, which is a city of about 60,000 inhabitants, distant three hundred miles from Saltillo, nearly six hundred miles from the Rio Grande, and five hundred from the city of Mexico.

Having made arrangements for the occupation of the state of Coahuila, and left with General Worth at Saltillo a squadron of dragoons, General Taylor returned to Monterey, where, on the 25th of November, he learned officially of the occupation of Tampico by the naval forces under Commodore Perry. On the requisition of the commodore, with the approval of General Taylor, a regiment and six companies from Taylor's army were ordered to Tampico to garrison that town.

On the 15th of December, General Taylor left Monterey for Victoria, the capital of Tamaulipas, which place he designed to occupy, and concentrate there a portion of his army. On his way thither he received information from General Worth at Saltillo, that Santa Anna, then in command of the Mexican army at San Luis, designed taking advantage of the diversion of force toward Victoria, by a rapid movement, strike a heavy blow at the American troops at Saltillo, and, if successful, another at General Wool's force at Parras. General Taylor, therefore, thought proper to return to Monterey with the regular forces, and thus be in a position to reinforce Saltillo, if necessary.   The volunteers under General Quitman were ordered to continue their march and effect a junction with General Patterson, at Victoria.   At the same time, Generals Butler and Wool moved rapidly from Monterey and Parras to join General Worth, who had advised them of a probable attack on his position.   General Taylor had proceeded beyond Monterey, on his way to Saltillo, when, on the 20th of December, he received information that the expected concentration and movement of the Mexican troops upon Saltillo had not taken place.   Deeming the force present and sent forward to that place sufficient to repel any demonstration from San Luis Potosi, General Taylor again marched with General Twiggs's division toward Victoria.

On the 29th of December, General Quitman entered Victoria without opposition.   The enemy had a body of 1,500 cavalry in the town, which fell back as the Americans approached.   General Taylor arrived there with the troops of General Twiggs on the 4th of January, and was joined on the same day by the force which General Patterson conducted from Matamoras.   The force collected at Victoria was over 5,000 strong.

While General Taylor was thus maturing his operations, the American government had determined to concentrate the largest possible number of regulars and experienced volunteers in the attack upon Vera Cruz, and the march thence to the city of Mexico.   General Scott was charged with the command of the expedition, and immediately took measures to secure its success.   On the 25th of November, General Scott wrote General Taylor from New York, informing him that he expected to be on the Rio Grande about the 20th of December, on his way to carry out the object of an expedition, the particulars of which, as despatches had been lost, he did not deem it prudent to communicate.   " I shall be obliged," he says, " to take from you most of the gallant officers and men (regulars and volunteers) whom you have so long and so nobly commanded.   I am afraid that I shall, by imperious necessity — the approach of yellow fever on the gulf coast — reduce you, for a time, to stand on the defensive.   This will be infinitely painful to you, and for that reason distressing to me.   But I rely upon your patriotism to submit to the temporary sacrifice with cheerfulness."

In consequence of the plan thus declared, the regular troops (with the exception of a very small body of the troops which composed his army in the month of November), the division of General Worth at Saltillo, of General Patterson at Victoria, the brigades of Generals Quitman and Twiggs at the same place, and all other corps which could possibly be drawn from the field of operations, of which the Rio Grande was the base, were ordered to Vera Cruz.   To maintain his position at Saltillo, General Taylor was left with about five thousand men, only five hundred being regulars.   On parting with the troops who had so faithfully served with him, he issued an order expressing his deep sensibility and attachment toward them, and his deep regret that he could not participate with those who were making their first campaign in its eventful scenes. To all, both officers and men, he extended "his heartfelt wishes for their continued success and happiness, confident that their achievements on another theatre would redound to the credit of their country and its arms."

In January, 1847, General Taylor left Victoria, and established his headquarters at Monterey, where, early in February, his force, including recent reinforcements of volunteers, amounted to between 6,000 and 7,000 men. Soon after reaching Monterey he received information that a party of dragoons had been surprised at Encarnacion, also that another party, with Captain Cassius M. Clay and Majors Borland and Gaines were taken prisoners.

While the United States were preparing to attack Vera Cruz, and endeavoring to maintain the positions gained by the northern divisions of the army, under Generals Taylor, Wool, and Kearny, Mexico was also preparing for a decisive blow. In December, the Mexican Congress assembled at the capital. Santa Anna was elected provisional president, and Gomez Farias vice president, of the republic. The command of the army was undertaken by Santa Anna personally, he having recently returned to Mexico from exile at Havana, and devoted himself with zeal to restore domestic order, to unite parties, to devise measures of finance, and to raise and equip troops. Notwithstanding every embarrassment, Santa Anna had concentrated at San Luis Potosi, before the end of January, 1847, an army of more than 21,000 men, prepared to march thence against the divisions of General Taylor's force between Saltillo and the Rio Grande. On the first of February the Mexican army was moving rapidly upon that town, upward of three hundred miles distant from San Luis. The march was arduous, from the great distance over a desert, want of water and provisions, and from the severity of the weather. On the 20th of February they reached Encarnacion, and the next day advanced on Saltillo.*

The army of Santa Anna was admirably equipped. It was composed of the flower of the Mexican nation, and numbered more than four to one of the army which it came to conquer. Hope and dire necessity both urged them to victory. The commander, Santa Anna, had well considered the advantages he would derive from this movement, if successful, and all the chances were in his favor. Could he have driven General Taylor from his position at Buena Vista, he would have swept down to Camargo, and over the whole valley of the Rio Grande. All the munitions of war of the Americans would have fallen into his hands. If defeated, Santa Anna well knew that his moral power over his army would be broken. The fate of his country seemed suspended on the issue of a single battle. His own fame, his place in history, were both to be decided in the coming conflict.†

* Fry's Life of Taylor.   † Mansfield.

General Wool had continued in command of the division of the American army at Saltillo.   Near the end of January, he advised General Taylor of the rumored advance of Santa Anna, then organizing his forces at San Luis, as has been mentioned.   In consequence of this information, although at that time indefinite, General Taylor determined at once to meet the enemy, if opportunity should be offered ; and leaving a garrison of fifteen hundred men at Monterey, he took up his line of march on the 31st with a reinforcement for the column of General Wool.   On the 2d of February, he reached Saltillo, and on the 4th he advanced to Agua Nueva, a strong position on the San Luis road, twenty miles south of Saltillo.   Here he encamped until the 21st, when he received intelligence that Santa Anna was advancing with his whole army.   Having carefully examined the various positions and defiles of the mountains, Taylor decided that Buena Vista, a strong mountain pass, eleven miles nearer Saltillo, was the most favorable point to make a stand against a force so overwhelming. He therefore fell back to that place, and at noon of the 21st, encamped to await the approach of Santa Anna, then within one day's march of this position.

The position of the American army at this moment was most critical. The regular troops had been withdrawn, with the exception of a few companies of artillery and dragoons.   The volunteers, of which the army was mainly composed, had received some instruction in the regular duties of the camp, but had not attained that perfection in discipline which gives confidence in military operations.[*]

The position selected by General Taylor to receive with his small army, the forces of the Mexican chief — five times the number of the Americans — was one of remarkable natural strength.   It was at a point where the main road from San Luis to Saltillo, passes between closely-approximating chains of mountains.   The bases of these mountains are cut, by the occasional torrents of rain, into numerous deep gullies, almost impassable, owing to the rugged and steep banks leaving between them elevated table-lands or plateaus, of various extent.   On the west of the road, and nearly parallel to it, between Agua Nueva and Buena Vista, is also a ditch, forming one of the mountain drains on that side.   The American army was drawn up at nearly right angles to the road, its chief force being on the east of it, occupying a large plateau commanding the mountain side. Facing the south, this force constituted the left wing.   A battery of light artillery occupied the road, and the right wing rested on the opposite hill. In this attitude, the Americans awaited the advance of the Mexicans, on the morning of the 22d of February, the birthday of Washington.

On the 21st, General Taylor had proceeded with a small force to Saltillo (nine miles from Buena Vista), to make some arrangements for the defence of the town, leaving General Wool in command of the troops.

[*] Mansfield.

Before those arrangements at Saltillo were completed, on the morning of the 22d, Taylor was advised that the enemy was in sight, advancing. Hastening to the battle-field, he found that the Mexican cavalry advance was in front, having marched from Encarnacion, over forty miles distant, at eleven o'clock on the day previous, and driving in an American mounted force left at Agua Nueva, to cover the removal of public stores.

The features of the ground occupied by the American troops were such as nearly to paralyze the artillery and cavalry of the Mexicans, while their infantry could not derive all the advantages of its numerical superiority. At eleven o'clock, General Taylor received from General Santa Anna, a summons to surrender at discretion, to which the American commander immediately replied, "declining to accede to the request." The enemy still forbore his attack, evidently waiting for the arrival of his rear columns. The Mexican light troops commenced the action by engaging the Americans on the extreme left, and kept up a sharp fire, climbing the mountain-side, and apparently endeavoring to gain the flank of the Americans. The skirmishing of the light troops was kept up until dark; when General Taylor became convinced that no serious attack would be made before morning, and returned, with a regiment and squadron of dragoons, to Saltillo. The troops bivouacked without fires, and laid upon their arms. A body of fifteen hundred Mexican cavalry under General Minon, had entered the valley through a narrow pass east of Saltillo, and had evidently been thrown in the rear of the Americans, to break up and harass the retreat which was so confidently expected by Santa Anna.

Having made the necessary dispositions for the protection of the rear, General Taylor returned to Buena Vista, on the morning of the 23d, ordering forward all the available troops from Saltillo. The action had commenced before his arrival on the field.

During the night of the 22d, the Mexicans had thrown a body of light troops on the mountain-side, with the purpose of outflanking the left of the Americans; and it was here that the action of the 23d, commenced at an early hour. The American riflemen in this position maintained their ground handsomely against a greatly superior force. About eight o'clock, a strong demonstration was made against the American centre, a heavy Mexican column moving along the road; which was soon dispersed by the fire from Captain Washington's battery. In the meantime, a large force of Mexican infantry and cavalry was concentrated under cover of the ridges, with the obvious intention of forcing the left of the Americans. It was found impossible to check the advance of the Mexican infantry, although the American artillery was served against it with great effect, under the orders of Captain O'Brien. When General Taylor arrived upon the field, the left wing of his army had become completely outflanked, and the enemy was pouring masses of infantry and cavalry along the base of the mountain; thus gaining the rear of the Americans in great force. Taylor immediately directed the left to be strengthened by detachments of Captains Bragg and Sherman's artillery, also by bodies of cavalry.   The action was for a long time warmly sustained at that point, the enemy making efforts both with infantry and cavalry, against the American line, and being always repulsed with heavy loss.

At one period, the position of that portion of the Mexican army which had gained the rear of the Americans was very critical, and it seemed doubtful whether it could regain the main body.   At that moment, General Taylor received from General Santa Anna a message by a staff-officer, desiring to know what he wanted.   Taylor despatched General Wool to the Mexican commander, and ordered his own troops to cease firing.   General Wool could not, however, cause the Mexicans to cease their fire, and returned, without having an interview with Santa Anna.   The extreme right of the Mexicans retreated along the base of the mountain, and finally, in spite of the efforts of the Americans, effected a junction with the remainder of the army.

During the day, the Mexican cavalry under General Minon, had ascended the elevated plain above Saltillo, and occupied the road from that city to the field of battle.   Several skirmishes took place between them and the small bodies of troops left by General Taylor to protect his rear. General Minon made one or two efforts with his cavalry to charge the artillery, but this body of Mexicans were finally driven back in a confused mass, and did not again appear upon the plain.

In the meantime the firing had partially ceased upon the principal field, at Buena Vista.   The enemy seemed to confine his efforts to the protection of his artillery, and General Taylor had left the plateau for a moment, when he was recalled thither by a heavy musketry fire.   He then discovered that a portion of his infantry, the Illinois and Kentucky volunteers, had engaged a greatly superior force of the enemy — evidently his reserve — and that they had been overwhelmed by numbers.   The moment was most critical.   Captain O'Brien had lost his two pieces of artillery, which had been taken by the Mexicans — his infantry support being entirely routed.   Captain Bragg, who had just arrived from the left, was ordered at once into battery, without any infantry to support him, and at the imminent risk of losing his guns, this officer came rapidly into action, the Mexican line being but a few yards from the muzzle of his pieces. The first discharge of canister caused the enemy to hesitate, the second and third drove him back in disorder, and saved the day.   The second Kentucky regiment, which had advanced beyond supporting distance in this affair, was driven back and closely pressed by the enemy's cavalry.   Taking a ravine which led in the direction of Captain Washington's battery, their pursuers became exposed to his fire, which soon checked and drove them back with loss.   In the meantime, the rest of the American artillery had taken position on the plateau, covered by the Mississippi and third Indiana regiments, the former of which had reached the ground in time to pour a fire into the right flank of the enemy, and thus contribute to his repulse. In this last conflict the Americans sustained a very heavy loss. Colonel Hardin of Illinois, and Colonels M'Kee and Clay of Kentucky, fell at this time, while gallantly leading their commands. Colonel Yell of Arkansas, and Adjutant Vaughan of Kentucky, had previously fallen.

No further attempt was made by the Mexicans to force the position of the Americans, and the approach of night gave an opportunity to pay proper attention to the wounded, and also to refresh the soldiers, who had been exhausted by incessant watchfulness and combat. Though the night was severely cold, the troops were compelled for the most part, to bivouack without fires, expecting that morning would renew the conflict. During the night the wounded were removed to Saltillo, and every preparation made to receive the enemy, should he again attack the American position. Seven fresh companies were drawn from the town, and Brigadier-General Marshall, with a reinforcement of Kentucky cavalry, and four pieces of artillery, was near at hand, when it was discovered that the enemy had abandoned his position during the night. Scouts soon ascertained that the Mexican army had fallen back upon Agua Nueva. The great disparity of numbers, and the exhaustion of Taylor's troops, rendered it inexpedient and hazardous to attempt pursuit. A staff officer was despatched to General Santa Anna to negotiate an exchange of prisoners, which was satisfactorily completed on the following day. The Americans collected and buried their own dead, and the Mexican wounded, of which a large number had been left upon the field, were removed to Saltillo, and rendered as comfortable as circumstances would permit.*

On the evening of the 26th it was ascertained that, excepting a small body of cavalry left at Agua Nueva, the Mexican army had retreated in the direction of San Luis Potosi. On the 27th, General Taylor advanced with his troops and resumed his former camp at Agua Nueva, the Mexican rear guard evacuating the place as the Americans approached, leaving a considerable number of wounded behind. It was Taylor's purpose to beat up the enemy's quarters at Encarnacion early the next morning, but upon examination, the weak condition of the cavalry horses rendered it unadvisable to attempt so long a march without water. Colonel Belknap, with a detachment of troops, was despatched to Encarnacion on the 1st of March. Some two hundred wounded and about sixty Mexican soldiers were found there, the army of Santa Anna, having passed on in the direction of Matehula, with greatly reduced numbers, and suffering much from hunger. The dead and dying were strewed upon the road, and crowded the buildings of the hacienda.

The American loss at the battle of Buena Vista, was 267 killed, 456 wounded, and 23 missing; that of the Mexicans in killed and wounded

* General Taylor's official despatch.

was estimated by General Taylor, and admitted by Santa Anna, to exceed 1500. At least 500 of their killed were left upon the field of battle. The loss of the Americans was especially severe in officers — 28 having been killed upon the field, and 41 wounded.

In a private letter to General E. G. W. Butler, General Taylor referred to certain incidents of the battle. Among other remarks he says : " For several hours the fate of the day was extremely doubtful ; so much so, that I was urged by some of the most experienced officers to fall back and take a new position. This I knew it would never do to attempt with volunteers, and at once declined it. Between the several deep ravines, there were portions of level land from one to four hundred yards in extent, which became alternately points of attack and defence, after our left was turned, by both sides. These extended along and near the base of the mountain for about two miles, and the struggle for them may be very appropriately compared to a game of chess. Night put a stop to the contest, and, strange to say, both armies occupied the same positions they did in the morning before the battle commenced. Our artillery did more than wonders.

" We lay on our arms all night, as we had done the two preceding ones, without fires, ready and expecting to renew the contest the next morning ; but we found at daylight the enemy had retreated during the night.

" I hope the greater portion of the good people of the country will be satisfied with what we have done on this occasion. I flatter myself that our compelling a Mexican army of more than twenty thousand men, completely organized, and led by their chief magistrate, to retreat, with less than five hundred regulars, and about four thousand volunteers, will meet their approval. I had not a single company of regular infantry ; the whole was taken from me."

The news of the victory of Buena Vista was received in the United States as the crowning evidence of Taylor's generalship. He had assumed the responsibility of holding his position beyond Monterey. Knowing his resources and trusting in his officers and troops, he hesitated not to risk everything on the field against the host of Santa Anna. He has himself done justice to the brilliant part which General Wool bore in the action, approving all the preliminary dispositions of that able commander. He has also borne testimony to the services of all others who took part in the action, and expressed his sympathies with the friends of those who had fallen. It was the province of the nation, in return, to acknowledge the surpassing merit of the commander-in-chief. That merit was acknowledged in every form of popular rejoicing and congratulation. Cities and states were emulous in exhibitions of sympathy for his trials, exultation for his success, and respect for his character.*

The importance of the victory at Buena Vista (says Mansfield) can

* Fry's Life of Taylor.

not be exaggerated. It secured the whole frontier of the Rio Grande, and struck terror and dismay into the hearts of the Mexican nation. It was, in fact, the first great turning point of the war.

General Taylor, on the 2d of March, intrusted to one of his aids, Mr. Thomas L. Crittenden, of Kentucky, the official reports of the battle of Buena Vista, to be conveyed to Washington. He was escorted by Major Giddings, commanding 260 infantry and two pieces of artillery, and having in charge also one hundred and fifty wagons. Near Ceralvo, on the road to Camargo, the escort was attacked by 1,600 Mexican cavalry and infantry, under Generals Urrea and Romaro. After a brief and gallant struggle the enemy was repulsed, with the loss of 45 killed and wounded. The Americans lost 17 men, of whom 15 were teamsters. General Taylor, subsequently hearing that Urrea was in command of a still larger force, pursued him with about 1,200 volunteers, and two companies of Bragg's artillery, as far as Caidereta, where he learned that the Mexicans had crossed the mountains. General Taylor then returned to the camp at Walnut Springs, three miles from Monterey, where he established his headquarters.

The operations of General Scott, at Vera Cruz and other points on the gulf of Mexico, and the brilliant series of successes of that officer and the troops under his command, in the march from Vera Cruz to the city of Mexico, terminating in the capture and occupation of that capital by the American troops, in September, transferred the seat of war to that quarter. Consequently, General Taylor remained for some months in comparative inactivity, at his headquarters near Monterey. Actual hostilities with Mexico having been practically brought to an end, with the exception of skirmishes with guerilla parties, General Taylor obtained permission to visit his family at Baton Rouge, in Louisiana, from whom he had now been absent for about two years.

Accordingly, in November, 1847, he left the command of the army with General Wool, and took his departure for the United States, by the way of Camargo, Matamoras, and Point Isabel, at which last place he embarked in a steamer for New Orleans, and arrived below that city on the 1st of December. He landed at the barracks, where he met his family, and remained two days. He was greeted by salutes of cannon, display of flags, and the cheers of the people. On the 3d the general proceeded to the city, where he was received with transports of enthusiasm and joy by his fellow-citizens anxious to welcome him to his home. Along the shores of the Mississippi, as far as the eye could reach, gay streamers floated on the breeze from ships of every nation, and the numerous steamboats on the river added to the interest of the scene.

General Taylor was accompanied by several officers of his staff, among whom was Major Bliss, assistant adjutant-general, who had accompanied him in all his campaigns and battles in Mexico. On landing at New

17

Orleans, a vast procession was formed, and the general was conducted to the St. Charles hotel, where he received the calls of several thousand citizens.   To the address of the mayor, welcoming him to the city, the general made a modest and appropriate reply, expressive of his gratitude at this reception by the people of New Orleans.   On the following day he visited the Roman catholic cathedral, and was welcomed in an eloquent address by Bishop Blanc.   A magnificent sword that had been voted by the legislature of Louisiana, was presented by Governor Johnson, with appropriate remarks, to which General Taylor replied in language of deep feeling at the honor done him.

On the 5th of December, General Taylor left the city in a steamer, for his home in Baton Rouge.   On the way thither he was greeted with the most enthusiastic cheers from people on the banks of the river, and on board of steamers and other vessels.   From that time he remained to enjoy the quiet of domestic retirement, of which he had so long been deprived, until summoned by the people to accept of new honors, and to enter upon the duties of the most important office in their gift.

The brilliant achievements of Taylor during his campaigns in Mexico, so much attracted the admiration of the people of the United States, that a strong desire was early manifested by his fellow-citizens of various political parties, to place him in nomination as a candidate for president of the republic.   His official despatches and private letters confirmed the favorable opinion generally entertained respecting his ability to fill the highest station with credit to himself and benefit to the nation — and the excellence of his private character, as well as his sterling good sense, was acknowledged by all.   Although his political opinions were known to coincide with those of the whig party, he had never taken an active part in political contests ; many of the democratic party, therefore, avowed their determination to support him as a candidate for the presidency, but the leaders of that party refused to acknowledge his claims.   A large portion of the whig party, particularly in the southern and southwestern states, early saw in the popularity attached to his name, the great probability of success in the presidential election if he could be made the candidate of the party, and consequently used every effort to effect such a result.   The attention, also, of citizens in several of the states, organized as the native American party, was turned toward General Taylor as a candidate for the presidency immediately after his brilliant victories on the Rio Grande and in Mexico.   One of the earliest meetings of the people in favor of his nomination for president, was held at Trenton, New Jersey, on the 11th of June, 1846 ; this was followed by a similar meeting in the city of New York, on the 18th of the same month.   Both of these meetings were called without distinction of party, soon after the reception of the news of the battles of Palo Alto and Resaca de la Palma.

Taylor's nomination for the presidency was proposed to him by one of the native American party, in March, 1847. While he did not positively refuse to allow his name to be used in that connexion, he stated in reply, April 28, 1847, that he could not, while the country was involved in war, and while his duty called him to take part in the operations against the enemy, acknowledge any ambition beyond that of bestowing all his best exertions toward obtaining an adjustment of our difficulties with Mexico. Subsequently he expressed a willingness to become a candidate for the presidency, provided that the call came from the spontaneous action and free will of the nation at large, and void of the slightest agency of his own.

The following letters, respecting his nomination and his political principles, give his views on those points.

"BATON ROUGE, LA., *January* 30, 1848.

"SIR : Your communication of the 15th instant has been received, and the suggestions therein offered duly considered.

"In reply to your inquiries, I have again to repeat, that I have neither the power nor the desire to dictate to the American people the exact manner in which they should proceed to nominate for the presidency of the United States. If they desire such a result, they must adopt the means best suited, in their opinion, to the consummation of the purpose ; and if they think fit to bring me before them for this office, through their legislatures, mass meetings, or conventions, I can not object to their designating these bodies as whig, democrat, or native. But in being thus nominated, I must insist on the condition—and my position on this point is immutable—that I shall not be brought forward by them as the candidate of their party, or considered as the exponent of their party doctrines.

"In conclusion, I have to repeat, that if I were nominated for the presidency, by any body of my fellow-citizens, designated by any name they might choose to adopt, I should esteem it an honor, and would accept such nomination, provided it had been made entirely independent of party considerations.

"I am, sir, very respectfully, your obedient servant, "Z. TAYLOR. "PETER SKEN SMITH, Esq., Philadelphia."

"BATON ROUGE, *April* 22, 1848.

"DEAR SIR : My opinions have been so often misconceived and misrepresented, that I deem it due to myself, if not to my friends, to make a brief exposition of them upon the topics to which you have called my attention.

"I have consented to the use of my name as a candidate for the presidency. I have frankly avowed my own distrust of my fitness for this high station ; but having, at the solicitation of many of my countrymen, taken my position as a candidate, I do not feel at liberty to surrender that position until my friends manifest a wish that I should retire from it. I will then most gladly do so. I have no private purposes to accomplish, no party projects to build up, no enemies to punish — nothing to serve but my country.

"I have been very often addressed by letter, and my opinions have been asked upon almost every question that might occur to the writers as affecting the interest of their country or their party. I have not always responded to these inquiries, for various reasons.

"I confess, while I have great cardinal principles which will regulate my political life, I am not sufficiently familiar with all the minute details of political legislation to give solemn pledges to exert myself to carry out this or defeat that measure. I have no concealment. I hold no opinion which I would not readily proclaim to my assembled countrymen ; but crude impressions upon matters of policy, which may be right to-day and wrong to-morrow, are perhaps not the best test of fitness for office. One who can not be trusted without pledges, can not be confided in merely on account of them.

"I will proceed, however, now to respond to your inquiries :—

"1. I reiterate what I have so often said : I am a whig. If elected, I would not be the mere president of a party. I would endeavor to act independent of party domination. I should feel bound to administer the government untrammelled by party schemes.

"2. THE VETO POWER.—The power given by the constitution to the executive to interpose his veto, is a high conservative power ; but, in my opinion, should never be exercised except in cases of clear violation of the constitution, or manifest haste and want of consideration by Congress. Indeed, I have thought that for many years past the known opinions and wishes of the executive have exercised undue and injurious influence upon the legislative department of the government ; and for this cause I have thought our system was in danger of undergoing a great change from its true theory. The personal opinions of the individual who may happen to occupy the executive chair, ought not to control the action of Congress upon questions of domestic policy ; nor ought his objections to be interposed where questions of constitutional power have been settled by the various departments of government, and acquiesced in by the people.

"3. Upon the subject of the tariff, the currency, the improvement of our great highways, rivers, lakes, and harbors, the will of the people, as expressed through their representatives in Congress, ought to be respected and carried out by the executive.

"4. THE MEXICAN WAR.—I sincerely rejoice at the prospect of peace. My life has been devoted to arms, yet I look upon war at all times and under all circumstances as a national calamity, to be avoided if compatible with the national honor. The principles of our government, as well as its true policy, are opposed to the subjugation of other nations and the dismemberment of other countries by conquest. In the language of the great Washington, ' Why should we quit our own to stand on foreign ground ?' In the Mexican war our national honor has been vindicated; and in dictating terms of peace, we may well afford to be forbearing and even magnanimous to a fallen foe.

" These are my opinions upon the subjects referred to by you, and any reports or publications, written or verbal, from any source, differing in any essential particular from what is here written, are unauthorized and untrue.

" I do not know that I shall again write upon the subject of national politics. I shall engage in no schemes, no combinations, no intrigues. If the American people have not confidence in me, they ought not to give me their suffrages. If they do not, you know me well enough to believe me, when I declare I shall be content. I am too old a soldier to murmur against such high authority. " Z. TAYLOR.

" To Captain J. S. ALLISON."

With the knowledge of General Taylor's political opinions repeatedly expressed in the above and other answers to inquiries made of him, his name was prominently brought before the whig national convention which met at Philadelphia on the 1st of June, 1848.

The first ballot taken in that convention showed the popularity of General Taylor, even in comparison with his distinguished rivals as candidates for the presidency. The votes stood for Zachary Taylor, 111; Henry Clay, 97; Winfield Scott, 43; Daniel Webster, 22; John M. Clayton, 4; John M'Lean, 2. Necessary for a choice, 140; the whole number of votes being 279.

On the second ballot the vote stood for Taylor, 118; Clay, 86; Scott, 49; Webster, 22; Clayton, 4. Third ballot, Taylor, 133; Clay, 74; Scott, 54; Webster, 17; Clayton, 1.

The fourth and final ballot gave Taylor 171; Clay, 35; Scott, 60; Webster, 14. It is worthy of notice, that the votes for General Taylor on the last ballot came from each of the thirty states represented in the convention; thus showing that he was truly a national candidate.

General Taylor was then declared duly nominated as the whig candidate for the presidency of the United States. Millard Fillmore, of the state of New York, was, on the second ballot, nominated by the same convention for vice-president.

Having duly accepted the nomination of the whig national convention, General Taylor remained with his family at Baton Rouge until the presidential election took place, in November, 1848. The result of that election, as shown by the votes of the people, and confirmed of course by the electoral colleges then chosen, which met in December following, was the election of Taylor and Fillmore, the whig candidates for president and vice-president, who each received 163 electoral votes, against 127 votes given for the democratic candidates, General Cass and General Butler.

The distinguishing traits of General Taylor's character, as described by a friend, are honesty, good judgment, benevolence, firmness, and energy. It were a waste of time to dwell upon these traits of his character, for his military career has afforded such abundant examples of his exercise of these qualities as to render them familiar to every one who has heard or read of the man. The following extracts from Taylor's official despatches at different periods of his life, are characteristic of his determination and unsurpassed bravery.

In his letter to General Howard, giving the details of his expedition against the British and Indians on Red river in September, 1814, he says : —

"I collected the officers together and put the following question to them : 'Are we able, 334 effective men, to fight the enemy with any prospect of success ?' They were of opinion the enemy was *at least three to one*, and that it was not practicable to effect the object. I then determined to drop down the river and erect a fort ; and should the enemy attempt to descend the river in force before the fort can be completed, *every foot of the way from the fort to the settlements shall be contested.*"

In his letter to the adjutant-general of the army, dated Point Isabel, May 7, 1846 (more than thirty years after the above), he uses similar language, viz. :—

"I shall march this day, with the main body of the army, to open a communication with Major Brown, and to throw forward supplies of ordnance and provisions. *If the enemy opposes my march, in whatever force, I shall fight him.*"

In person, General Taylor is about five feet eight inches in height, and slightly inclined to corpulency. His complexion is dark, his forehead high, and his eyes keen and penetrating, indicating uniform good humor, his face careworn, but extremely intelligent, and generally lit up with a benevolent smile. He dresses at all times with great simplicity, and is kind and affable in his manners. He has been but once married, and has had four children — one son and three daughters. Of the latter, one married Dr. Wood, of the U. S. army ; another (since deceased) married Colonel Jefferson Davis, of Mississippi, who commanded the Mississippi volunteers at Buena Vista ; the third married Colonel W. W. S. Bliss, of the army, who, as before mentioned, accompanied the general in his campaigns in Mexico. Colonel Bliss and lady reside with the president.

On the 24th of January, General Taylor took his departure for Washington, to enter upon the duties of the high office to which he had been elected by the suffrages of the people. On the day previous to his taking leave of his home and his immediate friends and neighbors, the citizens of Baton Rouge, without distinction of party, assembled spontaneously, to pay him their respects and bid him farewell. A large procession was formed, which proceeded to his residence where he was appropriately addressed on behalf of the citizens, by one of their number. To this address he made a brief but touching reply, in which he assured them that it was with feelings of no ordinary character, that he met with his fellow-citizens on such an occasion, many of whom he had been associated with more than a quarter of a century. Had he consulted his own wishes, he said he should have preferred the office he was then about to vacate, and have remained among his old friends ; but that as the people had, without his solicitation, seen fit to elevate him to another station, though he distrusted his abilities satisfactorily to discharge the great and important duties thus imposed upon him, yet he assured them that he should endeavor to fulfil them without regard to fear, favor, or affection from any one. In conclusion with his prayers for the welfare of his fellow-citizens of Baton Rouge, he bade them an affectionate farewell.

The day succeeding General Taylor's departure, Colonel Bliss, assistant adjutant-general, issued an order announcing the resignation of the general, and his final withdrawal from the military service of the army. In resigning his commission, General Taylor expressed his "regret at his separation from a service to which he was attached by so many pleasing and proud associations. To the officers and men who had served under his immediate orders, he expressed his hearty thanks for their zealous and cordial support in the execution of the duties confided to him during a long and eventful service. To them and to all he extended a heartfelt farewell, and his warmest wishes for their continued happiness and success in the arduous and honorable career which they had chosen." Thus terminated Taylor's connexion with the army, after a service of more than forty years.

On his journey to Washington, by way of the Mississippi and Ohio rivers, the Cumberland road, and the Baltimore and Ohio railroad, the president elect was met with the liveliest expressions of gratitude and respect by the people in the different places along his route. After a long and fatiguing journey, interrupted by the public demonstrations in the various cities and towns through which he passed, he arrived at Washington, on the evening of the 23d of February, the anniversary of the battle of Buena Vista — and was received with every demonstration of joy by the citizens and others assembled at the national capital. From the relay house, on the railroad, about thirty miles from Washington, he was attended by the mayor and several members of the city council. The delay at the relay house, where he was welcomed by deputations from Baltimore, caused his arrival at the metropolis after nightfall — but the stars shone brightly, and the railroad track was occasionally illuminated by bonfires on the route. By the roaring of cannon and flights of brilliant rockets was the general heralded into the city, and escorted by a large concourse of people to his quarters at Willard's hotel, on Pennsylvania avenue, where he remained until the day of his inauguration.

The joint committee of the senate and house of representatives appointed to wait on the president and vice-president elect and inform them of their election to those high offices, having accordingly waited on General Taylor, after his arrival at the seat of government, and through their chairman, Colonel Jefferson Davis of Mississippi (his son-in-law), performed that duty; " the president elect, in signifying his acceptance of the office to which he had been chosen by the people, evinced emotions of the profoundest gratitude, and acknowledged his distrust of his ability to fulfil the expectations upon which their confidence was based, but gave assurances of a fixed purpose to administer the government for the benefit and advantage of the whole country.

" In alluding to the fact to which his attention had been drawn, that the chairman of the committee represented a public body, a majority of whom were opposed in political opinion to the president elect, and accorded with that majority, he recognised in it the deference to the popular will constitutionally expressed, on which rests the strength and hope of the republic, and he said that it was to have been expected from the senate of the United States.

" He expressed an ardent wish that he might be able in any degree to assuage the fierceness of party, or temper with moderation the conflicts of those who are only divided as to the means of securing the public welfare.

" He said, having been reminded that he was about to occupy the chair once filled by Washington, that he could hope to emulate him only in the singleness of the aims which guided the conduct of the man who had no parallel in history, and no rival in the hearts of his countrymen.

" In conclusion, he announced his readiness to take the oath of office on the 5th of March, proximo, at such hour and place as might be designated."

The report of the committee being made to the senate on the 27th of February, that body appointed as a committee to make the necessary arrangements for the reception of the president elect on the 5th of March, Senators Reverdy Johnson, Jefferson Davis, and John Davis.

THE INAUGURATION.

At the appointed time, Monday, March, 5, 1849, the inauguration of General Zachary Taylor as president of the United States, took place, in front of the great portico of the capitol. The multitude of people assembled on the occasion from every part of the Union, for the purpose of witnessing the interesting ceremony, is supposed to have been much larger than was ever before collected in Washington. The weather, although the sky was clouded, was as pleasant as usual at this season of the year. At the break of day the strains of martial music resounded along the principal avenues of the city, and hundreds of national flags were unfolded to the breeze. The bells of the city then rang a stirring peal, and long before the usual hour of breakfast, the people were wending their way in immense masses to the capitol.

At nine o'clock, one hundred citizens who officiated as marshals on horseback, proceeded in a body to Willard's hotel, for the purpose of paying their respects to General Taylor. After the ceremony of introduction, the marshals retired to attend to their official duties, and the president elect, who was dressed in a plain suit of black, and in the enjoyment of his usual good health, returned to his apartments to prepare for the procession.

At half past eleven o'clock, the procession took up its line of march from the hotel to the capitol. The military of Washington, Baltimore, &c., who formed part of the procession, presented an imposing appearance. The carriage in which the president elect was escorted was drawn by four gray horses. Ex-President Polk, Mr. Speaker Winthrop, and Mr. Seaton, mayor of Washington, accompanied General Taylor in the carriage. Pennsylvania avenue, along which the procession passed, was thronged with thousands of people ; many of the roofs of the houses were also covered, and every window was occupied by spectators. The time occupied by the procession in reaching the east front of the capitol was about an hour, and after the conclusion of the inaugural ceremonies, the booming of artillery resounded through the city.

The senate being convened at eleven o'clock, after prayer by the chaplain, the Hon. David R. Atchison of Missouri, was chosen president, *pro tem.* The diplomatic corps, representing various foreign nations, were next announced. The brilliancy of some of their costumes appeared in fine contrast with the dark robes of the judges of the supreme court, seated opposite to them.

The late vice-president, Mr. Dallas, then conducted to the chair the Hon. Millard Fillmore, the vice-president elect, to whom the oath of office was administered by Mr. Atchison, after which, Mr. Fillmore delivered with calmness and dignity, an appropriate address, and took his seat as president of the senate.

At twelve o'clock, the members of the late executive cabinet appeared, and occupied places on the left of the vice-president.

All things were now in readiness for the appearance of the president elect, who, after an interval, entered the senate-chamber in company with Ex-President Polk, and took a seat which had been prepared for him ; Mr. Polk occupying another upon his left hand.

After a brief pause the order of procession was announced, and the company retired from the chamber of the senate in the order prescribed, to the east portico of the capitol, where an extensive staging had been erected. At about one o'clock, the president elect, in full view of at least twenty thousand people from all parts of the Union, pronounced his inaugural address. It was delivered in a remarkably distinct voice, and many parts of it were enunciated with a full and clear emphasis, and enthusiastically responded to by the cheers of the surrounding spectators. As soon as the applause which marked the conclusion of the address had subsided, the oath of office was administered to the president, by Chief-Justice Taney. The president then received congratulations from numerous persons present, Chief-Justice Taney and Ex-President Polk taking the lead.

The ceremonies at the capitol were terminated by salvos of artillery, and the president and the procession returned down the avenue leading from the capitol to the White house, appropriated to the residence of the successive presidents of the United States. At this mansion, the president received with his accustomed courtesy the salutes of some thousands of his fellow-citizens, and in the evening visited several balls given in honor of the occasion.

On the 6th of March, the president nominated to the senate the following gentlemen to compose his cabinet, and they were, the following day, confirmed by that body, viz. : John M. Clayton, of Delaware, secretary of state ; William M. Meredith, of Pennsylvania, secretary of the treasury ; George W. Crawford, of Georgia, secretary of war ; William B. Preston, of Virginia, secretary of the navy ; Thomas Ewing, of Ohio, secretary of the interior ; Jacob Collamer, of Vermont, postmaster-general ; Reverdy Johnson, of Maryland, attorney-general.

These officers, with the exception of Mr. Crawford, who arrived from Georgia a few days afterward, respectively took the oath of office and entered upon their duties on the 8th of March, 1849.

HISTORICAL SKETCH OF THE AMERICAN UNION.

A brief History of the Events and Circumstances which led to the Union of the States, and the formation of the Constitution.

In the early history of the New England colonies, we find the first instance of the association of the people of America for mutual defence and protection, while they owed allegiance to the British crown. In 1643, the colonies of Massachusetts, Plymouth, Connecticut, and New Haven, under the impression of danger from the surrounding tribes of Indians, entered into a league, offensive and defensive, firm and perpetual, under the name of the United Colonies of New England. They vested in an annual congress of commissioners, delegated from each colony, the authority to regulate their general concerns, and especially to levy war and make requisitions of men and money, upon the several members of the union in a ratio to their respective numbers. This confederacy subsisted for upward of forty years, and, for part of the time, with the countenance of the government in England, and was dissolved under King James II., in the year 1686.

This association is generally considered as the foundation of subsequent efforts for a more extensive and perfect union of the British North American colonies; and the people of this country continued, after the dissolution of this league, to afford other instructive precedents of associations for their safety. A congress of governors and commissioners from other colonies, as well as from New England, was occasionally held, the better to make arrangements for the protection of their interior frontier, of which we have an instance at Albany, in the year 1722; and a much more interesting congress was held at the same place in the year 1754, which consisted of commissioners from the colonies of New Hampshire, Massachusetts, Rhode Island, Connecticut, New York, Pennsylvania, and Maryland. It was called at the instance of the British government, to take into consideration the best means of defending America, as a war with France was then apprehended. The object of the British government, in calling this congress, was to effect treaties with the Indian tribes; but the commissioners, among whom was Dr. Franklin, and other distinguished men in the colonies, had more enlarged views.   They asserted and promulgated some invaluable truths, the proper reception of which in the minds of their countrymen prepared the way for their future independence and union.   The commissioners unanimously resolved that a UNION of the colonies was absolutely necessary for their preservation.   They likewise rejected all proposals for a division of the colonies into separate confederacies, and adopted a plan of federal government, drawn up by Dr. Franklin, consisting of a general council of delegates, to be chosen by the provincial assemblies, and a president general to be appointed by the crown.   In this council were proposed to be vested, subject to the negative of the president, many of the rights of war and peace, and the right to lay and levy imposts and taxes ; and the union was to embrace all the colonies from New Hampshire to Georgia.   But the times were not yet ripe, nor the minds of men sufficiently enlarged, for such a comprehensive proposition ; and this bold project for a continental union, had the singular fate of being rejected, not only by the king, but by every provincial assembly.   We were to remain some years longer separate and alien commonwealths, emulous of each other in obedience to the parent state, but jealous of each other's prosperity, and divided by policy, interest, prejudice, and manners.   So strong was the force of these considerations, and so exasperated were the people of the colonies against each other in their disputes about boundaries, that Dr. Franklin, in the year 1761, observed, that a union of the colonies was absolutely impossible, or at least without being forced by the most grievous tyranny and oppression.*

The seeds of union, however, had been sown, and its principles were to gather strength and advance toward maturity, when the season of common danger approached.   When the first attempt upon our liberties was made by the British government, by the passage of the stamp act, in 1765, a congress of delegates from nine colonies assembled in New York, in October of that year, at the instance and recommendation of Massachusetts.   The colonies of Massachusetts, Rhode Island, Connecticut, New York, New Jersey, Pennsylvania, Delaware, Maryland, and South Carolina, were represented.   This congress adopted a declaration of rights, in which the sole power of taxation was asserted to reside in the colonial legislatures, and they also declared, that the restrictions imposed by several late acts of parliament on the colonies were burdensome, and would render them unable to purchase the manufactures of Great Britain.   An address to the king, and a petition to each house of parliament, were adopted.

These state papers evince the talents, as well as firmness, tempered with wisdom and moderation, of this first American congress ; composed, as it was, of some of the most distinguished statesmen from the several colonies therein represented.†

* Kent's Historical Lecture in 1795.   † Pitkin.

The congress of 1765, was only a preparatory step to a more extensive and permanent union, which took place at Philadelphia, in September, 1774, and thereby laid the foundations of this great republic. The more serious and impending oppressions of the British parliament at this last critical era, induced the twelve colonies which spread over this vast continent, from Nova Scotia to Georgia, to an interchange of political opinions, and to concur in choosing and sending delegates to Philadelphia, " with authority and direction to meet and consult together for the common welfare." The assembling of this congress was first recommended by a town-meeting of the people of Providence, Rhode Island, followed by the colonial assemblies of Massachusetts and Virginia, and by other public bodies and meetings of the people. In some of the legislatures of the colonies, delegates were appointed by the popular or representative branch; and in other cases, they were appointed by conventions of the people in the colonies. The congress of delegates (calling themselves, in their more formal acts, " the delegates appointed by the *good people* of these colonies") assembled on the 4th of September, 1774; and having chosen officers, they adopted certain fundamental rules for their proceedings. All the colonies were represented, except Georgia.

Thus was organized, under the auspices, and with the consent, of the people, acting directly in their primary, sovereign capacity, and without the intervention of the functionaries to whom the ordinary powers of government were delegated in the colonies, the first general or national government, which has been very aptly called "the revolutionary government," since, in its origin and progress, it was wholly conducted upon revolutionary principles. The congress, thus assembled, exercised, *de facto* and *de jure*, a sovereign authority; not as the delegated agents of the governments *de facto* of the colonies, but in virtue of original powers derived from the people. The revolutionary government thus formed, terminated only when it was regularly superseded by the confederated government, under articles finally ratified, as we shall see, in 1781.*

The first and most important of their acts was a declaration, that in determining questions in this congress, each colony or province should have one vote; and this became the established course during the revolution. They proposed a general congress to be held at the same place in May, in the next year. They appointed committees to take into consideration their rights and grievances; asserted by number of declaratory resolutions, what they deemed to be the unalienable rights of English freemen; pointed out to their constituents the system of violence which was preparing against those rights; and bound them by the most sacred of all ties, the ties of honor and their country, to renounce commerce with Great Britain, as being the most salutary means to avert the one, and to secure the blessings of the other. These resolutions were received with univer-

* Judge Story's Commentaries.

sal and prompt obedience ; and the union being thus auspiciously formed, it was continued by a succession of delegates in Congress ; and through every period of the war, and through every revolution of our government, it has been revered and cultivated as the tutelary guardian of our liberties.[*]

In May, 1775, the second continental congress of delegates from all the colonies (except Georgia), assembled at Philadelphia, and were invested by the colonies with very ample discretionary powers.   These delegates were chosen, as the preceding had been, partly by the popular branch of the legislatures when in session, but principally by conventions of the people in the various states.   In July, Georgia acceded to, and completed the confederacy.   Hostilities had already commenced in the province of Massachusetts Bay, and the unconditional sovereignty of the British parliament over the colonies was to be asserted by an appeal to arms.   Congress, charged with the general interests and superintending direction of the Union, and supported by the zeal and confidence of their constituents, prepared for defence.   They published a declaration of the causes and necessity of taking up arms, and forthwith proceeded to levy and organize an army, to prescribe rules for the regulation of their land and naval forces, to emit a paper currency, contract debts, and exercise all the other prerogatives of an independent sovereignty, till at last, on the 4th day of July, 1776, they took a separate and equal station among the powers of the earth, by declaring the united colonies to be FREE AND INDEPENDENT STATES.

This memorable declaration, in imitation of that published by the United Netherlands on a similar occasion, recapitulated the oppressions of the British king, asserted it to be the natural right of every people to withdraw from tyranny, and made a solemn appeal to mankind, in vindication of the necessity of the measure.   By this declaration, made in the name, and by the authority, of the PEOPLE, these United States were absolved from all allegiance to the British crown, and all political connexion between them and the state of Great Britain was totally dissolved.   The principles of self-preservation, and of social happiness, gave a clear sanction to this act of separation.   When the government established over any people becomes incompetent, or destructive to the ends for which it was instituted, it is the right and the duty of such people, founded on the law of nature, and the reason and practice of mankind, to throw off such government, and provide new guards for their future security.

The establishment of the republics of Holland and Switzerland bears a striking analogy to that of the United States, in the causes which produced them, and in the manner in which they were conducted.   The United Netherlands were formerly a part of the immense dominions of the Spanish empire ; but the violent government of Philip the Second, and the unrelenting intolerance of the inquisition, drove those distant provinces to

* Kent.

union and resistance.   In 1579, by the celebrated treaty of Utrecht, they entered into a league for their mutual defence, and that treaty was always considered as the bond of their union, and the foundation of their republic. But although they had for sometime made open resistance to the force of Spain, yet it was not till the 26th of July, 1581, after all hopes of reconciliation were lost, and the authority of Philip had been for some time virtually renounced, that the confederated provinces, equally distinguished for their forbearance and firmness, solemnly declared themselves independent states, and absolved from all allegiance to the Spanish crown.   It is well known that Spain continued to make long and powerful efforts to reduce them to obedience, till at last, exhausted herself, she was reluctantly compelled to a permanent recognition of their independence at the treaty of Westphalia.   Similar to that of the Netherlands was the case of Switzerland, which formerly fell under the dominion of the German empire, acknowledging the counts of Hapsburg for her protectors, and faithfully preserving her allegiance after that family, under the well-known name of the house of Austria, succeeded to the imperial crown.   The tyranny of the imperial bailiffs became insupportable, and three of the Swiss cantons threw off the Austrian yoke in the year 1308, and confederated together for their common defence.   The house of Austria carried on an implacable war against them for more than a century.   That celebrated confederacy, which originally consisted of only the three cantons of Uri, Schweitz, and Underwalden, kept continually increasing in strength, by the accession of other cantons from conquest or alliance ; but the union of the thirteen cantons was not completed for two centuries, nor was their independence fully and finally acknowledged by the house of Austria, till the treaty of Westphalia, in 1648.[*]

To return to the history of our own government : the general sentiment of the importance of the union appears evident in all the early proceedings of Congress.   In July, 1775, a year before the declaration of independence, Dr. Franklin submitted to the consideration of Congress, a sketch of articles of confederation between the colonies, to continue until their reconciliation with Great Britain, and in failure of that event, to be perpetual.   This plan appears to have never been discussed in Congress.[†] But during the time that the declaration of independence was under consideration, Congress took measures for the formation of a constitutional plan of union.   On the 11th of June, 1776, it was resolved that a committee should be appointed to prepare and digest the form of a confederation to be entered into between the colonies ; and the day following a committee, consisting of one member from each colony, was appointed, to perform that duty. Upon the report of this committee, which was laid aside on the 20th of August, 1776, and not resumed till the 7th of April, 1777, the subject was from time to time debated, until the 15th of November, 1777, when a copy

---

[*] Kent's Historical Lecture.   [†] J. Q. Adams's Jubilee Discourse, 1839.

of the articles of confederation being made out, the same was finally agreed to. Congress, at the same time, directed that the articles should be proposed to the legislatures of all the United States, to be considered, and, if approved of by them, they were advised to authorize their delegates to ratify the same in the Congress of the United States ; which being done, the same should become conclusive. On the 29th of November ensuing, a committee of three was appointed, to procure a translation of the articles to be made into the French language, and to report an address to the inhabitants of Canada, &c. On the 26th of June, 1778, the form of a ratification of the articles of confederation was adopted, and it was ordered that the whole should be engrossed on parchment, with a view that the same should be signed by the delegates, in virtue of the powers furnished by the several states.*

On the 9th of July, 1778, the articles were signed by the delegates of New Hampshire, Massachusetts Bay, Rhode Island, Connecticut, New York, Pennsylvania, Virginia, and South Carolina. The delegates from New Jersey, Delaware, and Maryland, informed Congress that they had not yet received powers to ratify and sign. North Carolina and Georgia were not represented—and the ratification of New York was conditional, that all the other states should ratify.

The delegates from North Carolina signed the articles on the 21st of July, 1778 ; those of Georgia on the 24th of the same month ; those of New Jersey on the 26th of November, 1778 ; those of Delaware on the 22d of February, and 5th of May, 1779 ; but Maryland held out to the last, and positively refused the ratification, until the question of the conflicting claims of the Union and of the separate states, to the property of the crown-lands, should be adjusted. This was finally accomplished by cessions from the claiming states to the United States, of the unsettled lands, for the benefit of the whole Union.

The cessions of the claiming states of the crown-lands to the Union, originated the territorial system, and, eventually, in the ordinance for the government of the Northwestern territory (passed by Congress in July, 1786). It also removed the insuperable objection of the state of Maryland to the articles of confederation ; and her delegates signed them on the 1st of March, 1781, four years and four months after they had been submitted by Congress to the sovereign states, with a solemn averment that they could no longer be deferred ; that they seemed essential to the very existence of the Union as a free people ; and that, without them, they might be constrained to bid adieu to independence, to liberty, and safety.†

The confederation being thus finally complete, by the ratification of the delegates from Maryland, on the 1st of March, 1781, the event was joyfully announced by Congress, and, on the 2d of March, that body assembled under the new powers.‡

* Force's National Calendar, 1830.   † Adams's Jubilee Discourse.
‡ For the Articles of Confederation, see Vol. I., pages 1–7, of this work.

It will be observed, that the term of the continental Congress is properly divided into two periods, namely : the first extending from the first meeting, on the 4th of September, 1774, until the ratification of the confederation, on the 1st of March, 1781 ; the second, from the 1st of March, 1781, until the organization of the government under the constitution, on the 4th of March, 1789. The first period may be called that of " the revolutionary national government ;" the second was that of " the confederation."

The question naturally presents itself, if the declaration is to be considered as a national act, in what manner did the colonies become a nation, and in what manner did Congress become possessed of this national power ? The true answer must be, that as soon as Congress assumed powers and passed measures, which were in their nature national, to that extent the people, from whose acquiescence and consent they took effect, must be considered as agreeing to form a nation. The Congress of 1774, looking at the general terms of the commissions under which the delegates were appointed, seem to have possessed the power of concerting such measures as they deemed best to redress the grievances, and preserve the rights and liberties, of all the colonies. The Congress of 1775 and 1776 were clothed with more ample powers, and the language of their commissions generally was sufficiently broad to embrace the right to pass measures of a national character and obligation. The Congress of 1775 accordingly assumed at once the exercise of some of the highest functions of sovereignty. They took measures for national defence and resistance ; they followed up the prohibitions upon trade and intercourse with Great Britain ; they raised a national army and navy, and authorized limited national hostilities against Great Britain ; they raised money, emitted bills of credit, and contracted debts upon national account ; they established a national postoffice ; and, finally, they authorized captures and condemnation of prizes in prize courts, with a reserve of appellate jurisdiction to themselves.

The same body, in 1776, took bolder steps, and exerted powers which could in no other manner be justified or accounted for, than upon the supposition that a national union for national purposes already existed, and that the Congress was invested with sovereign power over all the colonies, for the purpose of preserving the common rights and liberties of all. The validity of these acts was never doubted or denied by the people. On the contrary, they became the foundation upon which the superstructure of the liberties and independence of the United States has been erected.

From the moment of the declaration of independence, if not for most purposes at an antecedent period, the united colonies must be considered as being a nation *de facto*, having a general government over it, created and acting by the general consent of the people of the colonies. The powers of that government were not, and indeed could not be, well defined. But still its exclusive sovereignty, in many cases, was firmly es-

18

tablished ; and its controlling power over the states was in most, if not in all national measures, universally admitted.   The articles of confederation were not ratified so as to become obligatory upon all the states, until March, 1781.   In the intermediate time, Congress continued to exercise the powers of a general government, whose acts were binding on all the states.   In respect to foreign governments, we were politically known as the United States only ; and it was in our national capacity, as such, that we sent and received ambassadors, entered into treaties and alliances, and were admitted into the general community of nations, who might exercise the right of belligerents, and claim an equality of sovereign powers and prerogatives.*

The continental congress, upon trial, soon found that the powers derived from the articles of confederation were inadequate to the legitimate objects of an effective national government.   Defects were more particularly manifest, whenever it became necessary to legislate upon the subject of commerce and that of taxes ; and it was at length indispensably necessary to amend the articles in such a way as to give authority and force to the national will in matters of trade and revenue.   This was from time to time attempted, until the present constitution of the United States was adopted.   The most important movements in Congress showing the progress of constitutional legislation, were on the 3d of February, 1781, April 18, 1783, April 26, 1783, April 30, 1784, March 3, 1786, September 29, 1786, and October 23, 1786.†

Peace came (in 1783).   The heroic leader of the revolutionary armies surrendered his commission.   The armies were disbanded, but they were not paid.   Mutiny was suppressed ; but not until Congress had been surrounded by armed men, demanding justice, and appealed in vain for protection to the sovereign state within whose jurisdiction they were sitting. A single frigate, the remnant of a gallant navy, which had richly shared the glories, and deeply suffered the calamities of the war, was dismantled and sold.   The expenses of the nation were reduced to the minimum of a peace establishment, and yet the nation was not relieved.   The nation wanted a government founded on the principles of the Declaration of Independence—a government constituted by the people.

In the congress of the confederation, the master-minds of James Madison and Alexander Hamilton were constantly engaged through the closing years of the Revolutionary war, and those of peace which immediately succeeded.   That of John Jay was associated with them shortly after the peace, in the capacity of secretary to the congress for foreign affairs. The incompetency of the articles of confederation for the management of the affairs of the Union at home and abroad, was demonstrated to them by the painful and mortifying experience of every day.   Washington, though in retirement, was brooding over the cruel injustice suffered by his asso-

* Story's Commentaries.   † Force's Calendar, 1830.

ciates in arms, the warriors of the revolution; over the prostration of the public credit and the faith of the nation, in the neglect to provide for the payment even of the interest upon the public debt; over the disappointed hopes of the friends of freedom; in the language of the address from Congress to the states, of the 18th of April, 1783—"the pride and boast of America, that the rights for which she contended were the rights of human nature."

At his residence of Mount Vernon, in March, 1785, the first idea was started of a revisal of the articles of confederation, by an organization of means differing from that of a compact between the state legislatures and their own delegates in Congress. A convention of delegates from the state legislatures, independent of the Congress itself, was the expedient which presented itself for effecting the purpose, and an augmentation of the powers of Congress for the regulation of commerce, as the object for which this assembly was to be convened. In January, 1786, the proposal was made and adopted in the legislature of Virginia, and communicated to the other state legislatures.

The convention was held at Annapolis, in September of that year. It was attended by delegates from only five of the central states, who, on comparing their restricted powers with the glaring and universally-acknowledged defects of the confederation, reported only a recommendation for the assemblage of another convention of delegates to meet at Philadelphia in May, 1787, from all the states, and with enlarged powers.

The constitution of the United States was the work of this convention. But in its construction, the convention immediately perceived that they must retrace their steps, and fall back from a league of friendship between sovereign states, to the constituent sovereignty of *the people*—from *power* to *right*—from the irresponsible despotism of state sovereignty, to the self-evident truths of the Declaration of Independence. From the day of that declaration, the constituent power of the people had never been called into action. A confederacy had been substituted in the place of a government, and state sovereignty had usurped the constituent sovereignty of the people.

The convention assembled at Philadelphia had themselves no direct authority from the people. Their authority was all derived from the state legislatures. But they had the articles of confederation before them, and they saw and felt the wretched condition into which they had brought the whole people, and that the Union itself was in the agonies of death. They soon perceived that the indispensably-needed powers were such as no state government; no combination of them was, by the principles of the Declaration of Independence, competent to bestow. They could emanate only from the people. A highly respectable portion of the assembly, still clinging to the confederacy of states, proposed, as a substitute for the constitution, a mere revival of the articles of confederation, with a grant of additional powers to the Congress. Their plan was respectfully and thoroughly discussed ; but the want of a government, and of the sanction of the people to the delegation of powers, happily prevailed. A constitution for the people, and the distribution of legislative, executive, and judicial powers, was prepared. It announced itself as the work of the people themselves ; and as this was unquestionably a power assumed by the convention, not delegated to them by the people, they religiously confined it to a simple power to propose, and carefully provided that it should be no more than a proposal, until sanctioned by the confederation Congress, by the state legislatures, and by the people of the several states, in conventions specially assembled, by authority of their legislatures, for the single purpose of examining and passing upon it.

And thus was consummated the work, commenced by the Declaration of Independence ; a work in which the people of the North American Union, acting under the deepest sense of responsibility to the Supreme Ruler of the universe, had achieved the most transcendent act of power that social man, in his mortal condition, can perform ; even that of dissolving the ties of allegiance by which he is bound to his country—of renouncing that country itself—of demolishing its government, of instituting another government, and of making for himself another country in its stead.

The revolution itself was a work of thirteen years—and had never been completed until that day (when Washington was inaugurated, on the 30th of April, 1789). The Declaration of Independence and the constitution of the United States, are parts of one consistent whole, founded upon one and the same theory of government, then new, not as a theory, for it had been working itself into the mind of man for many ages, and been especially expounded in the writings of Locke, but had never before been adopted by a great nation in practice.[*]

Proceedings of commissioners from certain states, assembled at Annapolis, in September, 1786, to consider on the best means of remedying the defects of the federal government.

Annapolis, in the state of Maryland, September 11, 1786.—At a meeting of commissioners from the states of New York, New Jersey, Pennsylvania, Delaware, and Virginia : present, *New York :* Alexander Hamilton, Egbert Benson ; *New Jersey :* Abraham Clark, William C. Houston, James Schureman ; *Pennsylvania :* Tench Coxe ; *Delaware :* George Read, John Dickinson, Richard Basset ; *Virginia :* Edmund Randolph, James Madison, jr., Saint George Tucker.

Mr. Dickinson was unanimously elected chairman. The commissioners produced their credentials from their respective states, which were read. After a full communication of sentiments, and deliberate consideration of what would be proper to be done by the commissioners now assembled,

[*] Adams's Jubilee Discourse.

it was unanimously agreed, that a committee be appointed to prepare a draught of a report to be made to the states having commissioners attending at this meeting. Adjourned till Wednesday morning.

Wednesday, Sept. 13.—Met agreeable to adjournment. The committee appointed for that purpose reported the draught of the report, which being read, the meeting proceeded to the consideration thereof, and after some time spent therein, adjourned till to-morrow morning.

Thursday, Sept. 14.—Met agreeable to adjournment. The meeting resumed the consideration of the draught of the report, and after some time spent therein, and amendments made, the same was unanimously agreed to, and is as follows, to wit :—

To the honorable the legislatures of Virginia, Delaware, Pennsylvania, New Jersey, and New York, the commissioners from the said states, respectively, assembled at Annapolis, humbly beg leave to report :—

That, pursuant to their several appointments, they met at Annapolis, in the state of Maryland, on the 11th day of September, instant, and having proceeded to a communication of their powers, they found that the states of New York, Pennsylvania, and Virginia, had, in substance, and nearly in the same terms, authorized their respective commissioners " to meet such commissioners as were or might be appointed by the other states in the union, at such time and place as should be agreed upon by the said commissioners, to take into consideration the trade and commerce of the United States, to consider how far a uniform system in their commercial intercourse and regulations, might be necessary to their common interest and permanent harmony, and to report to the several states such an act relative to this great object, as, when unanimously ratified by them, would enable the United States, in Congress assembled, effectually to provide for the same."

That the state of Delaware had given similar powers to their commissioners, with this difference only, that the act to be framed in virtue of these powers, is required to be reported " to the United States, in Congress assembled, to be agreed to by them, and confirmed by the legislatures of every state."

That the state of New Jersey had enlarged the object of their appointment, empowering their commissioners " to consider how far a uniform system in their commercial regulations, and *other important matters*, might be necessary to the common interest and permanent harmony of the several states ;" and to report such an act on the subject, as, when ratified by them, " would enable the United States, in Congress assembled, effectually to provide for the exigencies of the Union."

That appointments of commissioners have also been made by the states of New Hampshire, Massachusetts, Rhode Island, and North Carolina, none of whom, however, have attended ; but that no information has been received by your commissioners of any appointment having been made by the states of Connecticut, Maryland, South Carolina, or Georgia.

That the express terms of the powers to your commissioners supposing a deputation from all the states, and having for object the trade and commerce of the United States, your commissioners did not conceive it advisable to proceed on the business of their mission under the circumstances of so partial and defective a representation.

Deeply impressed, however, with the magnitude and importance of the object confided to them on this occasion, your commissioners can not forbear to indulge an expression of their earnest and unanimous wish, that speedy measures may be taken to effect a general meeting of the states, in a future convention, for the same and such other purposes as the situation of public affairs may be found to require.

If, in expressing this wish, or in intimating any other sentiment, your commissioners should seem to exceed the strict bounds of their appointment, they entertain a full confidence, that a conduct dictated by an anxiety for the welfare of the United States, will not fail to receive an indulgent construction.

In this persuasion, your commissioners submit an opinion, that the idea of extending the powers of their deputies to other objects than those of commerce, which has been adopted by the state of New Jersey, was an improvement on the original plan, and will deserve to be incorporated into that of a future convention. They are the more naturally led to this conclusion, as, in the course of their reflections on the subject, they have been induced to think that the power of regulating trade is of such comprehensive extent, and will enter so far into the general system of the federal government, that to give it efficacy, and to obviate questions and doubts concerning its precise nature and limits, may require a correspondent adjustment of other parts of the federal system.

That there are important defects in the system of the federal government, is acknowledged by the acts of all those states which have concurred in the present meeting ; that the defects, upon a closer examination, may be found greater and more numerous than even these acts imply, is at least so far probable, from the embarrassments which characterize the present state of our national affairs, foreign and domestic, as may reasonably be supposed to merit a deliberate and candid discussion, in some mode which will unite the sentiments and councils of all the states. In the choice of the mode, your commissioners are of opinion, that a convention of deputies from the different states, for the special and sole purpose of entering into this investigation, and digesting a plan for supplying such defects as may be discovered to exist, will be entitled to a preference, from considerations which will occur without being particularized.

Your commissioners decline an enumeration of those national circumstances on which their opinion respecting the propriety of a future convention, with more enlarged powers, is founded ; as it would be a useless intrusion of facts and observations, most of which have been frequently the subject of public discussion, and none of which can have escaped the penetration of those to whom they would, in this instance, be addressed. They are, however, of a nature so serious, as, in the view of your commissioners, to render the situation of the United States delicate and critical, calling for an exertion of the united virtue and wisdom of all the members of the confederacy.

Under this impression, your commissioners, with the most respectful deference, beg leave to suggest their unanimous conviction, that it may essentially tend to advance the interests of the Union, if the states, by whom they have been respectively delegated, would themselves concur, and use their endeavors to procure the concurrence of the other states, in the appointment of commissioners, to meet at Philadelphia on the second Monday in May next, to take into consideration the situation of the United States, to devise such further provisions as shall appear to them necessary to render the constitution of the federal government adequate to the exigencies of the Union ; and to report such an act for that purpose, to the

United States, in Congress assembled, as, when agreed to by them, and afterward confirmed by the legislatures of every state, will effectually provide for the same.

Though your commissioners could not, with propriety, address these observations and sentiments to any but the states they have the honor to represent, they have nevertheless concluded, from motives of respect, to transmit copies of this report to the United States, in Congress assembled, and to the executives of the other states.

By order of the commissioners.
Dated at Annapolis, September 14th, 1786.

In Congress, Wednesday, February 21, 1787.—The report of a grand committee, consisting of Messrs. Dane, Varnum, S. M. Mitchell, Smith, Cadwallader, Irvine, N. Mitchell, Forrest, Grayson, Blount, Bull, and Few, to whom was referred a letter of the 14th September, 1786, from J. Dickinson, written at the request of commissioners from the states of Virginia, Delaware, Pennsylvania, New Jersey, and New York, assembled at the city of Annapolis, together with a copy of the report of the said commissioners to the legislatures of the states by whom they were appointed, being an order of the day, was called up, and which is contained in the following resolution, viz. :—

Congress having had under consideration the letter of John Dickinson, Esq., chairman of the commissioners who assembled at Annapolis, during the last year ; also the proceedings of the said commissioners, and entirely coinciding with them, as to the inefficiency of the federal government, and the necessity of devising such further provisions as shall render the same adequate to the exigencies of the Union, do strongly recommend to the different legislatures to send forward delegates, to meet the proposed convention, on the second Monday in May next, at the city of Philadelphia.

The delegates for the state of New York thereupon laid before Congress instructions which they had received from their constituents, and in pursuance of the said instructions, moved to postpone the further consideration of the report, in order to take up the following proposition, viz. :—

" That it be recommended to the states composing the Union, that a convention of representatives from the said states respectively, be held at ——, on ——, for the purpose of revising the articles of confederation and perpetual union between the United States of America, and reporting to the United States, in Congress assembled, and to the states respectively, such alterations and amendments of the said articles of confederation, as the representatives, met in such convention, shall judge proper and necessary to render them adequate to the preservation and support of the Union."

On the question to postpone, for the purpose abovementioned, the yeas and nays being required by the delegates for New York, the question was lost by the following vote, three states only voting in the affirmative. The names of the members who voted in the affirmative are in *italic*.

Massachusetts : Messrs. *King, Dane ; Connecticut :* Messrs. *Johnson*, S. Mitchell ; *New York,* Messrs. *Smith, Benson ; New Jersey :* Messrs. *Cadwallader*, Clark, Schureman ; *Pennsylvania :* Messrs. Irvine, *Meredith*, Bingham ; *Delaware :* Mr. N. Mitchell ; *Maryland :* Mr. Forrest ; *Virginia :* Messrs. *Grayson, Madison ; North Carolina :* Messrs. Blount, Hawkins ; *South Carolina :* Messrs. Bull, Kean, Huger, Parker ; *Georgia :* Messrs. *Few*, Pierce.

A motion was then made by the delegates for Massachusetts, to postpone the further consideration of the report, in order to take into consideration a motion which they read in their place; this being agreed to, the motion of the delegates for Massachusetts was taken up, and being amended was agreed to, as follows :—

"Whereas, there is provision in the articles of confederation and perpetual union, for making alterations therein, by the assent of a Congress of the United States, and of the legislatures of the several states; and whereas, experience hath evinced that there are defects in the present confederation, as a mean to remedy which, several of the states, and particularly the state of New York, by express instructions to their delegates in Congress, have suggested a convention for the purposes expressed in the following resolution : and such convention appearing to be the most probable means of establishing, in these states, a firm national government:

"*Resolved*, That, in the opinion of Congress, it is expedient that, on the second Monday in May next, a convention of delegates who shall have been appointed by the several states, be held at Philadelphia, for the sole and express purpose of revising the articles of confederation, and reporting to Congress, and the several legislatures, such alteration and provisions therein, as shall, when agreed to in Congress, and confirmed by the states, render the federal constitution adequate to the exigencies of the government, and the preservation of the Union."

In compliance with the recommendation of Congress, delegates were chosen in the several states, for the purpose of revising the articles of confederation, who assembled in Philadelphia, on the second Monday in May, 1787.   General Washington was chosen president of the convention. On the 17th of September, 1787, the convention having agreed upon the several articles of the federal constitution, it was adopted and signed by all the members present.

On Friday, the 28th of September, 1787, the Congress having received the report of the convention, with the constitution, recommended for ratification by the several states, and by Congress, adopted the following resolution :—

"*Resolved, unanimously*, That the said report, with the resolutions and letters accompanying the same, be transmitted to the several legislatures, in order to be submitted to a convention of delegates chosen in each state by the people thereof, in conformity to the resolves of the convention, made and provided in that case."

The constitution having been ratified by the number of states required, the following proceedings took place in the old Congress, preparatory to organizing the new government.

Saturday, September, 13, 1788.—On the question to agree to the following proposition, it was resolved in the affirmative, by the unanimous votes of nine states, viz., of New Hampshire, Massachusetts, Connecticut, New York, New Jersey, Pennsylvania, Virginia, South Carolina, and Georgia.

"Whereas, the convention assembled in Philadelphia, pursuant to the resolution of Congress, of the 21st of February, 1787, did, on the 17th of September, in the same year, report to the United States, in Congress assembled, a constitution for the people of the United States ; whereupon, Congress, on the 28th of the same September, did resolve unanimously, 'that the said report, with the resolutions and letter accompanying the same, be transmitted to the several legislatures, in order to be submitted to a convention of delegates, chosen in each state by the people thereof, in conformity to the resolves of the convention, made and provided in that case ;' and whereas the constitution so reported by the convention, and by Congress transmitted to the several legislatures, has been ratified in the manner therein declared to be sufficient for the establishment of the same, and such ratifications, duly authenticated, have been received by Congress, and are filed in the office of the secretary, therefore—

" *Resolved*, That the first Wednesday in January next be the day for appointing electors in the several states which before the said day shall have ratified the said constitution ; that the first Wednesday in February next be the day for the electors to assemble in their respective states, and vote for a president ; and that the first Wednesday in March next be the time, and the present seat of Congress [New York] the place, for commencing proceedings under the said constitution."

Delegates to the Convention which met at Philadelphia, in May, 1787, to frame a new Constitution.

New Hampshire, on the 27th of June, 1787, appointed John Langdon, John Pickering, Nicholas Gilman, and Benjamin West.

Massachusetts, on the 9th of April, 1787, appointed Francis Dana, Elbridge Gerry, Nathaniel Gorham, Rufus King, and Caleb Strong.

Connecticut, on the second Thursday of May, 1786, appointed William Samuel Johnson, Roger Sherman, and Oliver Ellsworth.

New York, on the 6th of March, 1787, appointed Robert Yates, John Lansing, jr., and Alexander Hamilton.

New Jersey, on the 23d of November, 1780, appointed David Brearly, William Churchill Houston, William Paterson, and John Neilson ; and on the 8th of May, 1787, added William Livingston and Abraham Clark ; and on the 5th of June, 1787, added Jonathan Dayton.

Pennsylvania, on the 30th of December, 1786, appointed Thomas Mifflin, Robert Morris, George Clymer, Jared Ingersoll, Thomas Fitzsimons, James Wilson, and Governeur Morris ; and on the 28th of March, 1787, added Benjamin Franklin.

Delaware, on the 3d of February, 1787, appointed George Read, Gunning Bedford, jr., John Dickinson, Richard Bassett, and Jacob Broom.

Maryland, on the 26th of May, 1787, appointed James M'Henry, Daniel of St. Thomas Jenifer, Daniel Carroll, John Francis Mercer, and Luther Martin.

Virginia, on the 16th of October, 1786, appointed George Washington, Patrick Henry, Edmund Randolph, John Blair, James Madison, jr., George Mason, and George Wythe. Patrick Henry having declined his appointment as deputy, James M'Clurg was nominated to supply his place.

North Carolina, in January, 1787, elected Richard Caswell, Alexander Martin, William Richardson Davie, Richard Dobbs Spaight, and Willie Jones. Richard Caswell having resigned, William Blount was appointed a deputy in his place. Willie Jones having also declined his appointment, was supplied by Hugh Williamson.

South Carolina, on the 8th of March, 1787, appointed John Rutledge, Charles Pinckney, Charles Cotesworth Pinckney, and Pierce Butler.

Georgia, on the 10th of February, 1787, appointed William Few, Abraham Baldwin, William Pierce, George Walton, William Houston, and Nathaniel Pendleton.

Dates of the Ratification of the Constitution by the Thirteen Old States.

Delaware	December...7, 1787	South Carolina	May	23, 1788
Pennsylvania	December..12, 1787	New Hampshire	June	21, 1788
New Jersey	December..18, 1787	Virginia	June	26, 1788
Georgia	January....2, 1788	New York	July	26, 1788
Connecticut	January....9, 1788	North Carolina	November 21, 1789
Massachusetts	February...6, 1788	Rhode Island	May	29, 1790
Maryland	April.....28, 1788			

States since admitted into the Union by acts of Congress.

Vermont	March	4, 1791	Alabama	December 14, 1819
Kentucky	June	1, 1792	Maine	March 15, 1820
Tennessee	June	1, 1796	Missouri	August 10, 1821
Ohio	February	19, 1803	Arkansas	June 14, 1836
Louisiana	April	8, 1812	Michigan	January 26, 1837
Indiana	December	11, 1816	Florida	March 3, 1845
Mississippi	December	10, 1817	Texas	December 24, 1845
Illinois	December	3, 1818	Iowa, 1846	Wisconsin, 1848

CONGRESS AT ALBANY, 1754.

THE day appointed for the meeting of the commissioners, at Albany, in the state of New York, was the 14th of June, 1754, but they did not assemble until the 19th of June, when it was found that seven colonies were represented, viz :—

NEW YORK.
James Delancy,
Joseph Murray,
William Johnson,
John Chambers,
William Smith.

MASSACHUSETTS.
Samuel Welles,
John Chandler,
Thomas Hutchinson.
Oliver Partridge,
John Worthington.

NEW HAMPSHIRE.
Theodore Atkinson,
Richard Wibird,
Meshech Weare,
Henry Sherburne.

CONNECTICUT.
William Pitkin,
Roger Wolcott,
Elisha Williams.

RHODE ISLAND.
Stephen Hopkins,
Martin Howard.

PENNSYLVANIA.
John Penn,
Benjamin Franklin,
Richard Peters,
Isaac Norris.

MARYLAND.
Benjamin Tasker,
Abraham Barnes.

The whole number of commissioners appointed was twenty-five, who all attended, as above named. Virginia and New Jersey, though expressly invited, did not attend.

Having completed a treaty with the Indians, the commissioners took up the subject of a plan of union. A committee, consisting of one member from each colony, was appointed to draw a plan, viz. : Messrs. Hutchinson of Massachusetts, Atkinson of New Hampshire, Pitkin of Connecticut, Hopkins of Rhode Island, Smith of New York, Franklin of Pennsylvania, and Tasker of Maryland.

Several plans were proposed, but an outline presented by Dr. Franklin, before he arrived in Albany, was preferred by the committee, and reported to the Congress on the 28th of June. The debates on the various topics embraced in the plan of union continued for twelve days, when the one reported, substantially as drawn by Doctor Franklin, was adopted; and the Congress adjourned on the 11th of July. This scheme of general government received the assent of all the commissioners, except those from Connecticut. Indeed, Governor Hutchinson, in his history of Massachusetts, says the vote was unanimous in the Congress; but this is contradicted by the Connecticut historians. It was, however, to be of no force unless confirmed by the several colonial assemblies—and not one of them, when the report was made by their delegates, inclined to part with so great a share of power as was to be given to this general government. The plan met with no better fate in England, where it was laid before the king and the board of trade. Doctor Franklin says : " The colonial assemblies all thought there was too much *prerogative* in it, and in England it was thought to have too much of the *democratic* in it." Considering the rejection by the two parties, for opposite reasons, it was Franklin's opinion, thirty years afterward, that his plan was near the true medium. It is remarkable how nearly the basis approaches the constitution of the United States.*

CONGRESS AT NEW YORK, 1765.

THE proposal for holding a congress of delegates from the respective colonies, in consequence of the passage of the stamp act and other oppressive measures of the British parliament, was made by the corresponding committee of the New York assembly (appointed in October, 1764), and was repeatedly agitated in the different colonial legislatures. In June, 1765, the popular branch of the legislature of Massachusetts issued a circular letter proposing " a meeting of committees from the house of representatives or burgesses of the several British colonies on this continent, to consult together on the circumstances of the colonies, and the difficulties to which they are and must be reduced by the operation of the acts of parliament, for levying duties and taxes on the colonies ; and to consider of a general and united, dutiful, loyal, and humble representation of their condition to his majesty and to the parliament, and to implore relief ; also, that such meeting be at the city of New York, on the first Tuesday of October next." In consequence of the circular letter referred to, the following gentlemen met at New York, on the 7th of October, 1765, viz. :—

MASSACHUSETTS.
James Otis,
Oliver Partridge,
Timothy Ruggles.

RHODE ISLAND.
Metcalf Bowler,
Henry Ward.

CONNECTICUT.
Eliphalet Dyer,
David Rowland,
William S. Johnson.

NEW YORK.
Robert R. Livingston,
John Cruger,
Philip Livingston,
William Bayard,
Leonard Lispenard.

NEW JERSEY.
Robert Ogden,
Hendrick Fisher,
Joseph Borden.

PENNSYLVANIA.
John Dickinson,
John Morton,
George Bryan.

DELAWARE.
Thomas M'Kean,
Cæsar Rodney.

MARYLAND.
William Murdock,
Edward Tilghman,
Thomas Ringgold.

SOUTH CAROLINA.
Thomas Lynch,
Christopher Gadsden,
John Rutledge.

* See Pitkin's Political History, and Franklin's Works.

New Hampshire, Virginia, North Carolina, and Georgia, were not represented ; but their assemblies wrote that they would agree to whatever was done by the Congress.

Timothy Ruggles, of Massachusetts, was, by ballot, chosen chairman of the Congress, and John Cotton, clerk.*

This Congress continued in session, from day to day, until the 24th of October, 1765, and their proceedings were approved by all of the delegates, except Mr. Ruggles, of Massachusetts, and Mr. Ogden, of New Jersey, both of whom left New York without signing the address or petitions. The proceedings of the Congress were afterward sanctioned by the various colonial assemblies.

CONTINENTAL CONGRESS.

Presidents of the Continental Congress, from 1774 to 1788.

	FROM	ELECTED.
Peyton Randolph	Virginia	September...5, 1774
Henry Middleton	South Carolina	October...22, 1774
Peyton Randolph	Virginia	May.....10, 1775
John Hancock	Massachusetts	May.....24, 1775
Henry Laurens	South Carolina	November..1, 1777
John Jay	New York	December 10, 1778
Samuel Huntington	Connecticut	September 28, 1779
Thomas M'Kean	Delaware	July.....10, 1781
John Hanson	Maryland	November..5, 1781
Elias Boudinot	New Jersey	November..4, 1782
Thomas Mifflin	Pennsylvania	November..3, 1783
Richard Henry Lee	Virginia	November 30, 1784
Nathaniel Gorham	Massachusetts	June.......6, 1786
Arthur St. Clair	Pennsylvania	February...2, 1787
Cyrus Griffin	Virginia	January..22, 1788

Sessions of the Continental Congress.

The sessions of the continental Congress were commenced as follows : September 5, 1774, also May 10, 1775, at *Philadelphia*; December 20, 1776, at *Baltimore ;* March 4, 1777, at *Philadelphia ;* September 27, 1777, at *Lancaster*, Penn. ; September 30, 1777, at *York*, Penn. ; July 2, 1778, at *Philadelphia ;* June 30, 1783, at *Princeton*, New Jersey ; November 26, 1783, at *Annapolis*, Maryland ; November 1, 1784, at *Trenton* New Jersey ; January 11, 1785, at *New York*, which, from that time, continued to be the place of meeting till the adoption of the constitution of the United States. From 1781 to 1788, Congress met annually on the first Monday in November, pursuant to the articles of confederation.

* Journal of the First American or Stamp-Act Congress, of 1765, published in Niles's Register, 1812, and by E. Winchester, New York, 1845.

DECLARATION OF INDEPENDENCE,

JULY 4th, 1776.

THE UNANIMOUS DECLARATION OF THE THIRTEEN UNITED STATES OF AMERICA IN CONGRESS ASSEMBLED.

WHEN, in the course of human events, it becomes necessary for one people to dissolve the political bands which have connected them with another, and to assume among the powers of the earth the separate and equal station to which the laws of nature and of nature's God entitled them, a decent respect to the opinions of mankind requires that they should declare the causes which impel them to the separation.

We hold these truths to be self-evident : that all men are created equal ; that they are endowed by their Creator with certain unalienable rights ; that among these are life, liberty, and the pursuit of happiness ; that, to secure these rights, governments are instituted among men, deriving their just powers from the consent of the governed ; that, whenever any form of government becomes destructive of these ends, it is the right of the people to alter or to abolish it, and to institute new government, laying its foundation on such principles, and organizing its powers in such form, as to them shall seem most likely to effect their safety and happiness. Prudence, indeed, will dictate that governments long established should not be changed for light and transient causes ; and, accordingly, all experience hath shown that mankind are more disposed to suffer, while evils are sufferable, than to right themselves by abolishing the forms to which they are accustomed. But when a long train of abuses and usurpations, pursuing invariably the same object, evinces a design to reduce them under absolute despotism, it is their right, it is their duty, to throw off such government, and to provide new guards for their future security. Such has been the patient sufferance of these colonies, and such is now the necessity which constrains them to alter their former systems of government. The history of the present king of Great Britain is a history of repeated injuries and usurpations, all having in direct object the establishment of an absolute tyranny over these states. To prove this, let facts be submitted to a candid world :—

He has refused his assent to laws the most wholesome and necessary for the public good.

He has forbidden his governors to pass laws of immediate and pressing importance, unless suspended in their operation till his assent should be obtained ; and, when so suspended, he has utterly neglected to attend to them.

He has refused to pass other laws for the accommodation of large districts of people, unless those people would relinquish the right of representation in the legislature—a right inestimable to them, and formidable to tyrants only.

He has called together legislative bodies at places unusual, uncomfortable, and distant from the repository of their public records, for the sole purpose of fatiguing them into compliance with his measures.

He has dissolved representative houses repeatedly for opposing with manly firmness his invasions on the rights of the people.

He has refused, for a long time after such dissolutions, to cause others to be elected ; whereby the legislative powers, incapable of annihilation, have returned to the people at large for their exercise—the state remaining, in the meantime, exposed to all the dangers of invasion from without and convulsions within.

He has endeavored to prevent the population of these states—for that purpose obstructing the laws of naturalization of foreigners, refusing to pass others to encourage their migration hither, and raising the conditions of new appropriations of lands.

He has obstructed the administration of justice, by refusing his assent to laws for establishing judiciary powers.

He has made judges dependent on his will alone for the tenure of their offices and the amount and payment of their salaries.

He has erected a multitude of new offices, and sent hither swarms of officers to harass our people and eat out their substance.

He has kept among us, in times of peace, standing armies, without the consent of our legislatures.

He has affected to render the military independent of, and superior to, the civil power.

He has combined with others to subject us to a jurisdiction foreign to our constitution and unacknowledged by our laws—giving his assent to their acts of pretended legislation.

For quartering large bodies of armed troops among us ;

For protecting them, by a mock trial, from punishment for any murders which they should commit on the inhabitants of these states ;

For cutting off our trade with all parts of the world ;

For imposing taxes on us without our consent;

For depriving us, in many cases, of the benefits of trial by jury ;

For transporting us beyond seas to be tried for pretended offences ;

For abolishing the free system of English laws in a neighboring province, establishing therein an arbitrary government, and enlarging its boundaries, so as to render it at once an example and fit instrument for introducing the same absolute rule into these colonies ;

For taking away our charters, abolishing our most valuable laws, and altering, fundamentally, the *forms* of our governments ;

For suspending our own legislatures, and declaring themselves invested with power to legislate for us in all cases whatsoever.

He has abdicated government here by declaring us out of his protection and waging war against us.

He has plundered our seas, ravaged our coasts, burnt our towns, and destroyed the lives of our people.

He is at this time transporting large armies of foreign mercenaries to complete the works of death, desolation, and tyranny, already begun with circumstances of cruelty and perfidy scarcely paralleled in the most barbarous ages, and totally unworthy the head of a civilized nation.

He has constrained our fellow-citizens, taken captive on the high seas, to bear arms against their country, to become the executioners of their friends and brethren, or to fall themselves by their hands.

He has excited domestic insurrections among us, and has endeavored to bring on the inhabitants of our frontiers the merciless Indian savages, whose known rule of warfare is an undistinguished destruction of all ages, sexes, and conditions.

In every stage of these oppressions, we have petitioned for redress in the most humble terms.   Our repeated petitions have been answered only by repeated injury.   A prince, whose character is thus marked by every act which may define a tyrant, is unfit to be the ruler of a free people.

Nor have we been wanting in attentions to our British brethren.   We have warned them, from time to time, of attempts, by their legislature, to extend an unwarrantable jurisdiction over us.   We have reminded them of the circumstances of our emigration and settlement here.   We have appealed to their native justice and magnanimity, and we have conjured them, by the ties of our common kindred, to disavow these usurpations, which would inevitably interrupt our connexions and correspondence.   They, too, have been deaf to the voice of justice and of consanguinity.   We must, therefore, acquiesce in the necessity which denounces our separation, and hold them, as we hold the rest of mankind, enemies in war, in peace, friends.

We, therefore, the representatives of the United States of America, in general Congress assembled, appealing to the Supreme Judge of the World for the rectitude of our intentions, do, in the name, and by the authority of the good people of these colonies, solemnly publish and declare that these united colonies are, and of right ought to be, free and independent states ; that they are absolved from all allegiance to the British crown, and that all political connexion between them and the state of Great Britain is, and ought to be, totally dissolved ; and that, as free and independent states, they have full power to levy war, conclude peace, contract alliances, establish commerce, and to do all other acts and things which independent states may of right do.   And for the support of this declaration, with a firm reliance on the protection of Divine Providence, we mutually pledge to each other our lives, our fortunes, and our sacred honor.

The foregoing declaration was, by order of Congress, engrossed and signed by the following members :—

JOHN HANCOCK.

NEW HAMPSHIRE.

JOSIAH BARTLETT,
WILLIAM WHIPPLE,
MATTHEW THORNTON.

MASSACHUSETTS BAY.

SAMUEL ADAMS,
JOHN ADAMS,
ROBERT TREAT PAINE,
ELBRIDGE GERRY.

RHODE ISLAND.

STEPHEN HOPKINS,
WILLIAM ELLERY.

CONNECTICUT.

ROGER SHERMAN,
SAMUEL HUNTINGTON,
WILLIAM WILLIAMS,
OLIVER WOLCOTT.

NEW YORK.

WILLIAM FLOYD,
PHILIP LIVINGSTON,
FRANCIS LEWIS,
LEWIS MORRIS.

NEW JERSEY.

RICHARD STOCKTON,
JOHN WITHERSPOON,
FRANCIS HOPKINSON,
JOHN HART,
ABRAHAM CLARK.

PENNSYLVANIA.

ROBERT MORRIS,
BENJAMIN RUSH,
BENJAMIN FRANKLIN,
JOHN MORTON,
GEORGE CLYMER,
JAMES SMITH,
GEORGE TAYLOR,
JAMES WILSON,
GEORGE ROSS.

DELAWARE.

CÆSAR RODNEY,
GEORGE READ,
THOMAS M'KEAN.

MARYLAND.

SAMUEL CHASE,
WILLIAM PACA,

THOMAS STONE,   [ton
CHARLES CARROLL, of Carroll-

VIRGINIA.

GEORGE WYTHE,
RICHARD HENRY LEE,
THOMAS JEFFERSON,
BENJAMIN HARRISON,
THOMAS NELSON, JR.
FRANCIS LIGHTFOOT LEE,
CARTER BRAXTON,

NORTH CAROLINA.

WILLIAM HOOPER,
JOSEPH HEWES,
JOHN PENN.

SOUTH CAROLINA.

EDWARD RUTLEDGE,
THOMAS HEYWARD, JR.
THOMAS LYNCH, JR.
ARTHUR MIDDLETON.

GEORGIA.

BUTTON GWINNETT,
LYMAN HALL,
GEORGE WALTON.

John Hancock

Rob Morris

Benjamin Rush

Benj. Franklin

Elbridge Gerry

Oliver Wolcott

Sam Adams

Chas

Carter Braxton

John Morton

Joseph Hewes

Caesar Rodney

George Wythe

John Penn

Ged Read

Rich and Henry Lee

Tho M. Kean

Wm Hooper

Tho Heyward junr

Thos Lynch

Francis Lightfoot Lee

Wm Paca

Thomas Lynch

Abra Clark

Arthur Middleton

Button Gwinnett

Wm Whipple

Lyman Hall

Phil. Livingston

Fran Lewis

Lewis Morris

John Adams

Fras Payne

Geo Clymer

Josiah Bartlett

Matthew Thornton Rich'd Stockton

Step. Hopkins Jn° Witherspoon

Fras Hopkinson

William Ellery John Hart

Roger Sherman James Wilson

Charles Carroll of Carrollton Tho Stone

Th. Jefferson

Francis Lightfoot Lee Geo Taylor Tho Nelson jr

ARTICLES OF CONFEDERATION.

TO ALL TO WHOM THESE PRESENTS SHALL COME, WE, THE UNDERSIGNED, DELEGATES OF THE STATES AFFIXED TO OUR NAMES, SEND GREETING.

WHEREAS, the delegates of the United States of America in Congress assembled did, on the fifteenth day of November, in the year of our Lord one thousand seven hundred and seventy-seven, and in the second year of the independence of America, agree to certain articles of confederation and perpetual Union between the states of New Hampshire, Massachusetts Bay, Rhode Island and Providence Plantations, Connecticut, New York, New Jersey, Pennsylvania, Delaware, Maryland, Virginia, North Carolina, South Carolina, and Georgia, in the words following, viz. :—

Articles of Confederation and perpetual Union between the States of New Hampshire, Massachusetts Bay, Rhode Island and Providence Planta-tions, Connecticut, New York, New Jersey, Pennsylvania, Delaware, Maryland, Virginia, North Carolina, South Carolina, and Georgia.

ARTICLE 1. The style of this confederacy shall be, "The United States of America."

ARTICLE 2. Each state retains its sovereignty, freedom, and independence, and every power, jurisdiction, and right, which is not by this confederation expressly delegated to the United States in Congress assembled.

ARTICLE 3. The said states hereby severally enter into a firm league of friendship with each other for their common defence, the security of their liberties, and their mutual and general welfare; binding themselves to assist each other against all force offered to, or attacks made upon them, or any of them, on account of religion, sovereignty, trade, or any other pretence whatever.

ARTICLE 4. The better to secure and perpetuate mutual friendship, and intercourse among the people of the different states in this Union, the free inhabitants of each of these states, paupers, vagabonds, and fugitives from justice, excepted, shall be entitled to all privileges and immunities of free citizens in the several states; and the people of each state shall have free ingress and regress to and from any other state, and shall enjoy therein all the privileges of trade and commerce subject to the same duties, impositions, and restrictions, as the inhabitants thereof respectively, provided that such restrictions shall not extend so far as to prevent the removal of property imported into any state to any other state, of which the owner is an inhabitant; provided also, that no imposition, duties, or restriction, shall be laid by any state on the property of the United States or either of them.

If any person guilty of or charged with treason, felony, or other high misdemeanor, in any state, shall flee from justice, and be found in any of the United States, he shall, upon demand of the governor or executive power of the state from which he fled, be delivered up and removed to the state having jurisdiction of his offence.

Full faith and credit shall be given in each of these states to the records, acts, and judicial proceedings of the courts and magistrates of every other state.

ARTICLE 5. For the more convenient management of the general interests of the United States, delegates shall be annually appointed in such manner as the legislature of each state shall direct to meet in Congress on the first Monday in November, in every year, with a power reserved to each state to recall its delegates or any of them, at any time within the year, and to send others in their stead for the remainder of the year.

No state shall be represented in Congress by less than two, nor by more than seven members; and no person shall be capable of being a delegate for more than three years in any term of six years; nor shall any person, being a delegate, be capable of holding any office under the United States, for which he, or another for his benefit, receives any salary, fees, or emoluments of any kind.

Each state shall maintain its own delegates in a meeting of the states, and while they act as members of the commitee of the states.

In determining questions in the United States in Congress assembled, each state shall have one vote.

Freedom of speech and debate in Congress shall not be impeached or questioned in any court or place out of Congress; and the members of Congress shall be protected in their persons from arrests and imprisonments, during the time of their going to and from and attendance on Congress, except for treason, felony, or breach of the peace.

ARTICLE 6. No state, without the consent of the United States in Congress assembled, shall send any embassy to, or receive any embassy from, or enter into any conference, agreement, alliance, or treaty, with any king, prince, or state; nor shall any person holding any office of profit or trust under the United States, or any of them, accept of any present, emolument, office or title of any kind whatever, from any king, prince, or foreign state; nor shall the United States in Congress assembled, or any of them, grant any title of nobility.

No two or more states shall enter into any treaty, confederation, or alliance whatever, between them, without the consent of the United States in Congress assembled, specifying accurately the purposes for which the same is to be entered into and how long it shall continue.

No state shall lay any imposts or duties, which may interfere with any stipulations in treaties entered into by the United States in Congress assembled, with any king, prince, or state, in pursuance of any treaties already proposed by Congress to the courts of France and Spain.

No vessel-of-war shall be kept up in time of peace by any state, except such number only as shall be deemed necessary by the United States in Congress assembled for the defence of such state or its trade; nor shall any body of forces be kept up by any state in time of peace, except such number only as in the judgment of the United States in Congress assembled, shall be deemed requisite to garrison the forts necessary for the defence of such state ; but every state shall always keep up a well-regulated and disciplined militia, sufficiently armed and accoutred, and shall provide and have constantly ready for use, in public stores, a due number of field-pieces and tents, and a proper quantity of arms, ammunition, and camp equipage.

No state shall engage in any war without the consent of the United States in Congress assembled, unless such state be actually invaded by enemies or shall have received certain advice of a resolution being formed by some nation of Indians to invade such state, and the danger is so imminent as not to admit of a delay till the United States in Congress assembled can be consulted ; nor shall any state grant commissions to any ships or vessels-of-war, nor letters of marque or reprisal, except it be after a declaration of war by the United States in Congress assembled, and then only against the kingdom or state, and the subjects thereof, against which war has been so declared, and under such regulations as shall be established by the United States in Congress assembled, unless such state be infested by pirates, in which case vessels-of-war may be fitted out for that occasion, and kept so long as the danger shall continue, or until the United States in Congress assembled shall determine otherwise.

ARTICLE 7. When land forces are raised by any state for the common defence, all officers of or under the rank of colonel, shall be appointed by the legislature of each state respectively, by whom such forces shall be raised, or in such manner as such state shall direct, and all vacancies shall be filled up by the state which first made the appointment.

ARTICLE 8. All charges of war, and all other expenses that shall be incurred for the common defence or general welfare, and allowed by the United States in Congress assembled, shall be defrayed out of a common treasury, which shall be supplied by the several states in proportion to the value of all land within each state granted to or surveyed for any person, as such land and the buildings and improvements thereon shall be estimared according to such mode as the United States in Congress assembled shall from time to time direct and appoint.

The taxes for paying that proportion shall be laid and levied by the authority and direction of the legislatures of the several states, within the time agreed upon by the United States in Congress assembled.

ARTICLE 9. The United States in Congress assembled shall have the sole and exclusive right and power of determining on peace and war, except in the cases mentioned in the sixth article—of sending and receiving ambassadors—entering into treaties and alliances ; provided, that no treaty of commerce shall be made whereby the legislative power of the respective states shall be restrained from imposing such imposts and duties on foreigners as their own people are subjected to, or from prohibiting the exportation or importation of any species of goods or commodities whatsoever—of establishing rules for deciding in all cases, what captures on land or water shall be legal, and in what manner prizes taken by land or naval forces in the service of the United States shall be divided or appropriated—of granting letters of marque and reprisal in times of peace—appointing courts for the trial of piracies and felonies committed on the high seas, and establishing courts for receiving and determining finally appeals in all cases of captures : provided, that no member of Congress shall be appointed a judge of any of the said courts.

The United States in Congress assembled shall also be the last resort on appeal in all disputes and differences now subsisting or that hereafter may arise between two or more states concerning boundary, jurisdiction, or any other cause whatever ; which authority shall always be exercised in the manner following : whenever the legislative or executive authority or lawful agent of any state in controversy with another shall present a petition to Congress, stating the matter in question, and praying for a hearing, notice thereof shall be given by order of Congress to the legislative or executive authority of the other state in controversy, and a day assigned for the appearance of the parties, by their lawful agents, who shall then be directed to appoint by joint consent commissioners or judges to constitute a court for hearing and determining the matter in question ; but if they can not agree, Congress shall name three persons out of each of the United States, and from the list of such persons each party shall alternately strike out one, the petitioners beginning until the number shall be reduced to thirteen ; and from that number not less than seven nor more than nine names, as Congress shall direct shall, in the presence of Congress, be drawn out by lot ; and the persons whose names shall be so drawn, or any five of them, shall be commissioners or judges, to hear and finally determine the controversy, so always as a major part of the judges, who shall hear the cause, shall agree in the determination : and if either party shall neglect to attend at the day appointed, without showing reasons which Congress shall judge sufficient, or being present shall refuse to strike, the Congress shall proceed to nominate three persons out of each state, and the secretary of Congress shall strike in behalf of such party absent or refusing ; and the judgment and sentence of the court to be appointed in the manner before prescribed, shall be final and conclusive , and if any of the parties shall refuse to submit to the authority of such court, or to appear, or defend their claim or cause, the court shall nevertheless proceed to pronounce sentence or judgment, which shall in like manner be final and decisive, the judgment or sentence and other proceedings, being in either case transmitted to Congress, and lodged among the acts of Congress for the security of the parties concerned : provided, that every commissioner, before he sits in judgment, shall take an oath, to be administered by one of the judges of the supreme or superior court of the state, where the cause shall be tried, " well and truly to hear and determine the matter in question, according to the best of his judgment, without favor, affection, or hope of reward :" provided also, that no state shall be deprived of territory for the benefit of the United States.

All controversies concerning the private right of soil, claimed under different grants of two or more states, whose jurisdiction as they may respect such lands and the states which passed such grants are adjusted, the said grants or either of them being at the same time claimed to have originated antecedent to such settlement of jurisdiction, shall, on the petition of either party to the Congress of the United States, be finally determined, as near as may be, in the same manner as is before prescribed for deciding disputes respecting territorial jurisdiction between different states.

The United States in Congress assembled shall also have the sole and exclusive right and power of regulating the alloy and value of coin struck by their own authority, or by that of the respective states—fixing the standard of weights and measures throughout the United States—regulating the trade and managing all affairs with the Indians not members of any of the states ; provided that the legislative right of any state within its own limits be not infringed or violated—establishing and regulating postoffices from one state to another throughout all the United States, and exacting such postage on the papers passing through the same, as may be requisite to defray the expenses of the said office—appointing all officers of the land forces in the service of the United States excepting regimental officers—appointing all the officers of the naval forces, and commissioning all officers whatever in the service of the United States—making rules for the government and regulation of the said land and naval forces, and directing their operations.

The United States in Congress assembled shall have authority to appoint a committee to sit in the recess of Congress, to be denominated " a committee of the states," and to consist of one delegate from each state ; and to appoint such other committees and civil officers as may be necessary for managing the general affairs of the United States, under their direction—to appoint one of their number to preside, provided that no person be allowed to serve in the office of president more than one year in any term of three years—to ascertain the necessary sums of money to be raised for the service of the United States, and to appropriate and apply the same for defraying the public expenses—to borrow money or emit bills on the credit of the United States, transmitting every half year to the respective states an account of the sums of money so borrowed or emitted —to build and equip a navy—to agree upon the number of land forces, and to make requisitions from each state for its quota, in proportion to the number of white inhabitants in such state ; which requisition shall be binding, and thereupon the legislature of each state shall appoint the regimental officers, raise the men, and clothe, arm, and equip them, in a soldier-like manner, at the expense of the United States ; and the officers and men so clothed, armed, and equipped, shall march to the place appointed, and within the time agreed on by the United States in Congress assembled : but if the United States in Congress assembled, shall, on consideration of circumstances, judge proper that any state should not raise men or should raise a smaller number than its quota, and that any other state should raise a greater number of men than the quota thereof, such extra number shall be raised, officered, clothed, armed, and equipped, in the same manner as the quota of such state, unless the legislature of such state shall judge that such extra number can not safely be spared out of the same ; in which case they shall raise, officer, clothe, arm, and equip, as many of such extra number as they judge can be safely spared. And the officers and men so clothed, armed, and equipped, shall march to the place appointed, and within the time agreed on by the United States in Congress assembled.

The United States in Congress assembled shall never engage in a war, nor grant letters of marque and reprisal in time of peace, nor enter into any treaties or alliances, nor coin money, nor regulate the value thereof, nor ascertain the sums and expenses necessary for the defence and welfare of the United States or any of them, nor emit bills, nor borrow money on the credit of the United States, nor appropriate money, nor agree upon the number of vessels-of-war to be built or purchased, or the number of land or sea forces to be raised, nor appoint a commander-in-chief of the army or navy, unless nine states assent to the same ; nor shall a question on any other point, except for adjourning from day to day, be determined, unless by the votes of a majority of the United States in Congress assembled.

The Congress of the United States shall have power to adjourn to any time within the year, and to any place within the United States, so that no period of adjournment be for a longer duration than the space of six months ; and shall publish the journal of their proceedings monthly, except such parts thereof relating to treaties, alliances, or military operations, as in their judgment require secresy ; and the yeas and nays of the delegates of each state on any question shall be entered on the journal, when it is desired by any delegate ; and the delegates of a state, or any of them, at his or their request, shall be furnished with a transcript of the said journal, except such parts as are above excepted, to lay before the legislatures of the several states.

ARTICLE 10. The committee of the states, or any nine of them, shall be authorized to execute, in the recess of Congress, such of the powers of Congress as the United States in Congress assembled, by the consent of nine states, shall from time to time, think expedient to vest them with ; provided that no power be delegated to the said committee, for the exercise of which, by the articles of confederation, the voice of nine states in the Congress of the United States assembled is requisite.

ARTICLE 11. Canada, acceding to this confederation, and joining in the measures of the United States, shall be admitted into, and entitled to, all the advantages of this Union ; but no other colony shall be admitted into the same unless such admission be agreed to by nine states.

ARTICLE 12. All bills of credit emitted, moneys borrowed, and debts contracted, by or under the authority of Congress, before the assembling of the United States, in pursuance of the present confederation, shall be deemed and considered as a charge against the United States, for payment and satisfaction whereof the said United States and the public faith are hereby solemnly pledged.

ARTICLE 13. Every state shall abide by the decision of the United States in Congress assembled, on all questions which, by this confederation, are submitted to them. And the articles of this confederation shall be inviolably observed by every state, and the Union shall be perpetual ; nor shall any alteration at any time hereafter be made in any of them, unless such alteration be agreed to in a Congress of the United States, and be afterward confirmed by the legislature of every state.

And whereas it has pleased the great Governor of the world to incline the hearts of the legislatures we respectively represent in Congress, to approve of and to authorize us to ratify the said articles of confederation and perpetual Union : *know ye*, that we, the undersigned delegates, by virtue of the power and authority to us given for that purpose, do, by these presents, in the name and in behalf of our respective constituents, fully and entirely ratify and confirm each and every of the said articles of confederation and perpetual Union, and all and singular the matters and things therein contained ; and we do further solemnly plight and engage the faith of our respective constituents, that they shall abide by the determinations of the United States in Congress assembled, on all questions which, by the said confederation, are submitted to them ; and that the articles thereof shall be inviolably observed by the states we respectively represent ; and that the Union be perpetual.

In witness whereof, we have hereunto set our hands, in Congress
Done at Philadelphia, in the state of Pennsylvania, the ninth day of July,
in the year of our Lord one thousand seven hundred and seventy-eight,
and in the third year of the independence of America.

NEW HAMPSHIRE.
JOSIAH BARTLETT,
JOHN WENTWORTH, JR.

MASSACHUSETTS BAY.
JOHN HANCOCK,
SAMUEL ADAMS,
ELBRIDGE GERRY,
FRANCIS DANA,
JAMES LOVELL,
SAMUEL HOLTEN.

RHODE ISLAND.
WILLIAM ELLERY,
HENRY MARCHANT,
JOHN COLLINS.

CONNECTICUT.
ROGER SHERMAN,
SAMUEL HUNTINGTON,
OLIVER WOLCOTT,
TITUS HOSMER,
ANDREW ADAMS.

NEW YORK.
JAMES DUANE,
FRANCIS LEWIS,
WILLIAM DUER,
GOUVERNEUR MORRIS.

NEW JERSEY.
JOHN WITHERSPOON,
NATH. SCUDDER.

PENNSYLVANIA.
ROBERT MORRIS,
DANIEL ROBERDEAU,
JONATHAN BAYARD SMITH,
WILLIAM CLINGAN,
JOSEPH REED.

DELAWARE.
THOMAS M'KEAN,
JOHN DICKINSON,
NICHOLAS VAN DYKE.

MARYLAND.
JOHN HANSON,
DANIEL CARROLL.

VIRGINIA.
RICHARD HENRY LEE,
JOHN BANISTER,
THOMAS ADAMS,
JOHN HARVIE,
FRANCIS LIGHTFOOT LEE.

NORTH CAROLINA.
JOHN PENN,
CONSTABLE HARNETT,
JOHN WILLIAMS.

SOUTH CAROLINA.
HENRY LAURENS,
WILLIAM HENRY DRAYTON,
JOHN MATTHEWS,
RICHARD HUTSON,
THOMAS HEYWARD, JR.

GEORGIA.
JOHN WALTON,
EDWARD TELFAIR,
EDWARD LANGWORTHY.

CONSTITUTION OF THE UNITED STATES,

COPIED FROM, AND COMPARED WITH, THE ROLL IN THE DEPARTMENT
OF STATE.

WE the people of the United States, in order to form a more perfect union, establish justice, insure domestic tranquillity, provide for the common defence, promote the general welfare, and secure the blessings of liberty to ourselves and our posterity, do ordain and establish this constitution for the United States of America.

ARTICLE I.

SECTION 1. All legislative powers herein granted shall be vested in a Congress of the United States, which shall consist of a senate and house of representatives.

SECTION 2. The house of representatives shall be composed of members chosen every second year by the people of the several states, and the electors in each state shall have the qualifications requisite for electors of the most numerous branch of the state legislature.

No person shall be a representative who shall not have attained to the age of twenty-five years, and been seven years a citizen of the United States, and who shall not, when elected, be an inhabitant of that state in which he shall be chosen.

Representatives and direct taxes shall be apportioned among the several states which may be included within this Union, according to their respective numbers,* which shall be determined by adding to the whole number of free persons, including those bound to service for a term of years, and excluding Indians not taxed, three fifths of all other persons. The actual enumeration shall be made within three years after the first meeting of the Congress of the United States, and within every subsequent term of ten years, in such manner as they shall by law direct. The number of representatives shall not exceed one for every thirty thousand,† but each state shall have at least one representative ; and until such enumeration shall be made, the state of New Hampshire shall be entitled to choose three, Massachusetts eight, Rhode Island and Providence Plantations one, Connecticut five, New York six, New Jersey four, Pennsylvania eight, Delaware one, Maryland six, Virginia ten, North Carolina five, South Carolina five, and Georgia three.

* The constitutional provision, that direct taxes shall be apportioned among the several states according to their respective numbers, to be ascertained by a census, was not intended to restrict the power of imposing direct taxes to states only.—*Loughborough* vs. *Blake*, 5 *Wheaton*, 319.

† See laws United States, vol. ii., chap. 124 ; iii., 261 ; iv., 332. Acts of 17th Congress, 1st session, chap. x. ; and of the 22d and 27th Congress.

When vacancies happen in the representation from any state, the executive authority thereof shall issue writs of election to fill such vacancies.

The house of representatives shall choose their speaker and other officers ; and shall have the sole power of impeachment.

SECTION 3. The senate of the United States shall be composed of two senators from each state, chosen by the legislature thereof, for six years ; and each senator shall have one vote.*

Immediately after they shall be assembled in consequence of the first election, they shall be divided as equally as may be into three classes. The seats of the senators of the first class shall be vacated at the expiration of the second year, of the second class at the expiration of the fourth year, and of the third class at the expiration of the sixth year, so that one third may be chosen every second year ; and if vacancies happen by resignation, or otherwise, during the recess of the legislature of any state, the executive thereof may make temporary appointments until the next meeting of the legislature, which shall then fill such vacancies.

No person shall be a senator who shall not have attained to the age of thirty years, and been nine years a citizen of the United States, and who shall not, when elected, be an inhabitant of that state for which he shall be chosen.

The vice-president of the United States shall be president of the senate, but shall have no vote, unless they be equally divided.

The senate shall choose their other officers, and also a president pro-tempore, in the absence of the vice-president, or when he shall exercise the office of president of the United States.

The senate shall have the sole power to try all impeachments : When sitting for that purpose, they shall be on oath or affirmation.   When the president of the United States is tried, the chief justice shall preside : And no person shall be convicted without the concurrence of two thirds of the members present.

Judgment in cases of impeachment shall not extend further than to removal from office, and disqualification to hold and enjoy any office of honor, trust or profit under the United States : but the party convicted shall nevertheless be liable and subject to indictment, trial, judgment and punishment, according to law.

SECTION 4. The times, places and manner of holding elections for senators and representatives, shall be prescribed in each state by the legislature thereof ; but the Congress may at any time by law make or alter such regulations, except as to the places of choosing senators.

The Congress shall assemble at least once in every year, and such meeting shall be on the first Monday in December, unless they shall by law appoint a different day.

SECTION 5. Each house shall be the judge of the elections, returns and qualifications of its own members, and a majority of each shall constitute a quorum to do business , but a smaller number may adjourn from day to day, and may be authorized to compel the attendance of absent members, in such manner, and under such penalties as each house may provide.

Each house may determine the rules of its proceedings,† punish its

---

* See art. v., clause 1.

† To an action of trespass against the sergeant-at-arms of the house of representatives of the United States for assault and battery and false imprisonment, it is a legal justification and bar to plead that a Congress was held and sitting during the period of the trespasses complained, and that the house of representatives had resolved that the plaintiff had been guilty of a breach of the privileges of the house, and of a high contempt of the dignity

members for disorderly behavior, and, with the concurrence of two thirds, expel a member.

Each house shall keep a journal of its proceedings, and from time to time publish the same, excepting such parts as may in their judgment require secresy; and the yeas and nays of the members of either house on any question shall, at the desire of one fifth of those present, be entered on the journal.

Neither house, during the session of Congress, shall, without the consent of the other, adjourn for more than three days, nor to any other place than that in which the two houses shall be sitting.

SECTION 6. The senators and representatives shall receive a compensation for their services, to be ascertained by law, and paid out of the treasury of the United States. They shall in all cases, except treason, felony and breach of the peace, be privileged from arrest during their attendance at the session of their respective houses, and in going to and returning from the same; and for any speech or debate in either house, they shall not be questioned in any other place.

No senator or representative shall, during the time for which he was elected, be appointed to any civil office under the authority of the United States, which shall have been created, or the emoluments whereof shall have been increased during such time; and no person holding any office under the United States, shall be a member of either house during his continuance in office.

SECTION 7. All bills for raising revenue shall originate in the house of representatives; but the senate may propose or concur with amendments as on other bills.

Every bill which shall have passed the house of representatives and the senate, shall, before it become a law, be presented to the president of the United States; if he approve he shall sign it, but if not he shall return it, with his objections to that house in which it shall have originated, who shall enter the objections at large on their journal, and proceed to reconsider it. If after such reconsideration two thirds of that house shall agree to pass the bill, it shall be sent, together with the objections, to the other house, by which it shall likewise be reconsidered, and if approved by two thirds of that house, it shall become a law. But in all such cases the votes of both houses shall be determined by yeas and nays, and the names of the persons voting for and against the bill shall be entered on the journal of each house respectively. If any bill shall not be returned by the president within ten days (Sunday excepted) after it shall have been presented to him, the same shall be a law, in like manner as if he had signed it, unless the Congress by their adjournment prevent its return, in which case it shall not be a law.

Every order, resolution, or vote to which the concurrence of the senate

and authority of the same; and had ordered that the speaker should issue his warrant to the sergeant-at-arms, commanding him to take the plaintiff into custody wherever to be found, and to have him before the said house to answer to the said charge; and that the speaker did accordingly issue such a warrant, reciting the said resolution and order, and commanding the sergeant-at-arms to take the plaintiff into custody, &c., and deliver the said warrant to the defendant: by virtue of which warrant the defendant arrested the plaintiff, and conveyed him to the bar of the house, where he was heard in his defence touching the matter of said charge, and the examination being adjourned from day to day, and the house having ordered the plaintiff to be detained in custody, he was accordingly detained by the defendant until he was finally adjudged to be guilty and convicted of the charge aforesaid, and ordered to be forthwith brought to the bar and reprimanded by the speaker, and then discharged from custody, and after being thus reprimanded, was actually discharged from the arrest and custody aforesaid.—*Anderson vs. Dunn,* 6 *Wheaton,* 204.

and house of representatives may be necessary (except on a question of adjournment) shall be presented to the president of the United States; and before the same shall take effect, shall be approved by him, or being disapproved by him, shall be repassed by two thirds of the senate and house of representatives, according to the rules and limitations prescribed in the case of a bill.

SECTION 8. The Congress shall have power to lay and collect taxes,[*] duties, imposts and excises, to pay the debts and provide for the common defence and general welfare of the United States; but all duties, imposts and excises shall be uniform throughout the United States;

To borrow money on the credit of the United States;

To regulate commerce with foreign nations, and among the several states, and with the Indian tribes;

To establish an uniform rule of naturalization,[†] and uniform laws on the subject of bankruptcies[‡] throughout the United States;

To coin money, regulate the value thereof, and of foreign coin, and fix the standard of weights and measures;

To provide for the punishment of counterfeiting the securities and current coin of the United States;

To establish postoffices and postroads;

To promote the progress of science and useful arts, by securing for limited times to authors and inventors the exclusive right to their respective writings and discoveries;

To constitute tribunals inferior to the supreme court;

To define and punish piracies and felonies committed on the high seas, and offences against the law of nations;[||]

To declare war, grant letters of marque and reprisal, and make rules concerning captures on land and water;

To raise and support armies, but no appropriation of money to that use shall be for a longer term than two years;

To provide and maintain a navy;

To make rules for the government and regulation of the land and naval forces;

To provide for calling forth the militia to execute the laws of the Union, suppress insurrections and repel invasions;

---

[*] The power of Congress to *lay and collect taxes, duties,* &c., extends to the District of Columbia, and to the territories of the United States, as well as to the states.—*Loughborough* vs. *Blake,* 5 *Wheaton,* 318. But Congress are not bound to extend a direct tax to the district and territories.—*Id.,* 318.

[†] Under the constitution of the United States, the power of naturalization is exclusively in Congress.—*Chirac* vs. *Chirac,* 2 *Wheaton,* 259.
See laws United States, vol. ii., chap. 30; ii., 261; iii., 71; iii., 288; iii., 400; iv., 564; vi., 32.

[‡] Since the adoption of the constitution of the United States, a state has authority to pass a bankrupt law, provided such law does not impair the obligation of contracts within the meaning of the constitution (art. i., sect. 10), and provided there be no act of Congress in force to establish a uniform system of bankruptcy conflicting with such law.—*Sturgess* vs. *Crowninshield,* 4 *Wheaton,* 122, 192.
See laws United States, vol. ii., chap. 368, sect. 2: iii., 66; iii., 158.

[||] The act of the 3d March, 1819, chap. 76, sect. 5, referring to the law of nations for a definition of the crime of piracy, is a constitutional exercise of the power of Congress to define and punish that crime.—*United States* vs. *Smith,* 5 *Wheaton,* 153, 157.
Congress have power to provide for the punishment of offences committed by persons on board a ship-of-war of the United States, wherever that ship may lie. But Congress have not exercised that power in the case of a ship lying in the waters of the United States, the words within fort, arsenal, dockyard, magazine, or in *any other place or district of country under the sole and exclusive jurisdiction of the United States,* in the third section of the act of 1790, chap. 9, not extending to a ship-of-war, but only to objects in their nature, fixed and territorial.—*United States* vs. *Bevans,* 3 *Wheaton,* 890.

To provide for organizing, arming, and disciplining, the militia, and for governing such part of them as may be employed in the service of the United States, reserving to the states respectively, the appointment of the officers, and the authority of training the militia according to the discipline prescribed by Congress ;*

To exercise exclusive legislation in all cases whatsoever, over such district (not exceeding ten miles square) as may, by cession of particular states, and the acceptance of Congress, become the seat of the government of the United States,† and to exercise like authority over all places purchased by the consent of the legislature of the state in which the same shall be, for the erection of forts, magazines, arsenals, dockyards, and other needful buildings ;—And

To make all laws which shall be necessary and proper for carrying into execution the foregoing powers, and all other powers vested by this constitution in the government of the United States, or in any department or officer thereof.‡

SECTION 9. The migration or importation of such persons as any of the states now existing shall think proper to admit, shall not be prohibited by

---

* Vide amendments, art. ii.

† Congress has authority to impose a direct tax on the District of Columbia, in proportion to the census directed to be taken by the constitution.—*Loughborough* vs. *Blake*, 5 *Wheaton*, 317.

But Congress are not bound to extend a direct tax to the district and territories.—*Id.*, 322.

The power of Congress to exercise exclusive jurisdiction in all cases whatsoever within the District of Columbia, includes the power of taxing it.—*Id.*, 324.

‡ Whenever the terms in which a power is granted by the constitution to Congress, or whenever the nature of the power itself requires that it should be exercised exclusively by Congress, the subject is as completely taken away from the state legislatures as if they had been expressly forbidden to act on it.—*Sturgess* vs. *Crowninshield*, 4 *Wheaton*, 193.

Congress has power to incorporate a bank.—*McCulloch* vs. *State of Maryland*, 4 *Wheaton*, 316.

The power of establishing a corporation is not a distinct sovereign power or end of government, but only the means of carrying into effect other powers which are sovereign. Whenever it becomes an appropriate means of exercising any of the powers given by the constitution to the government of the Union, it may be exercised by that government.—*Id.*, 411, 421.

If a certain means to carry into effect any of the powers expressly given by the constitution to the government of the Union, be an appropriate measure, not prohibited by the constitution, the degree of its necessity is a question of legislative discretion, not of judicial cognizance.—*Id.*, 421.

The act of the 19th April, 1816, chap. 44, to incorporate the subscribers to the bank of the United States, is a law made in pursuance of the constitution.—*Id.*, 424.

The bank of the United States has constitutionally a right to establish its branches or offices of discount and deposite within any state.—*Id.*, 424.

There is nothing in the constitution of the United States similar to the articles of confederation, which excludes incidental or implied powers.—*Id.*, 403.

If the *end* be legitimate, and within the scope of the constitution, all the *means* which are appropriate, which are plainly adapted to that end, and which are not prohibited, may constitutionally be employed to carry it into effect.—*Id.*, 421.

The powers granted to Congress are not exclusive of similar powers existing in the states, unless where the constitution has expressly in terms given an exclusive power to Congress, or the exercise of a like power is prohibited to the states, or there is a direct repugnancy or incompatibility in the exercise of it by the states.—*Houston* vs. *Moore*, 5 *Wheaton*, 49.

The example of the first class is to be found in the exclusive legislation delegated to Congress over places purchased by the consent of the legislature of the state in which the same shall be for forts, arsenals, dockyards, &c. Of the second class, the prohibition of a state to coin money or emit bills of credit. Of the third class, the power to establish a uniform rule of naturalization, and the delegation of admiralty and maritime jurisdiction.—*Id.*, 49.

In all other classes of cases the states retain concurrent authority with Congress.—*Id.*, 48.

But in cases of concurrent authority, where the laws of the states and of the Union are in direct and manifest collision on the same subject, those of the Union being the supreme law of the land, are of paramount authority, and the state so far, and so far only as such incompatibility exists, must necessarily yield.—*Id.*, 49.

The state within which a branch of the United States bank may be established, can not,

20

the Congress prior to the year one thousand eight hundred and eight, but
a tax or duty may be imposed on such importation, not exceeding ten dollars for each person.

The privilege of the writ of habeas corpus shall not be suspended,
unless when in cases of rebellion or invasion the public safety may require it.

No bill of attainder or ex post facto law shall be passed.

No capitation, or other direct, tax shall be laid, unless in proportion to
the census or enumeration hereinbefore directed to be taken.

No tax or duty shall be laid on articles exported from any state.

No preference shall be given by any regulation of commerce or revenue
to the ports of one state over those of another : nor shall vessels bound to,
or from, one state, be obliged to enter, clear, or pay duties in another.

No money shall be drawn from the treasury, but in consequence of appropriations made by law ; and a regular statement and account of the
receipts and expenditures of all public money shall be published from time
to time.

No title of nobility shall be granted by the United States : And no person holding any office of profit or trust under them, shall, without the consent of the Congress, accept of any present, emolument, office, or title, of
any kind whatever, from any king, prince, or foreign state.

SECTION 10. No state shall enter into any treaty, alliance, or confederation ; grant letters of marque and reprisal ; coin money ; emit bills of
credit ; make anything but gold and silver coin a tender in payment of
debts ; pass any bill of attainder, ex post facto law, or law impairing the
obligation of contracts,* or grant any title of nobility.

without violating the constitution, tax that branch.—*McCulloch* vs. *State of Maryland*, 4
Wheaton, 425.

The state governments have no right to tax any of the constitutional means employed by
the government of the Union to execute its constitutional powers.—*Id.*, 427.

The states have no power by taxation, or otherwise, to retard, impede, burden, or in any
manner control, the operation of the constitutional laws enacted by Congress, to carry into
effect the powers vested in the national government.—*Id.*, 436.

This principle does not extend to a tax paid by the real property of the bank of the United States, in common with the other real property in a particular state, nor to a tax imposed on the proprietary which the citizens of that state may hold in common with the
other property of the same description throughout the state.—*Id.*. 436.

* Where a law is in its nature a *contract*, where absolute rights have vested under that
contract, a repeal of the law can not divest those rights.—*Fletcher* vs. *Peck*, 6 *Cranch*, 88.

A party to a contract can not pronounce its own deed invalid, although that party be a
sovereign state.—*Id.*, 88.

A *grant* is a *contract executed*.—*Id.*, 89.

A law annulling conveyance is unconstitutional, because it is a law impairing the obligation of contracts within the meaning of the constitution of the United States.—*Id.*

The court will not declare a law to be unconstitutional, unless the opposition between the
constitution and the law be clear and plain.—*Id.*, 87.

An act of the legislature of a state, declaring that certain lands which should be purchased for the Indians should not thereafter be subject to any tax, constituted a contract
which could not, after the adoption of the constitution of the United States, be rescinded
by a subsequent legislative act ; such rescinding act being void under the constitution of the
United States.—*State of New Jersey* vs. *Wilson*, 7 *Cranch*, 164.

The present constitution of the United States did not commence its operation until the
first Wednesday in March, 1789, and the provision in the constitution, that " no state shall
make any law impairing the obligation of contracts," does not extend to a state law enacted
before that day, and operating upon rights of property vesting before that time.—*Owings* vs.
Speed, 5 *Wheaton*, 420, 421.

An act of a state legislature, which discharges a debtor from all liability for debts contracted previous to his discharge, on his surrendering his property for the benefit of his
creditors, is a law impairing " the obligations of contracts," within the meaning of the constitution of the United States, so far as it attempts to discharge the contract ; and it makes
no difference in such a case, that the suit was brought in a state court of the state of which
both the parties were citizens where the contract was made, and the discharge obtained,

No state shall, without the consent of the Congress, lay any imposts or duties on imports or exports, except what may be absolutely necessary for executing its inspection laws : and the net produce of all duties and imposts, laid by any state on imports or exports, shall be for the use of the treasury of the United States ; and all such laws shall be subject to the revision and control of the Congress.

No state shall, without the consent of Congress, lay any duty of tonnage, keep troops, or ships-of-war in time of peace, enter into any agreement or compact with another state, or with a foreign power, or engage in war, unless actually invaded, or in such imminent danger as will not admit of delay.

ARTICLE II.

SECTION 1. The executive power shall be vested in a president of the United States of America. He shall hold his office during the term of four years,* and, together with the vice-president, chosen for the same term, be elected, as follows :

Each state shall appoint, in such manner as the legislature thereof may direct,† a number of electors, equal to the whole number of senators and representatives to which the state may be entitled in the Congress : but no senator or representative, or person holding an office of trust or profit under the United States, shall be appointed an elector.

[‡The electors shall meet in their respective states, and vote by ballot for two persons, of whom one at least shall not be an inhabitant of the same state with themselves. And they shall make a list of all the persons voted for, and of the number of votes for each ; which list they shall sign and certify, and transmit sealed to the seat of the government of the United States, directed to the president of the senate. The president of the senate shall, in the presence of the senate and house of representatives, open all the certificates, and the votes shall then be counted. The person having the greatest number of votes shall be the president, if such number be a majority of the whole number of electors appointed ; and if there be more than one who have such majority, and have an equal number of votes, then the house of representatives shall immediately choose by ballot one of them for president ; and if no person have a majority, then from the five highest on the list the said house shall in like manner choose the president. But in choosing the president, the votes shall be taken by states, the representation from each state having one vote ; a quorum for this purpose shall consist of a member or members from two thirds of the states, and a majority of

and where they continued to reside until the suit was brought.—*Farmers and Mechanics' Bank* vs. *Smith*, 6 *Wheaton*, 131.

The act of New York, passed on the 3d of April, 1811 (which not only liberates the person of the debtor, but discharges him from all liability for any debt contracted previous to his discharge, on his surrendering his property in the manner it prescribes), so far as it attempts to discharge the contract, is a law impairing the obligation of contracts within the meaning of the constitution of the United States, and is not a good plea in bar of an action brought upon such contract.—*Sturgess* vs. *Crowninshield*, 4 *Wheaton*, 122, 197.

Statutes of limitation and usury laws, unless retroactive in their effect, do not impair the obligation of contracts, and are constitutional.—*Id.*, 206.

A state bankrupt or insolvent law (which not only liberates the person of the debtor, but discharges him from all liability for the debt), so far as it attempts to discharge the contract, is repugnant to the constitution of the United States, and it makes no difference in the application of this principle, whether the law was passed *before* or *after* the debt was contracted.—*McMillan* vs. *McNeill*, 4 *Wheaton*, 209.

The charter granted by the British crown to the trustees of Dartmouth college, in New Hampshire, in the year 1769, is a contract within the meaning of that clause of the constitution of the United States (art. i., sect. 10) which declares, that no state shall make any law impairing the obligations of contracts. The charter was not dissolved by the revolution.—*College* vs. *Woodard*, 4 *Wheaton*, 518.

An act of the state legislature of New Hampshire, altering the charter of Dartmouth college in a material respect, without the consent of the corporation, is an act impairing the obligation of the charter, and is unconstitutional and void.—*Id.*, 518.

* See laws United States, vol. ii., chap. 109, sect. 12.
† See laws United States, vol. ii., chap. 109
‡ Vide amendments, art. xii.

all the states shall be necessary to a choice. In every case, after the choice of the president, the person having the greatest number of votes of the electors shall be the vice-president. But if there should remain two or more who have equal votes, the senate shall choose from them by ballot the vice-president.*]

The Congress may determine the time of choosing the electors,† and the day on which they shall give their votes; which day shall be the same throughout the United States.‡

No person except a natural born citizen, or a citizen of the United States, at the time of the adoption of this constitution, shall be eligible to the office of president; neither shall any person be eligible to that office who shall not have attained to the age of thirty-five years, and been fourteen years a resident within the United States.

In case of the removal of the president from office, or of his death, resignation,§ or inability to discharge the powers and duties of the said office, the same shall devolve on the vice-president, and the Congress may by law provide for the case of removal, death, resignation or inability, both of the president and vice-president, declaring what officer shall then act as president, and such officer shall act accordingly, until the disability be removed, or a president shall be elected.‖

The president shall, at stated times, receive for his services, a compensation, which shall neither be increased nor diminished during the period for which he shall have been elected, and he shall not receive within that period any other emolument from the United States, or any of them.

Before he enter on the execution of his office, he shall take the following oath or affirmation:—" I do solemnly swear (or affirm) that I will faithfully execute the office of president of the United States, and will to the best of my ability, preserve, protect and defend the constitution of the United States."

SECTION 2. The president shall be commander-in-chief of the army and navy of the United States, and of the militia of the several states, when called into the actual service of the United States;¶ he may require the opinion, in writing, of the principal officer in each of the executive departments, upon any subject relating to the duties of their respective offices, and he shall have power to grant reprieves and pardons for offences against the United States, except in cases of impeachment.

He shall have power, by and with the advice and consent of the senate, to make treaties, provided two thirds of the senators present concur; and he shall nominate, and by and with the advice and consent of the senate, shall appoint ambassadors, other public ministers and consuls, judges of the supreme court, and all other officers of the United States, whose appointments are not herein otherwise provided for, and which shall be es-

---

* This clause is annulled. See amendments, art. xii.
† See laws United States, vol. ii., chap. 104, sect. 1.
‡ See laws United States, vol. ii., chap. 109, sect. 2.
§ See laws United States, vol. ii., chap. 104, sect. 11.
‖ See laws United States, vol. ii., chap. 109, sect. 9; and vol. iii., chap. 403.
¶ The act of the state of Pennsylvania, of the 28th March, 1814 (providing, sect. 21, that the officers and privates of the militia of that state neglecting or refusing to serve when called into actual service, in pursuance of any order or requisition of the president of the United States, shall be liable to the penalties defined in the act of Congress of 28th February, 1795, chap. 277, or to any penalty which may have been prescribed since the date of that act, or which may hereafter be prescribed by any law of the United States, and also providing for the trial of such delinquents by a state court-martial, and that a list of the delinquents fined by such court should be furnished to the marshal of the United States, &c.; and also to the comptroller of the treasury of the United States, in order that the further proceedings directed to be had thereon by the laws of the United States might be completed), is not repugnant to the constitution and laws of the United States.—*Houston* vs. *Moore,* 5 *Wheaton,* 1, 12.

tablished by law : but the Congress may by law vest the appointment of such inferior officers, as they think proper, in the president alone, in the courts of law, or in the heads of departments.

The president shall have power to fill up all vacancies that may happen during the recess of the senate, by granting commissions which shall expire at the end of their next session.

SECTION 3. He shall from time to time give to the Congress information of the state of the Union, and recommend to their consideration such measures as he shall judge necessary and expedient ; he may, on extraordinary occasions, convene both houses, or either of them, and in case of disagreement between them, with respect to the time of adjournment, he may adjourn them to such time as he shall think proper ; he shall receive ambassadors and other public ministers ; he shall take care that the laws be faithfully executed, and shall commission all the officers of the United States.

SECTION 4. The president, vice-president and all civil officers of the United States, shall be removed from office on impeachment for, and conviction of, treason, bribery, or other high crimes and misdemeanors.

ARTICLE III.

SECTION 1. The judicial power of the United States, shall be vested in one supreme court, and in such inferior courts as the Congress may from time to time ordain and establish.* The judges, both of the supreme and inferior courts, shall hold their offices during good behavior, and shall, at stated times, receive for their services, a compensation, which shall not be diminished during their continuance in office.†

SECTION 2. The judicial power shall extend to all cases, in law and equity, arising under this constitution, the laws of the United States, and treaties made, or which shall be made, under their authority ;—to all cases affecting ambassadors, other public ministers and consuls ;—to all cases of admiralty and maritime jurisdiction ;—to controversies to which the United States shall be a party ;—to controversies between two or more states ;—between a state and citizens of another state ;—between citizens of different states,‡—between citizens of the same state claiming lands under grants of different states, and between a state, or the citizens thereof, and foreign states, citizens or subjects.§

In all cases affecting ambassadors, other public ministers and consuls, and those in which a state shall be party, the supreme court shall have original jurisdiction. In all the other cases before mentioned, the supreme court shall have appellate jurisdiction, both as to law and fact, with such exceptions, and under such regulations as the Congress shall make.‖

* Congress may constitutionally impose upon the judges of the supreme court of the United States the burden of holding circuit courts.—*Stuart* vs. *Laird*, 1 *Cranch*, 299.

† See laws of the United States, vol. ii., chap. 20.

‡ A citizen of the District of Columbia is not a citizen of a state within the meaning of the constitution of the United States.—*Hepburn et al* vs. *Ellzey*, 2 *Cranch*, 445.

§ The supreme court of the United States has not power to issue a *mandamus* to a *secretary of state* of the United States, it being an exercise of original jurisdiction not warranted by the constitution, notwithstanding the act of Congress.—*Marbury* vs. *Madison*, 1 *Cranch*, 137.

See a restriction of this provision.—Amendments, art. xi.

‖ The appellate jurisdiction of the supreme court of the United States extends to a final judgment or decree in any suit in the highest court of law, or equity of a state, where is drawn in question the validity of a treaty, &c.—*Martin* vs. *Hunter's lessee*, 1 *Wheaton*, 304. Such judgment, &c., may be re-examined by writ of error, in the same manner as if rendered in a circuit court.—*Id.*

If the cause has been once remanded before, and the state court decline or refuse to carry

The trial of all crimes, except in cases of impeachment, shall be by jury ; and such trial shall be held in the state where the said crimes shall have been committed ; but when not committed within any state, the trial

into effect the mandate of the supreme court thereon, this court will proceed to a final decision of the same, and award execution thereon.

Quere.—Whether this court has authority to issue a mandamus to the state court to enforce a former judgment ?—*Id.*, 362.

If the validity or construction of a treaty of the United States is drawn in question, and the decision is against its validity, or the title specially set up by either party under the treaty, this court has jurisdiction to ascertain that title, and determine its legal validity, and is not confined to the abstract construction of the treaty itself.—*Id.*, 362.

Quere.—Whether the courts of the United States have jurisdiction of offences at common law against the United States ?—*United States* vs. *Coolidge*, 1 *Wheaton*, 415.

The courts of the United States have exclusive jurisdiction of all seizures made on land or water for a breach of the laws of the United States, and any intervention of a state authority, which by taking the thing seized out of the hands of the United States' officer, might obstruct the exercise of this jurisdiction, is illegal.—*Slocum* vs. *Mayberry et al*, 2 *Wheaton*, 1, 9.

In such a case the court of the United States have cognizance of the seizure, may enforce a redelivery of the thing by attachment or other summary process.—*Id.*, 9.

The question under such a seizure, whether a forfeiture has been actually incurred, belongs exclusively to the courts of the United States, and it depends upon the final decree of such courts, whether the seizure is to be deemed rightful or tortuous.—*Id.*, 9, 10.

If the seizing officer refuse to institute proceedings to ascertain the forfeiture, the district court may, on application of the aggrieved party, compel the officer to proceed to adjudication, or to abandon the seizure.—*Id.*, 10.

The jurisdiction of the circuit court of the United States extends to a case between citizens of Kentucky, claiming lands exceeding the value of five hundred dollars, under different grants, the one issued by the state of Kentucky, and the other by the state of Virginia, upon warrants issued by Virginia, and locations founded thereon, prior to the separation of Kentucky from Virginia. It is the grant which passes the *legal* title to the land, and if the controversy is founded upon the conflicting grants of different states, the judicial power of the courts of the United States extends to the case, whatever may have been the equitable title of the parties prior to the grant.—*Colson et al* vs. *Lewis*, 2 *Wheaton*, 377.

Under the judiciary of 1789, chap. 20. sect. 25, giving appellate jurisdiction to the supreme court of the United States, from the final judgment or decree of the highest court of law or equity of a state, in certain cases the writ of error may be directed to any court in which the record and judgment on which it is to act may be found ; and if the record has been remitted by the highest court, to another court of the state, it may be brought by the writ of error from that court.—*Gelston* vs. *Hoyt*, 3 *Wheaton*, 246, 303.

The remedies in the courts of the United States at common law and in equity are to be, not according to the practice of state courts, but according to the principles of common law and equity as defined in England. This doctrine reconciled with the decisions of the courts of Tennessee, permitting an equitable title to be asserted in an action at law.—*Robinson* vs. *Campbell*, 3 *Wheaton*, 221.

Remedies in respect to real property, are to be pursued according to the *lex loci rei sitae.*—*Id.*, 219.

The courts of the United States have *exclusive* cognizance of questions of forfeiture upon all seizures made under the laws of the United States, and it is not competent for a state court to entertain or decide such question of forfeiture. If a sentence of condemnation be definitively pronounced by the proper court of the United States, it is conclusive that a forfeiture is incurred ; if a sentence of acquittal, it is equally conclusive against the forfeiture, and in either case the question can not be again litigated in any common law for ever.—*Gelston* vs. *Hoyt*, 3 *Wheaton*, 246, 311.

Where a seizure is made for a supposed forfeiture under a law of the United States, no action of trespass lies in any common-law tribunal, until a final decree is pronounced upon the proceeding *in rem* to enforce such forfeiture : for it depends upon the final decreee of the court proceeding *in rem*, whether such seizure is to be deemed rightful or tortuous, and the action, if brought before such decree is made, is brought too soon.—*Id.*, 313.

If a suit be brought against the seizing officer for the supposed trespass while the suit for the forfeiture is depending, the fact of such pending may be pleaded in abatement, or as a temporary bar of the action. If after a decree of condemnation, then that fact may be pleaded as a bar : if after an acquittal with a certificate of reasonable cause of seizure, then that may be pleaded as a bar. If after an acquittal without such certificate, then the officer is without any justification for the seizure, and it is definitively settled to be a tortuous act. If to an action of trespass in a state court for a seizure, the seizing officer plead the fact of forfeiture in his defence without averring a *lis pendens*, or a condemnation, or an acquittal, with a certificate of reasonable cause of seizure, the plea is bad: for it attempts to put in issue the question of forfeiture in a state court.—*Id.*, 314.

Supposing that the third article of the constitution of the United States which declares, that "the judicial power shall extend to all cases of admiralty and maritime jurisdiction" shall be at such place or places as the Congress may by law have directed.*

SECTION 3. Treason against the United States, shall consist only in

vested in the United States exclusive jurisdiction of all such cases, and that a murder committed in the waters of a state where the tide ebbs and flows, is a case of admiralty and maritime jurisdiction ; yet Congress have not, in the 8th section of the act of 1790, chap. 9, " for the punishment of certain crimes against the United States," so exercised this power, as to confer on the courts of the United States jurisdiction over such murder.—*United States* vs. *Bevans*, 3 *Wheaton*, 336, 387.

Quere.—Whether courts of common law have concurrent jurisdiction with the admiralty over murder committed in bays, &c., which are enclosed parts of the sea ?—*Id.*, 387.

The grant to the United States in the constitution of all cases of admiralty and maritime jurisdiction, does not extend to a cession of the waters in which those cases may arise, or of general jurisdiction over the same. Congress may pass all laws which are necessary for giving the most complete effect to the exercise of the admiralty and maritime jurisdiction granted to the government of the Union ; but the general jurisdiction over the place subject to this grant, adheres to the territory as a portion of territory not yet given away, and the residuary powers of legislation still remain in the state.—*Id.*, 389.

The supreme court of the United States has constitutionally appellate jurisdiction under the judiciary act of 1789, chap. 20, sect. 25, from the final judgment or decree of the highest court of law or equity of a state having jurisdiction of the subject matter of the suit, where is drawn in question the validity of a treaty or statute of, or an authority exercised under, the United States, and the decision is against their validity : or where is drawn in question the validity of a statute of, or an authority exercised under any state, on the ground of their being repugnant to the constitution, treaties, or laws of the United States, and the decision is in favor of such their validity : or of the constitution, or of a treaty, or statute of, or commission held under the United States, and the decision is against the title, right, privilege, or exemption, specially set up or claimed by either party under such clause of the constitution, treaty, statute, or commission.—*Cohens* vs. *Virginia*, 6 *Wheaton*, 264, 375.

It is no objection to the exercise of this appellate jurisdiction, that one of the parties is a state, and the other a citizen of that state.—*Id.*

The circuit courts of the Union have chancery jurisdiction in every state : they have the same chancery powers, and the same rules of decision in equity cases, in all the states.—*United States* vs. *Howland*, 4 *Wheaton*, 108, 115.

Resolutions of the legislature of Virginia of 1810, upon the proposition from Pennsylvania to amend the constitution, so as to provide an impartial tribunal to decide disputes between the state and federal judiciaries.—*Note to Cohens* vs. *Virginia. Notes* 6 *Wheaton*, 358.

Where a cause is brought to this court by writ of error, or appeal from the highest court of law, or equity of a state, under the 25th section of the judiciary act of 1789, chap. 20, upon the ground that the validity of a statute of the United States was drawn in question, and that the decision of the state court was against its validity, &c., or that the validity of the statute of a state was drawn in question as repugnant to the constitution of the United States, and the decision was in favor of its validity, it must appear from the record, that the act of Congress, or the constitutionality of the state law, was drawn in question.—*Miller* vs. *Nicholls*, 4 *Wheaton*, 311, 315.

But it is not required that the record should in terms state a misconstruction of the act of Congress, or that it was drawn into question. It is sufficient to give this court jurisdiction of the cause, that the record should show that an act of Congress was applicable to the case.—*Id.*, 315.

The supreme court of the United States has no jurisdiction under the 25th section of the judiciary act of 1789, chap. 20, unless the judgment or decree of the state court be a final judgment or decree. A judgment reversing that of an inferior court, and awarding a *venire facias de novo*, is not a final judgment.—*Houston* vs. *Moore*, 3 *Wheaton*, 433.

By the compact of 1802, settling the boundary line between Virginia and Tennessee, and the laws made in pursuance thereof, it is declared that all claims and titles to land derived from Virginia, or North Carolina, or Tennessee, which have fallen into the respective states, shall remain as secure to the owners thereof, as if derived from the government within whose boundary they have fallen, and shall not be prejudiced or affected by the establishment of the line. Where the titles of both the plaintiff and defendant in ejectment were derived under grant from Virginia to lands which fell within the limits of Tennessee, it was held that a prior settlement right thereto, which would in *equity* give the party a title, could not be asserted as a sufficient title in an action of ejectment brought in the circuit court of Tennessee.—*Robinson* vs. *Campbell*, 3 *Wheaton*, 212.

Although the state courts of Tennessee have decided that, under their statutes (declaring an elder grant founded on a junior entry to be void), a junior patent, founded on a prior entry, shall prevail *at law* against a senior patent founded on a junior entry, this doctrine has never been extended beyond cases within the express provision of the statute of Tennessee, and could not apply to titles deriving all their validity from the laws of Virginia, and confirmed by the compact between the two states.—*Id.*, 212.

* See amendments, art vi.

levying war against them, or in adhering to their enemies, giving them aid and comfort.

No person shall be convicted of treason unless on the testimony of two witnesses to the same overt act, or on confession in open court.

The Congress shall have power to declare the punishment of treason, but no attainder of treason shall work corruption of blood, or forfeiture except during the life of the person attainted.*

ARTICLE IV.

Section 1. Full faith and credit shall be given in each state to the public acts, records, and judicial proceedings of every other state.† And the Congress may by general laws prescribe the manner in which such acts, records and proceedings shall be proved, and the effect thereof.‡

Section 2. The citizens of each state shall be entitled to all privileges and immunities of citizens in the several states.

A person charged in any state with treason, felony, or other crime, who shall flee from justice, and be found in another state, shall on demand of the executive authority of the state from which he fled, be delivered up, to be removed to the state having jurisdiction of the crime.

No person held to service or labor in one state, under the laws thereof escaping into another, shall, in consequence of any law or regulation therein, be discharged from such service or labor, but shall be delivered up on claim of the party to whom such service or labor may be due.

Section 3. New states may be admitted by the Congress into this Union ; but no new state shall be formed or erected within the jurisdiction of any other state ; nor any state be formed by the junction of two or more states, or parts of states, without the consent of the legislatures of the states concerned as well as of the Congress.

The Congress shall have power to dispose of and make all needful rules and regulations respecting the territory or other property belonging to the United States ; and nothing in this constitution shall be so construed as to prejudice any claims of the United States, or of any particular state.

Section 4. The United States shall guaranty to every state in this Union a republican form of government, and shall protect each of them against invasion ; and on application of the legislature, or of the executive (when the legislature can not be convened) against domestic violence.

ARTICLE V.

The Congress, whenever two thirds of both houses shall deem it necessary, shall propose amendments to this constitution, or, on the application of the legislatures of two thirds of the several states, shall call a convention for proposing amendments, which, in either case, shall be valid to all intents and purposes, as part of this constitution, when ratified by the legislatures of three fourths of the several states, or by conventions in three fourths thereof, as the one or the other mode of ratification may be proposed by the Congress ; provided that no amendment which may be made

* See laws of the United States, vol. ii., chap. 36.
† A judgment of a state court has the same credit, validity, and effect, in every other court within the United States, which it had in the court where it was rendered ; and whatever pleas would be good to a suit thereon in such state, and none others can be pleaded in any other court within the United States.—*Hampton* vs. *McConnell*, 3 *Wheaton*, 234.

The record of a judgment in one state is conclusive evidence in another, although it appears that the suit in which it was rendered, was commenced by an attachment of property, the defendant having afterward appeared and taken defence.—*Mayhew* vs. *Thacher*, 6 *Wheaton*, 129.

‡ See laws United States, vol. ii., chap. 38 ; and vol. iii., chap. 409.

prior to the year one thousand eight hundred and eight shall in any manner affect the first and fourth clauses in the ninth section of the first article ; and that no state, without its consent, shall be deprived of its equal suffrage in the senate.*

ARTICLE VI.

All debts contracted and engagements entered into, before the adoption of this constitution, shall be as valid against the United States under this constitution, as under the confederation.

This constitution, and the laws of the United States which shall be made in pursuance thereof ; and all treaties made, or which shall be made, under the authority of the United States, shall be the supreme law of the land ;† and the judges in every state shall be bound thereby, anything in the constitution or laws of any state to the contrary notwithstanding.‡

The senators and representatives before mentioned, and the members of the several state legislatures, and all executive and judicial officers, both of the United States and of the several states, shall be bound by oath or affirmation, to support this constitution ;§ but no religious test shall ever be required as a qualification to any office or public trust under the United States.

ARTICLE VII.

The ratification of the conventions of nine states, shall be sufficient for the establishment of this constitution between the states so ratifying the same.

Done in convention by the unanimous consent of the states present, the seventeenth day of September, in the year of our Lord one thousand seven hundred and eighty-seven and of the independence of the United States of America the twelfth. In witness whereof we have hereunto subscribed our names.

Go. WASHINGTON,
President, and deputy from Virginia.

NEW HAMPSHIRE.
JOHN LANGDON,
NICHOLAS GILMAN.

MASSACHUSETTS.
NATHANIEL GORHAM.
RUFUS KING.

CONNECTICUT.
WILLIAM SAMUEL JOHNSON,
ROGER SHERMAN.

NEW YORK.
ALEXANDER HAMILTON.

NEW JERSEY.
WILLIAM LIVINGSTON,
DAVID BREARLEY,
WILLIAM PATERSON,
JONATHAN DAYTON.

PENNSYLVANIA.
BENJAMIN FRANKLIN,
THOMAS MIFFLIN,
ROBERT MORRIS,
GEORGE CLYMER,
THOMAS FITZSIMONS,
JARED INGERSOLL,
JAMES WILSON.
GOUVERNEUR MORRIS.

DELAWARE.
GEORGE REED,
GUNNING BEDFORD, JR.,
JOHN DICKINSON,
RICHARD BASSETT,
JACOB BROOM.

MARYLAND.
JAMES M'HENRY,
DANIEL OF ST. THO. JENIFER,
DANIEL CARROLL.

VIRGINIA.
JOHN BLAIR,
JAMES MADISON, JR.

NORTH CAROLINA.
WILLIAM BLOUNT,
RICHARD DOBBS SPAIGHT,
HUGH WILLIAMSON.

SOUTH CAROLINA.
JOHN RUTLEDGE,
CHARLES C. PINCKNEY
CHARLES PINCKNEY
PIERCE BUTLER.

GEORGIA.
WILLIAM FEW,
ABRAHAM BALDWIN.

Attest :   WILLIAM JACKSON, *Secretary.*

* See ante art. i., sect. 3, clause 1.

† An act of Congress repugnant to the constitution can not become a law.—*Marbury vs. Madison*, 1 *Cranch*, 176.

‡ The courts of the United States are bound to take notice of the constitution.—*Marbury vs. Madison*, 1 *Cranch*, 178.

A contemporary exposition of the constitution, practised and acquiesced under for a period of years, fixes its construction.—*Stuart vs. Laird*, 1 *Cranch*, 299.

The government of the Union, though limited in its powers, is supreme within its sphere of action, and its laws, when made in pursuance of the constitution, form the supreme law of the land.—*McCulloch vs. State of Maryland*, 4 *Wheaton*, 405.

§ See laws of the United States, vol. ii., chap. I.

AMENDMENTS*

TO THE CONSTITUTION OF THE UNITED STATES, RATIFIED ACCORDING TO THE PROVISIONS OF THE FIFTH ARTICLE OF THE FOREGOING CONSTITUTION.

ARTICLE THE FIRST. Congress shall make no law respecting an establishment of religion, or prohibiting the free exercise thereof; or abridging the freedom of speech, or of the press ; or the right of the people peaceably to assemble, and to petition the government for a redress of grievances.

ARTICLE THE SECOND. A well-regulated militia, being necessary to the security of a free state, the right of the people to keep and bear arms, shall not be infringed.

ARTICLE THE THIRD. No soldier shall, in time of peace be quartered in any house, without the consent of the owner, nor in a time of war, but in a manner to be prescribed by law.

ARTICLE THE FOURTH. The right of the people to be secure in their persons, houses, papers, and effects, against unreasonable searches and seizures, shall not be violated, and no warrants shall issue, but upon probable cause, supported by oath or affirmation, and particularly describing the place to be searched, and the persons or things to be seized.

ARTICLE THE FIFTH. No person shall be held to answer for a capital, or otherwise infamous crime, unless on a presentment or indictment of a grand jury, except in cases arising in the land or naval forces, or in the militia, when in actual service in time of war or public danger ; nor shall any person be subject for the same offence to be twice put in jeopardy of life or limb ; nor shall be compelled in any criminal case to be a witness against himself, nor be deprived of life, liberty, or property, without due process of law ; nor shall private property be taken for public use, without just compensation.

ARTICLE THE SIXTH. In all criminal prosecutions, the accused shall enjoy the right to a speedy and public trial, by an impartial jury of the state and district wherein the crime shall have been committed, which district shall have been previously ascertained by law, and to be informed of the nature and cause of the accusation ; to be confronted with the witnesses against him ; to have compulsory process for obtaining witnesses in his favor, and to have the assistance of counsel for his defence.

ARTICLE THE SEVENTH. In suits at common law, where the value in controversy shall exceed twenty dollars, the right of trial by jury shall be preserved, and no fact tried by a jury, shall be otherwise re-examined in any court of the United States, than according to the rules of the common law.†

ARTICLE THE EIGHTH. Excessive bail shall not be required, nor excessive fines imposed, nor cruel and unusual punishments inflicted.

---

* Congress, at its first session, begun and held in the city of New York, on Wednesday, the 4th of March, 1789, proposed to the legislatures of the several states twelve amendments to the constitution, ten of which, only, were adopted.

† The act of assembly of Maryland, of 1793, chap. 30, incorporating the bank of Columbia, and giving to the corporation a summary process by execution in the nature of an attachment against its debtors who have, by an express consent in writing, made the bonds, bills, or notes, by them drawn or endorsed, negotiable at the bank, is not repugnant to the constitution of the United States or of Maryland.—*Bank of Columbia* vs. *Okely*, 4 *Wheaton*, 236, 249.

But the last provision in the act of incorporation, which gives this summary process to the bank, is no part of its corporate franchise and may be repealed or altered at pleasure by the legislative will.—*Id.*, 245.

ARTICLE THE NINTH. The enumeration in the constitution, of certain rights, shall not be construed to deny or disparage others retained by the people.

ARTICLE THE TENTH. The powers not delegated to the United States, by the constitution, nor prohibited by it to the states, are reserved to the states respectively, or to the people.*

ARTICLE THE ELEVENTH.† The judicial power of the United States shall not be construed to extend to any suit in law or equity, commenced or prosecuted against one of the United States by citizens of another state, or by citizens or subjects of any foreign state.

ARTICLE THE TWELFTH.‡ The electors shall meet in their respective states, and vote by ballot for president and vice-president, one of whom, at least, shall not be an inhabitant of the same state with themselves; they shall name in their ballots the person voted for as president, and in distinct ballots the person voted for as vice-president, and they shall make distinct lists of all persons voted for as president, and of all persons voted for as vice-president, and of the number of votes for each, which lists they shall sign and certify, and transmit sealed to the seat of the government of the United States, directed to the president of the senate;§—the president of the senate shall, in the presence of the senate and house of representatives, open all the certificates and the votes shall then be counted;—the person having the greatest number of votes for president, shall be the president, if such number be a majority of the whole number of electors appointed; and if no person have such majority, then from the persons having the highest numbers not exceeding three on the list of those voted for as president, the house of representatives shall choose immediately, by ballot, the president. But in choosing the president, the votes shall be taken by states, the representation from each state having one vote; a quorum for this purpose shall consist of a member or members from two

* The powers granted to Congress are not exclusive of similar powers existing in the states, unless where the constitution has expressly in terms given an exclusive power to Congress, or the exercise of a like power is prohibited to the states, or there is a direct repugnancy or incompatibility in the exercise of it by the states.—*Houston* vs. *Moore*, 5 *Wheaton*, 1, 12.

The example of the first class is to be found in the exclusive legislation delegated to Congress over places purchased by the consent of the legislature of the state in which the same shall be for forts, arsenals, dockyards, &c. Of the second class, the prohibition of a state to coin money or emit bills of credit. Of the third class, the power to establish a uniform rule of naturalization, and the delegation of admiralty and maritime jurisdiction.—*Id.*, 49.

In all other classes of cases, the states retain concurrent authority with Congress.—*Id.* 49.

But in cases of concurrent authority, where the laws of the states and the Union are in direct and manifest collision on the same subject, those of the Union being the supreme law of the land are of paramount authority, and the state laws so far, and so far only as such incompatibility exists, must necessarily yield.—*Id.*, 49.

There is nothing in the constitution of the United States similar to the articles of confederation, which excludes incidental or implied powers.—*McCulloch* vs. *State of Maryland*, 4 *Wheaton*, 406.

If the *end* be legitimate, and within the scope of the constitution, all the *means* which are appropriate, which are plainly adapted to that end, and which are not prohibited, may constitutionally be employed to carry it into effect.—*Id.*, 421.

The act of Congress of 4th May, 1812, entitled, "An act further to amend the charter of the city of Washington," which provides (sect. 6) that the corporation of the city shall be empowered for certain purposes and under certain restrictions, to authorize the drawing of lotteries, does not extend to authorize the corporation to force the sale of the tickets in such lottery in states where such sale may be prohibited by the state laws.—*Cohens* vs. *Virginia*, 6 *Wheaton*, 264, 375.

† This amendment was proposed at the first session of the third Congress. See ante art. iii., sect. 2, clause 1.

‡ Proposed at the first session of the eighth Congress. See ante art. ii., sect. 1, clause 3. Annulled by this amendment.

§ See laws of the United States, vol. ii., chap. 109, sect. 5.

thirds of the states, and a majority of all the states shall be necessary to a choice.   And if the house of representatives shall not choose a president whenever the right of choice shall devolve upon them, before the fourth day of March next following, then the vice-president shall act as president, as in the case of the death or other constitutional disability of the president.   The person having the greatest number of votes as vice-president, shall be the vice-president, if such number be a majority of the whole number of electors appointed, and if no person have a majority, then from the two highest numbers on the list, the senate shall choose the vice-president ; a quorum for the purpose shall consist of two thirds of the whole number of senators, and a majority of the whole number shall be necessary to a choice.   But no person constitutionally ineligible to the office of president shall be eligible to that of vice-president of the United States.

NOTE.—Another amendment was proposed as article xiii., at the second session of the eleventh Congress, but not having been ratified by a sufficient number of states, has not yet become valid as a part of the constitution of the United States.   It is erroneously given as a part of the constitution, in page 74, vol i., laws of the United States.

I have examined and compared the foregoing print of the constitution of the United States, and the amendments thereto, with the rolls in this office, and find it a faithful and literal copy of the said constitution and amendments, in the text and punctuation thereof.   It appears that the first ten amendments, which were proposed at the first session of the first Congress of the United States, were finally ratified by the constitutional number of states, on the 15th day of December, 1791 ; that the eleventh amendment, which was proposed at the first session of the third Congress, was declared, in a message from the president of the United States to both houses of Congress, dated 8th January, 1798, to have been adopted by three fourths, the constitutional number of states ; and that the twelfth amendment, which was proposed at the first session of the eighth Congress, was adopted by three fourths, the constitutional number of states, in the year one thousand eight hundred and four, according to a public notice thereof, by the secretary of state, under date the 25th of September, of the same year.

                                                            DANIEL BRENT, *Chief Clerk.*

Department of State, Washington, 25th Feb., 1828.

₊ For history of the formation of the constitution, the declaration of independence, and the articles of confederation, see vol. ii., end of the messages.

SUCCESSIVE ADMINISTRATIONS, FROM 1789 TO 1846.

FIRST ADMINISTRATION—1789 to 1797.—EIGHT YEARS.

PRESIDENT: GEORGE WASHINGTON, *Virginia.*
VICE-PRESIDENT: JOHN ADAMS, *Massachusetts.*
SECRETARIES OF STATE: Thomas Jefferson, of Va., Sept. 26, 1789; Edmund Randolph, of Va., Jan. 2, 1794; Timothy Pickering, of Pa., Dec. 10, 1795.
SECRETARIES OF THE TREASURY: Alexander Hamilton, of New York, Sept. 11, 1789; Oliver Wolcott, of Conn., Feb. 3, 1795.
SECRETARIES OF WAR: Henry Knox, of Mass., Sept. 12, 1789; Timothy Pickering, of Mass., Jan. 2, 1795; James M'Henry, of Md., Jan. 27, 1796.
SECRETARIES OF THE NAVY: No navy department during this administration.
POSTMASTERS-GENERAL: Samuel Osgood, of Mass., Sept. 26, 1789; Timothy Pickering, of Mass., Nov. 7, 1794; Joseph Habersham, of Ga., Feb. 25, 1795.

Years.	Expenditures.	Public Debt.	Total.
1789—The expenditures from 4th March, 1789, to 31st December, 1791, are			
1790	included in 1791.		
1791	$1,921,589 52	$5,285,949 50	$7,207,539 02
1792	1,877,913 68	7,263,655 99	9,141,569 67
1793	1,710,070 26	5,819,505 29	7,529,575 55
1794	3,500,546 65	5,801,578 09	9,302,124 74
1795	4,350,658 04	6,084,411 61	10,435,069 65
1796	2,531,930 40	5,835,846 44	8,367,776 84
	$15,892,708 55	$36,090,946 92	$51,983,655 47

SECOND ADMINISTRATION—1797 to 1801.—FOUR YEARS.

PRESIDENT: JOHN ADAMS, *Massachusetts.*
VICE-PRESIDENT: THOMAS JEFFERSON, *Virginia.*
SECRETARIES OF STATE: Timothy Pickering, continued in office; John Marshall, of Va., May 13, 1800.
SECRETARIES OF THE TREASURY: Oliver Wolcott continued in office; S. Dexter, of Mass., Dec. 31, 1800.
SECRETARIES OF WAR: James M'Henry continued in office; S. Dexter, of Mass., May 13, 1800; Roger Griswold, of Conn., Feb. 3, 1801.
SECRETARIES OF THE NAVY: George Cabot, of Mass., May 3, 1789, declined; Benjamin Stoddart, of Maryland, May 21, 1798.
POSTMASTER-GENERAL: Joseph Habersham, continued.

Years.	Expenditures.	Public Debt.	Total.
1797	$2,833,590 96	$5,792,421 82	$8,626,012 78
1798	4,623,223 54	3,990,294 14	8,613,517 68
1799	6,480,166 72	4,596,876 78	11,077,043 50
1800	7,411,369 97	4,578,369 95	11,989,739 92
	$21,348,351 19	$18,957,962 69	$40,306,313 88

THIRD ADMINISTRATION—1801 to 1809.—EIGHT YEARS.

PRESIDENT: THOMAS JEFFERSON, *Virginia.*
VICE-PRESIDENTS: AARON BURR, *New York*; GEORGE CLINTON, *New York.*
SECRETARY OF STATE: James Madison, of Virginia, March 5, 1801.
SECRETARIES OF THE TREASURY: S. Dexter continued in office; Albert Gallatin, of Pa., Jan. 26, 1802.
SECRETARY OF WAR: Henry Dearborn, of Mass., March 4, 1801.
SECRETARIES OF THE NAVY: Benjamin Stoddart continued in office; Robert Smith, of Maryland, Jan. 28, 1802.

POSTMASTERS-GENERAL : Joseph Habersham continued in office; Gideon Granger, Conn., Jan. 26, 1802.

Years.	Expenditures.	Public Debt.	Total.
1801	$4,981,669 90	$7,291,707 04	$12,273,376 94
1802	3,737,079 91	9,539,004 76	13,276,084 67
1803	4,002,824 24	7,256,159 43	11,258,983 67
1804	4,452,857 91	8,171,787 45	12,624,645 36
1805	6,357,234 62	7,369,889 79	13,727,124 41
1806	6,080,209 36	8,989,884 61	15,070,093 97
1807	4,984,572 89	6,307,720 10	11,292,292 99
1808	6,504,338 85	10,260,245 35	16,764,584 20
	$41,100,787 68	$65,186,398 53	$106,287,186 21

FOURTH ADMINISTRATION—1809 TO 1817.—EIGHT YEARS.

PRESIDENT: JAMES MADISON, *Virginia.*
VICE-PRESIDENTS: GEORGE CLINTON, *New York;* ELBRIDGE GERRY, *Mass.*
SECRETARIES OF STATE: Robert Smith, of Md., 6th March, 1809; James Monroe, of Va., Nov. 25, 1811.
SECRETARIES OF THE TREASURY: Albert Gallatin continued in office; George W. Campbell, of Tenn., Feb. 9, 1814; Alexander J. Dallas, of Pa., Oct. 6, 1814.
SECRETARIES OF WAR: Wm. Eustis, of Mass., March 7, 1809; John Armstrong, of N. Y., Jan. 19, 1813; James Monroe, of Va., Sept. 26, 1814; Wm. H. Crawford, of Ga., March 2, 1815.
SECRETARIES OF THE NAVY: Paul Hamilton, of S. C., March 7, 1809; William Jones, of Pa., Jan. 12, 1813; Benjamin W. Crowninshield, of Mass., Dec. 19, 1841.
POSTMASTERS-GENERAL: Gideon Granger continued in office; R. J. Meigs, of Ohio, March 17, 1814.

Years	Expenditures.	Public Debt.	Total,
1809	$7,414,672 14	$6,452,554 16	$13,867,226 30
1810	5,311,082 28	8,008,904 46	13,319,986 74
1811	5,592,604 86	8,009,204 05	13,601,808 91
1812	17,829,498 70	4,449,622 45	22,279,121 15
1813	28,082,391 92	11,108,128 44	39,190,520 36
1814	30,127,686 28	7,900,543 94	38,028,230 22
1815	26,953,571 00	12,628,922 35	39,582,493 35
1816	23,373,432 58	24,871,062 93	48,244,495 51
	$144,684,939 76	$83,428,942 78	$228,113,882 54

FIFTH ADMINISTRATION—1817 TO 1825.—EIGHT YEARS.

PRESIDENT: JAMES MONROE, *Virginia.*
VICE-PRESIDENT: DANIEL D. TOMPKINS, *New York.*
SECRETARY OF STATE: John Q. Adams, of Mass., March 3, 1817.
SECRETARY OF THE TREASURY: Wm. H. Crawford, of Ga., March 5, 1817.
SECRETARIES OF WAR: Isaac Shelby, of Ky., March 5, 1817, declined the appointment; John C. Calhoun, of S. C., Dec. 16, 1817.
SECRETARIES OF THE NAVY: Benjamin W. Crowninshield, continued in office; Smith Thompson, of N. Y., Nov. 30, 1818; S. L. Southard, of N. J., Dec. 9, 1823.
POSTMASTERS-GENERAL: Return J. Meigs continued in office; John M'Lean, of Ohio, Dec. 9, 1823.

Years.	Expenditures.	Public Debt.	Total.
1817	$15,454,609 92	$25,423,036 12	$40,877,646 04
1818	13,808,673 78	21,296,201 62	35,104,875 40
1819	16,300,273 44	7,703,926 29	24,004,199 73
1820	13,134,530 57	8,628,494 28	21,763,024 85
1821	10,723,479 07	8,367,093 62	19,090,572 69
1822	9,827,580 55	7,848,949 12	17,676,529 67
1823	9,784,154 59	5,530,016 41	15,314,171 00
1824	15,330,144 71	16,568,393 76	31,898,538 47
	$104,363,446 63	$101,366,111 22	$205,729,557 85

SIXTH ADMINISTRATION—1824 TO 1829.—FOUR YEARS.

PRESIDENT: JOHN QUINCY ADAMS, *Massachusetts.*
VICE-PRESIDENT: JOHN C. CALHOUN, *South Carolina.*
SECRETARY OF STATE: Henry Clay, of Ky., March 8, 1825.
SECRETARY OF THE TREASURY: Richard Rush, of Penn., March 7, 1825.
SECRETARIES OF WAR. Jas. Barbour, of Va., March 7, 1825; Peter B. Porter, of N. Y., May 26, 1828.
SECRETARY OF THE NAVY. Samuel L. Southard, continued in office.
POSTMASTER-GENERAL: John M'Lean continued in office.

Years	Expenditures.	Public Debt.	Total.
1825	$11,490,459 94	$12,095,344 78	$23,585,804 72
1826	13,062,316 27	11,041,082 19	24,103,398 46
1827	12,653,096 65	10,003,668 39	22,656,765 04
1828	13,296,041 45	12,163,438 07	25,459,479 52
	$50,501,914 31	$45,303,533 43	$95,805,447 74

SEVENTH ADMINISTRATION—1829 TO 1837.—EIGHT YEARS.

PRESIDENT: ANDREW JACKSON, *Tennessee.*
VICE-PRESIDENTS: JOHN C. CALHOUN, *South Carolina;* MARTIN VAN BUREN, *New York.*
SECRETARIES OF STATE: Martin Van Buren, of New York, March 6, 1829; Ed. Livingston, of La., 1831; Louis M'Lane, of Del., 1833; John Forsyth, of Ga., 1834.
SECRETARIES OF THE TREASURY: Samuel D. Ingham, of Pa., March 6, 1829; Louis M'Lane, of Del., 1831; Wm. J. Duane, of Pa., 1833; Roger B. Taney, of Md., 1833—not confirmed by the senate; Levi Woodbury, of N. H., 1834.
SECRETARIES OF WAR: John H. Eaton, of Tenn., March 9, 1829; Lewis Cass, of Ohio, 1831.
SECRETARIES OF THE NAVY: John Branch, of N. C., March 9, 1829; Levi Woodbury, of N. H., 1831; Mahlon Dickerson, of N. J., 1834.
POSTMASTERS-GENERAL: Wm. T. Barry, of Ky., March 9, 1829; Amos Kendall, of Ky., 1835.

Years.	Expenditures.	Public Debt.	Total.
1829	$12,660,490 62	$12,383,867 78	$25,044,358 40
1830	13,229,533 33	11,355,748 22	24,585,281 55
1831	13,864,067 90	16,174,378 22	30,038,446 12
1832	16,516,388 77	17,840,309 29	34,356,698 06
1833	22,713,755 11	1,543,543 38	24,257,298 49
1834	18,425,417 25	6,176,565 19	24,601,982 44
1835	17,514,950 28	58,191 28	17,573,141 56
1836	29,621,807 82		29,621,807 82
	$144,546,404 08	$65,532,603 36	$210,079,007 44

EIGHTH ADMINISTRATION—1837 TO 1841.—FOUR YEARS.

PRESIDENT: MARTIN VAN BUREN, *New York.*
VICE-PRESIDENT: RICHARD M. JOHNSON, *Kentucky.*
SECRETARY OF STATE: John Forsyth, appointed June 27, 1834, resigned March 3, 1841.
SECRETARY OF THE TREASURY: Levi Woodbury, appointed June 27, 1834, resigned March 2, 1841.
SECRETARY OF WAR: Joel R. Poinsett, appointed March 7, 1837, resigned March 2, 1841.
SECRETARIES OF THE NAVY: Mahlon Dickerson, appointed June 30, 1834, resigned June, 1838; James K. Paulding, appointed *from* June 30, 1838; resigned March 2, 1841.
POSTMASTERS-GENERAL: Amos Kendall, appointed May 1, 1835, resigned; John M. Niles, appointed *from* May 25, 1840, resigned March 1, 1841.

Years	Expenditures.	Public Debt.	Total.
1837	$31,793,587 24	$21,823 91	$31,815,410 15
1838	31,578,785 08	5,605,720 27	37,184,505 35
1839	25,488,547 73	11,127,987 42	36,616,534 15
1840	23,327,772 11	4,086,614 70	27,414,386 81
	$112,188,692 16	$20,842,146 30	$133,030,836 46

NINTH ADMINISTRATION—1841 TO 1845.—FOUR YEARS.

PRESIDENT: GEN. WILLIAM HENRY HARRISON, *Ohio.* Died April 4, 1841.
VICE-PRESIDENT: JOHN TYLER, *Virginia.*
PRESIDENT: JOHN TYLER, *Virginia* (from April 4, 1841).
SECRETARIES OF STATE: Daniel Webster, appointed March 5, 1841, resigned May 8, 1843; Hugh S. Legaré, appointed May 9, 1843, died June 20, 1843; Abel P. Upshur, appointed June 24, 1843, died February 28, 1844; John Nelson, acting, February 29, 1844; John C. Calhoun, appointed March 6, 1844, resigned March 1, 1845.
SECRETARIES OF THE TREASURY: Thomas Ewing, appointed March 5, 1841, resigned; Walter Forward, appointed September 13, 1841, resigned; George M. Bibb, appointed June 15, 1844, resigned March 3, 1845.
SECRETARIES OF WAR: John Bell, appointed March 5, 1841, resigned; John C. Spencer, appointed October 12, 1841, transferred to treasury department; James M. Porter, appointed March 8, 1843, rejected by the senate; William Wilkins, appointed February 15, 1844, resigned March 3, 1845.
SECRETARIES OF THE NAVY: George E. Badger, appointed March 5, 1841, resigned; Abel P. Upshur, appointed September, 13, 1841, transferred to department of state; David Henshaw, appointed July 24, 1843, rejected by the senate; Thomas W. Gilmer, appointed February 15, 1844, died February 28, 1844; John Y. Mason, appointed March 14, 1844, resigned March 3, 1845.
POSTMASTERS-GENERAL: Francis Granger, appointed March 6, 1841, resigned; Charles A. Wickliffe, appointed September 13, 1841, resigned March 3, 1845.

Years	Expenditures.	Public Debt.	Total.
1841	$26,196,840 29	$5,600,689 74	$31,797,530 03
1842	24,361,336 59	8,575,539 94	32,936,876 53
1st Jan. to Jan. 30, 1843	11,256,508 60	861,596 55	12,118,105 15
For the year ending Jan. 30, 1844	20,650,198 01	2,991,802 84	33,642,010 85
From July to Dec. 31, 1844	11,700,159 50	1,538,478 06	13,238,637 56
	$94,164,952 99	$29,568,207 13	$123,838,160 12

TENTH ADMINISTRATION—1845 TO 1849.

PRESIDENT: JAMES KNOX POLK, *Tennessee.*
VICE-PRESIDENT: GEORGE M. DALLAS, *Pennsylvania.*
SECRETARY OF STATE: James Buchanan, of Pennsylvania, appointed March 5, 1845.
SECRETARY OF THE TREASURY: Robert J. Walker, of Mississippi, appointed March 5, 1845.
SECRETARY OF WAR: William L. Marcy, of New York, appointed March 5, 1845.
SECRETARY OF THE NAVY: George Bancroft, of Massachusetts, appointed March, 1845. JOHN Y. MASON, of Virginia, appointed 1846.
POSTMASTER-GENERAL: Cave Johnson, of Tennessee, appointed March 5, 1845.

PUBLIC MINISTERS OF THE UNITED STATES, TO FOREIGN COUNTRIES, FROM 1789 TO 1846.

To Great Britain.

Gouverneur Morris, of New Jersey, commissioner, October 13, 1789.

Thomas Pinckney, of South Carolina, minister plenipotentiary, January 12, 1792.

John Jay, of New York, envoy extraordinary, April 19, 1794.

Rufus King, of New York, minister plenipotentiary, May, 20, 1796.

James Monroe, of Virginia, minister plenipotentiary, April 18, 1803.

James Monroe and William Pinkney, jointly and severally, ministers plenipotentiary and extraordinary, May 12, 1806.

William Pinkney, of Maryland, minister plenipotentiary, May 12, 1806, renewed February 26, 1808.

John Quincy Adams, of Massachusetts, envoy extraordinary and minister plenipotentiary, February 28, 1815.

Richard Rush, of Pennsylvania, envoy extraordinary and minister plenipotentiary, December 16, 1817.

Rufus King, of New York, envoy extraordinary and minister plenipotentiary, May 5, 1825.

Albert Gallatin, of Pennsylvania, envoy extraordinary and minister plenipotentiary, May 10, 1826.

James Barbour, of Virginia, envoy extraordinary and minister plenipotentiary, May 23, 1828.

Louis M'Lane, of Delaware, envoy extraordinary and minister plenipotentiary, February 10, 1830.

Martin Van Buren, of N. Y., envoy extraordinary and minister plenipotentiary, 1831.

Aaron Vail, of New York, chargé d'affaires, 1832.

Andrew Stevenson, of Virginia, envoy extraordinary and minister plenipotentiary, 1836.

Edward Everett, of Massachusetts, envoy extraordinary and minister plenipotentiary, 1841.

Louis M'Lane, of Maryland, envoy extraordinary and minister plenipotentiary, 1845.

To France.

William Short, of Virginia, chargé d'affaires, April 6, 1790.

Gouverneur Morris, of New Jersey, minister penipotentiary, January 12, 1792.

James Monroe, of Virginia, minister plenipotentiary, May 28, 1790.

Charles Cotesworth Pinckney, of South Carolina, minister plenipotentiary, September 9, 1796.

Charles Cotesworth Pinckney, Elbridge Gerry, and John Marshall, jointly and severally, envoys extraordinary and ministers plenipotentiary, June 5, 1797.

Oliver Ellsworth, Patrick Henry, and William Vans Murray, envoys extraordinary and ministers plenipotentiary, February 26, 1799.

William Richardson Davie, of North Carolina, in place of Patrick Henry, December 10, 1799.

James A. Bayard, of Delaware, minister plenipotentiary, February 19, 1801.

Robert R. Livingston, of New York, minister plenipotentiary, October 2, 1801.

John Armstrong, of New York, minister plenipotentiary, June 30, 1804.

Joel Barlow, of Connecticut, minister plenipotentiary, February, 27, 1811.

William H. Crawford, of Georgia, minister plenipotentiary, April 9, 1813.

Albert Gallatin, of Pennsylvania, envoy extraordinary and minister plenipotentiary, February 28, 1815.

James Brown, of Louisiana, envoy extraordinary and minister plenipotentiary, December 9, 1823.

William C. Rives, of Virginia, envoy extraordinary and minister plenipotentiary, February 10, 1830.

Edward Livingston, of Louisiana, envoy extraordinary and minister plenipotentiary, 1833.

Lewis Cass, of Ohio, envoy extraordinary and minister plenipotentiary, 1836.

William R. King, of Alabama, envoy extraordinary and minister plenipotentiary, 1844.

To Spain.

William Carmichael, of Maryland, chargé d'affaires, April 11, 1790.
William Carmichael and William Short, commissioners, March 16, 1792.
William Short, of Virginia, minister resident, May 28, 1794.
Thomas Pinckney, of South Carolina, envoy extrordinary, November 24, 1794.
David Humphreys, of Connecticut, minister plenipotentiary, May 20, 1796.
Charles Pinckney, of South Carolina, minister plenipotentiary, June 6, 1801.
James Monroe, of Virginia, minister extraordinary and plenipotentiary, October 14, 1804.
James Bowdoin, of Massachusetts, minister plenipotentiary, November 22, 1804.
George W. Erving, of Massachusetts, minister plenipotentiary, August 10, 1814.
John Forsyth, of Georgia, minister plenipotentiary, February 16, 1819.
Hugh Nelson, of Virginia, envoy extraordinary and minister plenipotentiary, June 15, 1823.
Alexander Hill Everett, of Massachusetts, envoy extraordinary and minister plenipotentiary, March 9, 1825.
Cornelius P. Van Ness, of Vermont, envoy extraordinary and minister plenipotentiary, February 10, 1830.
William T. Barry, of Ky., envoy extraordinary and minister plenipotentiary, 1835.
John H. Eaton, of Tenn., envoy extraordinary and minister plenipotentiary, 1836.
Aaron Vail, of New York, chargé d'affaires, 1840.
Washington Irving, of N. Y., envoy extraordinary and minister plenipotentiary, 1842.
Romulus M. Saunders, of North Carolina, envoy extraordinary and minister plenipotentiary, 1546.

To the Netherlands.

William Short, of Virginia, minister resident, January 16, 1792.
John Quincy Adams, of Massachusetts, minister resident, May 30, 1794.
William Vans Murray, of Maryland, minister resident, March 2, 1797.
William Eustis, of Massachusetts, envoy extraordinary and minister plenipotentiary, December 10, 1814.
Alexander H. Everett, of Massachusetts, chargé d'affaires, November 30, 1818.
Christopher Hughes, of Maryland, chargé d'affaires, March 9, 1825.
Albert Gallatin and William Pitt Preble, agents in the negotiation and upon the umpirage relating to the northeastern boundary of the United States, May 9, 1828.
William Pitt Preble, of Maine, envoy extraordinary and minister plenipotentiary, February 10, 1830.
Auguste Davezac, of Louisiana, chargé d'affaires, 1831.
Harmanus Bleecker, of New York, chargé d'affaires, 1839.
Christopher Hughes, of Maryland, chargé d'affaires, 1842.
Auguste Davezac, of New York, chargé d'affaires, 1845.

To Portugal.

David Humphreys, of Connecticut, minister resident, February 21, 1791.
John Quincy Adams, of Massachusetts, minister plenipotentiary, May 30, 1796.
William Smith, of South Carolina, minister plenipotentiary, July 10, 1797.
Thomas Sumpter, of S. Carolina, minister plenipotentiary (in Brazil), March 7, 1809.
John Graham, of Virginia, minister plenipotentiary (in Brazil), January 6, 1819.
Henry Dearborn, senior, of New Hampshire, envoy extraordinary and minister plenipotentiary, May 7, 1822.
Thomas L. L. Brent, of Virginia, chargé d'affaires, March 9, 1825.
Edward Kavenagn, of Maine, chargé d'affaires, 1835.
Washington Barrow, chargé d'affaires, 1841.
Abraham Rencher, of North Carolina, chargé d'affaires, 1843.

To Prussia.

John Quincy Adams, of Massachusetts, minister plenipotentiary, June 1, 1797.
Henry Clay (secretary of state), special commissioner, with full power to conclude a treaty with the government of Prussia, April 18, 1828.
Henry Wheaton, of Rhode Island, minister plenipotentiary, 1837.
Andrew J. Donelson, of Tennessee, minister plenipotentiary, 1846.

To Austria.

Henry A. Muhlenberg, of Pennsylvania, minister plenipotentiary, 1838.
Daniel Jenifer, of Maryland, minister plenipotentiary, 1841.
William A. Stiles, of Georgia, chargé d'affaires, 1845.

To Russia.

John Quincy Adams, of Massachusetts, minister plenipotentiary, June 27, 1809.
James A. Bayard, of Delaware, envoy extraordinary and minister plenipotentiary, February 28, 1815.
William Pinkney, of Maryland, envoy extraordinary and minister plenipotentiary, April 26, 1815.
George W. Campbell, of Tennessee, envoy extraordinary and minister plenipotentiary, April 16, 1818.
Henry Middleton, of South Carolina, envoy extraordinary and minister plenipotentiary, April 6, 1820.
John Randolph, of Virginia, envoy extraordinary and minister plenipotentiary, 1830.
James Buchanan, of Penn., envoy extraordinary and minister plenipotentiary, 1831.
William Wilkins, of Penn., envoy extraordinary and minister plenipotentiary, 1834.
John Randolph Clay, of Pennsylvania, chargé d'affaires, 1836.
George M. Dallas, Penn., envoy extraordinary and minister plenipotentiary, 1837.
Churchill C. Cambreleng, of New York, envoy extraordinary and minister plenipotentiary, 1840.
Charles S. Todd, of Ky., envoy extraordinary and minister plenipotentiary, 1841.

To Sweden.

Jonathan Russell, of Rhode Island, minister plenipotentiary, January 18, 1814.
Christopher Hughes, jr., of Maryland, chargé d'affaires, January 21, 1819.
William C. Somerville, of Maryland, chargé d'affaires, March 9, 1825.
John James Appleton, of Massachusetts, chargé d'affaires, May 2, 1826.
Christopher Hughes, of Maryland, chargé d'affaires, March 3, 1830.
George W. Lay, of New York, chargé d'affaires, 1842.
Henry W. Ellsworth, of Indiana, chargé d'affaires, 1845.

Negotiators of the Treaty of Ghent.

John Quincy Adams, Albert Gallatin, and James A. Bayard, envoys extraordinary and ministers plenipotentiary, April 17, 1813. (See vol. 1, pages 363, 366.)
Henry Clay and Jonathan Russell were added to this commission on the 18th of January, 1814.

To Denmark.

Henry Wheaton, of New York, chargé d'affaires, March 3, 1827.
Jonathan F. Woodside, of Ohio, chargé d'affaires, 1835.
William W. Irwin, of Pennsylvania, chargé d'affaires, 1843.

To Belgium.

Hugh S. Legaré, of South Carolina, chargé d'affaires, 1832.
Virgil Maxcy, of Maryland, chargé d'affaires, 1837.
Henry W. Hilliard, of Alabama, chargé d'affaires, 1842.
Thomas G. Clemson, of Pennsylvania, chargé d'affaires, 1844.

To the Two Sicilies.

John Nelson, of Maryland, chargé d'affaires, 1831.
Enos T. Throop, of New York, chargé d'affaires, 1838.
William Boulware, of Virginia, chargé d'affaires, 1841.
William H. Polk, of Tennessee, chargé d'affaires, 1845.

To Sardinia.

H. Y. Rogers, chargé d'affaires, 1840.
Ambrose Baber, of Georgia, chargé d'affaires, 1841.
Robert Wickliffe, jr., of Kentucky, chargé d'affaires, 1843.

To Turkey.

David Porter, of Maryland, chargé d'affaires, 1831.
David Porter, minister resident, 1839.
Dabney S. Carr, of Maryland, minister resident, 1843.

To Guatemala (Central America).

William Miller, of North Carolina, chargé d'affaires, March 7, 1825.
John Williams, of Tennessee, chargé d'affaires, December 9, 1825.
William B. Rochester, of New York, chargé d'affaires, March 3, 1827.
Charles G. DeWitt, of New York, chargé d'affaires, 1833.
John L. Stephens, of New York, minister resident, 1839.

To Mexico.

Andrew Jackson, of Tennessee, envoy extraordinary and minister plenipotentiary, January 27, 1823. (*Declined the appointment.*)

Ninian Edwards, of Illinois, envoy extraordinary and minister plenipotentiary, March 4, 1824.

Joel R. Poinsett, of South Carolina, envoy extraordinary and minister plenipotentiary, March 8, 1825.

Anthony Butler, of Mississippi, chargé d'affaires, March 12, 1830.

Powhattan Ellis, of Miss., envoy extraordinary and minister plenipotentiary, 1837.

Waddy Thompson, of S. C., envoy extraordinary and minister plenipotentiary, 1842.

Wilson Shannon, of Ohio, envoy extraordinary and minister plenipotentiary, 1844.

John Slidell, of Louisiana, envoy extraordinary and minister plenipotentiary, 1845.

To the Republic of Colombia.

Richard C. Anderson, of Virginia, minister plenipotentiary, January 27, 1823.

Beaufort T. Watts, of South Carolina, chargé d'affaires, March 3, 1827.

William Henry Harrison, of Ohio, envoy extraordinary and minister plenipotentiary, May 24, 1828.

Thomas P. Moore, of Kentucky, envoy extraordinary and minister plenipotentiary, March 13, 1829.

To Brazil.

Condy Raguet, of Pennsylvania, chargé d'affaires, March 9, 1825.

William Tudor, chargé d'affaires, December 27, 1827.

Ethan A. Brown, of Ohio, chargé d'affaires, 1830.

William Hunter, of Rhode Island, chargé d'affaires, 1834.

William Hunter, of Rhode Island, minister plenipotentiary, 1841.

George H. Proffit, of Indiana, minister plenipotentiary, 1843.

Henry A. Wise, of Virginia, minister plenipotentiary, 1844.

To the Republic of Buenos Ayres.

Cæsar A. Rodney, of Delaware, minister plenipotentiary, January 27, 1823.

John M. Forbes, of Florida, chargé d'affaires, March 9, 1825.

Francis Baylies, of Massachusetts, chargé d'affaires, 1832.

William Brent, jr., of Virginia, chargé d'affaires, 1844.

To the Republic of Chili.

Heman Allen, of Vermont, minister plenipotentiary, January 27, 1823.

Samuel Larned, of Rhode Island, chargé d'affaires, February 9, 1828.

John Harum, of Ohio, chargé d'affaires, 1830.

Richard Pollard, of Virginia, chargé d'affaires, 1834.

John S. Pendleton, of Virginia, chargé d'affaires, 1841.

William Crump, of Virginia, chargé d'affaires, 1844.

To Peru.

James Cooley of Ohio, chargé d'affaires, May 2, 1826.

Samuel Larned, of Rhode Island, chargé d'affaires, December 29, 1828.

Emanuel J. West, of Illinois, chargé d'affaires, March 12, 1830.

Samuel Larned, of Rhode Island, chargé d'affaires, 1831.

James B. Thornton, of New Hampshire, chargé d'affaires, 1836.

James C. Pickett, of Virginia, chargé d'affaires, 1838.

Albert G. Jewett, of Maine, chargé d'affaires, 1845.

To Venezuela.

J. G. A. Williamson, of North Carolina, chargé d'affaires, 1835.

Allen A. Hall, of Tennessee, chargé d'affaires, 1841.

Benjamin G. Shields, of Alabama, chargé d'affaires, 1845.

To New Grenada.

Robert B. M'Afee, of Kentucky, chargé d'affaires, 1832.

James Semple, of Illinois, chargé d'affaires, 1837.

William M. Blackford, of Virginia, chargé d'affaires, 1842.

Benjamin A. Bidlack, of Pennsylvania, chargé d'affaires, 1845.

Assembly of American nations, proposed to be held at Panama.

Richard C. Anderson, of Virginia, and John Sergeant, of Pennsylvania, envoys extraordinary and ministers plenipotentiary, March 14, 1826.

Joel R. Poinsett, of South Carolina, envoy extraordinary and minister plenipotentiary, February 12, 1827.

To Texas.

Alcee Labranche, of Louisiana, chargé d'affaires, 1837.
George H. Flood, of Ohio, chargé d'affaires, 1840.
Joseph Eve, of Kentucky, chargé d'affaires, 1841.
William S. Murphy, of Ohio, chargé d'affaires, 1843.
Andrew J. Donelson, of Tennessee, chargé d'affaires, 1845.

To China.

Caleb Cushing, of Massachusetts, commissioner, 1843.
Alexander H. Everett, of Massachusetts, commissioner, 1845.

To Sandwich Islands.

George Brown, of Massachusetts, commissioner, 1843.
Anthony Ten Eyck, of Michigan, commissioner, 1845.

The pay of ministers plenipotentiary is $9,000 per annum, salary, beside $9,000 for an outfit. Secretaries of legation receive $2,000, and chargé d'affaires, $4,500 per annum. To entitle any chargé d'affaires, or secretary of any legation or embassy to any foreign country, or secretary of any minister plenipotentiary, to the above compensation, they must respectively be appointed by the president of the United States, by and with the advice and consent of the senate; but in the recess of the senate, the president is authorized to make such appointments, which must be submitted to the senate at the next session thereafter, for their advice and consent; and no compensation is allowed to any chargé d'affaires, or any secretary of legation, embassy, or minister, who shall not be so appointed.

Consuls of the United States, generally so called, are, in effect, agents for commerce and seamen; which latter denomination, for particular reasons, is given to some of this class of public officers. They receive no yearly salaries (except at Paris and London, Tangier, Tunis, and Tripoli, where they have an annual salary of $2,000), and their compensation is derived from the fees which are allowed by law. The amount of these fees depends, of course, upon the state of foreign trade, which is perpetually fluctuating. Consuls of the United States, for commercial purposes, are regularly admitted and recognised, as to their official functions, in the ports of Christian Europe; but in the colonies of the European nations, agents for commerce and seamen mostly exercise the duties of their station under courtesy, without any formal recognition; and, in some instances, from the jealousy of colonial policy, they have not been permitted to exercise them at all. In their public capacity, consuls and agents for commerce and seamen are principally occupied in verifying, in different forms, the legality of the trade of the United States with foreign nations, and in relieving and sending home American seamen, who, by accident or misfortune, are left destitute within the jurisdiction of their several consulates and agencies.

The compensation of the following public officers of the United States is at present fixed by law at the amounts stated :—

President of the United states, $25,000 per annum; vice-president, $5,000 per annum; secretaries of state, treasury, navy, and war, each, $6,000 per annum; postmaster-general, $6,000 per annum; attorney-general, $4,000 per annum; chief justice of the supreme court, $5,000 per annum; associate justices, $4,500 per annum.

From the first Congress, in 1789, inclusive, until March 4, 1795, senators and representatives received each $6 per diem, and $6 for every twenty miles travel. From March 4, 1795, to March 4, 1796, senators received $7, and representatives $6 per diem. From March 4, 1796, until December 4, 1815, the per diem was $6, and the mileage $6, to senators and representatives. From December 4, 1815, until March 4, 1817, each senator and representative received $1,500 per annum, with a proportional deduction for absence, from any cause but sickness. The president of the senate pro tempore, and speaker of the house, $3,000 per annum, each. From March 4, 1817, the compensation to members of both houses has been $8 per diem, and $8 for every twenty miles travel; and to the president of the senate pro tempore, and speaker of the house, $16 per diem.

MINISTERS, &c., TO FOREIGN COUNTRIES, FROM 1845 TO 1849.

MINISTERS PLENIPOTENTIARY.

Great Britain.—George Bancroft, of Massachusetts, 1846.
France.—Richard Rush, of Pennsylvania, 1847.
Prussia.—Edward A. Hannegan, of Indiana, 1849.
Russia.—Ralph J. Ingersoll, of Connecticut, 1846,
   "   Arthur P. Bagby, of Alabama, 1848.
Brazil.—David Tod, of Ohio, 1847.
Empire of Germany.—Andrew J. Donelson, of Tennessee, 1848.

CHARGE D'AFFAIRES.

Denmark.—R. P. Flenihen, of Pennsylvania, 1847.
Two Sicilies.—John Rowan, of Kentucky, 1848.
Sardinia.—Nathaniel Niles, of Vermont, 1848.
Portugal.—George W. Hopkins, of Virginia, 1847.
Central America.—Elijah Hise, of Kentucky, 1848.
Rome.—J. L. Martin, of Pennsylvania, 1848.
   "   Lewis Cass, jr., of Michigan, 1849.
Mexico.—Nathan Clifford, of Maine, 1848.
Argentine Republic (Buenos Ayres).—William A. Harris, of Virginia, 1846.
Chili.—Seth Barton, of Louisiana, 1847.
Peru.—John Randolph Clay, of Pennsylvania, 1847.
Bolivia.—John Appleton, of Maine, 1848.
Ecuador.—Vanbrugh Livingston, of New York, 1848.

COMMISSIONERS.

China.—John W. Davis, of Indiana, 1848.
Mexico.—Nicholas P. Trist, of Virginia, 1847.

ASSOCIATE JUSTICE OF THE SUPREME COURT.

Robert C. Grier, of Pennsylvania, appointed 1846.

SUMMARY OF THE CENSUS OF THE UNITED STATES,
JUNE 1, 1840.

Free or Non-Slaveholding States.

States and Territories.	Whites.	Free Colored.	Slaves.	Total.
Maine	500,438	1,355		501,793
New Hampshire	284,036	537	1	284,574
Vermont	291,218	730		291,948
Massachusetts	729,030	8,668		737,698
Rhode Island	105,587	3,238	5	108,830
Connecticut	301,856	8,105	17	309,978
Total, New England	2,212,165	22,633	23	2,234,821
New York	2,378,890	50,027	4	2,428,921
New Jersey	351,588	21,044	674	373,306
Pennsylvania	1,676,115	47,854	64	1,724,033
Ohio	1,502,122	17,342	3	1,519,467
Indiana	678,698	7,165	3	685,866
Illinois	472,254	3,598	331	476,183
Michigan	211,560	707		212,267
Wisconsin	30,749	185	11	43,112
Iowa	42,924	172	16	30,945
Total, Free States	9,557,065	170,727	1,129	9,728,921

Slaveholding States.

States and Territories.	Whites.	Free Colored.	Slaves.	Total.
Delaware	58,561	16,919	2,605	78,085
Maryland	318,204	62,078	89,737	470,019
District of Columbia	30,657	8,361	4,694	43,712
Virginia	740,968	49,842	448,987	1,239,797
North Carolina	484,870	22,732	245,817	753,419
South Carolina	259,084	8,276	327,038	594,398
Georgia	407,695	2,753	280,944	691,392
Florida	27,943	817	25,717	54,477
Alabama	335,185	2,039	253,532	590,756
Mississippi	179,074	1,369	195,211	375,654
Louisiana	158,457	25,502	168,451	352,411
Arkansas	77,174	465	19,935	97,574
Tennessee	640,627	5,524	183,059	829,210
Kentucky	590,253	7,317	182,258	779,828
Missouri	323,888	1,574	58,240	383,702
Total, Slave States	4,632,640	215,568	2,486,226	7,334,434
Total, United States	14,189,705	386,295	2,487,355	17,063,355

PROGRESS OF POPULATION IN THE UNITED STATES FOR FIFTY YEARS, FROM 1790 TO 1840.

First Census, August 1, 1790.

	Whites.	Free Colored.	Slaves.	Total.
Free States	1,900,772	26,831	40,850	1,968,453
Slave States	1,271,692	32,635	645,047	1,961,374
Total	3,172,464	59,446	697,897	3,929,827

Second Census, August 1, 1800.

	Whites.	Free Colored.	Slaves.	Total.
Free States	2,601,509	47,154	35,946	2,684,609
Slave States	1,702,980	61,241	857,095	2,621,316
Total	4,304,489	108,395	893,041	5,305,925

Third Census, August 1, 1810.

	Whites.	Free Colored.	Slaves.	Total.
Free States	3,653,219	78,181	27,510	3,758,910
Slave States	2,208,785	108,265	1,163,854	3,480,904
Total	5,862,004	186,446	1,191,364	7,239,814

Fourth Census, August 1, 1820.

	Whites.	Free Colored.	Slaves.	Total.
Free States	5,030,371	102,893	19,108	5,152,372
Slave States	2,842,340	135,434	1,524,580	4,502,224
Total	7,872,711	238,197	1,543,688	9,654,596

Fifth Census, June 1, 1830.

	Whites.	Free Colored.	Slaves.	Total.
Free States	6,876,620	137,529	3,568	7,017,717
Slave States	3,660,758	182,070	2,005,475	5,848,303
Total	10,537,378	319,599	2,009,043	12,866,020

Sixth Census, June 1, 1840.

	Whites.	Free Colored.	Slaves.	Total.
Free States	9,557,065	170,727	1,129	9,728,921
Slave States	4,632,640	215,568	2,486,226	7,334,434
Total	14,189,705	386,295	2,487,355	17,063,355

OCCUPATIONS OF THE PEOPLE, BY THE CENSUS OF 1840.

Number of Persons employed in	Agriculture.	Manufactures.	Commerce.
New England States	414,138	187,258	17,157
Middle States	808,633	333,947	50,077
Southern States	955,729	87,955	12,962
Southwestern States	650,546	37,899	14,496
Northwestern States	890,905	144,690	22,315
Total, 1840	3,719,951	791,749	117,607
Total, 1820	2,070,646	349,506	72,493

Other Occupations, by the Census of 1840.

Number of Persons employed in Mining in the United States	15,211
"　　　"　　　"　　　Navigation of the Ocean	56,021
"　　　"　　　"　　　Internal Navigation	33,076
"　　　"　　　"　　　Learned Professions, including Engineers	65,235

SYNOPSIS OF THE CONSTITUTIONS OF THE SEVERAL UNITED STATES.

ADOPTION OF THE FIRST STATE CONSTITUTIONS.

THE continental Congress, on the 10th of May, 1776, recommended to the assemblies and conventions of the several colonies where no governments sufficient to the exigencies of their affairs had been established, to adopt such systems as, in the opinion of the representatives of the people, would best conduce to the happiness and safety of their constituents in particular, and British America in general.

The difficulties in forming state governments or constitutions, were much less than in forming a system embracing all the states. The people had long been familiar with the civil institutions of their respective states, and could, with comparative ease, make such alterations as would suit their new political situation. The people of Connecticut and Rhode Island had, from their first settlement, chosen all their rulers, and in these states, a change of forms was only requisite.

Massachusetts, after the alteration of her charter by parliament, continued her old system as far as practicable, agreeably to the advice of Congress, until she was able and had leisure to form a new and more permanent one. From the peculiar situation of New Hampshire, Virginia, and South Carolina, Congress in November, 1775, recommended to them, if they judged it necessary for their peace and security, to establish governments, to continue during the disputes with Great Britain. In pursuance of these recommendations, the states of New Hampshire, South Carolina, Virginia, and New Jersey, established new systems of government before the declaration of independence. They were followed by four other states, during the year 1776, and with the exception of that of Virginia, these state systems of government were expressly limited in their duration to the continuance of the dispute between the colonies and Great Britain. In all the constitutions thus formed, except that of Pennsylvania, the legislative power was vested in two branches.*

Vermont did not become a member of the Union until 1791. That state was originally settled under grants from New Hampshire, and principally by the hardy yeomanry of New England, who became acquainted with the country in the war of 1756. It was a long time known by the name of "the New Hampshire grants," and its inhabitants were called "the green-mountain boys." It was claimed by New York, under the old

* Pitkin's History of the United States.

grant to the duke of York ; and in 1764, on an *exparte* application to the king and council, the country, as far east as Connecticut river, was placed under the jurisdiction of that province. This was done without the knowledge and contrary to the wishes of the inhabitants, who at the revolution declared themselves independent, and in 1777 established a temporary government. They afterward requested to be admitted a member of the confederacy, but were opposed by New Hampshire and New York, and Congress were unwilling to offend those states. A frame of state government was established July 4, 1786, and in 1790 New York was induced, by the payment of $30,000 to withdraw its claims, and in 1791 Vermont was admitted into the Union.

The following are the dates when the first constitutions of the old states were adopted :—

New Hampshire, January 5......1776	Delaware, September...........1776
South Carolina, March 24.......1776	North Carolina, December.......1776
Virginia, June 29...............1776	New York, April...............1777
New Jersey, July 2.............1776	Massachusetts, March..........1780
Maryland, August 14...........1776	Vermont, July 4...............1786
Pennsylvania, September........1776	Georgia, May.................1789

A synopsis or outline of the principal features of the Constitutions of each of the United States.

MAINE.

THE constitution of this state was formed in 1819, and went into operation in 1820.

The legislative power is vested in a senate and a house of representatives, both elected annually by the people, on the second Monday of September. These two bodies are together styled *the Legislature of Maine.*

The number of representatives can not be less than 100, nor more than 200. A town having 1,500 inhabitants is entitled to send one representative ; having 3,750, two ; 6,775, three : 10,500, four ; 15,000, five ; 20,250, six ; 26,250, seven ; but no town can ever be entitled to more than seven representatives. The number of senators can not be less than twenty, nor more than thirty-one.

The legislature meets (at Augusta) annually, in the month of May ; it formerly met in January.

The executive power is vested in a governor, who is elected annually by the people, on the second Monday in September, and his term of office commences on the first Wednesday in January. A council of seven members is elected annually, by joint ballot of the senators and representatives, to advise the governor in the executive part of government.

The right of suffrage is granted to every male citizen aged twenty-one years' or upward (excepting paupers, persons under guardianship, and Indians not taxed), having had his residence established in the state for the term of three months next preceding an election.

The judicial power is vested in a supreme judicial court, and such other courts as the legislature may, from time to time, establish. All the judges are appointed by the governor, with the advice and consent of the council ; and they hold their offices during good behavior, but not beyond the age of seventy years.

NEW HAMPSHIRE.

A constitution was established in 1784; and in 1792, this constitution was altered and amended by a convention of delegates held at Concord, and is now in force.

The legislative power is vested in a senate and house of representatives, which, together, are styled *the General Court of New Hampshire.*

Every town, or incorporated township, having 150 ratable polls, may send one representative; and for every 300 additional polls, it is entitled to an additional representative.

The senate consists of twelve members, who are chosen by the people in districts.

The executive power is vested in a governor and a council, which consists of five members.

The governor, council, senators, and representatives, are all elected annually, by the people, on the second Tuesday in March, and their term of service commences on the first Wednesday in June.

The general court meets annually (at Concord) on the first Wednesday in June.

The right of suffrage is granted to every male inhabitant of twenty-one years of age, excepting paupers, and persons excused from paying taxes at their own request.

The judiciary power is vested in a superior court, and a court of common pleas. The judges are appointed by the governor and council, and hold their offices during good behavior, but not beyond the age of seventy years.

VERMONT.

The first constitution of this state was formed in 1777, and revised in 1786; the one now in operation was adopted on the 4th of July, 1793, and an amendment establishing a senate was adopted in January, 1836.

The legislative power is now vested in a senate and house of representatives, elected by the people annually, on the first Tuesday in September.

The senate consists of thirty members; each county being entitled to at least one, and the remainder to be apportioned according to population; and the house of representatives is composed of one member from each town. The senators must be thirty years of age, and the lieutenant-governor is *ex-officio* president of the senate.

The legislature is styled *the General Assembly of the State of Vermont,* and meets annually, on the second Thursday of October, at *Montpelier.*

The executive power is vested in a governor, or, in his absence, a lieutenant-governor, both elected annually by the people, on the first Tuesday in September, and their term of office expires on the second Thursday in October.

The judiciary powers are vested in a supreme court, consisting of five judges, chosen every year by the legislature; in a county court, consisting of three judges, chosen in the same manner (one of the judges of the supreme court being chief-justice), who hold courts twice a year, in their respective counties, and in justices of the peace, appointed in the same manner.

The constitution grants the right of suffrage to every man, of the full age of twenty-one years, who has resided in the state for the space of one whole year, next before the election of representatives, and is of quiet and peaceable behavior.

A council of censors, consisting of thirteen persons, are chosen every seven years (first elected in 1799), on the last Wednesday in March, and meet on the first Wednesday in June. Their duty is to inquire whether the constitution has been preserved inviolate; whether the legislative and executive branches of government have performed their duty as guardians of the people; whether the public taxes have been justly laid and collected; in what manner the public moneys have been disposed of; and whether the laws have been duly executed.

MASSACHUSETTS.

The constitution of this state was formed in 1780, and amended, by a state convention and the people, in 1821. Several amendments have since been recommended by the legislature, and adopted by the people.

The legislative power is vested in a senate and house of representatives, which together are styled *the General Court of Massachusetts*.

The senate consists of forty members, who are chosen annually by the people, by districts, or counties, according to population.

The house of representatives consists of members chosen annually by the cities and towns, according to population, every town having 300 ratable polls electing one representative, and for every 450 more, one additional representative. Any town having less than 300 polls, to be represented as many years within ten years, as 300 is contained in the product of the number of polls in said town, multiplied by ten. When there is a surplus of polls over a sufficiency for one or more representatives, multiply the surplus by ten, and divide by 450, and the quotient will show how many years of the decennial period the town shall be allowed an additional representative.

The supreme executive magistrate is styled the *Governor of the Commonwealth of Massachusetts*, and has the title of "*His Excellency.*" The governor is elected annually by the people, and at the same time a lieutenant-governor is chosen, who has the title of "*His Honor.*" The governor is assisted in the executive department, particularly in appointments to office, by a council of nine members, who are chosen by the joint ballot of the senators and representatives, from the senators; and in case the persons elected councillors decline the appointment, others are chosen by the legislature from the people at large.

The annual election is held on the second Monday in November, and the general court meets at *Boston*, on the first Wednesday of January.

The right of suffrage is granted to every male citizen twenty-one years of age and upward (excepting paupers and persons under guardianship), who has resided within the commonwealth one year, and within the town or district in which he may claim a right to vote, six calendar months next preceding any election, and who has paid a state or county tax, assessed upon him within two years next preceding such election; and also every citizen who may be by law exempted from taxation, and who may be in all other respects qualified as abovementioned.

The judiciary is vested in a supreme court, a court of common pleas, and such other courts as the legislature may establish. The judges are appointed by the governor, by and with the advice and consent of the council, and hold their offices during good behavior.

RHODE ISLAND.

The charter granted to the colony of Rhode Island, by King Charles II., in 1663, formed the basis of the state government, until the present constitution was framed, which was adopted in November, 1842, and went into effect on the first Tuesday of May, 1843.

By this constitution the legislative power is vested in a senate and house of representatives, who are together styled *the General Assembly of the State of Rhode Island and Providence Plantations.*

The senate consists of the governor, lieutenant-governor, and one senator from each of the thirty-one towns in the state.

The house of representatives consists of sixty-nine members, apportioned among the towns according to population. Each town is to have at least one, and no town more than twelve representatives.

The executive power is vested in a governor, being, with the lieutenant-governor, senators, and representatives, elected annually by the people, on the first Wednesday of April, for the year commencing the first Tuesday of May, when the general assembly meets at *Newport;* and adjourned sessions are held alternately at *Providence, East Greenwich,* and *Bristol.* The judges and other public officers, except those chosen by the people, are appointed annually by the general assembly.

The judicial powers are vested in a supreme court, consisting of a chief-justice and three associate justices, who hold their offices until they are removed by a resolution passed by both houses of the assembly, and in a court of common pleas for each county, consisting of a justice of the supreme court, and two associate justices.

The right of suffrage is vested in all male *native* citizens of the United States, who have resided in the state two years, and in the town where they propose to vote, six months; who have been registered in the town clerk's office at least seven days before the election; have paid within one year a tax of one dollar, or have done military duty within the preceding year; likewise, in all male citizens (naturalized foreigners) of the United States, who in addition to the preceding qualifications, possess real estate in the town or city, worth $134 over all incumbrances, or which rents for $7 per annum.

CONNECTICUT.

The charter granted in 1662 by Charles II., formed the basis of the government of Connecticut till 1818, when the present constitution was framed.

The legislative power is vested in a senate and house of representatives, which together are styled *the General Assembly.*

The members of the house of representatives are chosen by the different towns in the state; the more ancient towns, the majority of the whole number, send each two representatives; the rest only one each. The present number is 220.

The senate must consist of not less than eighteen, nor more than twenty-four members, who are chosen by districts. The present number is twenty-one.

The executive power is vested in a governor. A lieutenant-governor is also chosen, who is president of the senate, and on whom the duties of the governor devolve, in case of his death, resignation, or absence.

The representatives, senators, governor, and lieutenant-governor, are all elected annually by the people, on the first Monday in April.

The general assembly has one stated session every year, on the first Wednesday in May, alternately at *Hartford* and at *New Haven.*

Every white male citizen of the United States, who shall have gained a settlement in this state, attained the age of twenty-one years, and resided in the town in which he may offer himself to be admitted to the privilege of an elector, at least six months preceding, and have a freehold estate of the yearly value of seven dollars, in this state; or having been enrolled in the militia, shall have performed military duty therein for the term of one year next preceding the time he shall offer himself for admission, or being liable thereto, shall have been, by authority of law, excused therefrom; or shall have paid a state tax within the year next preceding the time he shall present himself for such admission, and shall sustain a good moral character; shall, on the taking such an oath as may be prescribed by law, be an elector.

The judicial power is vested in a supreme court of errors, a superior court, and such inferior courts as the general assembly may, from time to time, establish. The judges are appointed by the general assembly; and those of the supreme and superior courts hold their offices during good behavior, but not beyond the age of seventy years.

No person is compelled to join, support, or to be classed with, or associated to, any congregation, church, or religious association. But every person may be compelled to pay his proportion of the expenses of the society to which he may belong; he may, however, separate himself from the society by leaving a written notice of his wish with the clerk of such society.

NEW YORK.

THE present constitution of the state of New York, was formed in 1846.

Every male citizen, twenty-one years of age, ten days a citizen, one year next preceding any election an inhabitant of the state, for the last four months a resident of the county where he may offer his vote, and for thirty days next preceding the election, a resident of the district of his candidate, may vote in the election district of which he shall at the time be a resident, and not elsewhere. No man of color shall vote unless he shall have been for three years a resident of the state, and, for one year next preceding the election, shall have owned a freehold worth two hundred and fifty dollars above all incumbrances, and shall have paid a tax thereon. And no person of color shall be taxed unless he shall own such real estate. Persons convicted of any infamous crime, and those who have made, or become directly or indirectly interested in any bet upon an election. may by a law be deprived of their vote therein.

The state shall be divided into thirty-two districts, each of which shall choose one senator to serve for two years. A census of the state shall be taken in 1855, and in every ten years afterward. The legislature, at the next session after such census, shall reorganize the districts on the basis of population, excluding aliens and persons of color not taxed; and the districts shall remain unaltered until the next census. Members of the assembly, one hundred and twenty-eight in number, and apportioned among the several counties according to the population, excluding aliens and persons of color not taxed, shall be elected annually and by single districts. Each county, except Hamilton, shall have at least one member of the assembly; and no new county shall be made unless its population entitle it to a member. The pay of the senators and representatives shall not be more than three dollars a day, with one dollar for every ten miles of travel, nor exceed in the whole three dollars per diem allowance. In extra sessions it shall be three dollars a day. The speaker shall receive one third additional to his per-diem allowance. No member of the legislature shall, during his term, be appointed to any office ; and no one holding office under the United States, and no member of Congress shall belong to the legislature. The election shall be on the Tuesday succeeding the first Monday in November ; and the legislature shall assemble on the first Tuesday of the following January. The assembly may *impeach* by a majority vote of all the members elected.

The governor and lieutenant-governor, chosen by a plurality of votes, shall hold office for two years. In case two persons have an equal and the highest vote, the legislature, at its next session, by joint ballot shall decide between them. They must be thirty years old, citizens of the United States, and have been, for five years next preceding their election, residents in the state. The governor may veto a bill ; but two thirds of both houses may pass it again, notwithstanding his veto. The lieutenant-governor shall be president of the senate, with only a casting vote ; and if the office of governor be vacant, he, and, after him, the president of the senate, shall act as governor. The secretary of state, comptroller, treasurer, attorney-general, state-engineer, and surveyor, shall be chosen at a general election, and hold office for two years. The treasurer may be suspended from office by the governor, during the recess of the legislature, and until thirty days after the beginning of the next session. At the first election, three canal commissioners, and three inspectors of prisons shall be chosen, to hold office one, two, and three years, respectively, as shall be determined by lot ; and afterward one shall be elected annually to hold office for three years. The inspectors shall have charge of the stateprisons, and shall appoint all officers therein.

The court of appeals shall consist of eight judges, four to be elected by the people of the state, to serve eight years, and four selected from the justices of the supreme court, having the shortest time to serve. The judges shall be so classified that every two years one shall leave office, and a new judge be elected to serve eight years. The state shall be divided into eight judicial districts, of which New York city shall be one ; where the number of judges is to be fixed by law. The other districts shall each elect four justices of the supreme court to serve eight years. The justices shall have general jurisdiction in law and equity, and shall be so classified that every two years one in each district shall go out of office. Each county, except the city and county of New York, shall elect one county judge for four years, who shall act as surrogate and hold the county court. Counties of more than forty thousand inhabitants may elect a separate surrogate. Towns may elect justices of the peace to serve four years. Cities may have inferior local courts of civil and criminal jurisdiction. Tribunals of conciliation may be established whose judgment shall be binding only upon parties who voluntarily submit their matters in dispute, and agree to abide the result. A clerk of the court of appeals, to be *ex-officio* clerk of the supreme court, shall be chosen by the people for three years. Sheriffs, county-clerks, coroners, and district attorneys, shall be chosen by counties once in three years, and as often as vacancies happen Sheriffs shall hold no other office, and be ineligible for the next three years after the termination of their office.

From June 1, 1846, there shall be paid each year out of the net revenue of the state canals, one million, three hundred thousand dollars, until June 1, 1855 ; and from that time one million, seven hundred thousand dollars a year, as a sinking fund for the payment of the canal debt of the

state. Afterward, from the remaining revenues of the canals, there shall be
paid from June 1, 1846, until the canal debt is extinguished, three hundred and fifty thousand dollars a year ; and afterward, one million, five
hundred thousand dollars a year, for the redemption of the general fund
and all contingent debts. Of the balance of the canal revenues, a sum not
above two hundred thousand dollars a year (which may, if necessary, after
eight years be increased to three hundred and fifty thousand dollars per
annum, and which, after the above debts are paid, and certain now unfinished canals completed, may be still further increased to six hundred and
seventy-two thousand, five hundred dollars a year), shall be devoted to pay
the necessary expenses of the state ; and the balance shall be expended
to complete the still unfinished canals. The principal and income of these
sinking funds shall be sacredly applied to the purposes for which they
were created ; and, if either proves insufficient, its revenues shall be sufficiently increased by taxes to preserve perfectly the public faith. The
state canals shall never be sold, leased, or otherwise disposed of.

The state shall never give its credit to any individual or corporation ;
nor shall it ever contract a debt, except to meet casual deficits in the revenue, or to suppress insurrection, or for defence in war, unless such debt
be authorized for some single work by a law which shall provide by a direct annual tax, to be irrepealable until the debt is extinguished, for the
payment of the interest annually, and of the principal within eighteen
years, and which shall be passed by yeas and nays, and be submitted to
the people, and receive a majority of all the votes at a general election,
to be held not less than three months after its passage, and at which no
other law or any amendment to the constitution is voted for ; and, on its
final passage by the legislature, the question shall be taken by yeas and
nays, and three fifths of all the members elected shall form a quorum. All
moneys arising from such loan shall be applied only to the objects of the
loan. No payment shall be made out of the funds of the state, unless by
a law distinctly specifying the sum and object of the appropriation. Public moneys or property can not be appropriated for local or private purposes, except by a two thirds vote of the members elected to each branch
of the legislature.

Corporations, with the individual liability of the corporators, may be
formed under general laws which may be altered or repealed. They shall
not be created by special act, except for municipal purposes, and when
the objects of the corporation can not be gained under general laws. No
special charter shall be granted for banking purposes ; and after January
1, 1850, stockholders in banks shall be individually liable, to the amount
of their stock, for debts incurred after that date. If a bank is insolvent,
the bill-holders shall be preferred creditors.

The capital of the common school and literary funds shall be preserved
inviolate, and its revenue applied to the support of common schools and
academies. All persons, from scruples of conscience, averse to bearing
arms, shall be excused therefrom upon such conditions as may be pro-
scribed by law. No one shall be incompetent as a witness on account
of his opinions upon religion. In all libel cases the truth may be given
in evidence, and the jury shall have the right to decide the law and the
fact. All feudal tenures, with all their incidents, are abolished ; except
such rents and services certain as have been lawfully created or reserved.
No lease or grant of agricultural land for more than twelve years, hereafter made, in which any rent or service is reserved, shall be valid.

Amendments to the constitution must be agreed to by a majority vote of the members elected to each of the two houses ; be entered on their journals with the yeas and nays ; be referred to the legislature to be chosen at the next general election of senators, and published three months previous to such election ; be passed by a majority of all the members elected to this legislature ; be then submitted to the people, and if a majority approve the amendments, they shall become a part of the constitution. In 1866, and every twentieth year thereafter, and at such times as the legislature may provide, the question of a revision of the constitution shall be submitted to the people ; and, if a majority decide in favor of a convention, the legislature at its next session shall provide for the election of delegates thereto.

NEW JERSEY.

THE original constitution of New Jersey was formed in 1776, and no revision of it took place until the adoption of the present constitution, in 1844, except that the legislature undertook to explain its provisions in particular parts.

In May, 1844, a convention of delegates, chosen by the people, assembled at Trenton. and prepared the draught of a new constitution, which was submitted to the people on the 13th of August, was adopted by a large majority, and went into operation on the 2d of September, 1844.

The legislative power is vested in a senate and general assembly, who are styled *the Senate and General Assembly of the State of New Jersey*, under which title laws are enacted.

The senate consists of one senator from each county, elected by the people for three years, one third going out each year. Their present number is nineteen.

The general assembly consists of not more than sixty, chosen annually by the people of each county, by apportionment according to the number of inhabitants.

The members of the senate and of the general assembly are elected on the second Tuesday of October, and meet at *Trenton* on the second Tuesday in the next January, when the legislative year commences.

Charters for banks and money corporations require the assent of three fifths of the members elected to each house, and are limited to twenty years.

The executive power is vested in a governor, elected by the people once in three years, at the general election. He has the power of nominating and appointing to office, with the advice and consent of the senate, the chancellor, justices of the supreme court, judges of the court of errors and appeals, and all other officers not otherwise provided for by law.

The judicial power is vested in a court of errors and appeals, composed of the chancellor, the judges of the supreme court, and six other judges ; a court for the trial of impeachments ; a court of chancery ; a supreme court, of five judges ; and courts of common pleas. The chancellor and judges of the supreme court hold their offices for seven years ; the six judges of the court of errors and appeals, for six years, one judge vacating his seat each year in rotation.

The right of suffrage is exercised by every white male citizen of the United States, who has resided in the state one year, and in the county where he votes five months (paupers, idiots, insane persons, and criminals excepted).

22

PENNSYLVANIA.

The first constitution of Pennsylvania was adopted in 1776; a second one in 1790; and the present amended constitution was adopted in 1838.

The legislative power is vested in a general assembly, consisting of a senate and house of representatives.

The senators are chosen for three years, one third being elected annually, by the people, by districts. Their number can not be greater than one third, nor less than one fourth of the number of representatives. The present number is thirty-three.

The representatives are chosen annually on the second Tuesday of October, by the citizens of Philadelphia, and each county respectively, apportioned according to the number of taxable inhabitants. The number can not be less than sixty nor more than one hundred; which latter is the present number chosen.

The general assembly meets annually at *Harrisburg*, on the first Tuesday of January, unless sooner convened by the governor.

The supreme executive power is vested in a governor, who is chosen on the 2d Tuesday in October, and who holds his office during three years from the third Tuesday of January next after his election; and he can not hold it longer than six years in any term of nine years.

The judicial power is vested in a supreme court, in courts of oyer and terminer, and general jail delivery, in a court of common pleas, orphans' court, register's court, and court of quarter sessions of the peace for each county, in justices of the peace, and in such other courts as the legislature may from time to time establish.

The judges of the supreme court, court of common pleas, and other courts of record, are appointed by the governor, with the consent of the senate—the judges of the supreme court for fifteen years; the president judges of the court of common pleas, and other courts of record, for ten years; and the associate judges of the courts of common pleas, for five years.

The right of suffrage is exercised by every white freeman of the age of twenty-two years, having resided in the state one year, and in the election district where he offers his vote ten days immediately preceding such election, and within two years paid a state or county tax, which shall have been assessed at least ten days before the election. White freemen, citizens of the United States, between the ages of twenty-one and twenty-two years, having resided in the state one year, may vote without paying taxes.

DELAWARE.

The constitution was formed in 1792, and amended in 1831.

The legislature is styled *the General Assembly*, and consists of a senate and house of representatives.

The senators are nine in number, namely, three from each county, and are elected for a term for four years.

The representatives are elected for a term of two years, and are twenty-one in number, seven from each county.

The general assembly meets at *Dover*, biennially, on the first Tuesday in January, unless sooner convened by the governor.

The general election is held biennially, on the second Tuesday in November.

The executive power is vested in a governor, who is elected by the people for a term of four years, and is not eligible for a second term.

The judicial power is vested in a court of errors and appeals, a superior court, a court of chancery, an orphans' court, a court of oyer and terminer, a court of general sessions of the peace and jail delivery, a register's court, justices of the peace, and such other courts as the general assembly may, by a vote of two thirds of each house, establish.

The right of suffrage is granted to every white male citizen of the age of twenty-two years, or upward, having resided in the state one year next before the election, and the last month in the county where he votes ; and having within two years paid a county tax. Also, to every white male citizen over twenty-one, and under twenty-two years of age, having resided as aforesaid, without payment of any tax.

MARYLAND.

The constitution of this state was first formed in 1776, since which time many amendments have been made by the legislature, which has the power, if amendments are passed by one legislature and confirmed by the next in succession.

By the constitution as it stands at present, the legislative power is vested in a senate consisting of twenty-one members, and a house of representatives of seventy-nine members, and these two branches united are styled *the General Assembly of Maryland.*

The senators are elected by the people, one from each county, and one from the city of Baltimore, and hold their seats for six years, one third being chosen biennialy.

The members of the house of delegates are elected annually by the people ; the city of Baltimore to send six delegates ; counties having more than 35,000 inhabitants, six delegates ; less than 35,000 and more than 25,000, five delegates ; less than 25,000 and more than 15,000, four delegates ; less than 15,000, three delegates.

The executive power is vested in a governor, who is chosen by the people, and holds his office for three years from the first Monday of January, but is ineligible for the next succeeding term. The state is divided into three districts, and the governor is taken from each of the districts, alternately. The governor nominates, and with the consent of the senate, appoints all officers whose offices are created by law.

The annual election is held on the first Wednesday in October, and the general assembly meets at *Annapolis*, on the last Monday in December.

The judicial power is vested in a court of chancery, a court of appeals of six judges, county courts, and orphans' courts. The state is divided into six judicial districts, and for each district there are a chief judge and two associates, who constitute the county courts for the respective counties in the district. The six chief judges constitute the court of appeals for the state. The chancellor and judges hold their offices during good behavior.

The constitution grants the right of suffrage to every free, white male citizen, above twenty-one years of age, having resided twelve months in the state, and six months in the county, or in the city of Annapolis or Baltimore, next preceding the election at which he offers to vote.

VIRGINIA.

The old constitution of this state was formed in 1776, and continued in operation until 1830, when the present amended constitution was formed by a convention, and accepted by the people.

By this constitution the legislative power is vested in a senate and a house of delegates, which are together styled *the General Assembly of Virginia.*

The house of delegates consists of 134 members, chosen annually; thirty-one from the twenty-six counties west of the Allegany mountains; twenty-five from the fourteen counties between the Allegany mountains and Blue Ridge, forty-two from the twenty-nine counties east of the Blue Ridge, and above tide-water, and thirty-six from the counties, cities, towns and boroughs, lying upon tide-water.

The senate consists of thirty-two members : thirteen from the counties west of the Blue Ridge. and nineteen from the counties, cities, towns, and boroughs, east thereof. The senators are elected for four years; and the seats of one fourth of them are vacated every year. In all elections to any office or place of trust, honor, or profit, the votes are given openly, or *viva voce*, and not by ballot.

A reapportionment for representation in both houses, is to take place every ten years, commencing in 1841, until which time there is to be no change in the number of delegates and senators from the several divisions, and after 1841, the number of delegates is never to exceed 150, nor that of the senators 36.

The time of election of delegates is fixed by the general assembly, and at present takes place in April.

The general assembly meets annually at *Richmond*, on the first Monday in December.

The executive power is vested in a governor, elected by the joint vote of the two houses of the general assembly. He holds his office three years, commencing on the first of January next succeeding his election, or on such other days as may be from time to time prescribed by law; and he is ineligible for the three years next after the expiration of his term of office.

There is a council of state, consisting of three members, elected for three years by the joint vote of the two houses, the seat of one being vacated annually. The senior councillor is lieutenant-governor.

The judges of the supreme court of appeals and of the superior courts, are elected by a joint vote of both houses of the general assembly, and hold their offices during good behavior, or until removed by a concurrent vote of both houses; but two thirds of the members present must concur in such vote, and the cause of removal be entered on the journals of each house.

The right of suffrage is extended to every white male citizen of the commonwealth, resident therein, aged twenty-one years and upward, who is qualified to exercise the right of suffrage according to the former constitution and laws; or who owns a freehold of the value of twenty-five dollars; or who has a joint interest to the amount of twenty-five dollars, in a freehold; or who has a life estate in, or reversionary title to, land of the value of fifty dollars, having been so possessed for six months; or who shall own and be in the actual occupation of a leasehold estate, having the title recorded two months before he shall offer to vote—of a term originally not less than five years, and of the annual value or rent of two hundred dollars; or who for twelve months before offering to vote, has been a housekeeper and head of a family, and shall have been assessed with a part of the revenue of the commonwealth, within the preceding year, and actually paid the same.

NORTH CAROLINA.

The constitution of North Carolina was originally framed and adopted in December, 1776, and certain amendments agreed upon by a convention in 1835, and ratified by the people, went into operation on the first of January, 1836.

The legislative power is vested in a body styled *the General Assembly*, consisting of a senate and house of commons, both elected biennially by the people.

The senate consists of fifty members, elected by districts, laid off and apportioned according to the amount of taxes paid by the citizens into the treasury of the state.

The house of commons consists of one hundred and twenty members, chosen by counties, according to their federal population, that is, according to their respective numbers, determined by adding to the whole number of free persons (including those bound to service for a term of years, and excluding Indians not taxed) three fifths of all other persons (slaves).

All freemen (people of color excepted) of the age of twenty-one years, who have been inhabitants of any one district within the state for twelve months preceding the day of any election, and are possessed of a freehold within the same district, of fifty acres of land, for six months next before and at the day of election, are entitled to vote for senators. The constitution grants the right of voting for governor and members of the house of commons, to all freemen of the age of twenty-one years, who have been inhabitants of the state twelve months immediately preceding the election.

The executive power is vested in a governor, who is elected by the people biennially ; is to enter on the duties of his office on the first day of January next after his election ; but he is not eligible more than four years in any term of six years. He is assisted by a council of state of seven persons, elected by the legislature.

The time of holding the election for governor and members of the general assembly, is appointed by the legislature ; at present it is fixed for the first Thursday in August, biennially. All elections by the people are by ballot. The general assembly meets biennially, at *Raleigh*, on the third Monday in November.

The judicial power is vested in a supreme court of three judges, and in a superior or circuit court of seven judges ; besides inferior courts. The state is divided into seven circuits, in which the superior court is held half yearly in the several counties. As judges of the superior courts of law they have jurisdiction of all pleas, whether brought before them by original or mesne process, or by *certiorari* writs of error, or appeal from any inferior court, also of all pleas of the state, and criminal matters. As judges of the courts of equity, they have all the powers of courts of chancery. The judges of the supreme and superior courts are elected by the legislature, in joint ballot, and hold their offices during good behavior.

SOUTH CAROLINA.

The first constitution of this state was formed in 1775 ; the present constitution was adopted in 1790.

The legislative authority is vested in a general assembly, consisting of a senate and a house of representatives.

The senate consists of forty-five members, who are elected by districts for four years, one half being chosen biennially.

The house of representatives consists of one hundred and twenty-four members, who are apportioned among the several districts, according to the number of white inhabitants and taxation, and are elected for two years. The representatives and one half of the senators are chosen every second year, on the second Monday in October, and the day following.

The executive power is vested in a governor, who is elected for two years, by a joint vote of the senate and house of representatives, at every first meeting of the house of representatives. A governor, after having performed the duties of the office for two years, can not be re-elected till after the expiration of four years.

At the time of the election of governor, a lieutenant-governor is chosen in the same manner, and for the same period.

The general assembly meets annually, at *Columbia*, on the fourth Monday in November.

The judicial power is vested in such superior and inferior courts of law and equity as the legislature shall, from time to time, direct and establish. In December, 1835, a change was made in the judiciary, though the judges remained the same. The old court of appeals of three judges was abolished, and two of the judges were made chancellors in equity, and the other one of the common law judges. The present court of appeals is constituted of the judges of the courts of law, and chancellors, who meet twice a year at Columbia, and twice a year at Charleston. There are four chancellors in equity, and seven judges of the general sessions and common pleas. The chancellor and judges are appointed by joint ballot of the senate and house of representatives, and hold their offices during good behavior.

The constitution grants the right of suffrage to every free white male citizen, of the age of twenty-one years, having resided in the state two years previous to the day of election, and having been possessed of a freehold of fifty acres of land, or a town lot, at least six months before such election, or (not having such freehold or town lot) having been a resident in the election district in which he offers his vote, six months before said election, and having paid a tax the preceding year, of three shillings sterling toward the support of the government.

GEORGIA.

The first constitution of Georgia was formed in 1777; a second in 1785; and a third, the one now in operation, in 1798.

The legislative power is vested in a senate and house of representatives, which together are styled *the General Assembly.*

The members of both houses are chosen annually, by the people, on the first Monday in October. The number of representatives is in proportion to population, including three fifths of all the people of color ; but each county is entitled to at least one member. The constitution was altered by the legislature in 1844, so as to divide the state into forty-seven senatorial districts, and to reduce the number of representatives from 201 to 130. The legislature have the power of altering the constitution, provided two thirds of each branch agree on amendments proposed by one legislature, and confirmed by their successors by a two-third vote, at the following session.

The executive power is vested in a governor, who was formerly elected by the general assembly ; but he is now (and since 1824) elected by the people, on the first Monday in October ; and he holds the office for two years.

The general assembly meets at *Milledgeville*, on the first Monday in November, unless convened at another time by the governor.

The judicial power is vested in a superior court, and in such inferior jurisdictions as the legislature may, from time to time, ordain and establish ; and the superior and inferior courts sit twice in each county every year. The state is divided into eleven circuits, with a judge of the superior court for each circuit. An inferior court is held in each county, composed of five justices, elected by the people every four years. These courts possess the powers of courts of probate. The judges of the superior court are elected by the legislature for three years ; the justices of the inferior courts, and justices of the peace are elected quadrennially by the people ; and the clerks of the superior and inferior courts, biennially.

The constitution grants the right of suffrage to all citizens and inhabitants who have attained the age of twenty-one years, and have paid all the taxes which may have been required of them, and which they may have had opportunity of paying, agreeably to law, for the year preceding the election, and shall have resided six months within the county.

FLORIDA.

The constitution of this state was formed by a convention of delegates chosen by the people, and was adopted by said convention in January, 1839, but Florida remained under a territorial government until the 3d of March, 1845, when it was admitted into the Union as a state by act of Congress.

The legislative power is vested in a *General Assembly*, consisting of a senate and house of representatives. The senators are elected by the people, in districts, for two years, one half of the number going out of office every year. The present number of senators is seventeen. The representatives are elected by the people, by counties, annually, their number never to exceed sixty ; at present, forty-one are chosen. The annual election takes place on the first Monday in October, and the legislature meets at *Tallahassee* on the first Monday in November of each year.

The executive power is vested in a governor, who is chosen by the people once in four years, and he is not eligible for the four years next succeeding his term of office.

The judicial power is vested in a supreme court, having appellate jurisdiction only, and composed of the circuit judges for five years after the election of those judges, and thereafter until the general assembly shall otherwise provide ; also in circuit courts, the state being divided into four circuits, in each of which a judge of the supreme court has jurisdiction. These judges have also equity powers until a separate chancery court shall be established by the legislature. The judges are elected by the legislature, at first for five years ; after that term, during good behavior. There are also courts of probate, held by a judge of probate, one being appointed for each county in the state.

The right of suffrage may be exercised by every free white male, aged twenty-one years, or upward, who has resided in Florida for two years, and in the county for six months, and who shall be enrolled in the militia, or by law exempted from serving therein. The general assembly shall provide for the registration of all qualified voters.

No laws shall be passed to emancipate slaves, or to prohibit the immigration of persons bringing slaves with them. The general assembly may prevent free colored persons from entering the state.

No act of incorporation shall be passed or altered, except by the assent of two thirds of each branch of the legislature. No bank charter shall be granted for more than twenty years, nor shall it ever be extended or renewed. The capital of a bank shall not exceed one hundred thousand dollars, nor shall a dividend be made, exceeding ten per cent. a year. Stockholders shall be individually liable for the debts of the bank, and no notes shall be issued for less than five dollars. The credit of the state shall not be pledged in aid of any corporation whatsoever.

For an amendment of the constitution, two thirds of both houses of the general assembly must assent ; the proposed alteration must then be published six months before the succeeding election, and then be again approved by a two-third vote in the succeeding assembly.

ALABAMA.

The legislative power is vested in two branches, a senate and house of representatives, which together are styled, *the General Assembly of the State of Alabama.*

The representatives are elected annually, and are apportioned among the different counties in proportion to the white population ; the whole number can not exceed one hundred, nor fall short of sixty. The present number is one hundred. The senators are elected for three years, and one third of them are chosen every year. Their number can not be more than one third, nor less than one fourth of the number of representatives. There are thirty-three at present.

The executive power is vested in a governor, who is elected by the people for two years ; and is eligible four years out of six.

The representatives and one third of the senators are elected annually on the first Monday in August, and the day following ; and the governor is elected biennially at the same time.

The general assembly meets annually, formerly at *Tuscaloosa,* in future at *Montgomery,* on the fourth Monday in October.

The right of suffrage is possessed by every white male citizen of twenty-one years of age, who has resided within the state one year preceding an election, and the last three months within the county, city, or town, in which he offers his vote.

The judicial power is vested in a supreme court (consisting of three justices), which has appellate jurisdiction only ; in a court of chancery, consisting of three chancellors, the state being divided into three chancery districts ; in circuit courts, each held by one judge, the state being divided into eight circuits, and such inferior courts as the legislature may establish. The judges of the supreme and circuit courts, and the chancellors, are elected by a joint vote of the two houses of the general assembly, for six years.

MISSISSIPPI.

The original constitution of this state was formed at the town of Washington, near Natchez, in August, 1817 ; and the present revised constitution was formed by a convention, at Jackson, in October, 1832.

The legislative power is vested in a senate and house of representatives, together styled *the Legislature of Mississippi.* The senators are chosen for four years, by the people, by districts, one half being elected biennially ; and their number can not be less than one fourth, nor more than one third of the whole number of representatives.

The representatives are chosen by the people, by counties, every two years, on the first Monday in November, and the day following ; their number not to be less than thirty-six nor more than one hundred, which last is the present number fixed. The legislature meets at Jackson, on the first Monday in January, biennially.

The executive power is vested in a governor, who is chosen by the people, qualified as electors, for two years, and can not hold the office more than four years, in any term of six years. The secretary of state, treasurer, and auditor of public accounts, are all chosen by the people, for two years.

The judicial power is vested in a high court of errors and appeals, held at least twice a year, consisting of three judges, chosen by the people for six years, one being elected in each of the three districts into which the state is divided, and one of the three judges being chosen biennially ; in a circuit court, held in each county at least twice in each year, the judges being chosen by the people of each judicial district, and holding their office four years ; in a superior court of chancery, the chancellor being chosen by the people of the whole state for six years ; in a court of probate, the judge being elected by the people of each county for two years ; justices of the peace and constables are also elected for two years.

Every free white male person, of the age of twenty-one years or upward, who shall be a citizen of the United States, and shall have resided in the state one year next preceding an election, and the last four months within the county, city, or town, in which he offers to vote, is a qualified elector. The mode of election is by ballot.

LOUISIANA.

The original constitution of this state was formed in 1812, and the present revised constitution formed by a convention of delegates in May, 1845, was accepted by the people in November, 1845.

The legislative power is vested in a senate and house of representatives, both together styled *the General Assembly of the State of Louisiana*.

The senators are elected by the people, by districts, for a term of four years, one half being chosen every two years, at the time of the election of representatives. The present number of senators is thirty-two.

The representatives are elected by the people by parishes, apportioned according to population, for a term of two years. Their present number is ninety-eight.

The executive power is vested in a governor, who is elected by the people for a term of four years ; and is ineligible for the next four years.

The biennial elections are held in November, and the sessions of the legislature are to be held biennially, at such place as may be fixed upon by the legislature, which must not be at New Orleans, or within sixty miles of that city. The sessions are to commence in January, and the period of the session is limited to sixty days.

The legislature is prohibited from granting any bank charters, or renewing any now in existence ; it is prohibited also from loaning the credit of the state, or borrowing money, except in case of war, invasion, or insurrection.

The judicial power is vested in a supreme court of five judges, which has appellate jurisdiction only, and such inferior courts as the legislature may establish. The state is divided into ten districts, in each of which there is a judge for the district courts. The life-tenure of the judges is abolished by the new constitution; those of the supreme court are to be appointed for eight years, and of the lower courts for six years. Sheriffs, coroners, clerks of court and justices of the peace, are to be elected by the people.

The right of suffrage is extended to all white males above twenty-one years of age, who have resided two consecutive years in the state; provided that no naturalized citizen can vote until two years after he becomes a citizen.

All citizens are disfranchised, both as to voting and holding office, who may fight, or in any way be connected with fighting a duel, either in or out of the state.

ARKANSAS.

The constitution of this state was formed by a convention of delegates, at Little Rock, in January, 1836.

The legislative power is vested in a general assembly, consisting of a senate and house of representatives.

The senators are elected by the people, by districts, for a term of four years; the representatives by counties, for two years. The senate consists of not less than seventeen nor more than thirty-three members; the house of representatives of not less than fifty-four, nor more than one hundred members.

The general elections are holden every two years, on the first Monday in October, and the general assembly meets biennially, at Little Rock, on the first Monday of November. All general elections are to be *viva voce*, until otherwise directed by law.

The executive power is vested in a governor, elected by the people once in four years; but he is not eligible for more than eight years in any term of twelve years.

The judicial power is vested in a supreme court of three justices, having appellate jurisdiction only, except in particular cases pointed out by the constitution; in circuit courts, of which there are seven in the state, each held by one judge; in county courts and justices of the peace.

The judges of the supreme and circuit courts are chosen by the general assembly, the former for a term of eight years, the latter for four years. Justices of the peace are elected by the people for a term of two years. Judges of the county courts are chosen by the justices of the peace.

Every white male citizen of the United States, who has been a citizen of the state of Arkansas for six months, is deemed a qualified elector, and entitled to vote at elections. Provided that soldiers and seamen of the army or navy of the United States are not so entitled.

TENNESSEE.

In 1796, the people of Tennessee, by a convention at Knoxville, formed a constitution; and Tennessee was, the same year, admitted into the Union as an independent state. On the third Monday in May, 1834, a convention met at Nashville, for the pupose of revising and amending the constitution; and the constitution, as amended by the convention, was ratified by the people in March, 1835.

The legislative authority is vested in a general assembly, consisting of a senate and house of representatives.

The number of representatives is apportioned among the several counties, according to the number of qualified voters, and can not exceed seventy-five (the present number), until the population shall be a million and a half, and can never afterward exceed ninety-nine.

The number of senators is apportioned among the several counties according to the number of voters, and can not exceed one third of the number of representatives. The present number is twenty-five.

The time for the election of the governor, senators, and representatives, is on the first Thursday in August, once in two years, and the time of the meeting of the general assembly is on the first Monday in October, next ensuing the election, at Nashville.

The supreme executive power is vested in a governor, who is chosen by the people for two years, and is not eligible more than six years in any term of eight.

Every free white man of the age of twenty-one years, being a citizen of the United States, and a citizen of the county wherein he may offer his vote, six months next preceding the day of election, is entitled to vote for civil officers.

The judicial power is vested in one supreme court, and such inferior courts as the legislature may, from time to time, ordain and establish, and in the judges thereof, and in justices of the peace.

The supreme court is composed of three judges, one of whom must reside in each of the three grand divisions of the state. The judges are elected by a joint vote of both houses of the general assembly, those of the supreme court for the term of twelve years, and those of the inferior courts for eight years. Attorneys for the state are elected in the same manner, for six years.

Ministers of the gospel are not eligible to a seat in either house of the legislature. No person who denies the being of a God, or a future state of rewards and punishments, can hold any civil office. Lotteries are prohibited; and persons who may be concerned in duels are disqualified for holding office in the state.

KENTUCKY.

On the separation of Kentucky from Virginia, in 1790, a constitution was adopted which continued in force till 1799, when a new one was formed instead of it; and this is now in force.

The legislative power is vested in a senate and house of representatives, which together are styled *the General Assembly of the Commonwealth of Kentucky.*

The representatives are elected annually, and are apportioned, every four years, among the different counties, according to the number of electors. Their present number is one hundred, which is the highest number that the constitution authorizes; fifty-eight being the lowest.

The senators are elected for four years, one quarter of them being chosen annually. Their present number is thirty-eight; and they can not exceed this number, nor fall short of twenty-four.

The executive power is vested in a governor, who is elected for four years, and is ineligible for the succeeding seven years after the expiration of his term of office. At the election of governor, a lieutenant-governor is also chosen, who is speaker of the senate, and on whom the duties of the governor devolve, in case of his absence or removal.

The representatives and one quarter of the members of the senate are elected annually by the people, on the first Monday in August; the governor is elected by the people, every fourth year, at the same time; and he commences the execution of his office on the fourth Tuesday succeeding the day of the commencement of the election at which he is chosen. The polls are kept open three days; and the votes are given openly, or *viva voce*, and not by ballot.

The general assembly meets at *Frankfort* annually, on the first Monday in December.

The constitution grants the right of suffrage to every free male citizen (people of color excepted) who has attained the age of twenty-one years, and has resided in the state two years, or in the county where he offers his vote, one year, next preceding the election.

The judiciary power is vested in a supreme court, styled the court of appeals, and in such inferior courts as the general assembly may, from time to time, erect and establish. The judges of the different courts, and justices of the peace, hold their offices during good behavior.

OHIO.

The constitution of this state was formed at Chillicothe, in 1802.

The legislative power is vested in a senate and house of representatives, which together are style *the General Assembly of the State of Ohio*.

The representatives are elected annually on the second Tuesday in October; and they are apportioned among the counties according to the number of white male inhabitants above twenty-one years of age. Their number can not be less than thirty-six, nor more than seventy-two.

The senators are chosen biennially, and are apportioned according to the number of white male inhabitants of twenty-one years of age. Their number can not be less than one third, nor more than one half of the number of representatives.

The executive power is vested in a governor, who is elected by the people for two years on the second Tuesday in October; and his term of service commences on the first Monday in December.

The general assembly meets annually, at *Columbus*, on the first Monday in December.

The right of suffrage is granted to all white male inhabitants above the age of twenty-one years, who have resided in the state one year next preceding the election, and who have paid, or are charged with, a state or county tax.

The judicial power is vested in a supreme court, in courts of common pleas for each county, and such other courts as the legislature may from time to time establish. The judges are elected by a joint ballot of both houses of the general assembly, for the term of seven years.

INDIANA.

The executive power is vested in a governor, who is elected by the people, for a term of three years, and may be once re-elected. At every election of governor, a lieutenant-governor is also chosen, who is president of the senate, and on whom, in case of the death, resignation, or removal of the governor, the powers and duty of governor devolve.

The legislative authority is vested in a *General Assembly*, consisting of a senate, the members of which are elected for three years, and a house of representatives, elected annually.

The number of representatives can never be less than thirty-six, nor more than one hundred ; and they are apportioned among the several counties according to the number of white male inhabitants above twenty-one years of age.   The number of senators, who are apportioned in like manner, can not be less than one third, nor more than one half, of the number of representatives.

The representatives and one third of the members of the senate are elected annually, on the first Monday in August ; and the governor is chosen on the same day, every third year.

The general assembly meets annually, at *Indianapolis*, on the first Monday in December.

The right of suffrage is granted to all male citizens of the age of twenty-one years or upward, who may have resided in the state one year immediately preceding an election.

The judiciary power is vested in one supreme court, in circuit courts, and in such other inferior courts as the general assembly may establish. The supreme court consists of three judges ; and each of the circuit courts consists of a president and two associate judges.   The judges are all appointed for the term of seven years.   The judges of the supreme court are appointed by the governor, with the consent of the senate ; the presidents of the circuit courts, by the legislature ; and the associate judges are elected by the people.

ILLINOIS.

THE original constitution of Illinois was framed in August, 1818. The present constitution was adopted by a state convention in August, 1847, and accepted by the people in March, 1848.

The legislative authority is vested in a general assembly, consisting of a senate, the members of which, twenty-five in number, are elected for four years, one half every two years ; and of a house of representatives, seventy-five in number, elected for two years.   These numbers to be increased after the population of the state shall be one million, but the number of representatives shall never exceed one hundred.   Senators must be thirty years of age. and five years inhabitants of the state.   Representatives must be twenty-five years of age, citizens of the United States, and three years inhabitants of the state.

The governor and lieutenant-governor, chosen by a plurality of votes, once in four years, on the Tuesday after the first Monday in November, shall be thirty-five years of age, citizen of the United States for fourteen years, and residents of the state for ten years.   The governor is not eligible for two consecutive terms.   A majority of members elected to both houses may defeat the governor's veto.   A majority of the members elected to each house, is required for the passage of any law.

The general assembly meets biennially at *Springfield*, on the first Monday in January ; and the governor is authorized to convene it on extraordinary occasions at other times.

All white male citizens, twenty-one years old, resident in the state for one year, may vote at elections.

The judicial power is vested in a supreme court of three judges, elected by the people, for a term of nine years at the first election, and afterward for three years ; also in circuit courts of one judge each, elected by the people in nine judicial circuits into which the state is divided ; and county courts of one judge each elected by the people for four years.

No state-bank can be created or revived. Acts creating banks must be submitted to the people. Stockholders are individually liable to the amount of their shares. Slavery and lotteries are prohibited. The credit of the state can not be lent. Corporations, not for banking purposes, may be established under general laws.

MICHIGAN.

THE constitution of Michigan was formed by a convention of delegates at Detroit, in May, 1835, and ratified by the people in October following. The legislative power is vested in a senate and house of representatives. The senators are elected by the people, by districts, for a term of two years, one half of the whole number, as nearly as may be, being chosen annually. The representatives are elected by the people, by counties, annually, and their number can not be less than forty-eight, nor more than one hundred ; the senators at all times are to be equal, as nearly as may be, to one third of the number of the house of representatives. The present number of senators is eighteen ; of representatives, fifty-three.

The annual election is held on the first Monday in November, and the following day. The legislature met at Detroit, until the year 1847, when the seat of government was permanently located at Lansing.

The supreme executive power is vested in a governor, elected by the people, who holds his office for two years, and a lieutenant-governor, who is chosen at the same time, in the same manner, and for the same term, as the governor. The lieutenant-governor is president of the senate.

The judicial power is vested in a supreme court, consisting of a chief-justice and three associate justices ; in a court of chancery, held by a chancellor, at five different parts of the state within the year, the state being divided into five chancery circuits ; in circuit courts, there being four judicial circuits, in each of which one of the judges of the supreme court sits as presiding judge (in each county one or two terms of the circuit court are held annually) ; also in county courts, and in such other courts as the legislature may from time to time establish. The judges of the supreme court are appointed by the governor and senate for the term of seven years. Judges of all county courts, associate judges of circuit courts, and judges of probate, are elected by the people for the term of four years. Each township is authorized to elect four justices of the peace, who hold their offices for four years.

In all elections, every white male above the age of twenty-one years, having resided in the state six months next preceding any election, is entitled to vote at such election. All votes are given by ballot, except for such township officers as may by law be directed to be otherwise chosen.

Slavery, lotteries, and the sale of lottery tickets, are prohibited.

MISSOURI.

THE constitution of this state was formed by a convention at St. Louis, in June, 1820. In January, 1846, a new constitution was formed by a state convention at Jefferson ; which was submitted to the people on the first Monday of August in the latter year, and rejected. The constitution adopted in 1820, is therefore, still in force, and the outlines thereof are as follows :—

The legislative power is vested in a senate and house of representatives, styled together *the General Assembly*. The senators, in number not fewer than fourteen, nor more than thirty-three, shall be thirty years old, have the qualification of representatives, be inhabitants of the state for four years, and shall be chosen by districts, for four years, one half every second year. The representatives, in number not more than one hundred, shall be chosen in counties every second year ; they must be free white male citizens of the United States, twenty-four years old, inhabitants of the state for two years and of the county for one year next before the election. Every free white male citizen of the United States, twenty-one years old, resident in the state one year before the election, and three months in the place where he offers his vote, may vote at elections.

The elections are held biennially, on the first Monday in August. The legislature meets every second year, on the first Monday in November, at the city of Jefferson.

The executive power is vested in a governor, who is elected by the people, once in four years, and is ineligible for the next four years. A lieutenant-governor is also chosen, for the same term, who is, *ex officio*, president of the senate. The governor and lieutenant-governor must be thirty-five years old, natives of the United States, or citizens thereof at the adoption of the constitution. The governor may veto a bill, but a majority of both houses may pass it, notwithstanding his veto. If the office of governor be vacant, it shall be filled by the lieutenant-governor, and after him by the president of the senate *pro tem*.

The supreme court consists of three judges, appointed by the governor and senate, and has appellate jurisdiction only. Circuit courts have exclusive criminal jurisdiction, unless deprived of it by law, and hear all civil cases not cognizable by a justice of the peace. The equity jurisdiction is divided between the circuit and supreme courts. Judges of the supreme court must be thirty years old, may hold office until sixty-five, and may be removed upon address of two thirds of both houses of the legislature.

One bank, and no more, may be established, with not more than five branches, and a total capital of not more than five millions of dollars, one half, at least, reserved to the state.

The general assembly, by a vote of two thirds of the members, may propose amendments to the constitution, and if, at the first session thereafter, they are confirmed by a vote of two thirds of the members, they become part of the constitution.

IOWA.

The constitution of the state of Iowa, was adopted by a state convention at Iowa city, on the 18th of May, 1846, and accepted by the people in August of the same year.

The general assembly consists of a senate and house of representatives, the sessions of which, held at *Iowa city*, are biennial, commencing on the first Monday in December after their election, which takes place on the first Monday of August, biennially. Senators, not less than one third, nor more than one half as numerous as the representatives, must be twenty-five years of age, chosen for four years, one half biennially. Representatives shall be chosen for two years ; they must be twenty-one years of age, and have resided in the state one year at least, and in their district thirty days previous to the election. The representatives shall not be less than twenty-six, nor more than thirty-nine, till the white population amounts to one hundred and seventy-five thousand ; afterward they shall not be less than thirty-nine, nor more than seventy-two.

Every white male citizen of the United States, twenty-one years old, idiots, insane, or infamous persons excepted, having resided in the state six months, and in the county where he claims to vote twenty days, has the right of suffrage.

The executive power is vested in a governor, chosen by a plurality of votes for a term of four years ; he must be thirty years old, and have resided in the state for two years. If the governor, for any cause, be disabled, the secretary of the state, and after him the president of the senate, and after him the speaker of the house, acts as governor.

The judicial authority is vested in a supreme court, consisting of a chief justice and two associates, elected by the general assembly for six years ; in district courts, the judges of which are elected by the people in their respective districts, each for five years ; and in justices of the peace.

No state debts can be created exceeding one hundred thousand dollars, except in case of war or insurrection, unless authorized by a special law approved by a majority of the votes of the people. No corporation with banking privileges shall be created, and private banking shall be prohibited by law. Other corporations may be organized under *general* laws, with certain restrictions. The state shall never become a stockholder in any corporation. A superintendent of public instruction is chosen by the people once in three years ; also a secretary of state, an auditor, and a treasurer, once in two years.

Neither slavery nor involuntary servitude, unless for the punishment of crimes, shall ever be tolerated in this state. To amend the constitution, the general assembly must submit the question of a convention to the people at the next general election ; and if a majority are in favor thereof, the assembly shall provide for the election of delegates to a convention to be held in six months after the vote of the people in favor thereof.

WISCONSIN.

The constitution was adopted by a state convention at Madison city, February 1, 1848. The legislature consists of a senate and assembly, and meets annually on the first Monday in January, at Madison.

The senators, in number not more than one third, nor fewer than one fourth, of the assembly, are chosen by the people, in districts for two years, one half each year. Members of the assembly, in number not fewer than fifty-four, nor more than one hundred, must be qualified electors in their districts, resident one year in the state, and chosen annually on the Tuesday succeeding the first Monday of November.

All males twenty-one years old, residents of the state for one year next before the election, who are white citizens of the United States, or white foreigners who have declared their intention to become citizens, or persons of Indian blood, once declared by the laws of the United States to be citizens, or civilized persons of Indian descent, not members of a tribe, may vote at elections.

The executive power is vested in a governor, who is chosen by the people, by a plurality of votes, for a term of two years. In default of the governor, his duties are discharged by a lieutenant-governor, who is chosen by a plurality of votes, for the same term and with the same qualifications as the governor, and is president of the senate, with a casting vote. The governor's *veto* may be overruled by a vote of two thirds of the members present in each house.

The judicial power is vested in a supreme court, in circuit courts, judges of probate, and justices of the peace, all elected by the people. Judges of the circuit courts are chosen at a separate election by the people, by circuits, for six years. The same judges sit as a supreme court, to try cases upon appeal, without a jury. The legislature may erect a separate supreme court, to consist of three judges chosen by the people for six years, in which case, the number of circuit judges may be reduced. Probate judges and justices of the peace are elected by the people for two years. In every organized county the legislature may appoint one or more persons, with powers not exceeding those of a circuit judge at chambers.

The credit of the state shall never be lent; nor shall any debt be contracted, nor money paid for internal improvements, unless the state hold trust property dedicated to such purposes. Except in case of war, invasion, or insurrection, no debt shall be contracted, exceeding one hundred thousand dollars. The legislature shall prevent towns and cities from contracting debts. No general or special law to create a bank or banks shall be passed, till a majority of the votes at a general election shall have been in favor of a bank, and until such a majority have afterward approved the act as passed. Corporations, except banks, may be created under general laws, but not by special acts, except in specified cases.

Slavery and imprisonment for debt are prohibited. A state superintendent of education shall be chosen by the people.

Amendments to the constitution agreed to by a majority of members of both houses of the legislature, if again approved by a majority of the succeeding legislature, shall be submitted to the people, and if approved by a majority of their votes, shall become a part of the constitution. A majority of each house may recommend a convention to change the constitution, and a majority of votes at a general election afterward, may authorize the calling of such convention.

TEXAS.

THE constitution of the state of Texas was adopted by a convention of delegates at the city of Austin, in August, 1845, and was approved by the people on the 13th of October following.

The legislative power is vested in a senate and house of representatives, styled together *the Legislature of the State of Texas.* The style of laws is, " Be it enacted by the legislature of the state of Texas."

The senators are elected by the people, by districts, for the term of four years, one half being chosen biennially ; their number is not to be less than nineteen, nor more than thirty-one. The representatives are elected for two years, by the people, by counties, apportioned according to their free population ; the number is not to be less than forty-five nor more than ninety.

Elections by the people are to be held in the several counties, cities, or towns, at such times as may be designated by law. The sessions of the legislature are to be held at the city of Austin, at such times as may be prescribed by law, until the year 1850, when the seat of government shall be permanently located by the votes of the people.

The executive power is vested in a governor, elected by the people, at

23

the time and places of elections for members of the legislature ; he holds his office for the term of two years, but is not eligible for more than four years in any term of six years.   At the same time, a lieutenant-governor is chosen for the same term, who is president of the senate, and succeeds the governor in case of death, resignation, removal from office, inability, refusal to serve, impeachment, or absence from the state, of the latter.

The judicial power is vested in a supreme court of three judges, in district courts, and in such inferior courts as the legislature may, from time to time, establish.   The judges of the supreme and district courts are appointed by the governor, with the advice and consent of two thirds of the senate ; and the judges hold their offices for six years.

The right of suffrage is granted to every free male person over the age of twenty-one years (Indians not taxed, Africans, and descendants of Africans, excepted), who shall have attained the age of twenty-one years, and who shall be a citizen of the United States, or who was, at the adoption of this constitution by the Congress of the United States, a citizen of the republic of Texas, and shall have resided in this state one year next preceding an election, and the last six months within the district, city, or town, in which he offers to vote ; provided that soldiers and seamen or marines of the army or navy of the United States, shall not be entitled to vote at any election created by this constitution.

The legislature shall have no power to pass laws for the emancipation of slaves, without the consent of their owners.   No banking or discounting company shall hereafter be created, renewed, or extended.   No person shall be imprisoned for debt.

COMPARATIVE VIEW OF THE STATE CONSTITUTIONS.

In the six New England states, the executive and legislative branches of the government are all elected annually.   The representation in the lower branch of the legislature is more numerous in those states than in the other states of the Union ; the representatives in the New England states being elected by *towns* to the house of representatives, while in all other parts of the Union the representation in that branch of the legislature is by *counties ; districts* in South Carolina, and *parishes* in Louisiana, being local divisions synonymous with counties.

An executive council, elected by the people, is peculiar to the state of New Hampshire.   There are, however, executive councils, elected by the legislature, in Maine, Massachusetts, Virginia, and North Carolina.

The governor possesses the veto power, or qualified negative, on bills and resolutions which have been passed by the legislature, in the following twelve states, viz.:   Maine, New Hampshire, Massachusetts, New York, Pennsylvania, Georgia, Mississippi, Louisiana, Michigan, Texas, Iowa, and Wisconsin ; in these states the executive veto can only be overruled by a two third vote of both branches of the legislature.

In the following ten, states the governor may return bills or resolutions passed by the legislature, but his veto may be overruled by a majority of the members elected to both houses, viz. : Vermont, Connecticut, New Jersey, Alabama, Florida, Arkansas, Kentucky, Indiana, Illinois, and Missouri.

In the following eight states, the approval of the governor is not required to bills or resolutions passed by the legislature, but the same may become laws, after receiving the signature of the speaker or presiding officer of each branch of the legislature, viz. : Rhode Island, Delaware, Maryland, Virginia, North Carolina, South Carolina, Tennessee, and Ohio.

In all of the states, except Virginia and South Carolina, the governor is elected by the people ; in those two states he is chosen by the legislature. Lieutenant-governors are chosen by the people in Massachusetts, Vermont, Rhode Island, Connecticut, New York, Kentucky, Indiana, Illinois, Wisconsin, Missouri, Michigan, and Texas ; in Virginia and South Carolina, by the legislature. In the other states, the office of lieutenant-governor does not exist.

In the New England states, a majority of all the votes given is required to constitute a choice, in elections generally, by the people ; there are exceptions in Maine, Vermont, and Connecticut, in elections for state senators, and in Connecticut, on second trials, at adjourned meetings, for the choice of representatives to the general assembly, in which cases a plurality of votes only is required for a choice. In Maine, New Hampshire, and Connecticut, members of Congress are also elected by plurality. In all of the states except those of New England, a plurality of votes given effects a choice in elections by the people.

In all of the states, at popular elections, the manner of voting is by ballot, except in Virginia, Kentucky, Missouri, and Arkansas, in which states, in all elections to any office of trust, honor, or profit, with exceptions as to electors of president and vice-president, the votes are given openly, or *viva voce*, and not by ballot.

North Carolina is now the only state which requires a freehold qualification for electors for either branch of the legislature, members of the senate in that state being chosen by freemen possessed of a freehold within the district where they reside and vote, of fifty acres of land. In Virginia, freeholders may vote for members of the house of delegates, in any county where they own a freehold of the value named in the constitution ; housekeepers and heads of families who shall have been assessed with a part of the revenue of the commonwealth, within the preceding year when they vote, are also entitled to vote at elections.

Persons of color are entitled to vote at elections in the states of Maine, New Hampshire, Vermont, Massachusetts, and Rhode Island. In the state of New York, they are also qualified to vote, if possessed of a freehold estate of the value of two hundred and fifty dollars, without any incumbrance. In all other states of the Union, persons of color, or those of African descent, are excluded from the right of voting at elections.

Ministers of the gospel are not eligible as legislators in Maryland, Virginia, North Carolina, Tennessee, and Texas. In South Carolina, Kentucky, Louisiana, Mississippi, and Missouri, they are eligible neither as governors nor legislators. In Delaware, they are not eligible to any office whatever.

New Hampshire and Massachusetts are the only states whose constitutions make provision for religious establishments. In New Hampshire the legislature is empowered to *authorize*, and in Massachusetts the legislature is enjoined to *require*, the several towns, parishes, &c., in the state to make adequate provision, at their own expense, for the support and maintenance of *protestant* teachers, or ministers of the gospel. The constitution of 'New Hampshire requires the governor, members of the council, and of both branches of the legislature, to be " of the *protestant* religion."

The *council of censors* is peculiar to Vermont; that body is chosen once in seven years, and among their other powers, they can call a convention to amend the constitution of the state.

Massachusetts and New Hampshire are the only states whose constitutions appoint *titles* to the officers of government. The governor of Massachusetts is entitled " *His Excellency*," and the lieutenant-governor " *His Honor.*" The governor of New Hampshire is entitled " *His Excellency.*"

CHRONOLOGICAL TABLE

Of the principal political and other Events in American History, from the Discovery in 1492 to 1849.

1492. Aug. 3, Columbus sets sail from Palos, in Spain.
" Oct. 12, First land discovered (one of the Bahamas).
" " 27, Cuba discovered.
" Dec. 6, Hayti or Hispaniola discovered.
1493. Jan. 16, Columbus returns to Spain.
" Sept. 25, Columbus sails from Cadiz on his second voyage.
" Dec. 8, Columbus lays the foundation of Isabella, in Hispaniola, the first European town in the New World.
1494. May 5, Jamaica discovered.
1496. Mar. 10, Columbus sails again for Spain.
1497. June 24, Newfoundland discovered by the Cabots.
1498. May 30, Columbus sails from Spain on his third voyage.
" July 31, Trinidad discovered.
" Aug. 1, America discovered by Columbus.
1499. June 16, America discovered by Americus Vespucius.
1500. Amazon river discovered by Pinzon.
" April 23, Brazil discovered by Cabral.
1502. May 11, Columbus sails on his last voyage.
" Aug. 14, Bay of Honduras discovered by Columbus.
1504. Sept. 2, Columbus returns to Spain.
1506. May 20, Columbus dies, in his fifty-ninth year.
1508. St. Lawrence river first navigated by Aubert.
1512. April 2, Florida discovered by Juan Ponce de Leon.
" Baracoa, the first town in Cuba, built by Diego Velasquez.
1513. Sept. 25, Pacific ocean discovered by Vasco Nunez de Balboa.
1516. Rio de la Plata discovered by Juan Diaz de Solis.
1517. Patent granted by Charles V. for an annual import of 4,000 negro slaves to Hispaniola, Cuba, Jamaica, and Puerto Rico.
" Yucatan discovered by Francis Hernandez Cordova.
1519. Mar. 13, Cortes lands at Tabasco, in Mexico.
" April 22, Cortes arrives at San Juan de Ulloa.
" Vera Cruz settled by Cortes.
" Nov. 8, Cortes enters Mexico.
1520. Montezuma dies.
" Nov. 7, Straits of Magellan discovered by Ferdinand Magellan.
1521. Aug. 13, Mexico taken by Cortes.
1522. Bermudas discovered by Juan Bermudez.
1525. First invasion of Peru by Pizarro and Almagro.
1528. Pizarro appointed governor of Peru.
1531. Second invasion of Peru by Pizarro.
1532. First colony founded in Peru by Pizarro.
1535. Chili invaded by Almagro.
1537. California discovered by Cortes.
1539. May 18, Ferdinand de Soto sails from Havana, on an expedition for the conquest of Florida.
1541. Aug. 6, Orellana explores the Amazon, and arrives at the ocean.
1545. Mines of Potosi, in South America, discovered.
1548. Platina discovered in the south of Mexico.
1563. Slaves first imported into the West Indies by the English.
1576. Elizabeth's and Frobisher's straits discovered by Martin Frobisher.
1585. June 26, Virginia visited by Sir Walter Raleigh.

1586.   Tobacco introduced into England by Mr. Lane.
1587.   Aug. 13, first Indian baptized in Virginia.
1602.   May 15, Cape Cod named by Bartholemew Gosnold.
"   " 21, Martha's Vineyard discovered by Gosnold.
1607.   May 13, Jamestown, Virginia, founded.
1608.   July 3, Quebec founded.
1609.   Hudson river discovered by Henry Hudson.
1611.   Lake Champlain discovered by Champlain.
1616.   Baffin's bay discovered by Baffin.
1617.   Pocahontas dies in England.
1619.   June 19, first general assembly in Virginia.
1619.   May 20, Long Island sound first navigated by Dermer.
1620.   Aug. 5, Puritans sail from Southampton, England, for America.
"   Nov. 10, Puritans anchor at Cape Cod.
"   " first white child born in New England.
"   Dec. 11, first landing at Plymouth.
"   " 25, first house built at Plymouth.
"   Slaves first introduced into Virginia by the Dutch.
1621.   May 12, first marriage at Plymouth.
1630.   Boston settled.
"   Oct. 19, first general court of Massachusetts colony, holden at Boston.
1631.   Delaware settled by the Swedes.
1632.   First church built at Boston.
1633.   First house erected in Connecticut, at Windsor.
1634.   Maryland settled.
"   Roger Williams banished from Massachusetts.
1636.   Hartford, Connecticut, settled.
"   Providence founded by Roger Williams.
1637.   First synod convened at Newtown (now Cambridge), Massachusetts.
1638.   New Haven founded.
"   Harvard college founded.
"   June 1, earthquake in New England.
1639.   Jan. 14, convention at Hartford, Connecticut, for forming a constitution.
"   April, first general election at Hartford.
"   First printing-press established at Cambridge, Massachusetts, by Stephen Day.
1642.   Oct. 9, first commencement at Harvard college.
1643.   May 19, union of the New England colonies.
1646.   First act passed by the general court of Massachusetts, for the spread of the gospel among the Indians.
1647.   May 19, first general assembly of Rhode Island.
1648.   First execution for witchcraft.
"   New London settled.
1650.   Harvard college chartered.
"   Constitution of Maryland settled.
1651.   Navigation-act passed by Great Britain.
1652.   First mint established in New England.
1654.   Yale college first projected by Mr. Davenport.
1663.   Jan. 26, earthquake felt in New England, New Netherlands, and Canada.
1664.   Aug. 27, surrender of New Amsterdam to the English.
1665.   June 12, New York city incorporated.
1672.   First copyright granted by Massachusetts.
1673.   Mississippi river explored by Marquette and Joliet.
1675.   June 24, commencement of King Philip's war.
1676.   Aug. 12, death of King Philip.
1681.   Mar. 4, grant of Pennsylvania to William Penn.
1682.   Oct. 24, arrival of William Penn in America.
"   Louisiana taken possession of by M. de la Sale.
1683.   First legislative assembly in New York.
"   Roger Williams dies, in his eighty-fourth year.
1686.   First episcopal society formed in Boston.
1687.   First printing-press established near Philadelphia, by William Bradford
1688.   New York and New Jersey united to New England.
1690.   Feb. 8, Schenectady burned by the French and Indians.
"   First paper-money issued by Massachusetts.
1692.   William and Mary college, Virginia, chartered.

1693. Episcopal church established at New York.
" First printing-press established in New York, by William Bradford.
1695. Rice introduced into Carolina.
1698. First French colony arrive at the mouth of the Mississippi.
1699. Captain Kidd, the pirate, apprehended at Boston.
1700. Episcopal church established in Pennsylvania.
1701. Oct., Yale college chartered and founded at Saybrook.
1702. Episcopal church established in New Jersey and Rhode Island.
1703. Culture of silk introduced into Carolina.
" Duty of £4 laid on imported negroes, in Massachusetts.
1704. Tonnage duty laid by Rhode Island on foreign vessels.
" Act " to prevent the growth of popery," passed by Maryland.
" First newspaper (Boston News Letter) published at Boston, by Batholomew Green.
1706. Bills of credit issued by Carolina.
1709. First printing-press in Connecticut, established at New London, by Thomas Short.
1711. South Sea Company incorporated.
1712. Free schools founded in Charlestown, Massachusetts.
1714. First schooner built at Cape Ann.
1717. Yale college removed from Saybrook to New Haven.
1718. Impost duties laid by Massachusetts on English manufactures and English ships.
1719. First presbyterian church founded in New York.
1720. Tea first used in New England.
1721. Inoculation for smallpox introduced into New England.
1722. Paper-money first issued in Pennsylvania.
1725. First newspaper in New York (the New York Gazette), published by William Bradford.
1726. First printing-presses established in Virginia and Maryland.
1727. Earthquake in New England.
1730. First printing-press and newspaper established at Charleston, South Carolina.
1732. Tobacco made a legal tender in Maryland at 1d. per pound, and corn at 20d. per bushel.
" Feb. 22, George Washington born.
" First printing-press and newspaper established at Newport, Rhode Island.
1733. Georgia settled.
" Freemason's lodge first held in Boston.
1737. Earthquake in New Jersey.
1738. College founded at Princeton, New Jersey.
1741. Jan. 1, General Magazine and Historical Chronicle, first published by Benjamin Franklin.
1742. Faneuil Hall erected at Boston.
1750. First theatrical performance in Boston.
1754. Columbia college founded in New York.
1755. Defeat of General Braddock.
" Sept. 8, battle of Lake George.
" Earthquake in North America.
" First newspaper (Connecticut Gazette) published at New Haven.
1756. May 17, war declared with France by Great Britain.
" First printing-press and newspaper established at Portsmouth, New Hampshire, by Daniel Fowle.
1758. July 26, Louisburg taken by the English.
" Aug. 27, Fort Frontenac taken by the English.
" Nov. 25, Fort Du Quesne (now Pittsburgh) taken by the English.
1759. Ticonderoga taken by the English.
" Sept. 18, Quebec taken by the English.
1761. Mar. 12, earthquake in New England.
1763. Feb. 10, treaty of peace signed at Paris, between the English and French.
" First newspaper published in Georgia.
1764. Mar., right to tax American colonies voted by house of commons.
" April 5, first act for levying revenue passed by parliament.
" " 21, Louisiana ordered to be given up to Spain.
1765. Stamp act passed by parliament.
" Mar. 22, stamp act receives the royal assent.

1765.	May 29, Virginia resolutions against the right of taxation.
"	June 6, general congress proposed by Massachusetts.
"	Oct. 7, congress of twenty-eight delegates convenes at New York, and publishes a declaration of rights.
1766.	Feb., Dr. Franklin examined before the house of commons, relative to the repeal of the stamp-act.
"	Mar. 18., stamp-act repealed.
1767.	Tax laid on paper, glass, painters' colors, and teas.
1769.	Dartmouth college incorporated.
"	American philosophical society instituted at Philadelphia.
1770.	Tea-plant introduced into Georgia.
1773.	Tea thrown overboard at Boston.
1774.	Boston port-bill passed.
"	Sept. 4, first continental Congress at Philadelphia.
"	Dr. Franklin dismissed from the postoffice.
1775.	April 19, battle of Lexington.
"	May 10, Ticonderoga taken by the provincials.
"	June 17, battle of Bunker's Hill.
"	July 2, General Washington arrives at Cambridge.
"	Dec. 13, resolution of Congress to fit out a navy of thirteen ships.
"	" 31, assault on Quebec, and death of General Montgomery.
1776.	Jan. 3, battle near Princeton.
"	March 17, Boston evacuated by the British.
"	July 4, declaration of independence.
"	Sept. 11, battle of Brandywine.
"	" 15, the British take possession of New York.
"	" 27, the British take possession of Philadelphia.
"	Oct. 4, battle of Germantown.
"	" 22, battle of Red Bank.
"	" 28, battle of White Plains.
"	Nov. 16, capture of Fort Washington by the British.
"	Dec. 26, battle of Trenton.
1777.	Sept. 19, battle near Stillwater.
1778.	June 28, battle at Monmouth courthouse.
"	Dec. 29, Savannah taken by the British.
1780.	Aug. 16, battle near Camden.
1781.	Bank of North America established.
"	Jan. 17, battle of Cowpens.
"	March 15, battle of Guilford.
"	Sept. 5, Fort Trumbull, Conn., taken by Arnold, and New London burnt.
"	" 8, battle at Eutaw.
"	Oct. 19, surrender of Lord·Cornwallis.
1782.	March 4, resolution of the house of commons in favor of peace.
"	April 19, independence of United States acknowledged by Holland.
"	July, evacuation of Savannah.
"	Dec. 14, evacuation of Charlestown.
1783.	Jan. 20, cessation of hostilities agreed on.
"	Feb. 5, independence of the United States acknowledged by Sweden.
"	" 25, " " " " Denmark.
"	March 24, " " " " Spain.
"	July, " " " " Russia.
"	April 11, proclamation of peace by Congress.
"	" 19, peace proclaimed in the army by Washington.
"	Sept. 3, definitive treaty of peace signed at Paris.
"	Oct. 18, proclamation for disbanding the army.
"	Nov. 2, Washington's farewell orders.
"	" 25, New York evacuated by the British.
1784.	Feb., first voyage to China from New York.
1785.	July 9, and Aug. 5, treaty with Prussia.
1786.	Shay's insurrection in Massachusetts.
"	Sept. 20, insurrection in New Hampshire.
1787.	Sept. 17, federal constitution agreed on by convention.
1788.	Federal constitution adopted.
1789.	March 3, George Washington elected president.
"	April 30, inauguration of George Washington.

1790. District of Columbia ceded by Virginia and Maryland.
" May 29, constitution adopted by Rhode Island.
1791. Mar. 4, Vermont admitted into the Union.
" Bank of the United States established.
" First folio Bible printed by Worcester of Mass.
1792. June 1, Kentucky admitted into the Union.
1793. Washington re-elected president.
" Death of John Hancock.
1794. Insurrection in Pennsylvania.
1796. June 1, Tennessee admitted into the Union.
" Dec. 7, Washington's last speech to Congress.
1797. March 4, John Adams inaugurated president.
1798. Washington reappointed commander-in chief.
1799. Dec. 14, death of George Washington.
1800. Seat of government removed to Washington.
" May 13, disbanding of the provisional army.
1801. March 4, Thomas Jefferson inaugurated president.
1802. July 20, Louisiana ceded to France by Spain.
1803. Feb. 19, Ohio admitted into the Union.
1803. April 30, Louisiana purchased by the United States.
" August, Commodore Preble bombards Tripoli.
1805. June 3, treaty of peace with Tripoli.
1806. Expedition of Lewis and Clark to the mouth of the Columbia.
1807. June 22, attack on the frigate Chesapeake.
" July 2, interdict to armed British vessels.
" Nov. 11, British orders in council.
" Dec. 17, Milan decree.
" " 22, embargo laid by the American government.
1808. Jan. 1, slave-trade abolished.
" April 17, Bayonne decree.
1809. March 1, embargo repealed.
" " 4, James Madison inaugurated president.
1810. March 23, Rambouillet decree.
1811. May 16, engagement between the frigate President and Little Belt.
" Nov. 7, battle of Tippecanoe.
1812. April 3, embargo laid for ninety days.
" June 19, proclamation of war. (War declared June 18th.)
" " 23, British orders in council repealed.
" Aug. 15, surrender of General Hull.
" Action between the frigates Constitution and Guerriere.
" Nov., defeat at Queenstown.
" Action between the Frolic and Wasp.
" " " United States and Macedonian.
" April 8, Louisiana admitted into the Union.
1813. April 27, capture of York, Upper Canada.
" May 27, battle of Fort George.
" June 1, Chesapeake captured by the Shannon.
" Sept. 10, Perry's victory on Lake Erie.
" Oct. 5, battle of the Thames.
" Dec. 13, Buffalo burnt.
1814. March 28, action between the frigates Essex and Phœbe.
" July 5, battle of Chippewa.
" " 25, battle of Bridgewater.
" August, Washington city captured, and capitol burnt.
" " 9, 11, Stonington bombarded.
" " 11, M'Donough's victory on Lake Champlain.
" Sept. 12, battle near Baltimore.
" Dec. 24, treaty of Ghent signed.
" " 25, battle of New Orleans.
1815. Feb. 17, treaty of Ghent ratified by the president.
" March, war declared with Algiers.
1817. Mar. 4, James Monroe inaugurated president.
" Dec. 10, Mississippi admitted into the Union.
1818. Dec. 3, Illinois " "
1819. Dec. 14, Alabama " "

1819.   May, first steamship sailed for Europe.
1820.   Mar. 15, Maine admitted into the Union.
1821.   July 1, Jackson takes possession of Florida.
"   Aug. 10, Missouri admitted into the Union.
"   First settlement of Liberia.
1824.   March 13, convention with Great Britain, for suppression of slave-trade.
"   April 5, convention with Russia in relation to the northwest boundary.
"   August 13, arrival of General Lafayette.
1825.   Mar. 4, John Quincy Adams inaugurated president.
"   Sept. 7, departure of General Lafayette.
1826.   July 4, death of Presidents Adams and Jefferson.
1829.   Feb. 20, resolutions passed by the Virginia house of delegates, denying the right of Congress to pass the tariff bill.
"   March 4, Andrew Jackson inaugurated president.
"   May 2, hail fell in Tuscaloosa, Alabama, to the depth of twelve inches.
"   " 17, death of John Jay, at Bedford, New York.
"   Sept. 15, slavery abolished in Mexico.
"   Nov. 9, separation of Yucatan from Mexico, and union with the republic of Central America.
"   Dec. 4, revolution commences in Mexico.
1830.   Jan. 20, General Bolivar resigns his military and civil commissions.
"   " 27, city of Guatemala nearly destroyed by earthquakes.
"   April 4, Yucatan declares its independence.
1831.   Jan. 12, remarkable eclipse of the sun.
"   July 4, death of James Monroe.
"   Oct. 1, free-trade convention at Philadelphia.
"   " 26, tariff convention at New York.
1832.   Feb. 6, attack on Qualla Battoo, in Sumatra, by U. S. frigate Potomac.
"   June 8, cholera breaks out at Quebec, in Canada; being its first appearance in America.
"   Aug. 27, capture of Blackhawk.
"   Sept. 26, university of New York organized.
"   Nov., union and state-rights convention of South Carolina.
"   Dec. 28, John C. Calhoun resigns the office of vice-president.
1833.   Mar. 1, new tariff-bill signed by the president.
"   " 4, Andrew Jackson inaugurated president for a second term.
"   " 11, state-rights convention of South Carolina.
"   " 29, Santa Anna elected president of Mexico.
"   May 16,   " inaugurated   "
"   Oct. 1, public deposites removed from the bank of the United States, by order of General Jackson.
"   Nov. 13, remarkable meteoric showers in the United States.
1834.   Mar. 28, vote of censure by the senate against General Jackson, for removing the deposites.
1835.   April 18, French indemnity-bill passes the chamber of deputies.
"   Dec. 16, great fire in New York.
1836.   April 21, battle of San Jacinto, in Texas.
"   June 14, Arkansas admitted into the Union.
"   Dec. 15, burning of the general postoffice and patent office, at Washington.
1837.   Jan. 26, Michigan admitted into the Union.
"   Mar. 4, Martin Van Buren inaugurated president of the United States.
1840.   Jan. 19, antarctic continent discovered by the U. S. exploring expedition.
"   June 30, sub-treasury bill becomes a law.
1841.   Mar. 4, William Henry Harrison inaugurated president of the United States.
"   April 4, death of President Harrison.
"   Aug. 9, sub-treasury bill repealed.
"   " 18, bankrupt act becomes a law.
1843.   March 3, bankrupt act repealed.
"   June 17, Bunker Hill monument celebration.
1845.   Mar. 1, Texas annexed to the United States.
"   " 3, Florida admitted into the Union.
"   " 4, James K. Polk inaugurated president.
"   June 18, death of Andrew Jackson.
"   Dec. 24, Texas admitted into the Union.

1846.   May 8, battle of Palo Alto, on the Rio Grande.

"   " 9, battle of Resaca de la Palma, do.

"   " 13, proclamation of war existing with Mexico.

"   June 18, United States senate advise the president to confirm the Oregon treaty with Great Britain.

"   July 28, new United States tariff bill passed.

"   Aug. 3, President Polk vetoes the river and harbor bill.

"   " 6, revolution in Mexico, in favor of Santa Anna.

"   " 8, President Polk vetoes the French spoliation bill.

"   " 10, Congress adjourns.

"   " 18, Brigadier-General Kearney of United States army, takes possession of Santa Fe.

"   " 19, Commodore Stockton blockades the Mexican ports on the Pacific.

"   Sept. 21, 22, 23, battles of Monterey, Mexico.

"   " 26, California expedition with Colonel Stevenson's regiment of 780 officers and men, sails from New York.

"   Oct. 25, Tabasco in Mexico, bombarded by Commodore Perry.

"   Nov. 14, Commodore Conner takes Tampico.

"   Dec. 6, General Kearney defeats the Mexicans at San Pasqual.

"   " 25, Colonel Doniphan defeats the Mexicans at Brazito, near El Paso.

"   " 28, Iowa admitted into the Union.

1847.   Jan. 8, Mexican Congress resolve to raise fifteen millions of dollars on the property of the clergy for the war with the United States.

"   " 8, 9, battles of San Gabriel and Mesa in California, fought by General Kearney, who defeats the Mexicans.

"   " 14, revolt of the Mexicans in New Mexico against the United States authorities.

"   " 24, battle of Canada, in New Mexico. Mexicans defeated by the Americans under Colonel Price.

"   Feb. 22, 23, battle of Buena Vista. Mexicans 21,000 in number, under General Santa Anna, defeated by 4,500 Americans under General Taylor.

"   " 28, battle of Sacramento. Colonel Doniphan, with 924 Americans, defeats 4,000 Mexicans.

"   Mar. 1, General Kearney declares California a part of the United States.

"   " 20, city and castle of Vera Cruz taken by the army and navy of the United States, under General Scott and Commodore Perry.

"   April 2, Alvarado taken by the Americans under Lieutenant Hunter.

"   " 18, battle of Cerro Gordo. Mexicans under Santa Anna defeated by the Americans under General Scott.

"   " 18, Tuspan in Mexico taken by Commodore Perry.

"   May 1, Smithsonian Institution at Washington, corner-stone laid.

"   Aug. 20, battles of Contreras and Churubusco, in Mexico. Mexicans defeated by Americans under General Smith, part of General Scott's command.

"   " 31, new constitution of Illinois adopted by state convention.

"   Sept. 8, battle of Molina del Rey, near the city of Mexico. The Americans under General Worth (part of Scott's command), defeat the Mexicans under General Santa Anna.

"   " 12, 14, battle of Chapultepec, near Mexico; the Americans, under Generals Scott, Worth, Pillow, and Quitman, defeat the Mexicans under Santa Anna. General Scott and American army enter the city of Mexico, on the 14th.

"   Sept. 13, to Oct. 12, siege of Puebla, held by the Americans against the Mexicans. The latter repulsed by the former, under Colonel Childs.

"   Oct. 9, the city of Huamantla, in Mexico, taken by the Americans, under General Lane.

"   " 20, port of Guayamas, in Mexico, bombarded and captured by the Americans.

"   Dec. 31, the several Mexican states occupied by the American army placed under military contributions.

1848.   Jan. 27, a national convention to nominate president and vice-president called by the whig members of Congress. At an adjourned meeting it was resolved that the convention meet at Independence Hall, Philadelphia.

1848.　　Feb. 18, By a general order, Major-General Scott turns over the command of the U. S. army in Mexico to Major-General Butler.

"　　May 22–26, the democratic national convention at Baltimore nominate General Lewis Cass of Michigan, for president, and General William O. Butler of Kentucky, for vice-president.

"　　" 25, Major-General Scott received by the municipal authorities of the city of New York. There was a large military and civic procession.

"　　" 29, Wisconsin admitted into the Union.

"　　" 30, treaty of peace between the United States and Mexico, which had been signed at Guadalupe Hidalgo, Feb. 2, 1848, afterward modified at Washington, and confirmed by the Mexican Congress; ratified by the American commissioners, Sevier and Clifford, and the Mexican minister of foreign relations, Don Luis de la Rosa. It was proclaimed in the United States, July 4, 1848.

"　　June 7, 8, the whig national convention meet at Philadelphia, and on the second day, fourth ballot, nominate General Zachary Taylor for president, and, on second ballot, Hon. Millard Fillmore for vice-president.

"　　" 22, 23, democratic convention at Utica, N. Y., nominate Martin Van Buren for president and Henry Dodge (who declined June 29) for vice-president.

"　　July 4, corner-stone of monument to General Washington, laid at the city of Washington. Oration by Hon. Robert C. Winthrop, speaker of the United States house of representatives.

"　　Aug. 13, Oregon territorial bill, with prohibition of slavery, passed by Congress.

"　　" 9, 10, free-soil convention at Buffalo, nominate Martin Van Buren, of New York, for president, and Charles Francis Adams, of Massachusetts, for vice-president. Sixteen states were represented by delegates.

"　　" 14, Adjournment of 30th Congress, 1st session.

"　　" 17, destructive fire at Albany, N. Y.

"　　Sept. 9, destructive fire at Brooklyn, N. Y.

"　　Nov. 7, presidential election.

"　　Dec. 4, meeting of the 30th Congress, second session.

"　　" 6, Taylor and Fillmore elected president and vice-president by the electoral colleges.

1849.　　March 5, inauguration of Zachary Taylor as president, and of Millard Fillmore as vice-president, of the United States.

THE END.

Im TheStory
personalised classic books

"Beautiful gift.. lovely finish. My Niece loves it, so precious!"

Helen R Brumfieldon

⭐⭐⭐⭐⭐

UNIQUE GIFT

FOR KIDS, PARTNERS AND FRIENDS

Timeless books such as:

Kids

Alice in Wonderland · The Jungle Book · The Wonderful Wizard of Oz
Peter and Wendy · Robin Hood · The Prince and The Pauper
The Railway Children · Treasure Island · A Christmas Carol

Adults

Romeo and Juliet · Dracula

Highly Customizable   **Change** Books Title   **Replace** Characters Names & Pictures   **Upload** Photo (for inside page)   **Add** Inscriptions

Visit
Im TheStory.com
and order yours today!

CPSIA information can be obtained
at www.ICGtesting.com
Printed in the USA
BVHW070847200819
556223BV00023B/3085/P